The Astrology 14 Horoscope

How to Cast and Interpret It

The Astrology 14 Horoscope

HOW TO CAST AND INTERPRET IT

Steven Schmidt

Illustrated by Mitzi Schmidt

The Bobbs-Merrill Company, Inc.
Indianapolis   New York

This book is for my children
Teri and Woody
(Aquarius and Taurus)
whose stars are bright in my sky

Contents

List of Illustrations

List of Tables

Acknowledgments

I wish to thank the following:

The many readers of my first book who have written to me in support of my attempt to update astrology. Most of them have asked for further details and for guidelines in casting their horoscopes according to my system. This book was written primarily for them.

The Carnegie Fund for Authors, whose Trustees awarded me a grant during the writing of this book to help me through a medical and financial emergency.

My wife, Mitzi, for her devotion, patience, and encouragement, and for illustrating this book.

Introduction

In my previous book, *Astrology 14: Your New Sun Sign*,* I began to bring astrology up to date. I did not create a wholly new system. I applied known scientific *facts* to astrology to update it and put it on a firmer scientific basis. My investigations had revealed that astrology, as it is practiced today, is deficient in three principal areas:

1. It still follows a twelve-sign system. Today there are not twelve but fourteen constellations in the Zodiac, and my system adds Cetus and Ophiuchus to the familiar twelve sun signs.

2. It has the sun entering Aries on March 21 (the vernal equinox, or first day of spring). Actually, because of a movement called the precession of the equinoxes, the sun now enters *Pisces* on March 21, making Pisces the first sun sign of the Zodiac.

3. In the interpretation of horoscopes, it still tries to force individuals into pre-established categories. The scientific method is to look first at the individuals, discover their similarities and differences, and *then* draw general conclusions as to the characters of the individuals.

In short, I concluded that traditional astrology is still working with data that were valid in Julius Caesar's time, but are now twenty centuries out of date! I attempted to correct these faults, and the result was *Astrology 14*.

The underlying theme of that book (and of the present one as well) is that astrology is not accepted as a true science because of its refusal to change. That is, astrology is *static*, and science must be *dynamic*—it must move with the times and with the universe, which are in a constant state

---

* New York: The Bobbs-Merrill Company, Inc., 1970.

of flux. Does astrology truly aspire to be a science? Or is it to remain simply a sort of parlor game whose rules must not be altered? Millions of people practice and follow astrology, and they take it very seriously indeed; most scientists and others of skeptical bent still tend to dismiss astrology as if it were a fortune-telling game.

Gibson Reaves, a professor of astronomy at the University of Southern California, was quoted in an article on my system* as stating that "astrology is essentially irrational, and to try to give it such a rational, scientific explanation would spoil it for most people, anyway."

If you believe that astrology is fun and games, and "essentially irrational," then you don't want its rules changed, any more than does a bridge or chess devotee. Attempts such as mine to make astrology more scientific, then, can have no appeal for you. Or if you have a vested interest in traditional astrology, as Carroll Righter does, you are obviously not going to welcome with open arms someone who says you have been doing it wrong and that your data are two thousand years out of date. Righter is quoted in the same *Time* article as "dismissing" my system as "meaningless."

On the other hand, people who take astrology seriously and are not averse to seeking new possibilities in a field that has tended, in the millennia since Babylon, to grow tradition-bound and rigid have approved of my approach. I receive letters every week from readers of *Astrology 14* who feel as I do about the need for a scientific astrology. But how, they ask, can we make use of this information? How can we cast our horoscopes in accordance with your updated system? I consider myself primarily a poet and novelist, but I could not in good conscience ignore such queries. They are not the least of my reasons for writing the present work.

The great psychologist Carl Jung once defined astrology as "an art on its way to becoming a science." I believe this to be true, and am doing what I can to further this necessary and important transformation—another reason for the existence of the work you are reading.

Astrology 14 was issued as a challenge to the astrology establishment. It created a controversy that is by no means settled yet. My system may be rejected by some, but I don't think it is possible to dismiss scientific facts of such magnitude. Early in this century, buggy-whip manufacturers no doubt would have liked to "dismiss" the upstart automobile—but progress has a way of going right on despite the denials of those who feel secure with the old and established; despite many who, emulating the ostrich, stick their heads in the sand and hope it will go away if they ignore it.

* "The Revised Zodiac," *Time*, November 23, 1970.

One reviewer of my previous book made a cogent criticism that has been echoed by a few other readers. "If the changed positions of the signs are to be taken seriously," Jim Floody wrote, "then revised charts and tables for all the planets would need to be made up. Schmidt calls for this, but he does little beyond presenting his new theories. They are not developed. . . . But if a change in astrological traditions of 2,000 years is to be validated, then there is a need for a more comprehensive exposition."

I have said that *Astrology 14* was issued as a challenge, and I hoped that established astrologers would accept this challenge, following my book with "how-to" publications adapted to the fourteen signs and the movement of the spring point from Aries to Pisces. However, so far no one seems to have taken up the challenge; at least I have heard of no such project. Clearly, it is my task to fill the gap between theory and practice.

In the pages that follow, you will learn how to cast your own horoscope, and those of your family and friends, including all fourteen sun signs and with the spring point in its proper present position. The tables and charts have been simplified—necessarily, as a detailed revision of the ephemerides and the tables of houses would fill a bookshelf. However, the information presented is as accurate as possible within the limitations of space. A chapter each is devoted to the placement on the chart and interpretation of your rising sign, sun, moon, and each of the planets. These will enable you to complete your chart. You will then be ready for the more interesting and subjective business of interpreting your horoscope in its totality.

The real art of astrology lies in the interpretation of the completed horoscope chart. It is based mainly on the relative positions of the heavenly bodies on your chart—that is, on the *aspects*: the number of degrees between one planet and another. The basic aspects, along with their meanings, are described in *Astrology 14*. For convenience, this information is repeated in the present work.

When you have plotted all the aspects, the great question remains: What do they *mean*? Some of the meanings of the aspects are clear and unequivocal; others, however, have been in dispute among astrologers for many years, and still are. This is why I stress the *subjectivity* of your interpretation. You know yourself better than anyone else does. In a case where a stranger—or even a close friend or relative—could only shrug or flip a coin, you should be able to tell which of two possible interpretations is the right one for you.

Much of the general and theoretical information presented in *Astrology 14* has not been repeated in this work. Therefore, I urge you to read my previous book before embarking upon the adventure of charting your horoscope, as confusion may otherwise result. However, realizing that *Astrology 14* may not be available to some readers, I have included enough essential information so that the present work may be read and used as an independent volume.

A criticism that I expected, but that has not been forthcoming, is that the lists of people born under each sun sign in *Astrology 14* are too short to be definitive—especially since I tried to follow the scientific method, which would demand a *large* sampling of individuals. To rectify this, I have greatly enlarged the "populations" listed in the other book, including at least one name for each day of the year.

Blank horoscope charts are printed at the end of the book for the convenience of the reader.

You are now ready to start out on an enterprise that may well affect your entire life. Many of you have charted horoscopes before—or paid to have it done for you by a professional astrologer—according to the traditional, twelve-sign system. Now, for the first time, you have the opportunity to erect your chart in accordance with data that have been corrected and updated for the twentieth century. You may, therefore, regard yourself as a pioneer of the new age that is dawning—the age of a truly scientific astrology.

The Astrology 14 Horoscope

How to Cast and Interpret It

1: The Rising Sign

DEFINITION

THE BASIC HOROSCOPE CHART for the system of Astrology 14 is shown in Figure 1. Like other such charts, it resembles a wheel, with fourteen (rather than twelve) spokes (known as *cusps*) radiating from a central hub. The circular hub, on which the name and birthdate of the subject of the horoscope are customarily written, actually represents the earth. Astrology was evolved in the dim past, when men believed the earth to be the center of the universe, fixed and unmoving, with the sun, moon, planets, and stars circling it in stately procession, rising in the east and setting in the west. It was not until fairly recently, in the times of Copernicus and Galileo, that men learned that the earth, like the other planets, actually revolves about the sun. However, to our eyes, the sun and other heavenly bodies still rise and set, and it is with this *apparent* motion that astrologers are concerned.

Since there are fourteen cusps (spokes) to this wheel, there are also fourteen spaces between them, and these spaces are known as the Houses. Each House occupies approximately 26 degrees of the 360 degrees that make up the circular horoscope. In the chapters that follow, you will learn how to place the sun, moon, and planets on the chart. Each, of course, will occupy a House, and the meaning of the planet will be affected by the House it occupies. However, each House has an intrinsic meaning of its own, whether it is empty on your chart or occupied by one or more planets. The fourteen Houses, along with the sun signs they correspond to and the life activities governed, are listed in Table 1.

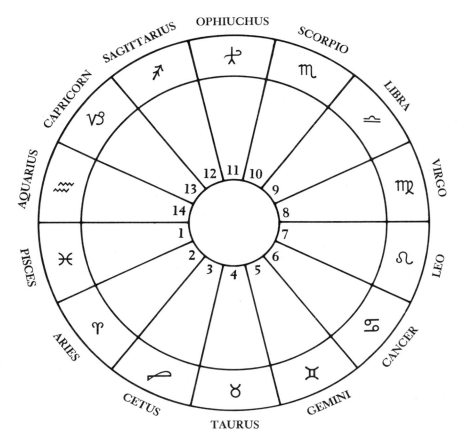

Figure 1. Basic Astrology 14 horoscope chart

A natal chart is a schematic representation of the heavens at the moment of your birth. To erect such a chart, an astrologer must know two basic facts: (1) the date of your birth including the time (to the minute, if possible) and (2) the *place* of your birth. The date tells the astrologer the subject's sun sign; that is, the zodiacal constellation (group of stars) through which the sun was apparently moving at the moment of birth. But the place of birth is just as important because he needs it to plot the subject's *ascendant** (or rising sign), upon which all the rest of the chart is based.

Let us assume, by way of an example, that you were born at noon on January 1 of a given year (say, 1940). You may be sure that many other babies were drawing their first breath, all over the world, at noon on that day. What makes your chart different from theirs? The fact that you were born in a different place makes your rising sign different from theirs. The rising sign is the sun sign (constellation) that was rising on the eastern horizon at the moment of your birth. Obviously, this sign will be different for a child born at noon in Los Angeles than for one born in New York, Paris, or Johannesburg, South Africa. But what if you and another child were born at the same time *and* in the same place? Would your horoscopes be identical? For our purposes, the answer is *yes*, they would be, since you both would have the same sun sign, rising sign, and aspects of the planets. This happens all the time, of course, especially for children born in large cities, and means that all of us have "time twins." Actually, it is rare for two children to be born at exactly the same moment in a given place. This is why astrologers plot the ascendant, or *degree* of the rising sign, as explained below. Even a few minutes' difference in time of birth makes your individual horoscope different from that of your "twin."

I have said that the remainder of the horoscope is based on the rising sign. This is because the rising sign always occupies the first House. The generalized horoscope shown in Figure 1 has Pisces in the first House, but this configuration would only be valid for a personal horoscope if Pisces is the subject's rising sign. Therefore, the rising sign must be calculated first. When it is known, the symbol for that sign is drawn in the first House—that is, at "nine o'clock" on a blank chart—and the symbols of

---

* Technically, the ascendant is the *degree* of the sign that is rising on the eastern horizon at the moment of birth. In erecting a personal horoscope, an astrologer plots the line to this degree of the rising sign, which becomes the first degree of the first House. In a general work such as the present one, however, it is impossible to be so precise. The terms *ascendant* and *rising sign* are not actually synonymous, and the latter will be used throughout. Thus, although the exact degree is not computed, the reader will know his rising sign, and his chart will be basically correct.

4 THE ASTROLOGY 14 HOROSCOPE

Table 1. THE HOUSES

House	Sign	Corresponds to*	Life Activity Governed
1st	♓	Pisces	Life of individual, including body and egocentric concerns; personal potential
2nd	♈	Aries	Money, financial concerns, physical possessions and securities
3rd	⬗	Cetus	Education and communications
4th	♉	Taurus	Relationships to environment and to friends and relatives of own generation
5th	♊	Gemini	Home of parents, ancestral influences, beginnings and endings
6th	♋	Cancer	Children, amusements, recreation and display
7th	♌	Leo	Health, work, domestic service, efficiency
8th	♍	Virgo	Marriage and other partnerships, friendships and enmities
9th	♎	Libra	Death and inheritances, sex expression, self-sacrifice
10th	♏	Scorpio	Travel, self-projection to new horizons
11th	⚕	Ophiuchus	Duty, higher life of spirit and intellect
12th	♐	Sagittarius	Career, material responsibility; social life and status; reputation, honors, etc.
13th	♑	Capricorn	Friends, group objectives; hopes, wishes; benefits
14th	♒	Aquarius	Trouble, imprisonment, self-betrayal; illness, escapism, disgrace

*The reader is reminded that the sun signs bear only a *nominal* relationship to the Houses. A horoscope always begins with the individual's ascendant in the first House, and the rising sign can be any of the fourteen zodiacal constellations. The relationships shown in this table, therefore, are valid only if Pisces is your rising sign.

the other signs are entered in the other Houses, proceeding counterclockwise from the first to the fourteenth House.

The easiest rising sign to compute is for someone born at dawn. If you were born at sunrise on January 1, your sun sign would be Sagittarius; and, although unseen, the rising sign would *also* be Sagittarius. Dawn births always have identical sun signs and rising signs, and the person in our example is then known as a *double* Sagittarius. However, if you were born even 45 minutes before or after sunrise, your sun sign and rising sign will probably be different.

Nearly everyone knows the date and year of his birth. Unfortunately, many do not know the exact *time* of birth, and this information is not always entered on birth certificates. In these cases, an astrologer usually bases his calculation of the subject's rising sign as 12 o'clock noon of his birthday.

COMPUTATION

Table 2, on p. 15 at the end of this chapter, will enable you to find your rising sign. Four dates are given for each month of the year. Find the date closest to your birthday; then find the *time* closest to the moment of your birth. If the time is unknown, use the time closest to 12:00 noon. In our example of someone born at noon on January 1, his rising sign would be Aquarius, whose time (11:39 A.M.) is closest to noon on that date.

The times given in Table 2 have been computed for 40 degrees north latitude, which includes the most densely populated areas of the United States. The constellations rise a little earlier or later north or south of that line, depending on the season of the year, but the times given will still be valid for most areas. These times will also hold good for readers born in southern Europe (Spain, Portugal, Italy, and Greece). Most of Europe lies to the north of 40 degrees north latitude, as does Canada; however, readers born in those areas will find that these times are generally valid.

INTERPRETATION

After you have used Table 2 to find your rising sign, and entered its symbol in the first House of a blank horoscope chart, fill in the symbols of the remaining signs in the outer rim of the wheel, moving counter-clockwise, until each House is occupied by a symbol. Our example of a subject born at noon on January 1, 1940, is illustrated in Figure 2. His rising sign (Aquarius) occupies his first House, Pisces is in the second House, Aries in the third, etc. With this much of your chart completed, the question naturally arises as to the *meaning* of your rising sign.

As mentioned above, a birth at or near sunrise will make the subject a *double* of his sun sign. This means that all of the basic characteristics of his sun sign, as described in Chapter 2, will be strengthened and intensified. The first House concerns the personal life of the subject, both mental and physical, with emphasis on his personal *potential*. Thus, both the strengths and weaknesses of your sun sign will be doubled if your rising sign and sun sign are the same.

Most of us, however, were not children of the dawn, and our sun sign differs from our rising sign. Basic interpretations of the rising signs are given below. These should not be read as individual entities, however; the

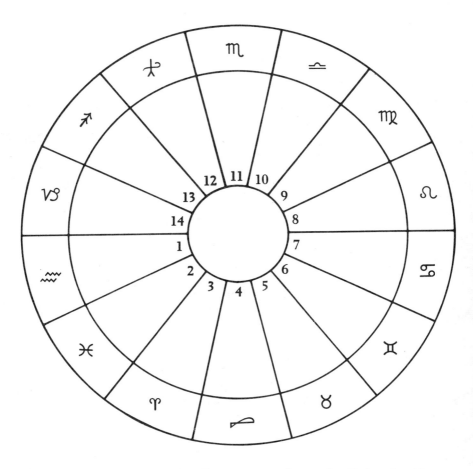

Figure 2. Basic chart of subject born at noon on January 1, with Aquarius rising

meaning of your rising sign should be compared with the meaning of your sun sign. Similar traits are strengthened, dissimilar ones weakened, and it is perfectly possible for opposing traits to cancel each other out. Much will depend on the placement of the sun, moon, and planets on your chart, which will be taken up in later chapters. We will proceed one step at a time, for, as Goethe said, to begin a long journey, it is only necessary to take the first step. This you have already done in finding your rising sign and placing it in the first House on your chart. The next step, after you have read the interpretation of your rising sign, will concern your sun sign, which is the subject of Chapter 2.

THE RISING SIGNS

PISCES ♓

Ruled by the planet Neptune, which is often concerned with *belief* in spiritual affairs, Pisces as your rising sign tends to strengthen whatever belief you may have—in a religion, a cause, a political party, or in yourself. Pisces adds a vein of iron to your personality, increasing your determination to succeed, your will power, and ambition. A Pisces type has strong potential for success. You have the drive and the ability to concentrate single-mindedly on your goal. However, your success will probably be earned at a considerable expenditure of time and energy, as Pisceans seldom figure in "overnight" success stories of the Cinderella type. On the contrary, you may have to struggle hard against poverty and adverse conditions before your goal is achieved. Reigning Neptune can either help or hinder your efforts, depending upon its aspects to other elements of your chart. Also, your single-minded drive toward your goal should not be made at the expense of family, friends, and other elements of your life. You would be wise to take up a hobby or side activity that is completely different from your principal occupation. Success is wonderful, but the heights can be lonely, as the hero of *Room at the Top* discovered. You may or may not be versatile, depending upon other elements in your horoscope. You have a good sense of humor, tending to be a prankster with a dead-pan expression; you delight in "putting on" your friends.

ARIES ♈

Ruled by Mars, the planet of war and conquest (often considered a necessary evil by astrologers), Aries rising tends to strengthen your ego and the power of your personality as it affects others. You have a strong sense of personal identity, and are unlikely to spend much time mulling over the existential question, "Who am I?" You *know* who you are, and your family, friends, and associates are not in much doubt, either! Aries types tend to have personal power in no small measure, then, and are also apt to be strongly creative. You would probably do well in politics if public affairs is your interest, but not in a subordinate position, as you are a natural leader. You hate to take orders or to follow a pre-established routine, and if you don't see an immediate opening in your field, you may very well create one! As a political, social, or business leader, you will not find it hard to gain support from others, as people are easily drawn by your personal magnetism. If a creative rather than a leadership role is more your cup of tea, you will probably succeed most readily in the field of literature. Aries types have few weaknesses, but they can succumb to a tendency toward dogmatism, of feeling that they are always right when it comes to their own field of interest. Even when finally convinced that a strongly held opinion is wrong, you probably find it very difficult to admit it.

CETUS ♋

Though ruled by mighty Jupiter, the greatest of the planets (called the "greater fortune" by astrologers), which usually provides power and good luck, Cetus rising often adds a note of repression to your activities. You have a great deal of natural charm, which flourishes in a cultural or artistic environment, but would be of no help at all in the political field, which is definitely *not* recommended for Cetus types. Instead, your proper arena is the performing arts, if you have talent to offer the public. You love the limelight and always enjoy being surrounded by interesting people. The graphic arts is another excellent field for your creativity, as you have a natural flair for color, design, and harmony. Many Cetus types have gained great distinction in both the performing and graphic arts. You have a tendency to be headstrong and opinionated, and this is aggravated by the fact that, beneath all the surface charm and glitter, you are basically unsure of yourself. Distractions and interruptions do not bother you, however, because you have the enviable ability to detach yourself completely from your surroundings, and are able to work unruffled in the midst of chaos. This trait can help you greatly in your career, of course, but it may be misinterpreted by others, to whom your detached objectivity may appear as callous indifference to others.

TAURUS ♉

Ruled by Venus, the planet commonly associated with love (and also with music by astrologers), Taurus rising usually bodes well for your romantic interests. It also tends to make you possessive—not only of your beloved and your friends, but of opinions, beliefs, and material possessions as well. Like any other trait, this can be good in moderation and bad if carried to an extreme. It is highly unlikely that you would ever be a spend-thrift; on the other hand, you may lose the people and things you love the most by clinging too closely to them. Taurus is the strongest sign for musical talent in the Zodiac, and this would probably be an excellent field for you to enter. Many Taurus types have achieved great success in musical careers, as both composers and performers. If you are talented, and other aspects on your chart are favorable, you could hardly go wrong in the world of music. Since music is closely associated with mathematics and the physical sciences, you could probably do well in either of these fields if your bent is more scientific than artistic. Politics, however, would be a doubtful choice as a career, as you have an innate shyness that makes you shun the limelight unless you are a musical performer. You tend to make friends slowly; once made, however, a friend is yours forever. You are equally implacable as an enemy.

GEMINI ♊

Ruled by fast-moving Mercury, the innermost planet—which is named for the god of thinkers, writers, and thieves—Gemini rising strengthens your intellect and the agility of your mind. You are versatile and can leap nimbly from one thought (or situation) to another. In fact, Gemini types are so adaptable that variety is their keynote; they are to be found in every field of human endeavor and activity. You are liable to be rest-less and may be thought of as a slow starter in your life activity. Although you can successfully do two things at one time, in the sense of holding down two jobs or "wearing two hats," you may very well drop both and move on to a pasture that looks greener to you. Gemini types are some-times thought of as two-faced or even fickle in their affections. This is because, in your youth, your curiosity and restlessness drive you to learn as much as you can about the world in the shortest possible time. Thus you may gain the reputation of being a job-hopper and a Don Juan in romantic affairs—here today, gone tomorrow. The mature Gemini type, however, his wild oats sown and much of his curiosity satisfied, tends to be remarkably steadfast. Out of the richness of your experience, you are able to choose the job, the spouse, and the environment that suit you best, and will probably stick to them forever. Beneath the surface flash and agility, you are consistent in your opinions and secretive about your innermost thoughts and feelings.

CANCER ♋

Ruled by that queen of the night, the moon, which is associated astrologically with the unconscious, Cancer rising tends to increase the sensitivity of your emotions. You can "feel for" people even when you don't understand them. In your thoughts, moods, and feelings, you are as changeable as a Gemini type; however, you tend to be much more conservative in your actions, sticking to a job you don't like, for example, rather than rushing off to take another that seems to hold out a brighter prospect. You have a strong sense of duty and responsibility. Barring accidents, Cancer types tend to be long-lived, and many of them retain a youthful outlook despite the years and decades. Accidents do occur, however, because you tend to compensate for the conservatism of your everyday life by being a daredevil, even reckless, in your choice of sports and outdoor activities. The more you feel held down in your job or home, the more likely you are to climb the most dangerous mountains in your spare time—so beware of overcompensation. You are at ease in social situations, with a sure instinct for the right dress and deportment. However, you seldom take the lead in conversation, remaining a little withdrawn and preferring to listen rather than talk. Like Pisces types, you have an impish sense of humor and love to play jokes on your friends.

LEO ♌

Ruled by the sun, which represents the male principle, consciousness (opposite to the unconscious, feminine moon), Leo rising strengthens the forcefulness of your personality and accents your extraverted side. Your keynote is *independence*, which makes you chafe against the restrictions of living in a society where we are all dependent upon one another. Since you don't hesitate to break a convention when it makes no sense to you, you are often thought of as a bohemian or simply as "a character" by your friends and associates. This has its disadvantages, of course, but it can also make you a pace-setter and a leader with a strong and colorful personality. Your more conventional associates may consider you a maverick, but society also recognizes the need for strongly independent and original thinkers and actors on the stage of the world. Your rewards will probably come late in life, but they will be great ones. Beware of a tendency to be discouraged if your independent way of life has led you down false trails that apparently go nowhere; it is always possible to make a fresh start at any age. You share with Aries types the trait of finding it difficult to admit mistakes, as your independence usually makes you anything but humble. Like Taurus, you are a wonderfully steadfast friend, but a hard enemy. There is little in between, as it is almost impossible for you to be neutral or noncommittal.

VIRGO ♍

Ruled by Mercury (which also rules Gemini), Virgo rising tends to increase your analytical ability. You are quick to size up a person or a situation, and your conclusion is nearly always right. You are strongly individualistic—you stand out in a crowd, usually have a nickname, and are familiar to everyone in your surroundings, whether they have actually met you or not. Many Virgo types have achieved success as actors and actresses, and they have definitely not been cast as *types!* Your ability to analyze can make you a valuable employee in many fields, but your marked individuality can be either a blessing or a curse. Whatever your field of interest, you find it extremely difficult to do things the way they have always been done; you immediately see possibilities for change and improvement, and are surprised and hurt when others don't see it your way. Your potential for success is great because you can both analyze an existing product or method and improve on it in an original and practical way. Be prepared for jealousy and resistance, however, as the great majority will always vote for the status quo rather than a bold, bright new idea. You may feel extremely discouraged at repeated failures and misunderstandings on the part of your associates, but after a short time you will bounce back with enthusiasm, ready to go on.

LIBRA ♎

Ruled by Venus, the planet of love, Libra rising tends to increase the strength and quality of your judgment. You are always able to balance two opposing points of view, no matter how strongly you feel about the subject. The influence of Venus should help your love life, other elements of your horoscope being favorable. You are something of a dandy in your choice of personal attire, and members of the opposite sex find you attractive (members of your own sex may consider you a little too cocksure). This sign bodes well for a political career or one in any division of the law. You would make a good lawyer and an even better judge. Venus is usually associated with musical talent, a trait you share with Taurus types. There is a split here. The talent of Taurus types tends to find expression in composing, conducting, and instrumental performance, but you are more likely to be a singer. You probably have an excellent natural singing voice and, with training, could have a successful career as a vocal artist. Although your potential for success is very good (as long as you keep your balance), your personality tends to be flawed by a single weakness: lack of self-confidence. If allowed to develop, this could lead to dogmatism in your views and even to neurosis. Use your ability to judge to find this weakness. Once it is corrected, you have little to fear.

SCORPIO ♏

Ruled by ruddy Mars, Scorpio rising increases the sensitivity of your feelings and emotions, especially where others are concerned. The aggressiveness usually associated with Mars may or may not be present, depending upon other elements of your horoscope. You have great empathy and, even more than Libra types, are able to appreciate the other person's point of view. This quality, although it makes you a marvelous spouse or friend, can lead to trouble, because it also makes it hard for you to recognize your enemies. If your Mars is strongly aspected, you would do well in a political career, especially since you have a genuine desire to benefit your fellow man. There is a streak of the poet, mystic, or philosopher in you, and you are strongly idealistic, both on a personal level and as concerns all mankind. This idealism can, of course, lead to rude awakenings, the world we all have to live in being anything but ideal at the moment! In extreme cases, your drive to bring things closer to your ideal can cause you crushing disappointment or even martyrdom. However, your goals are so positive and so high-minded that you tend to attract friends and, eventually, a spouse who feels as you do, and it *is* possible to approach the ideal in personal relationships where there are sympathy and flexibility on both sides.

OPHIUCHUS ♇

Ruled by far Pluto, which is usually associated with death and other disasters by astrologers, Ophiuchus rising actually tends to strengthen your resourcefulness. Pluto was discovered so recently that its influence is not known in any detail, and we may assume that it can be positive if well-aspected to other elements in your chart. You are versatile, and would probably have a good chance of success in the entertainment world. If you are musically talented, you have the ability to master several instruments and can sing and compose as well. You have a good deal of personal charm, and generally can "hold the floor" at a party. However, a career in politics is probably not advisable. Your ability to entertain does not extend to swaying voters or members of a political party to your way of thinking. Talent and sensitivity are so strongly indicated that, unless other elements in your horoscope tend to neutralize them, you will probably feel badly frustrated by what is considered a "normal" life in home, office, or factory. Not all of you can be professional entertainers, of course, but all of you *can* find an outlet—a means of expression for your creative talent and energy. I strongly advise you to find such an outlet, as its results can only be positive, whether you are destined for a quiet, private life or a career on the stages and screens of the world.

SAGITTARIUS ♐

Ruled by benevolent Jupiter, Sagittarius rising will strengthen your ability to perceive what is really going on around you at all times. You were born with your eyes wide open, and apparently have not blinked since. Jupiter is known as the "greater fortune" to astrologers and, unless adversely aspected by other elements, signifies good luck and the development of an expansive, generous personality. Like Scorpio types, you are sensitive to the needs of humanity, but (unlike them) you are more inclined to act on your beliefs. There is little of the poet or the contemplative philosopher in your makeup; you tend to be an extravert, and prefer the "real" world of people and events to the interior realm of more mystic and spiritual types. Although this would seem to indicate fitness for a political career, you would probably chafe against the restrictions of the "party line," which would often be in opposition to your own ideas for bettering the lot of mankind. You like to see *direct* results of your labors, and would probably be happier as a social worker, in the Peace Corps, or working for a nonprofit foundation with humanitarian ideals. Rewards may come easily to you, as our society recognizes "outer" accomplishments much more quickly than it does those of the spirit; however, for balance, you should try to develop your intuitive, "inner" nature.

CAPRICORN ♑

Ruled by Saturn (usually considered gloomy and cold by astrologers), Capricorn rising strengthens your sense of conservatism. You tend to make full use of whatever comes your way, mentally as well as materially. You are strongly realistic, and would probably make an excellent politician. Like other "split" signs, Capricorn types have a tendency to develop one side at the expense of the other. You are ambitious to climb to the heights of worldly success and recognition, but it is dangerous to do so without regard for the "watery" realm—the side of the unconscious and the creative spirit. A real asset is your ability to remain objective, although this may make you seem cold to your friends and associates. You also have an excellent sense of humor, which expresses itself in remarks that are dry and subtly witty. In addition to the danger of a one-sided development, you also may remain immature if you specialize too narrowly in one field. You have all the traits that usually indicate success and material prosperity, but must beware of the fate of many men and women of great accomplishment who remain childish in their personal lives, tending to pour everything into their professional careers. This tendency can be avoided, however, if you always strive for *balance* in everything you undertake.

AQUARIUS ♒

Ruled by Uranus (called "the disruptor" by astrologers), Aquarius rising is an aid to the acquiring of knowledge, especially in scientific or technical fields. Women as well as men with a strongly aspected Uranus are mechanically inclined and have the ability to make things work. You are attracted to the odd, the unusual, and the paradoxical—a proclivity that makes your friends consider you "a character" at times. You share a trait with Ophiuchus types in being well suited for the world of entertainment; in fact, you thrive in the limelight. However, you tend to be less versatile than Ophiuchans, and more nervous and temperamental. There is a definite need for you to stay in top condition, mentally as well as physically, if you are to achieve success as an entertainer or in any other field. Like Virgo types, you have a highly developed analytical ability, and there is a danger that you may carry this to extremes. Very little could be accomplished without analysis, of course, but the habit of overanalysis can destroy the pleasure of simple acceptance and enjoyment. You are a good conversationalist and tend to take an active part in discussions. Try to be a little less analytical and critical, and keep yourself in good condition, and your chances of success and happiness are excellent. For social harmony, always remember that the best habit is that of always trying to see the other person's point of view.

TABLE 2 15

Table 2. RISING SIGNS

Date	Time	Sign	Symbol	Date	Time	Sign	Symbol
Jan. 1	8:13 A.M.	Sagittarius	♐	Jan. 15	10:43 P.M.	Leo	♌
	9:56 A.M.	Capricorn	♑	cont.	12:26 A.M.	Virgo	♍
	11:39 A.M.	Aquarius	♒		2:09 A.M.	Libra	♎
	1:22 P.M.	Pisces	♓		3:52 A.M.	Scorpio	♏
	3:05 P.M.	Aries	♈		5:35 A.M.	Ophiuchus	⛎
	4:48 P.M.	Cetus	⟿				
	6:31 P.M.	Taurus	♉	Jan. 23	6:37 A.M.	Sagittarius	♐
	8:14 P.M.	Gemini	♊		8:20 A.M.	Capricorn	♑
	9:57 P.M.	Cancer	♋		10:03 A.M.	Aquarius	♒
	11:40 P.M.	Leo	♌		11:46 A.M.	Pisces	♓
	1:23 A.M.	Virgo	♍		1:29 P.M.	Aries	♈
	3:06 A.M.	Libra	♎		3:12 P.M.	Cetus	⟿
	4:49 A.M.	Scorpio	♏		4:55 P.M.	Taurus	♉
	6:32 A.M.	Ophiuchus	⛎		6:38 P.M.	Gemini	♊
					8:21 P.M.	Cancer	♋
Jan. 8	7:43 A.M.	Sagittarius	♐		10:04 P.M.	Leo	♌
	9:26 A.M.	Capricorn	♑		11:47 P.M.	Virgo	♍
	11:09 A.M.	Aquarius	♒		1:30 A.M.	Libra	♎
	12:52 P.M.	Pisces	♓		3:13 A.M.	Scorpio	♏
	2:35 P.M.	Aries	♈		4:56 A.M.	Ophiuchus	⛎
	4:18 P.M.	Cetus	⟿				
	6:01 P.M.	Taurus	♉	Feb. 1	7:38 A.M.	Capricorn	♑
	7:44 P.M.	Gemini	♊		9:21 A.M.	Aquarius	♒
	9:27 P.M.	Cancer	♋		11:04 A.M.	Pisces	♓
	11:10 P.M.	Leo	♌		12:47 P.M.	Aries	♈
	12:53 A.M.	Virgo	♍		2:30 P.M.	Cetus	⟿
	2:36 A.M.	Libra	♎		4:13 P.M.	Taurus	♉
	4:19 A.M.	Scorpio	♏		5:56 P.M.	Gemini	♊
	6:02 A.M.	Ophiuchus	⛎		7:39 P.M.	Cancer	♋
					9:22 P.M.	Leo	♌
Jan. 15	7:16 A.M.	Sagittarius	♐		11:05 P.M.	Virgo	♍
	8:59 A.M.	Capricorn	♑		12:48 A.M.	Libra	♎
	10:42 A.M.	Aquarius	♒		2:31 A.M.	Scorpio	♏
	12:25 P.M.	Pisces	♓		4:14 A.M.	Ophiuchus	⛎
	2:08 P.M.	Aries	♈		5:55 A.M.	Sagittarius	♐
	3:51 P.M.	Cetus	⟿				
	5:34 P.M.	Taurus	♉	Feb. 8	7:02 A.M.	Capricorn	♑
	7:17 P.M.	Gemini	♊		8:45 A.M.	Aquarius	♒
	9:00 P.M.	Cancer	♋		10:28 A.M.	Pisces	♓

Date	Time	Sign	Symbol	Date	Time	Sign	Symbol
Feb. 8	12:11 P.M.	Aries	♈	Mar. 1	6:58 A.M.	Aquarius	♒
cont.	1:54 P.M.	Cetus	⪕		8:41 A.M.	Pisces	♓
	3:37 P.M.	Taurus	♉		10:24 A.M.	Aries	♈
	5:20 P.M.	Gemini	♊		12:07 P.M.	Cetus	⪕
	7:03 P.M.	Cancer	♋		1:50 P.M.	Taurus	♉
	8:46 P.M.	Leo	♌		3:33 P.M.	Gemini	♊
	10:29 P.M.	Virgo	♍		5:16 P.M.	Cancer	♋
	12:12 A.M.	Libra	♎		6:59 P.M.	Leo	♌
	1:55 A.M.	Scorpio	♏		8:42 P.M.	Virgo	♍
	3:38 A.M.	Ophiuchus	⛎		10:25 P.M.	Libra	♎
	5:19 A.M.	Sagittarius	♐		12:08 A.M.	Scorpio	♏
					1:51 A.M.	Ophiuchus	⛎
Feb. 15	6:26 A.M.	Capricorn	♑		3:32 A.M.	Sagittarius	♐
	8:09 A.M.	Aquarius	♒		5:15 A.M.	Capricorn	♑
	9:52 A.M.	Pisces	♓				
	11:35 A.M.	Aries	♈	Mar. 8	6:19 A.M.	Aquarius	♒
	1:18 P.M.	Cetus	⪕		8:02 A.M.	Pisces	♓
	3:01 P.M.	Taurus	♉		9:45 A.M.	Aries	♈
	4:44 P.M.	Gemini	♊		11:28 A.M.	Cetus	⪕
	6:27 P.M.	Cancer	♋		1:11 P.M.	Taurus	♉
	8:10 P.M.	Leo	♌		2:54 P.M.	Gemini	♊
	9:53 P.M.	Virgo	♍		4:37 P.M.	Cancer	♋
	11:36 P.M.	Libra	♎		6:20 P.M.	Leo	♌
	1:19 A.M.	Scorpio	♏		8:03 P.M.	Virgo	♍
	3:02 A.M.	Ophiuchus	⛎		9:46 P.M.	Libra	♎
	4:43 A.M.	Sagittarius	♐		11:29 P.M.	Scorpio	♏
					1:12 A.M.	Ophiuchus	⛎
Feb. 22	7:36 A.M.	Aquarius	♒		2:53 A.M.	Sagittarius	♐
	9:19 A.M.	Pisces	♓		4:36 A.M.	Capricorn	♑
	11:02 A.M.	Aries	♈				
	12:45 P.M.	Cetus	⪕	Mar. 15	5:40 A.M.	Aquarius	♒
	2:28 P.M.	Taurus	♉		7:23 A.M.	Pisces	♓
	4:11 P.M.	Gemini	♊		9:06 A.M.	Aries	♈
	5:54 P.M.	Cancer	♋		10:49 A.M.	Cetus	⪕
	7:37 P.M.	Leo	♌		12:32 P.M.	Taurus	♉
	9:20 P.M.	Virgo	♍		2:15 P.M.	Gemini	♊
	11:03 P.M.	Libra	♎		3:58 P.M.	Cancer	♋
	12:46 A.M.	Scorpio	♏		5:41 P.M.	Leo	♌
	2:29 A.M.	Ophiuchus	⛎		7:24 P.M.	Virgo	♍
	4:10 A.M.	Sagittarius	♐		9:07 P.M.	Libra	♎
	5:53 A.M.	Capricorn	♑		10:50 P.M.	Scorpio	♏

TABLE 2 17

Date	Time	Sign	Symbol	Date	Time	Sign	Symbol
Mar. 15	12:33 A.M.	Ophiuchus	⚕	April 8	3:31 P.M.	Leo	♌
cont.	2:14 A.M.	Sagittarius	♐	cont.	5:14 P.M.	Virgo	♍
	3:57 A.M.	Capricorn	♑		6:57 P.M.	Libra	♎
					8:40 P.M.	Scorpio	♏
Mar. 23	6:42 A.M.	Pisces	♓		10:23 P.M.	Ophiuchus	⚕
	8:25 A.M.	Aries	♈		12:04 A.M.	Sagittarius	♐
	10:08 A.M.	Cetus	⬡		1:47 A.M.	Capricorn	♑
	11:51 A.M.	Taurus	♉		3:30 A.M.	Aquarius	♒
	1:34 P.M.	Gemini	♊				
	3:17 P.M.	Cancer	♋	April 15	4:32 A.M.	Pisces	♓
	5:00 P.M.	Leo	♌		6:15 A.M.	Aries	♈
	6:43 P.M.	Virgo	♍		7:58 A.M.	Cetus	⬡
	8:26 P.M.	Libra	♎		9:41 A.M.	Taurus	♉
	10:09 P.M.	Scorpio	♏		11:24 A.M.	Gemini	♊
	11:52 P.M.	Ophiuchus	⚕		1:07 P.M.	Cancer	♋
	1:33 A.M.	Sagittarius	♐		2:50 P.M.	Leo	♌
	3:16 A.M.	Capricorn	♑		4:33 P.M.	Virgo	♍
	4:59 A.M.	Aquarius	♒		6:16 P.M.	Libra	♎
					8:59 P.M.	Scorpio	♏
April 1	5:49 A.M.	Pisces	♓		9:42 P.M.	Ophiuchus	⚕
	7:32 A.M.	Aries	♈		11:23 P.M.	Sagittarius	♐
	9:15 A.M.	Cetus	⬡		1:06 A.M.	Capricorn	♑
	11:58 A.M.	Taurus	♉		2:49 A.M.	Aquarius	♒
	12:41 P.M.	Gemini	♊				
	2:24 P.M.	Cancer	♋	April 23	5:33 A.M.	Aries	♈
	4:07 P.M.	Leo	♌		7:16 A.M.	Cetus	⬡
	5:50 P.M.	Virgo	♍		8:59 A.M.	Taurus	♉
	7:33 P.M.	Libra	♎		10:42 A.M.	Gemini	♊
	9:16 P.M.	Scorpio	♏		12:25 P.M.	Cancer	♋
	10:59 P.M.	Ophiuchus	⚕		2:08 P.M.	Leo	♌
	12:40 A.M.	Sagittarius	♐		3:51 P.M.	Virgo	♍
	2:23 A.M.	Capricorn	♑		5:34 P.M.	Libra	♎
	4:06 A.M.	Aquarius	♒		7:17 P.M.	Scorpio	♏
					9:00 P.M.	Ophiuchus	⚕
					10:41 P.M.	Sagittarius	♐
April 8	5:13 A.M.	Pisces	♓		12:24 A.M.	Capricorn	♑
	6:56 A.M.	Aries	♈		2:07 A.M.	Aquarius	♒
	8:39 A.M.	Cetus	⬡		3:50 A.M.	Pisces	♓
	10.22 A.M.	Taurus	♉				
	12:05 P.M.	Gemini	♊	May 1	4:53 A.M.	Aries	♈
	1:48 P.M.	Cancer	♋				

Date	Time	Sign	Symbol
May 1	6:36 A.M.	Cetus	⊶
cont.	8:19 A.M.	Taurus	♉
	10:02 A.M.	Gemini	♊
	11:45 A.M.	Cancer	♋
	1:28 P.M.	Leo	♌
	3:11 P.M.	Virgo	♍
	4:54 P.M.	Libra	♎
	6:37 P.M.	Scorpio	♏
	8:20 P.M.	Ophiuchus	⛎
	10:01 P.M.	Sagittarius	♐
	11:44 P.M.	Capricorn	♑
	1:27 A.M.	Aquarius	♒
	3:10 A.M.	Pisces	♓
May 8	4:15 A.M.	Aries	♈
	5:58 A.M.	Cetus	⊶
	7:41 A.M.	Taurus	♉
	9:24 A.M.	Gemini	♊
	11:07 A.M.	Cancer	♋
	12:50 P.M.	Leo	♌
	2:23 P.M.	Virgo	♍
	4:16 P.M.	Libra	♎
	5:59 P.M.	Scorpio	♏
	7:42 P.M.	Ophiuchus	⛎
	9:23 P.M.	Sagittarius	♐
	11:06 P.M.	Capricorn	♑
	12:49 A.M.	Aquarius	♒
	2:32 A.M.	Pisces	♓
May 15	5:24 A.M.	Cetus	⊶
	7:07 A.M.	Taurus	♉
	8:50 A.M.	Gemini	♊
	10:33 A.M.	Cancer	♋
	12:16 P.M.	Leo	♌
	1:59 P.M.	Virgo	♍
	3:42 P.M.	Libra	♎
	5:25 P.M.	Scorpio	♏
	7:08 P.M.	Ophiuchus	⛎
	8:49 P.M.	Sagittarius	♐
	10:32 P.M.	Capricorn	♑
	12:15 A.M.	Aquarius	♒

Date	Time	Sign	Symbol
May 15	1:58 A.M.	Pisces	♓
cont.	3:41 A.M.	Aries	♈
May 23	4:43 A.M.	Cetus	⊶
	6:26 A.M.	Taurus	♉
	8:09 A.M.	Gemini	♊
	9:52 A.M.	Cancer	♋
	11:35 A.M.	Leo	♌
	1:18 P.M.	Virgo	♍
	3:01 P.M.	Libra	♎
	4:44 P.M.	Scorpio	♏
	6:27 P.M.	Ophiuchus	⛎
	8:08 P.M.	Sagittarius	♐
	9:51 P.M.	Capricorn	♑
	11:34 P.M.	Aquarius	♒
	1:17 A.M.	Pisces	♓
	3:00 A.M.	Aries	♈
June 1	4:04 A.M.	Cetus	⊶
	5:47 A.M.	Taurus	♉
	7:30 A.M.	Gemini	♊
	9:13 A.M.	Cancer	♋
	10:56 A.M.	Leo	♌
	12:39 P.M.	Virgo	♍
	2:22 P.M.	Libra	♎
	4:05 P.M.	Scorpio	♏
	5:48 P.M.	Ophiuchus	⛎
	7:29 P.M.	Sagittarius	♐
	9:12 P.M.	Capricorn	♑
	10:55 P.M.	Aquarius	♒
	12:38 A.M.	Pisces	♓
	2:21 A.M.	Aries	♈
June 8	5:18 A.M.	Taurus	♉
	7:01 A.M.	Gemini	♊
	8:44 A.M.	Cancer	♋
	10:27 A.M.	Leo	♌
	12:10 P.M.	Virgo	♍
	1:53 P.M.	Libra	♎
	3:36 P.M.	Scorpio	♏

TABLE 2 19

Date	Time	Sign	Symbol	Date	Time	Sign	Symbol
June 8	5:19 P.M.	Ophiuchus	⚕	July 1	8:56 A.M.	Leo	♌
cont.	7:02 P.M.	Sagittarius	♐	cont.	10:39 A.M.	Virgo	♍
	8:45 P.M.	Capricorn	♑		12:22 P.M.	Libra	♎
	10:28 P.M.	Aquarius	♒		2:05 P.M.	Scorpio	♏
	12:11 A.M.	Pisces	♓		3:48 P.M.	Ophiuchus	⚕
	1:54 A.M.	Aries	♈		5:31 P.M.	Sagittarius	♐
	3:37 A.M.	Cetus	⬗		7:14 P.M.	Capricorn	♑
					8:57 P.M.	Aquarius	♒
June 15	4:48 A.M.	Taurus	♉		10:40 P.M.	Pisces	♓
	6:31 A.M.	Gemini	♊		12:23 A.M.	Aries	♈
	8:14 A.M.	Cancer	♋		2:06 A.M.	Cetus	⬗
	9:57 A.M.	Leo	♌				
	11:40 A.M.	Virgo	♍	July 8	5:07 A.M.	Gemini	♊
	1:23 P.M.	Libra	♎		6:50 A.M.	Cancer	♋
	3:06 P.M.	Scorpio	♏		8:33 A.M.	Leo	♌
	4:49 P.M.	Ophiuchus	⚕		10:16 A.M.	Virgo	♍
	6:32 P.M.	Sagittarius	♐		11:59 A.M.	Libra	♎
	8:15 P.M.	Capricorn	♑		1:42 P.M.	Scorpio	♏
	9:58 P.M.	Aquarius	♒		3:25 P.M.	Ophiuchus	⚕
	11:41 P.M.	Pisces	♓		5:08 P.M.	Sagittarius	♐
	1:24 A.M.	Aries	♈		6:51 P.M.	Capricorn	♑
	3:07 A.M.	Cetus	⬗		8:34 P.M.	Aquarius	♒
					10:17 P.M.	Pisces	♓
June 23	4:19 A.M.	Taurus	♉		12:00 P.M.	Aries	♈
	6:02 A.M.	Gemini	♊		1:43 A.M.	Cetus	⬗
	7:45 A.M.	Cancer	♋		3:26 A.M.	Taurus	♉
	9:28 A.M.	Leo	♌				
	11:11 A.M.	Virgo	♍	July 15	4:42 A.M.	Gemini	♊
	12:54 P.M.	Libra	♎		6:25 A.M.	Cancer	♋
	2:37 P.M.	Scorpio	♏		8:08 A.M.	Leo	♌
	4:20 P.M.	Ophiuchus	⚕		9:51 A.M.	Virgo	♍
	6:03 P.M.	Sagittarius	♐		11:34 A.M.	Libra	♎
	7:46 P.M.	Capricorn	♑		1:17 P.M.	Scorpio	♏
	9:29 P.M.	Aquarius	♒		3:00 P.M.	Ophiuchus	⚕
	11:12 P.M.	Pisces	♓		4:43 P.M.	Sagittarius	♐
	12:55 A.M.	Aries	♈		6:26 P.M.	Capricorn	♑
	2:38 A.M.	Cetus	⬗		8:09 P.M.	Aquarius	♒
					9:52 P.M.	Pisces	♓
July 1	3:47 A.M.	Taurus	♉		11:35 P.M.	Aries	♈
	5:30 A.M.	Gemini	♊		1:18 A.M.	Cetus	⬗
	7:13 A.M.	Cancer	♋		3:01 A.M.	Taurus	♉

Date	Time	Sign	Symbol	Date	Time	Sign	Symbol
July 23	4:19 A.M.	Gemini	♊	Aug. 8	12:05 A.M.	Cetus	⊷
	6:02 A.M.	Cancer	♋	cont.	1:48 A.M.	Taurus	♉
	7:45 A.M.	Leo	♌		3:31 A.M.	Gemini	♊
	9:28 A.M.	Virgo	♍				
	11:11 A.M.	Libra	♎	Aug. 15	4:53 A.M.	Cancer	♋
	12:54 P.M.	Scorpio	♏		6:36 A.M.	Leo	♌
	2:37 P.M.	Ophiuchus	⚕		8:19 A.M.	Virgo	♍
	4:20 P.M.	Sagittarius	♐		10:02 A.M.	Libra	♎
	6:03 P.M.	Capricorn	♑		11:45 A.M.	Scorpio	♏
	7:46 P.M.	Aquarius	♒		1:28 P.M.	Ophiuchus	⚕
	9:29 P.M.	Pisces	♓		3:11 P.M.	Sagittarius	♐
	11:12 P.M.	Aries	♈		4:54 P.M.	Capricorn	♑
	12:55 A.M.	Cetus	⊷		6:37 P.M.	Aquarius	♒
	2:38 A.M.	Taurus	♉		8:20 P.M.	Pisces	♓
					10:03 P.M.	Aries	♈
Aug. 1	5:36 A.M.	Cancer	♋		11:46 P.M.	Cetus	⊷
	7:19 A.M.	Leo	♌		1:29 A.M.	Taurus	♉
	9:02 A.M.	Virgo	♍		3:12 A.M.	Gemini	♊
	10:45 A.M.	Libra	♎				
	12:28 P.M.	Scorpio	♏	Aug. 23	4:27 A.M.	Cancer	♋
	2:11 P.M.	Ophiuchus	⚕		6:10 A.M.	Leo	♌
	3:54 P.M.	Sagittarius	♐		7:53 A.M.	Virgo	♍
	5:37 P.M.	Capricorn	♑		9:36 A.M.	Libra	♎
	7:20 P.M.	Aquarius	♒		11:19 A.M.	Scorpio	♏
	9:03 P.M.	Pisces	♓		1:02 P.M.	Ophiuchus	⚕
	10:46 P.M.	Aries	♈		2:45 P.M.	Sagittarius	♐
	12:29 A.M.	Cetus	⊷		4:28 P.M.	Capricorn	♑
	2:12 A.M.	Taurus	♉		6:11 P.M.	Aquarius	♒
	3:55 A.M.	Gemini	♊		7:54 P.M.	Pisces	♓
					9:37 P.M.	Aries	♈
Aug. 8	5:12 A.M.	Cancer	♋		11:20 P.M.	Cetus	⊷
	6:55 A.M.	Leo	♌		1:03 A.M.	Taurus	♉
	8:38 A.M.	Virgo	♍		2:46 A.M.	Gemini	♊
	10:21 A.M.	Libra	♎				
	12:04 P.M.	Scorpio	♏	Sept. 1	5:43 A.M.	Leo	♌
	1:47 P.M.	Ophiuchus	⚕		7:26 A.M.	Virgo	♍
	3:30 P.M.	Sagittarius	♐		9:09 A.M.	Libra	♎
	5:13 P.M.	Capricorn	♑		10:52 A.M.	Scorpio	♏
	6:56 P.M.	Aquarius	♒		12:35 P.M.	Ophiuchus	⚕
	8:39 P.M.	Pisces	♓		2:18 P.M.	Sagittarius	♐
	10:22 P.M.	Aries	♈		4:01 P.M.	Capricorn	♑

TABLE 2 21

Date	Time	Sign	Symbol	Date	Time	Sign	Symbol
Sept. 1	5:44 P.M.	Aquarius	♒	Sept. 23	9:47 A.M.	Scorpio	♏
cont.	7:27 P.M.	Pisces	♓	cont.	11:30 A.M.	Ophiuchus	⛎
	9:10 P.M.	Aries	♈		1:13 P.M.	Sagittarius	♐
	10:53 P.M.	Cetus	⊂		2:56 P.M.	Capricorn	♑
	12:36 A.M.	Taurus	♉		4:39 P.M.	Aquarius	♒
	2:19 A.M.	Gemini	♊		6:22 P.M.	Pisces	♓
	4:02 A.M.	Cancer	♋		8:05 P.M.	Aries	♈
					9:48 P.M.	Cetus	⊂
Sept. 8	5:25 A.M.	Leo	♌		11:31 P.M.	Taurus	♉
	7:08 A.M.	Virgo	♍		1:14 A.M.	Gemini	♊
	8:51 A.M.	Libra	♎		2:57 A.M.	Cancer	♋
	10:34 A.M.	Scorpio	♏		4:40 A.M.	Leo	♌
	12:17 P.M.	Ophiuchus	⛎				
	2:00 P.M.	Sagittarius	♐	Oct. 1	5:55 A.M.	Virgo	♍
	3:43 P.M.	Capricorn	♑		7:38 A.M.	Libra	♎
	5:26 P.M.	Aquarius	♒		9:21 A.M.	Scorpio	♏
	7:09 P.M.	Pisces	♓		11:04 A.M.	Ophiuchus	⛎
	8:52 P.M.	Aries	♈		12:47 P.M.	Sagittarius	♐
	10:35 P.M.	Cetus	⊂		2:30 P.M.	Capricorn	♑
	12:18 A.M.	Taurus	♉		4:13 P.M.	Aquarius	♒
	2:01 A.M.	Gemini	♊		5:56 P.M.	Pisces	♓
	3:44 A.M.	Cancer	♋		7:39 P.M.	Aries	♈
					9:22 P.M.	Cetus	⊂
Sept. 15	5:02 A.M.	Leo	♌		11:05 P.M.	Taurus	♉
	6:45 A.M.	Virgo	♍		12:48 A.M.	Gemini	♊
	8:28 A.M.	Libra	♎		2:31 A.M.	Cancer	♋
	10:11 A.M.	Scorpio	♏		4:14 A.M.	Leo	♌
	11:54 A.M.	Ophiuchus	⛎				
	1:37 P.M.	Sagittarius	♐	Oct. 8	5:37 A.M.	Virgo	♍
	3:20 P.M.	Capricorn	♑		7:20 A.M.	Libra	♎
	5:03 P.M.	Aquarius	♒		9:03 A.M.	Scorpio	♏
	6:46 P.M.	Pisces	♓		10:46 A.M.	Ophiuchus	⛎
	8:29 P.M.	Aries	♈		12:29 P.M.	Sagittarius	♐
	10:12 P.M.	Cetus	⊂		2:12 P.M.	Capricorn	♑
	11:55 P.M.	Taurus	♉		3:55 P.M.	Aquarius	♒
	1:38 A.M.	Gemini	♊		5:38 P.M.	Pisces	♓
	3:21 A.M.	Cancer	♋		7:21 P.M.	Aries	♈
					9:04 P.M.	Cetus	⊂
Sept. 23	6:21 A.M.	Virgo	♍		10:47 P.M.	Taurus	♉
	8:04 A.M.	Libra	♎		12:30 A.M.	Gemini	♊

Date	Time	Sign	Symbol
Oct. 8 cont.	2:13 A.M.	Cancer	♋
	3:56 A.M.	Leo	♌
Oct. 15	7:01 A.M.	Libra	♎
	8:44 A.M.	Scorpio	♏
	10:27 A.M.	Ophiuchus	⛎
	12:10 P.M.	Sagittarius	♐
	1:53 P.M.	Capricorn	♑
	3:36 P.M.	Aquarius	♒
	5:19 P.M.	Pisces	♓
	7:02 P.M.	Aries	♈
	8:45 P.M.	Cetus	⎛
	10:28 P.M.	Taurus	♉
	12:11 A.M.	Gemini	♊
	1:54 A.M.	Cancer	♋
	3:37 A.M.	Leo	♌
	5:20 A.M.	Virgo	♍
Oct. 23	6:35 A.M.	Libra	♎
	8:18 A.M.	Scorpio	♏
	10:01 A.M.	Ophiuchus	⛎
	11:44 A.M.	Sagittarius	♐
	1:27 P.M.	Capricorn	♑
	3:10 P.M.	Aquarius	♒
	4:53 P.M.	Pisces	♓
	6:36 P.M.	Aries	♈
	8:19 P.M.	Cetus	⎛
	10:02 P.M.	Taurus	♉
	11:45 P.M.	Gemini	♊
	1:28 A.M.	Cancer	♋
	3:11 A.M.	Leo	♌
	4:54 A.M.	Virgo	♍
Nov. 1	6:11 A.M.	Libra	♎
	7:54 A.M.	Scorpio	♏
	9:37 A.M.	Ophiuchus	⛎
	11:20 A.M.	Sagittarius	♐
	1:03 P.M.	Capricorn	♑
	2:46 P.M.	Aquarius	♒
	4:29 P.M.	Pisces	♓
	6:12 P.M.	Aries	♈

Date	Time	Sign	Symbol
Nov. 1 cont.	7:55 P.M.	Cetus	⎛
	9:38 P.M.	Taurus	♉
	11:21 P.M.	Gemini	♊
	1:04 A.M.	Cancer	♋
	2:47 A.M.	Leo	♌
	4:30 A.M.	Virgo	♍
Nov. 8	5:50 A.M.	Libra	♎
	7:33 A.M.	Scorpio	♏
	9:16 A.M.	Ophiuchus	⛎
	10:59 A.M.	Sagittarius	♐
	12:42 P.M.	Capricorn	♑
	2:25 P.M.	Aquarius	♒
	4:08 P.M.	Pisces	♓
	5:51 P.M.	Aries	♈
	7:34 P.M.	Cetus	⎛
	9:17 P.M.	Taurus	♉
	11:00 P.M.	Gemini	♊
	12:43 A.M.	Cancer	♋
	2:26 A.M.	Leo	♌
	4:09 A.M.	Virgo	♍
Nov. 15	7:14 A.M.	Scorpio	♏
	8:57 A.M.	Ophiuchus	⛎
	10:40 A.M.	Sagittarius	♐
	12:23 P.M.	Capricorn	♑
	2:06 P.M.	Aquarius	♒
	3:49 P.M.	Pisces	♓
	5:32 P.M.	Aries	♈
	7:15 P.M.	Cetus	⎛
	8:58 P.M.	Taurus	♉
	10:41 P.M.	Gemini	♊
	12:24 A.M.	Cancer	♋
	2:07 A.M.	Leo	♌
	3:50 A.M.	Virgo	♍
	5:33 A.M.	Libra	♎
Nov. 23	6:54 A.M.	Scorpio	♏
	8:37 A.M.	Ophiuchus	⛎
	10:20 A.M.	Sagittarius	♐
	12:03 P.M.	Capricorn	♑

TABLE 2 23

Date	Time	Sign	Symbol	Date	Time	Sign	Symbol
Nov. 23	1:46 P.M.	Aquarius	♒	Dec. 8	11:17 P.M.	Cancer	♋
cont.	3:29 P.M.	Pisces	♓	cont.	1:00 A.M.	Leo	♌
	5:12 P.M.	Aries	♈		2:43 A.M.	Virgo	♍
	6:55 P.M.	Cetus	⊂⟋		4:26 A.M.	Libra	♎
	8:38 P.M.	Taurus	♉		6:09 A.M.	Scorpio	♏
	10:21 P.M.	Gemini	♊				
	12:04 A.M.	Cancer	♋	Dec. 15	7:26 A.M.	Ophiuchus	⚕
	1:47 A.M.	Leo	♌		9:09 A.M.	Sagittarius	♐
	3:30 A.M.	Virgo	♍		10:51 A.M.	Capricorn	♑
	5:13 A.M.	Libra	♎		12:34 P.M.	Aquarius	♒
					2:17 P.M.	Pisces	♓
Dec. 1	6:27 A.M.	Scorpio	♏		4:00 P.M.	Aries	♈
	8:10 A.M.	Ophiuchus	⚕		5:43 P.M.	Cetus	⊂⟋
	9:53 A.M.	Sagittarius	♐		7:27 P.M.	Taurus	♉
	11:36 A.M.	Capricorn	♑		9:10 P.M.	Gemini	♊
	1:19 P.M.	Aquarius	♒		10:52 P.M.	Cancer	♋
	3:02 P.M.	Pisces	♓		12:35 A.M.	Leo	♌
	4:45 P.M.	Aries	♈		2:18 A.M.	Virgo	♍
	6:28 P.M.	Cetus	⊂⟋		4:01 A.M.	Libra	♎
	8:11 P.M.	Taurus	♉		5:44 A.M.	Scorpio	♏
	9:54 P.M.	Gemini	♊				
	11:37 P.M.	Cancer	♋	Dec. 23	7:01 A.M.	Ophiuchus	⚕
	1:20 A.M.	Leo	♌		8:44 A.M.	Sagittarius	♐
	3:03 A.M.	Virgo	♍		10:27 A.M.	Capricorn	♑
	4:46 A.M.	Libra	♎		12:10 P.M.	Aquarius	♒
					1:53 P.M.	Pisces	♓
Dec. 8	7:50 A.M.	Ophiuchus	⚕		3:36 P.M.	Aries	♈
	9:33 A.M.	Sagittarius	♐		5:19 P.M.	Cetus	⊂⟋
	11:16 A.M.	Capricorn	♑		7:02 P.M.	Taurus	♉
	12:59 P.M.	Aquarius	♒		8:45 P.M.	Gemini	♊
	2:42 P.M.	Pisces	♓		10:28 P.M.	Cancer	♋
	4:25 P.M.	Aries	♈		12:11 A.M.	Leo	♌
	6:08 P.M.	Cetus	⊂⟋		1:54 A.M.	Virgo	♍
	7:51 P.M.	Taurus	♉		3:37 A.M.	Libra	♎
	9:34 P.M.	Gemini	♊		5:20 A.M.	Scorpio	♏

2: Your Sun Sign

OLD AND NEW SUN SIGNS

YOUR SUN SIGN is the sign (or constellation) in which the sun was apparently moving at the moment of your birth. The apparent motion of the sun has already been described. But what does it mean to say that the sun is "in" a certain sign? It simply means that, from our position on earth, the sun, in its yearly journey along the ecliptic, moves against a background of stars. In the dim past, when men first began to study the heavens systematically, it was found convenient to divide the stars into groups, which were called *constellations*, and lines were drawn to connect the stars of a group to form fanciful pictures of men, gods, and other creatures. For example: a cluster of stars through which the sun passes in the autumn was thought to resemble a scorpion; the ancients therefore embellished their representations of this constellation by drawing a scorpion —and to this day we call the constellation Scorpio.

How many constellations are there? There is a total of 89, covering the entire sphere of stars visible from the earth. However, early observers placed particular significance on the constellations that clustered around the ecliptic (or sun path). Because many of the constellations through which the sun passed were named after animals, they called the band on either side of the ecliptic the Zodiac ("circle of animals"). In very early times, it is known that there were 10 constellations (or *signs*) in the Zodiac. About two thousand years ago, when the system of astrology now generally in use was first set up, 12 zodiacal signs were recognized. Now, in the twentieth century, two more signs—Cetus and Ophiuchus—

have moved into the belt of the Zodiac, bringing the total to 14. The stars do move, although very slowly from our point of view, and it was the need to update astrology, so that it conforms to the appearance of the heavens today, that led me to write Astrology 14.

As I described in that book, the spring point or vernal equinox also moves, due to a motion called the precession of the equinoxes, so that the sun now enters Pisces on the first day of spring. Traditional astrology still has the sun entering Aries at the vernal equinox, as it did in the time of Julius Caesar. Pisces, therefore, occupies the first House of a generalized horoscope, and Aries occupies the second House (see Chapter 1).

One point should be made very clear. I have been accused, since the publication of Astrology 14, of changing the signs that people are used to and feel comfortable with. I have changed nothing. The system of Astrology 14 is based on scientific facts—astronomical facts that can easily be verified by consulting any manual of astronomy. Astrology, as it is practiced today, is two thousand years out of date; I have simply updated it and attempted to place astrology on a scientific basis in accordance with the universe as it now appears. For example: my birthdate is July 7. All my life I was told that Cancer is my sun sign. Astrology 14 reveals that the sun was actually in the constellation Gemini when I was born. True, Cancer would have been my sun sign had I been born twenty centuries ago, but—whatever the ups and downs of interpretation may be—it is a fact that Gemini is my sun sign. If you are not interested in such facts, or prefer to ignore them, then Astrology 14 is not for you. On the other hand, if you are willing to accept the facts of science, and believe that astrology can and should be transformed from an occult art into a true science, you must be willing to accept that your sun sign is probably different from the one you have been led to believe is yours. Not everyone's sun sign is different in Astrology 14, but even those that remain the same are interpreted differently, as will be seen below.

All of the "traditional" 12 sun signs are still in the Zodiac. To these have been added the signs of Cetus, the Whale (May 12 to June 6), and Ophiuchus, the Serpent-Slayer (December 6 to 31). Adding these two "new" signs means that each of the 14 sun signs occupies less space in the circle of the Zodiac—about 26 degrees each instead of the 30 degrees of traditional astrology. With the movement of the spring point from Aries to Pisces, the dates for all of the sun signs are changed. Table 3 lists the sun signs, old and new, along with their dates, for purposes of comparison.

Placing the sun on your chart, then, is a simple matter of finding your sun sign by looking up your birthdate in Table 3, then drawing the symbol of the sun (⊙) in the House occupied by that sign on your chart. Be sure

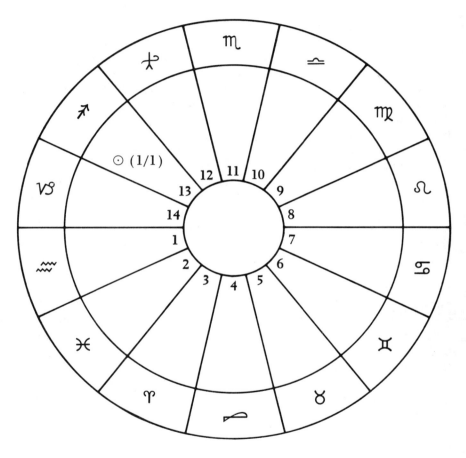

Figure 3. Placement of sun on chart of subject born on January 1, 1940, with Aquarius rising

Table 3. COMPARISON OF DATES

Sign	Sun Sign	Astrology 14	Traditional
♓	Pisces	March 21 to April 15	Feb. 20 to March 20
♈	Aries	April 16 to May 11	March 21 to April 20
⊷	Cetus	May 12 to June 6	—
♉	Taurus	June 7 to July 2	April 21 to May 21
♊	Gemini	July 3 to July 28	May 22 to June 21
♋	Cancer	July 29 to Aug. 23	June 22 to July 23
♌	Leo	Aug. 24 to Sept. 18	July 24 to Aug. 23
♍	Virgo	Sept. 19 to Oct. 14	Aug. 24 to Sept. 23
♎	Libra	Oct. 15 to Nov. 9	Sept. 24 to Oct. 23
♏	Scorpio	Nov. 10 to Dec. 5	Oct. 24 to Nov. 22
⚷	Ophiuchus	Dec. 6 to Dec. 31	—
♐	Sagittarius	Jan. 1 to Jan. 26	Nov. 23 to Dec. 21
♑	Capricorn	Jan. 27 to Feb. 21	Dec. 22 to Jan. 20
♒	Aquarius	Feb. 22 to March 20	Jan. 21 to Feb. 19

to include the date in parentheses beside the symbol. For our example of a subject born on January 1, 1940, the sun is placed in Sagittarius on his chart (Figure 3). Since his rising sign is Aquarius, Sagittarius occupies his thirteenth House.

Each of the 14 sun signs is described in the pages that follow, and a general interpretation of each sign is given. It should be remembered that, for greater accuracy, the interpretation of your rising sign (Chapter 1) must be compared with the interpretation of your sun sign. The number of degrees between your rising sign and sun sign is also important; this will be taken up under *Aspects*, in Chapter 12.

INTERPRETATION

In the system of Astrology 14, the interpretation of your sun sign is based upon individuals born under that sign. This is the exact opposite of the method of traditional astrology, which pushes people into predetermined niches according to the date of their birth. For example: people born under Leo, according to the old system, were thought to be strong, magnanimous, jovial, even-tempered, and extraverted. Why? Because Leo is ruled by the sun. The ruling planet *does* have an influence, of course, but common sense tells us it is ridiculous to use the above adjectives to describe millions of people—one-twelfth of the human race—simply because they were born between July 24 and August 23. Most of us have known people born in that time period who were not at all jovial and whose dispositions were anything but sunny!

If the old system is false, then, what does determine the characteristics of persons born under a certain sun sign? Astrology 14 follows the method of science, which studies the individual data first, *then* proceeds to draw general conclusions. Since my aim is to help put astrology on a scientific basis, I have at least made a beginning in that direction by establishing an astrological characterology that is based on the scientific method. That is, I have collected *people* born under each of the 14 sun signs—at least one name for each date of the year—and base my interpretations on a close study of each group. What do they have in common? How are the individuals born under Leo, say, different from those born under Virgo?

To aid my attempts to answer such questions, I have included among the famous names listed for each sign names of individuals known to me personally. This also underscores the fact that astrology applies equally to everyone—to the humble and obscure as well as the great and renowned.

Although they go beyond the interpretations given in *Astrology 14,* the conclusions I have drawn are, of course, tentative. A great deal more work and research are necessary before anything like firm interpretations can be made. Astrology is an ancient art, but Astrology 14 is a new departure, and has already stirred up a considerable controversy. I welcome other writers and astrologers to use my system, test it, and—if possible—disprove it. For another rule of the scientific method is that a theory is never considered absolute; it stands only as long as its statements hold true. Even the atomic theory, well-established by modern physics and mathematics—with the atomic bomb as a dramatic demonstration—is still only a *theory.* It could be scrapped tomorrow if facts about the structure of matter were discovered that the theory of atomic particles couldn't account for. With the present book, every reader can test the theory of Astrology 14 for himself—by casting his own horoscope. He can then compare the results with a horoscope cast by the traditional system, and decide for himself which fits him more accurately.

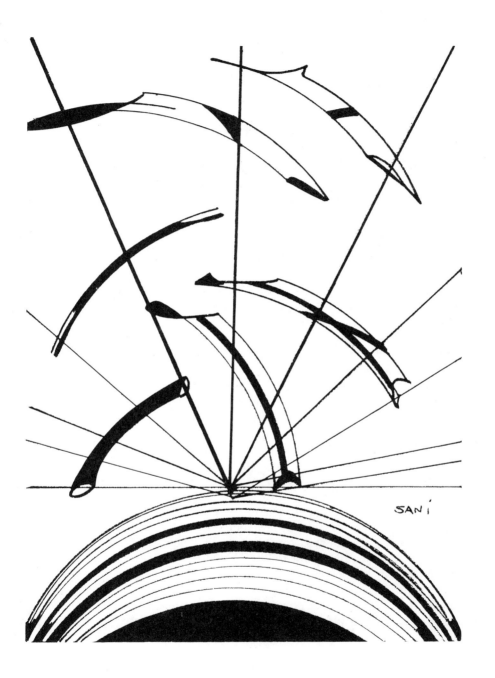

Pisces
(March 21 to April 15)

Pisces, the Fish, is the first sign of the Zodiac. It is, therefore, the spring sign, displacing Aries at the beginning of the zodiacal year, as already described. The vernal equinox, or first day of spring, is the midpoint between the winter solstice (shortest day of the year) and summer solstice (longest day of the year). That the spring point moves backward through the signs of the Zodiac, due to the precession of the equinoxes, is a fact recognized not only by astronomers, but by the followers of sidereal astrology, who should be given credit for this much of a scientific approach.

The ruling planet of Pisces is Neptune, a heavenly body much larger than the earth and much farther from the sun. Eighth of the nine known planets, it was named for the ancient god of the sea. Neptune (or Poseidon), like Saturn, was the ruler of a vast and mysterious realm. Even today, we know more about the surface of the moon than we do of the depths of the sea. Astrologically, the keywords of Neptune are *nebulousness* and *impressionability*, and it is usually associated with matters of the spirit, with belief that goes beyond rational science and everyday affairs. If Pisces is your sun sign, this planet is of particular importance in your horoscope (see Chapter 10).

In *Astrology 14*, I compared the traditional interpretation of the Piscean personality with my preliminary findings based on a study of 22 persons born under this sign. This material will not be repeated here; the interested reader is referred to my previous book (pp. 39–42).

I have enlarged the list of Pisceans to 47 individuals. The interpretation that follows is based on this extended list. It must be stressed that, except for the few known to me personally, these people were chosen at random—I made no attempt to "load the dice" to favor my interpretation.

My initial study found Pisceans to be determined, strong-willed, and ambitious, with versatility a secondary characteristic. Nothing in my further research disproves these basic findings. However, the influence of the ruling planet, Neptune, must always be kept in mind. Neptune is usually concerned with belief in spiritual affairs. We live in a materialistic age, one in which belief (in its traditional sense) has often gone by the boards. Many of you children of Pisces probably do not consider yourselves religious, do not attend church or temple, and profess to be willing to take on only one world at a time. How, then, is Neptune's influence felt by you? Modern psychology teaches us that nothing in the psyche dies or is ever really forgotten. Anything that is suppressed, forgotten, or "blocked" lives on in your unconscious mind, exerting an influence that is nonetheless real for being secret. You are a strong believer, whether you are consciously aware of it or not.

A point that should be mentioned in this context is that, in a time such as ours when "official" religion is in decline, many people seek substitutes for an organized, dogmatic faith. The current widespread interest in the occult is proof enough of this. As church attendance goes down, the popularity of magic, witchcraft, Satanism, the Tarot, etc., goes up. Zen Buddhism is having a fantastic success in the United States and Europe, considering its origins in the East. And, if you are honest with yourself, you will admit that there is something behind your interest in astrology. You may not be a "true believer," but your interest is at least strong enough to lead you to read this book!

It seems to be a basic rule of the human psyche that people need to believe in something.

"I believe in myself!" the strong-willed Piscean is likely to retort. That is true of most of you, but it is still a form of belief. Pisces, with Neptune ruling, tends to strengthen whatever belief you may hold: in yourself, in a cause or political party, or in a religion. Nearly everyone is ambitious to succeed at something, be it to bake the best cake at the county fair or to paint a greater masterpiece than Michelangelo's Sistine ceiling, but the circumstances of life thwart most of us, and our dreams go unfulfilled. You Piscean have an advantage here. The iron in your personality, your single-minded drive to succeed, often enables you to overcome obstacles that would discourage or completely stop another. There is an old saying that genius is 99 percent perspiration and only 1 percent inspiration; where this holds true, you will probably achieve the goal you are so determined to reach. Most likely you agree with Cassius when he tells his friend, "The fault, dear Brutus, is not in our stars but in ourselves, that we are underlings."

You are probably a pragmatist and think of yourself as hard-headed and realistic. You believe in the evidence of your senses, in hard facts and in solid results, and are willing to work long and hard once you have set a course for yourself. Despite the findings of modern science and philosophy, in which the universe appears to be more and more irrational, you firmly believe in a rational, ordered world, with cause-and-effect reigning supreme. You can point with pride to the achievements of modern civilization—much of it was built by people such as yourself, scratching cities out of jungles and throwing bridges across yawning gulfs. This is true, but it should also be remembered that a driving will can destroy as well as create. Otto von Bismarck (April 1), for example, did much to build Germany into a great nation, but his ruthless motto, "Blood and Iron," also led to suffering, death, and destruction.

Success, therefore, is almost certainly yours, or within your grasp, if the other elements in your horoscope are favorable. Your willingness to work long, hard hours will stand you in good stead because the children of Pisces are not generally the heroes of overnight success stories. You may have to struggle against poverty and other adverse conditions to reach your goal, but once it is attained, you will have all the more reason to take pride in your accomplishment. Neptune can either help or hinder your efforts, depending on its position with relation to other elements in your chart.

There is some danger that your single-minded drive to succeed may be at the expense of your family and friends. This is unlikely in most cases, however, because another trait of Pisces is *versatility*. Most of you are able to handle your main career, pursue a side occupation or hobby, and lead a full familial and social life—but beware of a tendency to lose yourself too completely in whatever occupies your time and energy at the moment.

Every personality has many sides, of course, and I do not wish to leave the impression of the Piscean as a dull, undeviating plodder, with everything sacrificed to success. Most of you have an excellent sense of humor, and are usually successful at not taking either yourselves or life in general too seriously. Your specialty is the dead-pan anecdote and the playing of subtle, often quite complicated practical jokes on your friends. You delight in putting them on, then observing the effect when the truth sinks in.

Pisces, then, is strong-willed, ambitious, clever, humorous, and versatile enough to achieve a successful, well-rounded life. It must be remembered, however, that this is only the basic interpretation of your sun sign. It must be compared with your rising sign (Chapter 1) and with all the other elements in your horoscope, which will be described in the chapters that follow.

RELATIONSHIP OF PISCES TO OTHER SIGNS

Compatible	Incompatible	Neutral
Pisces*	Taurus	Aries
Cetus	Gemini	Leo
Cancer	Virgo	Libra
Scorpio	Ophiuchus	Aquarius
Capricorn	Sagittarius	

* If born within 10 days of own birthdate.

PISCES
(March 21 to April 15)

March

21	Peter Brook (director)
22	Joseph Schildkraut (actor)
23	Joan Crawford (actress)
23	Wernher von Braun (rocket scientist)
24	Thomas E. Dewey (statesman)
25	Ed Begley (actor)
26	Robert Frost (poet)
27	Budd Schulberg (writer)
27	Gloria Swanson (actress)
28	Christian Herter (statesman)
28	Rudolf Serkin (pianist)
29	Pearl Bailey (singer)
29	Eugene McCarthy (U.S. Senator)
29	John Tyler (10th U.S. President)
30	Warren Beatty (actor)
30	Vincent Van Gogh (painter)
31	William Waldorf Astor (capitalist)

April

1	Vivian Heeschen (dream interpreter)
1	Debbie Reynolds (actress)
1	Edmond Rostand (poet/dramatist)
1	Prince Otto von Bismarck (statesman)
2	Walter Chrysler (auto manufacturer)
2	Emile Zola (writer)
3	Marlon Brando (actor)
3	Henry R. Luce (publisher)
4	Arthur Murray (dance instructor)
4	John H. Schmidt (engineer)
5	Bette Davis (actress)
5	Gregory Peck (actor)
5	Spencer Tracy (actor)
6	Edmund Bennett (lawyer)
7	Kurt von Schleicher (general/statesman)
8	Mary Pickford (actress)
9	Nikolai Lenin (founder of Soviet Union)
9	Paul Robeson (singer)
9	Helen Scheuchenpflug (housewife)
10	Clare Boothe Luce (writer/politician)
10	Omar Sharif (actor)
11	Dean Acheson (statesman)

12   Gerhardt Schmidt (Lutheran pastor)
12   Karl Schmidt (principal)
13   Thomas Jefferson (3rd U.S. President)
13   Lily Pons (singer)
14   Julie Christie (actress)
14   Rod Steiger (actor)
15   Henry James (writer)
15   Elizabeth Montgomery (actress)

Aries

(April 16 to May 11)

♈

Aries, the Ram, is the second sign of the Zodiac. For centuries it was retained as the first sign by astrologers who did not note (or ignored) the precession of the equinoxes. In the system of Astrology 14, Aries is placed in its proper position as the second sun sign of the zodiacal year.

The ruling planet of Aries is Mars, a neighbor to the earth but smaller and farther from the sun. Fourth of the nine known planets, it was named for the ancient god of war. Mars has been much in the news recently, and will probably be the next goal of our astronauts. Although photographs sent back by *Mariner* spacecraft show a pocked surface much like that of the moon, with no signs of intelligent life, an old legend persists that there was an ancient civilization on Mars, which died when the planet lost its oxygen (hence its reddish color). Mars has two satellites, Deimos and Phobos. These are so small that, a few years ago, a Russian scientist postulated that they might be artificial. However, when *Mariner* 9 went into orbit around Mars in 1971, it began to send back a series of remarkably clear pictures, including shots of these two moonlets. Deimos and Phobos are irregularly shaped chunks of rock, their surfaces pitted by meteorites.

The warlike god Mars (or Ares) represents the *masculine* principle—the exact opposite of the goddess Venus, who is symbolic of the feminine principle. Astrologically, this planet stands for such "masculine" qualities as energy, action, heat, aggression, and power. Mars is a powerful influence in any horoscope and, if Aries is your sun sign, this planet is of particular importance (see Chapter 6).

In *Astrology 14*, I compared the traditional interpretation of the Arian personality with my preliminary findings based on a study of 25 persons born under this sign. This material will not be repeated here; the interested reader is referred to my previous book (pp. 43–47).

I have enlarged the list of Arians to 42 individuals. The interpretation that follows is based on this extended list. It must be stressed that, except for the few known to me personally, these people were chosen at random—I made no attempt to "load the dice" to favor my interpretation.

My initial study found Arians to be creative, especially in the field of literature, with good omens for success in politics, but with a brooding, introspective side to their natures and a stubbornness that can harden into dogma. My further research has not indicated anything false in these preliminary interpretations. The influence of the ruling planet, however, must always be kept in mind. Mars is so powerful that in ancient times it was thought to be an evil planet (because of its association with war and its attendant suffering and destruction). Some of this feeling has come down to the present day, so that we find contemporary astrologers referring to Mars as "a necessary evil." This is not necessarily so. For one thing, the influence of any planet is not absolute; its effect in your chart is strongly dependent upon its relationship to the other elements. Also, aggression is an ambivalent drive (or emotion), and its effects can be either good or bad, depending upon the direction it takes. Adolf Hitler (April 20) was obviously aggressive, and his Mars running rampant ended in the destruction of most of Europe and the death of millions in World War II. On the other hand, man's aggressive drive is also responsible for the building of great civilizations. Without this drive, we certainly would not have seen men walking on the moon.

As a child of Aries, ruled by Mars, you have a strong sense of personal identity. Your ego is firmly established. You feel that you know who you are, whether or not you are clear on what you want and how to achieve it. Unlike the typical Piscean, who makes a point of stressing his belief in himself, you take your individualism so much for granted that it is generally unconscious. You know who you are, automatically, and the currently notorious "loss of identity" is no personal concern of yours. By the same token, you are not apt to spend much time or energy mulling over the existential question, Who am I? The problem of individual identity that is of such concern to modern philosophers and psychologists is probably a puzzle to you. "Don't they know?" you ask, shrug, then go about your own affairs. (This is not to imply a lack of interest in such fields as existentialism; indeed, an Arian friend of mine is a strong believer in this philosophy. It simply means that you don't feel personally involved in such concerns.)

This strength of ego gives the children of Aries the advantage of personal power. Whether quietly or noisily, you tend to dominate—or to exert a dominating influence—in your circle of family and friends. You know who you are, and they, too, are left in little doubt on this point.

This almost total reliance on the ego is, however, a weakness as well as a strength. It means that the unconscious mind is probably unreal to you. A dream, for instance, is "only a dream"—an oddity of sleep, of no concern to the highly conscious direction of your life. But Jung has taught us the importance of a balanced psyche, with the personality dominated neither by the ego nor by the unconscious, which must both work in harmony to produce a healthy, well-balanced, mature human being. Too much emphasis on any one element of the total psyche makes us one-sided, with consequent loss of vitality, or even neurosis.

This is demonstrated by the personality of Sigmund Freud (May 6), who regarded the unconscious as nothing but a repository for the forgotten and suppressed—a sort of dark cellar of the mind, choked with dust and full of broken, outmoded bits of experience. It is ironic that Freud, whose *Interpretation of Dreams* did so much to promote modern psychology, remained blind to the *positive* side of the unconscious, which is the source of psychic energy and the wellspring of all human creativity. But to Freud dreams were "nothing but" wish-fulfillments, and his refusal to listen to the views of his former disciples—Jung and Adler, among others—illustrates the dogmatism and rigidity that Arians are prone to when they are not well balanced.

The children of Aries are strongly creative, however, and literature seems to be their special field. Even those who are not primarily writers tend to write as a sideline or hobby, and they usually write long, fascinating letters, keep a voluminous diary, or both. If your bent is creative, then, the field of literature would be a good one for you to consider. The power of your ruling planet, Mars, can be put to good use as the drive behind a pen or typewriter.

Aries is also an excellent sun sign for political activity. We all have personalities that, primarily, are either introverted or extraverted. The more introverted, the more likely you are to be attracted by private life; the more extraverted, the more a public arena will appeal to you. If you feel at home in the limelight, a political career might be indicated for you—the power of ruling Mars can be at least as great an asset for someone in public life as it is for an artist or writer. As an Arian, however, you would probably chafe at the restrictions of a subordinate position; you hate to be ordered about or follow a dull routine, and you are a born leader. If you don't see an opening at or near the top of your chosen field, you may very well *create* one rather than submit to the laborious process of working your way up from lower echelons. Once you have achieved prominence in the political, social, or business field of your choice, you will find it easy to gain support from others, as people are drawn by the force of your personal magnetism.

Aries, then, is a sign of great power, be it in the public domain or in artistic and other private pursuits. With the driving power of ruling Mars, there is very little that can stop you once you've chosen a goal and started toward it. If you can remember to be wary of signs of dogmatism developing in your personality (such as feeling that you're never wrong

when it comes to the field of your expertise), there is no reason for you
not to achieve a full, happy, and prosperous life under our native star, the
sun. It must be remembered, however, that this is only the basic interpretation of your sun sign. It must be compared with your rising sign (Chapter 1)
and with all the other elements in your horoscope, which will be described
in the chapters to follow.

RELATIONSHIP OF ARIES TO OTHER SIGNS

Compatible	Incompatible	Neutral
Aries*	Gemini	Pisces
Taurus	Cancer	Cetus
Leo	Libra	Virgo
Ophiuchus	Sagittarius	Scorpio
Aquarius	Capricorn	

ARIES

(April 16 to May 11)

April

16	Charlie Chaplin (actor)
17	William Holden (actor)
17	Artur Schnabel (pianist)
17	Betty Shultz (typist)
18	Clarence Darrow (attorney)
18	Elizabeth Bolin Schmidt (housewife)
19	Jayne Mansfield (actress)
20	Lionel Hampton (musician)
20	Adolf Hitler (dictator)
21	Elizabeth II (queen of England)
22	J. Robert Oppenheimer (nuclear physicist)
23	James Buchanan (15th U.S. President)
23	Vladimir Nabokov (writer)
23	Sherman Pearl (writer)
23	Shirley Temple (actress)
24	Shirley MacLaine (actress)
24	Barbra Streisand (singer/actress)
25	Ella Fitzgerald (singer)
26	Stephen Funck (Lutheran pastor)
26	Anita Loos (writer)
26	Jorge Villaseñor, Jr. (cartoonist)
27	Ulysses S. Grant (18th U.S. President)
28	James Monroe (5th U.S. President)
29	Hirohito (emperor of Japan)
30	Fulton Lewis, Jr. (news commentator)

* If born within 10 days of own birthdate.

May

1	Mike Shrieves (history student)
1	Kate Smith (singer)
2	Bing Crosby (singer/actor)
2	Faisal (king of Iraq)
3	Richard Cure (businessman)
4	Audrey Hepburn (actress)
5	Karl Marx (philosopher)
5	Ken Petersen (teacher/writer)
5	Gordon Richards (jockey)
6	Sigmund Freud (psychoanalyst)
6	Orson Welles (actor)
7	Archibald MacLeish (poet)
8	Harry S Truman (33rd U.S. President)
9	Henry Kaiser (industrialist)
10	Fred Astaire (dancer)
11	Irving Berlin (composer)
11	Phil Silvers (comedian)

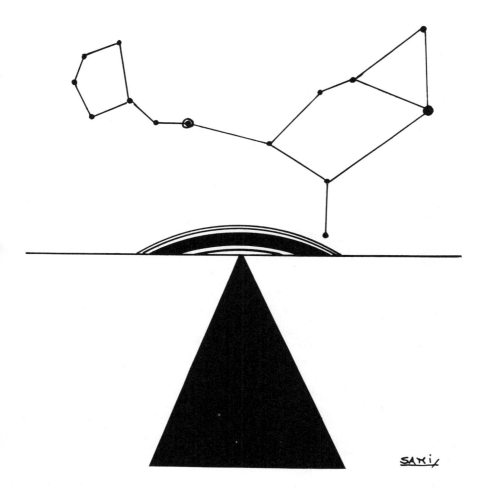

Cetus
(May 12 to June 6)

Cetus, the Whale, is the third sign of the Zodiac. It is one of the two "new" sun signs introduced by Astrology 14. Cetus is no newer than any of the other constellations, of course, but it is new to astrology, as it entered the Zodiac later than the traditional 12 signs. It is the largest of all the constellations, and although only a portion of its tail is in the Zodiac, it is farther into the belt than is Aries, which is apparently in the process of moving out.

Until the publication of my earlier book, Astrology 14, Cetus had not been recognized by astrologers as a zodiacal constellation. However, it was not completely ignored. In traditional astrology, Cetus ruled the marriage-decanate of Aquarius, through which the sun once passed from February 10 to 20. The old astrology considered Cetus to be representative of discord, a vast and evil influence in human affairs, and pictured it as a sea monster rather than the familiar whale. This beast was identified with the sea-denizen that swallowed Jonah and the monster to whom the maiden Andromeda was sacrificed. However, a new interpretation is necessary in this Age of Aquarius, especially since Cetus has been "promoted" from a mere decanate-ruler to a full-fledged sun sign.

The ruling planet of Cetus is Jupiter, the largest of all the planets that circle the sun. Fifth of the nine known planets, it was named for the chief god of the ancients (called Zeus by the Greeks), befitting its great size. Jupiter has no fewer than 12 moons, one of which (Titan) is large enough to have an atmosphere. Men probably will not be able to explore Jupiter directly—its gravity would crush a human being—so these moons will most likely be the bases for our astronauts when they have ventured beyond Mars and the asteroid belt.

Astrologically, Jupiter is the "greater fortune"—a powerful and beneficent influence in any horoscope. We derive the adjective "jovial" from another name for this god, Jove, indicating that people with a strongly placed Jupiter are usually good-natured, expansive, and generous. This planet is of particular importance if Cetus is your sun sign (see Chapter 7).

In Astrology 14, with no previous characteristics to compare for this sun sign, I provided some information on the whale as a mammal and

Cetus as a constellation. This material will not be repeated here; the interested reader is referred to my previous book (pp. 49–50).

My preliminary findings as to the children of Cetus were based on a study of 20 persons born under this sign. I have enlarged this list to 41 individuals, and the interpretation that follows is based on this extended list. It must be stressed that, except for the few known to me personally, these people were chosen at random—I made no attempt to "load the dice" to favor my interpretation.

My initial study found Cetaceans to be people of great natural charm, who find a natural environment in the arts, especially the performing arts and, to a lesser extent, the graphic arts (painting, drawing, and design). Politics, however, seemed definitely indicated *not* to be a career a child of Cetus could profitably take up. Further research has not shown anything false in these preliminary interpretations. The influence of the ruling planet, however, must always be kept in mind. Jupiter is a powerfully beneficent planet and, if in good relation to other elements of your horoscope, could conceivably "bless" a political career. For example: Tito (May 25) successfully ruled Yugoslavia for many years in an extremely tricky situation between the Soviet Union and the West. Sagittarius is also ruled by Jupiter, and the children of that sign are often prominent in public affairs (if not actually involved in politics). However, where Cetus is concerned, Jupiter also seems to have a *repressive* effect. The tragic example of John F. Kennedy (May 29), the only American President born under Cetus, could serve as a warning.

But Cetaceans are as strong in the entertainment world as they are weak politically. Nearly all of you have the magnetic charm characteristic of great performers, and most of you are also talented—another necessary trait for a career in the limelight. If you are an extraverted type, you love being the center of attention, whether before an audience or at home surrounded by your family and a wide circle of interesting friends. As I mentioned in my previous book, many children of Cetus have achieved unusual distinction as actors, singers, and dancers, not a few of them having been knighted or otherwise honored.

If you tend more to be an introverted type, your talent could probably be turned with profit to the graphic arts. Cetaceans seem to have a natural flair for color, design, and harmony. The current widespread interest in painting and drawing must number many Cetaceans among the millions of Sunday painters as well as professional artists. Even if you don't feel the brush or the pen to be your natural instrument, you probably decorate your home with taste and originality, and wear your clothes with dash and style.

What are the weaknesses of Cetus? They are not many, but mention should be made of them. Unlikelihood of success in politics has already been described. As far as your personality is concerned, you tend to be headstrong and sometimes too strongly opinionated. These traits, of course, are often associated with performers; you seldom get to see your name in lights without a certain force and drive to your character. However, it would be a good idea to question your motives occasionally, and to try to take a more liberal attitude toward the opinions of your associates, even if they differ strongly from your own.

This tendency to want always to have things your own way is aggravated by a basic sense of insecurity. You put up a brave front to the world. But beneath all your charm and surface brilliance of manner and effect, you are never quite sure of yourself, sometimes give way to self-doubts when alone too long, and need constant bolstering by your family, friends, associates, and fans, though few of them ever suspect this need.

Whatever career you follow is helped by your ability to dissociate yourself from your surroundings. Unlike the children of Scorpio, for example, you are not bothered by distractions and interruptions once you have set a task for yourself. You sail merrily along and can paint a picture, memorize a part in a play, or cook an omelet in the midst of chaos. This is an enviable trait, and often a necessary one in a world growing ever more crowded and with the level of noise pollution constantly increasing. However, like anything else, it can be pushed beyond reasonable limits. You are not callous, and you are sensitive to the needs of others when you are aware of them; however, your objectivity and ability to engross yourself in the task at hand are sometimes misinterpreted by others as indifference to their wants and needs. This is unjust, of course, but whoever said justice is necessarily present in our world? Look up from your work occasionally, and attend to those around you. They'll love you all the more for it, and you won't have any trouble picking up where you left off.

Cetus, then, is a sign of great personal charisma—of charm that not only attracts lovers and friends, but is a valuable concomitant to a career in the world of entertainment. Though ruling Jupiter has a repressive effect on political careers, Cetus is also an excellent sign for the arts, especially painting, drawing, and design. If you can overcome your secret doubts about yourself, and not become so lost in your activities that you fail to see the needs of loved ones, you can have a wonderful, colorful life, replete with friends and with days full of interesting events. It must be remembered, however, that this is only the basic interpretation of your sun sign. It must be compared with the rising sign (Chapter 1) and with all the other elements in your horoscope, which will be described in the chapters to follow.

RELATIONSHIP OF CETUS TO OTHER SIGNS

Compatible	Incompatible	Neutral
Cetus*	Cancer	Aries
Pisces	Leo	Taurus
Gemini	Scorpio	Libra
Virgo	Capricorn	Ophiuchus
Sagittarius		
Aquarius		

CETUS

(May 12 to June 6)

May

12	Dante Gabriel Rossetti (poet/painter)
12	Philip Wylie (writer)
13	Georges Braque (painter)
14	Bruce Rogers (designer)
15	James Mason (actor)
16	Philip Armour (meat packer)
17	Alfonso XIII (king of Spain)
18	Perry Como (singer)
18	Dame Margot Fonteyn (ballet dancer)
18	Bertrand Russell (philosopher)
19	Dame Nellie Melba (singer)
20	Allan Nevins (historian)
21	Geneva Bridges (housewife)
21	Robert Montgomery (actor)
22	Sir Arthur Conan Doyle (writer)
22	Lord Laurence Olivier (actor)
22	Richard Wagner (composer)
23	John Bardeen (physicist)
24	Bob Dylan (singer)
25	Josip Tito (president of Yugoslavia)
26	Peggy Lee (singer)
27	Hubert Humphrey (politician)
27	Georges Roualt (painter)
27	Herman Wouk (writer)
28	Carroll Baker (actress)
29	Bob Hope (entertainer)
29	John F. Kennedy (35th U.S. President)
30	Cornelia Otis Skinner (actress/writer)
31	Norman Vincent Peale (clergyman)

* If born within 10 days of own birthdate.

June

1	Pat Boone (singer)
1	Arlene Cure (housewife)
1	John Masefield (poet)
1	Marilyn Monroe (actress)
2	Sir Edward Elgar (composer)
3	Tony Curtis (actor)
3	Maurice Evans (actor)
3	Paulette Goddard (actress)
4	Rosalind Russell (actress)
5	Ruth Benedict (anthropologist)
6	Jacobus J. Fouche (president of South Africa)
6	Thomas Mann (writer)

Taurus
(June 7 to July 2)

Taurus, the Bull, is the fourth sign of the Zodiac. In traditional astrology, it was the second sun sign, following Aries. With Pisces in its proper position at the beginning of the zodiacal year and Cetus inserted after Aries, Astrology 14 places Taurus in its correct place as the fourth of the zodiacal constellations.

The ruling planet of Taurus is Venus, earth's other neighbor in the heavens, but closer to the sun and smaller than our planet. Second of the nine known planets, it was named for the goddess of love (the Greek Aphrodite). It is not only close to the earth but is nearest to terrestrial size of all the planets. It was thought for many years that Venus might, therefore, have a civilization similar to ours, and it was a favorite of writers of science fiction and fantasy, who depicted an idyllic setting of great forests and sunny meadows—the Earthly Paradise that earthmen have lost. Direct observation has been impossible, however, because the surface of Venus is always shrouded by a thick layer of clouds. Recent explorations by Russian robot spacecraft that have penetrated this veil indicate that the surface is extremely hot and the atmosphere unbreathable by humans. So much for our dreams of Arcadia! But the truth about Venus will not be known until our astronauts are able to go there.

The lovely goddess Venus (or Aphrodite) represents the *feminine* principle—the exact opposite of Mars, who is symbolic of the masculine principle. Astrologically, there is a close connection between these two planets, as they complement each other. Venus is known as the "lesser fortune" (Jupiter is the "greater fortune"). It is a beneficent planet in your horoscope (unless adversely aspected by other elements), and if Taurus is your sun sign, this planet is of particular importance (see Chapter 5).

In *Astrology 14*, I compared the traditional interpretation of the Taurean personality with my preliminary findings based on a study of 21 persons born under this sign. This material will not be repeated here; the interested reader is referred to my previous book (pp. 54–57).

I have enlarged the list of Taureans to 43 individuals. The interpretation that follows is based on this extended list. It must be stressed that, except for the few known to me personally, these people were chosen at random —I made no attempt to "load the dice" to favor my interpretation.

My initial study found Taureans to be people who love music and are almost always talented in this field, with mathematical ability a secondary trait. I also found the children of Taurus to have only one "bullish" trait— that of great physical strength—and to be generally shy in social situations and slow to make friends. The musical trait was so striking (14 of the 21 on my first list, or 67 percent, were connected with music in one way or another) that I concluded that Taurus must be the strongest sign for music in the Zodiac. Is this borne out by further research? In general, yes. In the larger list, 20 of the 43 are related to a musical career in some way, a little less than 50 percent. Although this is a lower percentage than that of my first list, it is still a definite indication that the children of Taurus have an affinity for music. With this modification, my further research has not indicated the initial interpretations to be false. The influence of the ruling planet, however, must always be kept in mind. Venus is associated with love, of course, as well as with music. If well aspected on your chart, it indicates a good probability of success in affairs of the heart. However, the reverse is also true. A badly aspected Venus can play havoc with your romance or marriage (as the statistics of divorce courts would seem to bear out).

Venus also has a tendency to make you possessive. Of course, like any other trait, this is good in moderation and bad if carried to extremes. You *should* be possessive of the people and things you love—but not to the extent of smothering or hoarding them. An age-old complaint of men is that the women they pursue tend to become clinging vines once they have been conquered. We all want to be held in loving arms, but no one enjoys being gripped in a vise of steel! Be careful, then, to moderate this trait if Venus is strongly placed in your horoscope, as it well may be if Taurus is your sun sign.

This tendency to possessiveness is usually expressed in a general sense of *conservatism*. That is, you tend to be not only possessive of your beloved and friends, but of opinions, beliefs, and material commodities as well. You are the sort of person who likes to play it "close to the vest"—to look things over and think them through before you come to a conclusion or decide on a course of action. This is good, of course, as far as it goes. It is highly unlikely, for instance, that you would ever develop into a spendthrift or a wastrel. Taureans are usually careful managers, and hardly ever have to be "dunned" into paying their bills on time. On the other hand, there is always the danger mentioned above of losing the people and things you love most by clinging too closely to them. Strive, then, for a balanced viewpoint. You sensibly realize that being conservative keeps you out of a lot of trouble—personally, financially, and otherwise—but you should be aware, too, that the element of risk in life can't be avoided. Indeed, it should not be; not always, at least. Few of us ever reach the summit of our ambitions or our heart's desire without being willing to take a chance or play a hunch, at least occasionally. Keep things organized and under control, but don't hesitate to reach out for the brass ring of opportunity when it appears. It may show up only once.

As indicated above, Taurus seems to be the strongest sign for musical talent in the Zodiac, so this would probably be an excellent field for you to enter. Many Taureans have achieved great success in musical careers, both as composers and performers, as our list clearly indicates. If you feel that you are talented, it seems that you could hardly go wrong in the world of music—always provided that talent is present and that the other aspects of your horoscope are favorable. If you don't feel that a musical career is right for you, you might investigate the fields of mathematics and the physical sciences; Taureans are often strong in these areas, too, as there is a close correlation between music and the world of numbers.

My son Sherwood (June 23) is a good example of this. In *Astrology 14*, I listed him as a mathematics student. He was in high school then, and planning a career as a computer programmer. He has now completed his first year of college, and has decided to major in music. Also, my father (June 25), an engineer and one of the most scientifically oriented men I've ever known, was an amateur pianist and a connoisseur of classical music.

As a child of Taurus, ruled by Venus, you tend to be not only conservative and possessive, but innately shy—especially in public or social situations. Unless you are a musical performer, you shun the limelight and prefer to keep to yourself. The field of politics is probably not your proper arena. You make friends slowly, and test both new acquaintances and possible lovers thoroughly before giving away any part of your heart. Once a friend is made, however, he is yours forever. You take seriously the advice of Polonius to his son Laertes:

> The friends thou hast, and their adoption tried,
> Grapple them to thy soul with hoops of steel;
> But do not dull thy palm with entertainment
> Of each new-hatch'd, unfledg'd comrade.

You are equally implacable as an enemy.

Taurus, then, is a sign of both conservatism and possessiveness, with musical talent and mathematical or scientific ability strongly indicated. You may not shine in the limelight or as the life of the party, but your innate conservatism and good sense can not only keep you out of trouble, but make for a quietly happy life, secure and steady. You probably don't have many friends, but they are close ones and as loyal to you as you are to them. The influence of your ruling Venus, combined with these conservative traits, indicates excellent prospects for a happy and lasting marriage. But don't hesitate to take a chance occasionally if the rewards seem to be worth it. It must be remembered, however, that this is only the basic interpretation of your sun sign. It must be compared with your rising sign (Chapter 1) and with all the other elements in your horoscope, which will be described in the chapters to follow.

RELATIONSHIP OF TAURUS TO OTHER SIGNS

Compatible	Incompatible	Neutral
Taurus*	Pisces	Cetus
Aries	Leo	Gemini
Cancer	Virgo	Scorpio
Libra	Ophiuchus	Sagittarius
Capricorn	Aquarius	

TAURUS
(June 7 to July 2)

June

7	Don Bridges (musician)
7	Dean Martin (singer)
8	Robert Schumann (composer)
9	Otto Nicolai (composer)
9	Carl Nielsen (composer)
9	Cole Porter (songwriter)
10	Judy Garland (singer)
10	Prince Philip (duke of Edinburgh)
11	Hazel Scott (singer)
11	Richard Strauss (composer)
12	Charles Kingsley (writer)
13	Winfield Scott (American general)
14	Burl Ives (actor/singer)
14	Harriet Beecher Stowe (writer)
15	Ernestine Schumann-Heink (singer)
16	Eduardo Frei Montalva (president of Chile)
17	John Lowell (statesman)
18	Paul McCartney (composer/singer)
19	Duchess of Windsor (socialite)
19	Guy Lombardo (bandleader)
20	Lillian Hellman (dramatist)
21	Jean-Paul Sartre (philosopher)
22	Gower Champion (dancer)
22	Giacomo Puccini (composer)

* If born within 10 days of own birthdate.

23 Don Drysdale (baseball player)
23 Duke of Windsor
23 Sherwood Schmidt (music student)
24 Alexandre Dumas (writer)
24 Phil Harris (actor/singer)
24 Sir John Ross (Arctic navigator)
25 George Abbott (director/dramatist)
25 Walther Nernst (physicist)
25 Hermann Oberth (space-science pioneer)
25 Emil J. Schmidt (engineer)
26 Jean Maury (French prelate)
27 Helen Keller (writer)
28 Richard Rodgers (composer)
29 Antoine de Saint-Exupéry (writer/aviator)
29 Nelson Eddy (singer)
30 Susan Hayward (actress)

July

1 Leslie Caron (dancer)
1 Naomi Jacob (writer)
2 Olav V (king of Norway)

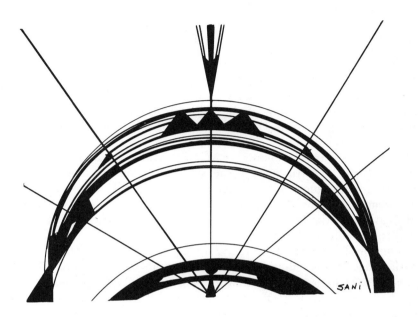

Gemini
(July 3 to July 28)

Gemini, the Twins, is the fifth sign of the Zodiac. In traditional astrology, it was the third sun sign, following Taurus. With Pisces in its proper position at the beginning of the zodiacal year and Cetus inserted after Aries, Astrology 14 places Gemini in its correct place as the fifth of the zodiacal constellations.

The ruling planet of Gemini is Mercury, which is closer to the sun and smaller than the earth. First of the nine known planets, it was named for the wing-footed messenger of the gods, whom the Greeks called Hermes. The planet Mercury is small, hot, and fast-moving. A surface temperature of 610°F. and the fact that it has no atmosphere make it highly unlikely that there is life on this planet.

The familiar figure of Mercury, usually pictured as a handsome youth with wings on his helmet and heels, was both the divine herald and the conductor of souls to the underworld. He represents the intellect and most types of mental or physical communication. Mercury was the god of thinkers and writers—and also of thieves. Astrologically, Mercury is one of the planets that can be either good or bad in your horoscope, depending on its relation to other elements. If well aspected, it increases the strength of your intellect and the agility of your mind; if badly aspected, it can increase a tendency to be fickle or two-faced. If Gemini is your sun sign, this planet is of particular importance in your horoscope (see Chapter 4).

In *Astrology 14*, I compared the traditional interpretation of the Geminian personality with my preliminary findings based on a study of 20 persons born under this sign. This material will not be repeated here; the interested reader is referred to my previous book (pp. 58–61).

I have enlarged the list of Geminians to 43 individuals. The interpretation that follows is based on this extended list. It must be stressed that, except for the few known to me personally, these people were chosen at random—I made no attempt to "load the dice" to favor my interpretation.

My initial study found Geminians to be keynoted by the word *variety*. There is some evidence for the dualism that traditional astrology associates with this sign, but it is slight. Further research has not indicated anything false in my initial interpretation, although the extended list shows a greater preponderance of writers: 11 of the 43 (a little more than 25 percent)

Geminians on the new list are writers, and some of the others, such as Carl Jung (July 26), wrote extensively in connection with their primary fields. This is hardly surprising, for Mercury rules the intellect and communication, both of which are basic to literature.

Gemini is my own sun sign. Hindsight is always easier than foresight, of course, but it does seem as I look back that I was fated to be a writer. A talent for drawing led everyone (myself included) to assume that I would be a commercial artist or cartoonist. I was also strongly attracted to music, but have no real talent for it except appreciation. I started college as an art major; however, a course in Shakespeare settled the matter for me. I switched my major to English, and have been writing ever since.

Their ruling planet Mercury makes Gemini types versatile and able to adapt quickly to new situations and environments. You can leap nimbly from one thought (or situation) to another, and in the fast-moving modern world this can often be an advantage. However, it is good not to be too facile. If carried to an extreme, this trait can make you appear to be two-faced to your associates and fickle to your partners in the arena of romance. "Be not the first by whom the new is tried," an old saw tells us, and adds: "Nor yet the last to lay the old aside." Geminians are hardly ever guilty of the latter. They are only too willing to try the new, whether in jobs, clothes, friends, or places of residence. This is one definition of progress, of course; if no one were willing to try new things, the human race would simply stand still. And it is exhilarating to be a pioneer—to venture into an area seldom or never explored—but don't forget, in your enthusiasm, that such an attitude can also leave you out on a limb.

The "quicksilver" influence of Mercury may make you restless. A typical Geminian may change schools, jobs, and friends so often that he actually gets behind slower-moving but steadier types, as we are reminded by the fable of the tortoise and the hare. Thus, ironically, the quick and versatile Geminian is often actually a slow starter in his major life activity. There is a good reason for this. Jung has stressed the difference between the tasks of the first half of life and those of the second, the two being divided by a crisis area that he calls *individuation*. Geminians seem to be especially affected by this. When young, their curiosity and restlessness lead them to try to learn as much about the world as they can in the shortest possible time. To their more conservative and single-minded fellows, they may appear to be job-hoppers in their careers and Don Juans when it comes to romance. What they are actually doing is *trying out the world*, and seeking their proper place in it—a process that may take some time. But what is time? To the Geminian, time, like money, is to be *spent*, and he will spend both lavishly if he feels he is on the track of something important or interesting.

The mature Gemini type, however, once he has passed the crisis of individuation, with his wild oats sown and the greater part of his curiosity about the world satisfied, tends to be remarkably steadfast. It may appear to others that you have wasted both time and money in your youth, but what you have gained is richness of experience and the poise of one who has seen life from all sides. You are then in a position to choose the job, the spouse, and the environment that suit you best, and you will probably stick to them forever.

There is naturally a danger that the fast-moving and wide-ranging Geminian may burn himself out before he ever reaches maturity. This does happen, as in the case of the great modern artist Amedeo Modigliani (July 12), who died at 36 after a brilliant but all-too-short career. But most Geminians are impatient of caution. If you never stick your head out, it'll never be lopped off. True, but who wants to stay in his hole (or rut) forever? Ruled by Mercury, you are excited by the variety, the color, and the infinite possibilities of life. You want to taste these, to see them close up, and above all to experience life as it is lived by others far from you in both space and time. Thus, the Gemini type is often an avid reader—especially of novels and history—as well as a traveler who will leave for Tierra del Fuego at the drop of a passport.

Gemini types are often described by the adjective "brilliant." Their agility and versatility sometimes put on a show that is dazzling to their more pedestrian fellows. A good example of this trait is the writer Aldous Huxley (July 28), who was certainly brilliant and versatile, and unafraid to venture into new realms (he was one of the first to explore the effects of "mind-expanding" drugs). But brilliance is only the strong reflection of light. A diamond is brilliant, but then so is the cheap tinsel that hangs on the Christmas tree. Whether there is real talent or genius beneath the surface flash and glitter is often difficult to tell, especially with young Geminians. Your family and close friends are usually the only ones who really know you. For beneath this sometimes dazzling display of fireworks on the surface, you are strongly consistent in your opinions and usually tend to be secretive about your innermost thoughts and feelings.

Gemini, then, is a sign of variety, versatility, and mental and verbal agility; of "brilliance" (whether real or only apparent); and of fickleness and a too facile approach to life if your Mercury is not in good aspect to other elements of your chart. A career that requires skill with words or almost any form of communications would seem to be indicated. If you can restrain your wilder impulses to see and know everything, there is nothing to prevent you from achieving a life rich in both material and spiritual rewards. It must be remembered, however, that this is only the basic interpretation of your sun sign. It must be compared with your rising sign (Chapter 1) and with all the other elements in your horoscope, which will be described in the chapters to follow.

RELATIONSHIP OF GEMINI TO OTHER SIGNS

Compatible	Incompatible	Neutral
Gemini*	Pisces	Taurus
Cetus	Aries	Cancer
Leo	Virgo	Libra
Scorpio	Sagittarius	Ophiuchus
Aquarius		Capricorn

GEMINI
(July 3 to July 28)

July

3	Franz Kafka (writer)
4	Louis Armstrong (musician)
4	Calvin Coolidge (30th U.S. President)
4	Eva Marie Saint (actress)
5	Henry Cabot Lodge (statesman)
6	Janet Leigh (actress)
7	Marc Chagall (painter)
7	Gustav Mahler (composer)
7	Steven Schmidt (writer)
7	Ringo Starr (musician)
8	Alvin B. Jessup (musician)
8	Nelson Rockefeller (politician)
9	Charles Funck (businessman)
10	David Brinkley (news commentator)
10	Max Meltcher (businessman)
10	Joe Verduce (businessman)
11	John Quincy Adams (6th U.S. President)
11	Winifred George (accountant)
12	Amedeo Modigliani (painter)
12	Benjamin Shillaber (writer/painter)
13	Dave Garroway (comedian)
14	Polly Bergen (actress)
14	Ingmar Bergman (filmmaker)
15	Henry Manning (Cardinal/writer)
16	Ginger Rogers (actress)
17	Phyllis Diller (comedienne)
17	Laurence Dooling (businessman)
17	Erle Stanley Gardner (writer)
17	Art Linkletter (entertainer)

* If born within 10 days of own birthdate.

18 John Glenn (astronaut)
18 Red Skelton (comedian)
19 A. J. Cronin (writer)
20 Wiley Rutledge (jurist)
21 Ernest Hemingway (writer)
22 Stephen Vincent Benét (writer)
23 Don Salvador de Madariaga (writer)
24 Lord Dunsany (writer)
25 Walter Brennan (actor)
26 Carl Jung (psychologist)
26 Jason Robards, Jr. (actor)
27 Anastasio Bustamente (statesman)
28 Aldous Huxley (writer)
28 Jacqueline Kennedy Onassis (socialite)

Cancer
(July 29 to August 23)

∽

Cancer, the Crab, is the sixth sign of the Zodiac. In traditional astrology, it was the fourth sun sign, following Gemini, and began with the summer solstice (June 22). With Pisces at the beginning of the zodiacal year and Cetus inserted between Aries and Taurus, Astrology 14 places Cancer in its correct place as the sixth of the zodiacal constellations.

The ruling planet of Cancer is the moon, our nearest neighbor in the sky. The moon has always been important in the eyes and thoughts of men, but our generation has had a closer look at it than any previous one, thanks to our space program. Astronauts Armstrong and Aldrin of *Apollo 11* were the first men to walk on the surface of our satellite, in 1969; other successful *Apollo* flights have been made since. Our lunar astronauts have found no traces of life on the airless moon, but the rocks and soil samples they have brought back have already yielded important information. The moon was apparently created at the same time as the earth, and was not born out of the "mother" planet; also, the old controversy as to the origin of the craters has been settled—they were caused by both volcanic and meteoric activity.

The moon is smaller than the earth and the other planets, but it is relatively large when compared to the size of other satellites as related to their planets. It has always exerted a strong effect upon mankind—an inspiration to lovers and poets, an "impossible" goal for explorers and scientists, a white lamp in the sky for night people. Its influence on the tides has been noted since early times, and its influence on the human psyche —though still only dimly understood—is just as strong. The term "lunatic" was coined in the Middle Ages because the full moon was thought to bring on madness; legends of werewolves and other "changelings" are still with us. Until recently, science has pooh-poohed such stories, but experiments in asylums have proved that inmates are affected by lunar influences, even when locked away from "the glimpses of the moon."

The moon has always been represented by goddesses, such as Diana and Selene, reflecting the feminine principle. It is opposite to the masculine sun just as feminine Venus is opposite to masculine Mars. Astrologically, the moon represents not only the feminine, but the unconscious in general, the emotions, birth, and growth, and it has always been associated with water. Its influence in your horoscope is second only to that of the sun and rising sign and, if Cancer is your sun sign, the moon is of particular importance (see Chapter 3).

In *Astrology 14*, I compared the traditional interpretation of the Cancerian personality with my preliminary findings based on a study of 25 persons born under this sign. This material will not be repeated here; the interested reader is referred to my previous book (pp. 62–66).

I have enlarged the list of Cancerians to 44 individuals. The interpretation that follows is based on this extended list. It must be stressed that, except for the few known to me personally, these people were chosen at random—I made no attempt to "load the dice" to favor my interpretation.

My initial study found Cancerians to be emotionally sensitive, changeable as Geminians (but much more conservative), with a strong sense of duty. They tend to be long-lived and to retain a youthful outlook throughout their lives, and compensate for their innate conservatism by being daredevils in their choice of sports. They are at ease in social situations and usually have an impish sense of humor. My further research has not indicated anything false in these preliminary interpretations. However, the influence of the moon, which rules this sign, must always be kept in mind. Its influence is as variable as its phases. The moon circles the earth every 28 days, "pulling" on first one continent, then another (actually, the moon and the earth revolve about a common center of gravity, but from our point of view the moon rises and sets like the sun). It is no wonder, then, that the children of Cancer are changeable!

The sensitivity of your emotions usually develops an empathy that is much needed in human affairs—you "feel for" people even when you don't understand them. More than any other sign except Scorpio, Cancerians are able to put themselves in the other fellow's place. Although, like Geminians, you may be prone to quick changes in your moods, thoughts, and feelings, you are unlike the Twins in being much more conservative in your actions. In an unhappy job situation, for example, Gemini is liable to throw up his hands and walk out; you may feel the same impulse, but will probably stick it out until you have found another job to go to. Thus, *caution* is one of the keywords of Cancer.

You have a strong sense of duty and responsibility. Married life, especially with a large family, suits you fine. Male or female, your interests tend to center in the home rather than in your place of business or club. A "snug harbor" is your ideal, and you find it hard to understand more restless types who want to be always on the go. Routine work does not bother you, if it is work of your own choosing, and you tend to be extremely steady as spouse, friend, or employee.

Longevity is another typical trait of Cancerians, along with a youthful attitude that enables you to bear your years gracefully, no matter how many. Barring accidents, you will probably live to play with grandchildren and great-grandchildren.

Obviously, accidents do occur, however, and the "minions of the moon" are slightly more prone to them than are the children of most other signs. The reason for this is that you tend to compensate for the caution and conservatism of your daily round by going in for dangerous forms of recreation when you play. Mountain-climbing, scuba-diving, fast cars and planes—these are often the delight of the Cancerian on vacation. This was brought home to me again recently when my wife and I were shopping for furniture. Our salesman was a tall, well-built young man and, learning that he was born under Cancer, I asked him if he went in for such sports. "You bet," he said, nodding emphatically. "Sky-diving, too. I love it!"

If you, too, go in for such sports, you would be well advised to pay close attention to your dreams. Our most direct link with the unconscious is, of course, our dreams, and Cancerians are particularly susceptible to the unconscious. Jung has written: "An acquaintance of mine once told me of a dream in which *he stepped out into space from the top of a mountain.* I explained to him something of the influence of the unconscious and warned him against dangerous mountaineering expeditions, for which he had a regular passion. But he laughed at such ideas. A few months later while climbing a mountain he actually did step off into space and was killed." I don't wish to belabor the point, but the death by drowning of my friend Jorge Villaseñor (August 23) has made me sensitive to such things (Jorge also enjoyed climbing mountains).

The meaning is clear: Beware of overcompensation for the quiet and conservatism of your daily life.

In social situations, you are generally at ease. You have a sure instinct for the right dress and demeanor, whatever the occasion. You remain a little withdrawn, however, and seldom take the conversational lead, preferring to listen rather than talk. Your sense of humor is well developed, usually taking the form of jokes played on your friends.

Cancer, then, is a sign of conservatism and sensitivity, especially where the emotions are concerned. You will probably succeed at any task that requires patience and long, steady effort. Though your moods may shift quickly, you are usually able to restrain impulses to blow up or walk out. Marriage is your natural arena, and the home is the center of your life. If you remember to curb your recklessness when away from home, there is no reason you can't lead a long, productive, and fully satisfying life. It must be remembered, however, that this is only the basic interpretation of your sun sign. It must be compared with your rising sign (Chapter 1) and with all the other elements in your horoscope, which will be described in the chapters to follow.

RELATIONSHIP OF CANCER TO OTHER SIGNS

Compatible	Incompatible	Neutral
Cancer*	Aries	Gemini
Pisces	Cetus	Leo
Taurus	Libra	Sagittarius
Virgo	Scorpio	Aquarius
Ophiuchus	Capricorn	

CANCER

(July 29 to August 23)

July

29	Dag Hammarskjöld (statesman)
29	Benito Mussolini (dictator)
30	Robert McCormick (editor/publisher)
31	Hank Bauer (baseball player)
31	Geraldine Chaplin (actress)

August

1	Herman Melville (writer)
2	James Baldwin (writer)
2	Peter O'Toole (actor)
3	Tony Bennett (singer)
3	Leon Uris (writer)
4	Ezra Taft Benson (politician)
5	Neil Armstrong (astronaut)
5	John Huston (director)
5	Robert Taylor (actor)
6	Lucille Ball (comedienne)
7	Ralph Bunche (statesman)
8	Andy Warhol (painter/filmmaker)
9	Léonide Massine (dancer/choreographer)
10	Eddie Fisher (singer)
10	Herbert Hoover (31st U.S. President)
11	Robert Burns (businessman)
11	Lloyd Nolan (actor)
12	George Hamilton (actor)
12	Jane Wyatt (actress)
13	Alfred Hitchcock (writer/director)
14	Sir Walter Besant (writer)
15	Princess Anne
15	Ethel Barrymore (actress)
16	Lois Brown (housewife)
16	Eydie Gorme (singer)
16	George Meany (labor leader)

* If born within 10 days of own birthdate.

17   Maureen O'Hara (actress)
17   Mae West (actress)
18   Hayley Mills (actress)
19   Bernard Baruch (financier)
19   Willy Shumaker (jockey)
20   Louise Funck (housewife)
20   Benjamin Harrison (23rd U.S. President)
21   Count Basie (musician)
21   Princess Margaret Rose
22   Ray Bradbury (writer)
22   Jackie Guthrie (housewife)
23   Gene Kelly (dancer)
23   Jorge Villaseñor (painter/sculptor)

Leo
(August 24 to September 18)

Leo, the Lion, is the seventh sign of the Zodiac. In traditional astrology, it was the fifth sun sign, following Cancer. With Pisces at the beginning of the zodiacal year and Cetus inserted between Aries and Taurus, Astrology 14 places Leo in its correct place as the seventh of the zodiacal constellations.

The ruling planet of Leo is the sun, center and source of energy for our solar system and giver of life to the earth (and, perhaps, to other planets as well). We know much more about the sun than did the ancients in the infancy of astrology, of course. This great blazing sphere that makes life possible is a middle-sized, yellow, type G star, midway between the brightest and dimmest stars in the observable universe; it is located on the outskirts of our galaxy, the Milky Way, which contains billions of stars—and there are billions of galaxies within reach of our telescopes! This is the sun seen in the perspective of modern astronomy. Of course, none of this was known when astrology was first developed. It was then thought that the earth was fixed, unmoving, at the center of the universe, with the sun, moon, planets, and stars revolving about it. A small, cozy place; it suited man's ego to be at the center of things. This is the universe of "common sense"—and it is still the universe of astrology.

The sun, anciently conceived as the flaming chariot of Apollo, is much larger than any of its planets. There is no doubt of its influence, for life on earth would be impossible without it. Astrologically, the sun represents the male principle and consciousness, as opposed to the moon, which represents the female principle and the unconscious. The sun's traits are the positive ones of power, vitality, and self-expression; however, its influence in your chart is not always beneficent—that depends on the aspects of other elements. Nevertheless, the sun is the single most important element in your horoscope, and is particularly significant if Leo is your sun sign.

It should always be kept in mind that the sign you were born under is your sun sign; that is, the zodiacal constellation through which the sun was passing at the moment of your birth. The whole science of astrology is based upon this point, so it is easy to see why the sun is considered of paramount importance in your horoscope.

In *Astrology 14*, I compared the traditional interpretation of the Leo personality with my preliminary findings based on a study of 21 persons born under this sign. This material will not be repeated here; the interested reader is referred to my previous book (pp. 67–70).

I have enlarged the list of Leos to 39 individuals. The interpretation that follows is based on this extended list. It must be stressed that, except for the few known to me personally, these people were chosen at random —I made no attempt to "load the dice" to favor my interpretation.

My initial study found Leos to be persons of strongly independent character, natural leaders and pace-setters, who make strong friends and equally strong enemies. There is nothing middling or wishy-washy about them, and it is almost impossible to feel neutral about a Leo—you either love him or hate him; few can remain indifferent. My further research has not indicated anything false in these preliminary interpretations. However, the influence of the sun, which rules this sign, must always be kept in mind. It strengthens the forcefulness of your personality and accents your extraverted side; that is, the sun affects your conscious ego, just as the moon affects the unconscious. As a result, Leo tries to lead a consciously directed life. He wants to be "in control" at all times, and is hyper-alert to the world around him. The outer scene, the environment, is more important to him than the workings of his own psyche. As a result, he tends to downgrade the unconscious, and pays little heed to dreams, hunches, or "visions"—these phantasmagoria are not *real* to him.

Often citing Jung, I have repeatedly stressed the importance of the unconscious. Its messages and warnings can be ignored only at our peril. Developing the wholeness of our personality is our main job in life, whether we are aware of it or not, and there is much more to the human psyche than the individual ego. On the contrary, the ego is like a tiny island in a vast sea: everything below the waters is the unconscious, but it is still us. Ignorance of the importance of the unconscious is usually the Achilles heel of Leo types. If they have a flaw, it is almost always to be found in this area (but it is probably their *only* flaw).

The marked independence of Leo makes you chafe against the restrictions of living in a society where we are all dependent upon one another. "No man is an island," wrote John Donne. You don't really want to be an island, of course, because you enjoy people and are most at home when surrounded by a crowd of them—especially if they admire you. But you would like to have the independence of an island, stand alone, and make or break your own laws.

Because of this "maverick" streak to your personality, you don't hesitate to break a social rule or convention when it makes no sense to you. Your friends and associates sometimes think of you as a bohemian or simply as "a character." This has its disadvantages, of course. A large and complex society places a premium on obedience to basic, conventional norms of behavior. The large group of young people known collectively as "hippies" are in conflict with the law and with social norms for this very reason.

On the other hand, society also recognizes the need for strongly independent and original thinkers and actors on the stage of the world. Little progress would be made if everyone conformed. For all the millions who thought it impossible for man to fly, there had to be a few like the Wright brothers, who thought flight possible, for our jet age to be created. Everyone has a right to his own ideas and to follow his individual star. This was stated beautifully by Howard Roark in his address to the court in Ayn Rand's novel, *The Fountainhead*.

Your rewards will probably come late in life, but they will be great ones. It's always easier to follow a beaten path than to hack out a new trail—but there's little personal satisfaction in doing what everyone else does. You must beware of a tendency to discouragement if your independent way of life has led you down paths that go nowhere. It is always possible to make a fresh start, begin again, at any age and no matter how many failures have gone before. Nearly all of the great discoveries in science and other fields were made after hundreds or thousands of trials that failed; the discoverers had the spirit and endurance to go on.

You share with Aries types the trait of finding it difficult to admit mistakes, as your independence usually makes you anything but humble.

Like Taurus, you are a wonderfully steadfast friend, but a hard enemy. There is little in between, as it is almost impossible for you to be neutral or noncommittal on any subject that interests you.

Leo, then, is a sign of independence, with emphasis on the conscious ego rather than the unconscious. It is a good sign for leadership—for pacesetters and discoverers—and, if other elements in your chart are favorable, you can develop a strong, colorful, and magnetic personality. The power is there; it need only be applied in the right direction. Pay attention to your dreams and hunches, however "unreal" these may seem to you, and there is nothing to prevent you from achieving a successful and prosperous life. It must be remembered, however, that this is only the basic interpretation of your sun sign. It must be compared with your rising sign (Chapter 1) and with all the other elements in your horoscope, which will be described in the chapters to follow.

RELATIONSHIP OF LEO TO OTHER SIGNS

Compatible	Incompatible	Neutral
Leo*	Cetus	Pisces

* If born within 10 days of own birthdate.

Aries   Taurus   Cancer
Gemini   Scorpio   Virgo
Libra   Ophiuchus   Capricorn
Sagittarius   Aquarius

LEO
(August 24 to September 18)

August

24 Charles McKim (architect)
25 Leonard Bernstein (composer/conductor)
25 Sean Connery (actor)
26 Prince Albert (prince consort)
27 Lyndon B. Johnson (36th U.S. President)
27 Martha Raye (comedienne)
27 Tuesday Weld (actress)
28 Charles Boyer (actor)
29 Ingrid Bergman (actress)
29 Kendall Sessions (writer)
30 Camden Benares (writer)
30 Roy Wilkins (NAACP official)
31 William Saroyan (writer)

September

1 Rocky Marciano (boxer)
1 Walter P. Reuther (labor leader)
2 Cleveland Amory (writer)
2 Marge Champion (dancer)
2 Mary Jane Schmidt (housewife)
3 Alan Ladd (actor)
4 Henry Ford II (industrialist)
5 John Cage (composer)
5 Carol Lawrence (singer)
6 Noel Villaseñor (engineering student)
7 Peter Lawford (actor)
8 Peter Sellers (actor)
9 Leo Tolstoy (writer)
10 Edmund O'Brien (actor)
11 D. H. Lawrence (writer)
12 Maurice Chevalier (singer)
12 Gerard George (businessman)
12 Louis MacNeice (poet/astrologer)
13 J. B. Priestley (writer)
14 Jan Masaryk (statesman)
15 William H. Taft (27th U.S. President)

16   Lauren Bacall (actress)
16   Sir Alexander Korda (producer)
17   Anne Bancroft (actress)
17   Roddy McDowall (actor)
18   Edwin McMillan (physicist)

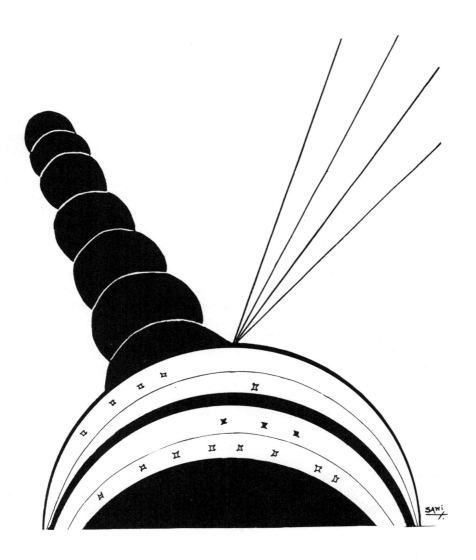

Virgo
(September 19 to October 14)

♍

Virgo, the Virgin, is the eighth sign of the Zodiac. In traditional astrology, it was the sixth sun sign, following Leo. With Pisces at the beginning of the zodiacal year and Cetus inserted between Aries and Taurus, Astrology 14 places Virgo in its correct place as the eighth of the zodiacal constellations.

The ruling planet of Virgo is Mercury, which is closer to the sun and smaller than the earth. First of the nine known planets, it was named for the wing-footed messenger of the gods, whom the Greeks called Hermes. The planet Mercury is small, hot, and fast-moving. A surface temperature of 610°F. and the fact that it has no atmosphere make it highly unlikely that there is life on this planet.

The familiar figure of Mercury, usually pictured as a handsome youth with wings on his helmet and heels, was both the divine herald and the conductor of souls to the underworld. He represents the intellect and most types of mental or physical communication. Mercury was the god of thinkers and writers—and also of thieves. Astrologically, Mercury is one of the planets that can be either good or bad in your horoscope, depending on its relation to other elements. If well aspected, it increases the strength of your intellect and the agility of your mind; if badly aspected, it can increase a tendency to be fickle or two-faced. If Virgo is your sun sign, this planet is of particular importance in your horoscope (see Chapter 4).

In *Astrology 14*, I compared the traditional interpretation of the Virgoan personality with my preliminary findings based on a study of 23 persons born under this sign. This material will not be repeated here; the interested reader is referred to my previous book (pp. 71–74).

I have enlarged the list of Virgoans to 43 individuals. The interpretation that follows is based on this extended list. It must be stressed that, except for the few known to me personally, these people were chosen at random—I made no attempt to "load the dice" to favor my interpretation.

My initial study found Virgoans to be strongly individualistic people, with a "one of a kind" flavor to their personalities of the type that often inspires affection and the bestowal of nicknames. They are in danger of loneliness and obscurity if they don't "make it" all the way, for it is difficult for them to fit into the mold of conformity. Further research has not indicated anything false in my initial interpretation. However, the influence of the ruling planet must always be kept in mind. Mercury, which also rules Gemini, can be a great help if you are involved in either written or oral communication. Many successful writers and actors have been born under either Gemini or Virgo. The main difference seems to be that, whereas Geminians tend to be creative and flexible, Virgoans receive strengthened analytical ability from their ruling planet.

The typical Virgoan is alert and quick to size up a person or situation. Although such "snap judgments" are often frowned upon, your conclusions are nearly always right. It's as if you had a built-in computer that is able to evaluate a large amount of data almost instantly, and come up with the right answer, long before a slow-thinking type can begin to make up his mind. This analytical ability makes you hard to fool in any situation, and it can be a definite asset in many fields of employment.

Your marked individuality makes you stand out in a crowd. You are definitely not one of the anonymous, "faceless" ones that throng the streets of every city; your personality makes a definite impression on everyone around you, whether they have actually been introduced to you or not. This charisma often leads to the bestowal of a nickname, which is used by everyone—sometimes to the point that your actual name is virtually forgotten!

A colorful and strongly individualistic personality is a marked asset for star performers in any field, of course, and especially in the world of theatre, motion pictures, and TV. Many Virgo types have achieved success as actors and actresses, and they have definitely not been cast as types! A Virgoan may have difficulty in breaking into his chosen field simply because he or she is so strongly individualistic. Most people tend to classify everyone they meet—to type them, put them in a pre-established slot— and potential employers are certainly not exempt from this tendency. Since Virgoans are difficult to classify, they may be rejected simply because they don't fit neatly into an employer's set of mental niches. The irony of this is that the rejected Virgoan would probably be a much more valuable employee than the "conformist" who is hired in his place. If this has happened to you, don't be discouraged. The more conformist our society becomes, the greater will be the need for individuals who think their own thoughts and are a potential fount of fresh ideas and original concepts— and eventually the value of this trait, along with your keen analytical ability, will be recognized and rewarded.

Nonconformists have always been more at home in the arts, of course, and an impressive number of distinguished artists have been born under Virgo. The great American novelist, William Faulkner (September 25), is a typically individualistic Virgoan. He now belongs to history, and his name is listed among the winners of the Nobel Prize, but when he started to write, he had all the difficulties of any young person trying to break into a highly competitive field. His first novel went the rounds of many publishers before an editor finally recognized its worth. This woman was impressed with the power of his style, but thought she saw some areas that could be improved upon. She wrote to Faulkner, stating that her firm would like to publish his novel, and included her list of suggested corrections. Most young writers, eager to see their work in print, would have been only too happy to comply. But Faulkner sent her letter back to her with a curt query scribbled across its bottom: "Who in the hell are you?"

A strongly individualistic attitude such as Faulkner's may not be the best way to win friends and influence people, but in his case it paid off. The Nobel Prize is not usually awarded to people who are willing to alter their work or their ideas to fit someone else's opinions. As a Virgoan, you are probably not interested in winning popularity contests anyway. Most of you know your worth and would rather follow your own star, even if you find yourself all alone on the path. A diamond in the rough is still a valuable gem, no matter how rough its setting may be.

These are some of the advantages of strong individuality. The disadvantages have also been mentioned, and are made obvious after a moment's reflection on the fate of the individual in a large, complex, and increasingly *organized* society. The more organized and complicated the machinery, the more difficult it is not to be simply a cog smoothly functioning with a multitude of other cogs. The more pessimistic (or antihuman) prophets among us have predicted a future society that will resemble nothing so much as a gigantic beehive or anthill; a world in which the evolution of the individual will have stopped and a *society* will evolve with human beings reduced to mere cells in its great body. *Cyborgs* have been suggested—living brains connected to a computer for greater efficiency. But I am one of the optimists who believe the human spirit is too strong to allow itself to be degraded to the level of a cell or an electronic circuit, and believe with Faulkner that man will not simply endure—he will prevail.

Virgo, then, is a sign of strong individualism, usually accompanied by marked analytical ability. You are a natural "idea man" and can be a definite asset to almost any type of organization that recognizes the value of novel methods and ideas, and does not expect you to fit into a preestablished niche. Your way may be difficult, however, for the majority usually side with the status quo and tend to resist bright, bold new ideas. Be prepared for this, and you will be able to bounce back with enthusiasm. It must be remembered, however, that this is only the basic interpretation of your sun sign. It must be compared with your rising sign

(Chapter 1) and with all the other elements in your horoscope, which will be described in the chapters to follow.

RELATIONSHIP OF VIRGO TO OTHER SIGNS

Compatible	Incompatible	Neutral
Virgo*	Pisces	Aries
Cetus	Taurus	Leo
Cancer	Gemini	Libra
Scorpio	Ophiuchus	Aquarius
Capricorn	Sagittarius	

VIRGO
(September 19 to October 14)

September

19	David McCallum (actor)
19	Joseph Pasternak (filmmaker)
20	Sophia Loren (actress)
21	H. G. Wells (writer)
22	Ruth Bultman (nurse)
22	Paul Muni (actor)
23	Walter Lippmann (writer)
23	Mickey Rooney (actor)
23	Romy Schneider (actress)
23	Katherine Zyskowski (housewife)
24	F. Scott Fitzgerald (writer)
24	Karen Wagner (housewife)
25	William Faulkner (writer)
26	T. S. Eliot (poet)
26	Pope Paul VI
27	George Raft (actor)
27	Cyril Scott (composer)
28	Al Capp (cartoonist)
28	Ed Sullivan (TV announcer)
29	Brigitte Bardot (actress)
30	Truman Capote (writer)
30	Deborah Kerr (actress)

October

1	Julie Andrews (singer)
1	Stanley Holloway (actor)
2	Groucho Marx (entertainer)
3	Emily Post (etiquette authority)
3	Gore Vidal (writer)

* If born within 10 days of own birthdate.

3   Thomas Wolfe (writer)
4   Rutherford B. Hayes (19th U.S. President)
5   Chester Arthur (21st U.S. President)
6   Jenny Lind (singer)
7   Niels Bohr (atomic research pioneer)
8   Eddie Rickenbacker (aviator)
9   John Lennon (musician)
10 Helen Hayes (actress)
10 Angela Lansbury (actress)
11 Robert Blau (physician)
11 Eleanor Roosevelt (stateswoman)
11 Pamela Villaseñor (dance student)
12 James MacDonald (politician)
13 Herblock (cartoonist)
13 Yves Montand (actor)
14 Dwight D. Eisenhower (34th U.S. President)

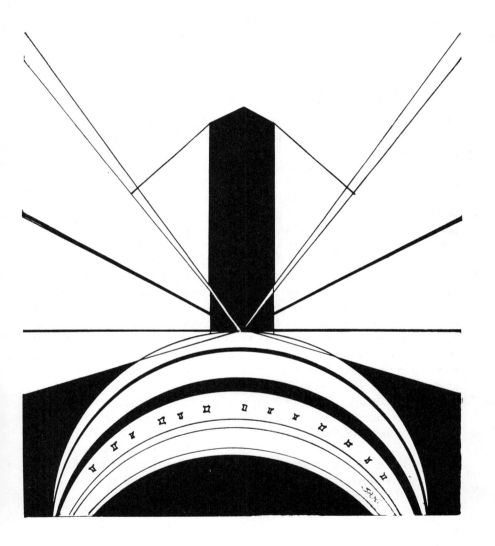

Libra
(October 15 to November 9)

Libra, the Scales, is the ninth sign of the Zodiac. In traditional astrology, it was the seventh sun sign, following Virgo. With Pisces at the beginning of the zodiacal year and Cetus inserted between Aries and Taurus, Astrology 14 places Libra in its correct place as the ninth of the zodiacal constellations.

The ruling planet of Libra is Venus, which also rules Taurus. Venus is one of earth's neighbors in the heavens, but is closer to the sun and smaller than our planet. Second of the nine known planets, it was named for the goddess of love (the Greek Aphrodite). It is not only close to the earth but is nearest to terrestrial size of all the planets. It was thought for many years that Venus might, therefore, have a civilization similar to ours, and was a favorite of writers of science fiction and fantasy, who depicted an idyllic setting of great forests and sunny meadows—the Earthly Paradise that earthmen have lost. Direct observation has been impossible, however, because the surface of Venus is always shrouded by a thick layer of clouds. Recent explorations by Russian robot spacecraft that have penetrated this veil indicate that the surface is extremely hot and the atmosphere unbreathable by humans. So much for our dreams of Arcadia! But the truth about Venus will not be known until our astronauts are able to go there.

The lovely goddess Venus (or Aphrodite) represents the *feminine* principle—the exact opposite of Mars, who is symbolic of the masculine principle. Astrologically, there is a close connection between these two planets, as they complement each other. Venus is known as the "lesser fortune" (Jupiter is the "greater fortune"). It is a beneficent planet in your horoscope (unless adversely aspected by other elements), and if Libra is your sun sign, this planet is of particular importance (see Chapter 5).

In *Astrology 14*, I compared the traditional interpretation of the Libran personality with my preliminary findings based on a study of 22 persons born under this sign. This material will not be repeated here; the interested reader is referred to my previous book (pp. 75–79).

I have enlarged the list of Librans to 50 individuals. The interpretation that follows is based on this extended list. It must be stressed that, except for the few known to me personally, these people were chosen at random —I made no attempt to "load the dice" to favor my interpretation.

My initial study found Librans to be people who have a well-developed quality of judgment, which makes them good candidates for careers in politics or the law. Like Taureans, they are also usually talented musically. Their weakness is a tendency to lack self-confidence, which may, if carried to an extreme, result in dogmatism or even neurosis. Nothing in my further research has indicated these preliminary findings to be false. However, we now have a larger group to work with, so let's see what can be said of the "typical" Libran.

The constellation Libra is symbolized by the scales of justice (incidentally, the only inorganic sign in the Zodiac). This sun sign does tend to increase the strength and quality of your judgment, but you usually have your own concept of justice, which may or may not agree with that of your society or your neighbors. Although your emotions are strong, as is only natural with Venus as your ruling planet, you are always able to balance two opposing points of view, no matter how strongly you feel about the subject at hand. If you are an extravert and find politics interesting, this would be an excellent field for you to enter. The path to political office is often through a legal career, of course. You would make a good lawyer and an even better judge. If the arts, rather than public life, appeal to you, you would probably do best in the field of music.

I have stated that Taurus is the strongest sign for musical talent. Since both Taurus and Libra are ruled by Venus, this is a trait you may very well share with Taurus types. Of the 50 Librans on the extended list, 13 (or 26 percent) are associated with music. Although this is not as high a percentage as was found on the list for Taurus, it is well above average. However, there is a split here. The musical talent of Taurus types tends to find expression in composing, conducting, and instrumental performance, but you are more likely to be a singer. Of the 13 musicians on the list, no less than 10 are singers! This would seem to indicate a strong possibility that, if music is your forte, you probably have an excellent natural singing voice and, with training, could have a successful career as a vocal artist.

Even if your place in life has already been established as an accountant, housewife, or whatever, you might gain great satisfaction from developing this vocal talent—in church choirs, little theatre groups, etc.—and who knows? It might lead to a new career!

Venus rules the heart as well as the vocal cords, of course. Another trait Libra shares with Taurus is a tendency to be possessive. Like any other trait, this is good in moderation and bad if carried to extremes. Hold fast to the people and things you love, but not *too* fast. A loved one or object can be like a nettle: it won't harm you if you hold it lightly, but can be prickly if your clutch is too tight. Your sense of judgment, however, usually prevents you from falling into such an impasse.

With Venus strongly aspected, as it often is if Libra is your sun sign, your chances for success in love and marriage are extremely good. The opposite sex usually finds you attractive, and you are aware of this without being overly self-conscious about it. You tend to be something of a dandy in your choice of personal attire. You are not far behind when a new style in clothing or hair arrangement comes into vogue. Your innate sense of judgment keeps you away from the bizarre and ridiculous, however, and your colorful and individualistic style of dress usually enhances your appeal to members of the opposite sex. On the other hand, members of your own sex may regard you as a little too cocksure in both dress and deportment.

As long as you keep your balance (which is usually not difficult for a Libran), your potential for success is very good in both your career and your personal life. The only flaw in your personality is a tendency to lack confidence in yourself, as mentioned above. The typical Libran has so much going for him that it is difficult for people born under other signs to understand this flaw. None of us is perfect, of course, but many Librans tend to strive for a perfection that is simply unattainable on the human scale. Such striving can only lead to frustration, and a feeling of frustration over an extended period can lead not only to loss of self-confidence but to neurosis. The corrective is to moderate the demands you make upon yourself. Life has much to offer, and it is good to set high goals, but reaching for *impossible* goals can only end in frustration and defeat.

Libra, then, is a strong sign for a career in politics, law, or music (especially vocal music). It also bodes well for success in the arena of love. Your strong sense of judgment should be used to avoid tendencies to lack confidence in yourself. With this one weakness overcome, there is nothing to stop you from attaining a richly rewarding life in both public and personal spheres. It must be remembered, however, that this is only the basic interpretation of your sun sign. It must be compared with your rising sign (Chapter 1) and with all the other elements in your horoscope, which will be described in the chapters to follow.

RELATIONSHIP OF LIBRA TO OTHER SIGNS

Compatible	Incompatible	Neutral
Libra*	Aries	Pisces
Taurus	Gemini	Cetus

* If born within 10 days of own birthdate.

Leo   Cancer   Virgo
Ophiuchus   Capricorn   Scorpio
Aquarius   Sagittarius

LIBRA
(October 15 to November 9)

October

15   John Kenneth Galbraith (economist)
16   David Ben-Gurion (statesman)
16   Eugene O'Neill (dramatist)
17   Montgomery Clift (actor)
17   Rita Hayworth (actress)
18   Sidney Kingsley (dramatist)
18   Melina Mercouri (actress)
19   General Yakubu Gowon (head of Military Council, Nigeria)
19   Lewis Mumford (writer)
20   Art Buchwald (columnist)
20   Daniel Sickles (politician/general)
21   Ted Shawn (dancer/choreographer)
22   Joan Fontaine (actress)
22   Giovanni Martinelli (singer)
23   Johnny Carson (entertainer)
24   Moss Hart (dramatist)
24   Dame Sybil Thorndike (actress)
25   Anthony Franciosa (actor)
25   Pablo Picasso (painter)
26   Jackie Coogan (actor)
26   Mahalia Jackson (singer)
27   Nanette Fabray (singer)
27   Theodore Roosevelt (26th U.S. President)
27   Dylan Thomas (poet)
28   Howard Hanson (composer)
28   Jonas Salk (polio vaccine discoverer)
29   Thomas Bayard (statesman)
29   Jon Vickers (singer)
30   John Adams (2nd U.S. President)
30   Maryalice Jessup (singer)
30   Ezra Pound (writer)
31   Michael Collins (astronaut)
31   Ethel Waters (singer/actress)

November

1   Jules Bastien-Lepage (painter)
1   Victoria de los Angeles (singer)
2   Warren Harding (29th U.S. President)

2   Burt Lancaster (actor)
2   James Polk (11th U.S. President)
3   André Malraux (writer)
3   James Reston (journalist)
4   Walter Cronkite (newscaster)
5   Bill Verduce (executive)
6   James Jones (writer)
7   Billy Graham (evangelist)
7   Joan Sutherland (singer)
8   Vincenzo Bellini (composer)
8   Anthony Castiglia (physician)
8   Katharine Hepburn (actress)
8   Lane Schmidt (teletypist)
9   Ed Wynn (comedian)

Scorpio
(November 10 to December 5)

♏

Scorpio, the Scorpion, is the tenth sign of the Zodiac. In traditional astrology, it was the eighth sun sign, following Libra. With Pisces at the beginning of the zodiacal year and Cetus inserted between Aries and Taurus, Astrology 14 places Scorpio in its correct place as the tenth of the zodiacal constellations.

The ruling planet of Scorpio is Mars, one of earth's neighbors in the heavens, but smaller and farther from the sun. Fourth of the nine known planets, it was named for the ancient god of war. Mars has been much in the news recently, and will probably be the next goal of our astronauts. Although photographs sent back by *Mariner* spacecraft show a pocked surface, much like that of the moon, an old legend persists that there was an ancient civilization on Mars, which died when the planet lost its oxygen (hence its reddish color). Mars has two satellites, Deimos and Phobos. These are so small that, a few years ago, a Russian scientist postulated that they might be artificial. However, when *Mariner* 9 went into orbit around Mars in 1971, it sent back a series of remarkably clear pictures, including shots of these two moonlets. Deimos and Phobos are irregularly shaped chunks of rock, their surfaces pitted by meteorites.

The warlike god Mars (or Ares) represents the *masculine* principle— the exact opposite of the goddess Venus, who is symbolic of the feminine principle. Astrologically, this planet stands for such "masculine" qualities as energy, action, heat, aggression, and power. Mars is a powerful influence in any horoscope and, if Scorpio is your sun sign, this planet is of particular importance (see Chapter 6).

In *Astrology* 14, I compared the traditional interpretation of the Scorpio personality with my preliminary findings based on a study of 21 persons born under this sign. This material will not be repeated here; the interested reader is referred to my previous book (pp. 80–84).

I have enlarged the list of Scorpios to 48 individuals. The interpretation that follows is based on this extended list. It must be stressed that, except for the few known to me personally, these people were chosen at random —I made no attempt to "load the dice" to favor my interpretation.

My initial study found Scorpios to be sensitive people, with a pronounced empathy for the feelings of others; they are the *humanists* of the Zodiac, usually with a streak of poetry or mysticism in their makeup. My further research has not indicated anything false in these preliminary interpretations. The influence of the ruling planet, however, must always be kept in mind. Mars is so powerful that in ancient times it was thought to be an evil planet (because of its association with war and its attendant suffering and destruction). Some of this feeling has come down to the present day, so that we find contemporary astrologers referring to Mars as "a necessary evil." This is not necessarily so. The influence of *any* planet is not absolute; its effect in your chart is strongly dependent upon its relationship to the other elements.

I hope that, in my description of Scorpio in *Astrology 14*, I have at least made a dent in the age-old superstition that Scorpios are extremely sexy or overly aggressive types. Nothing in my research has indicated that the children of Scorpio are sexier or more pugnacious than people born under any of the other 13 signs. This does not mean, on the other hand, that Scorpios are *not* sexy or aggressive. Everything depends on the entire horoscope. Remarks on the traits of this or any other sun sign, taken by themselves, can only be very general; the "other things being equal" proviso should always be kept in mind—and, as we know, in life other things are very seldom equal!

If your Mars is strongly placed with other elements of your horoscope, and if you tend to be an extravert, you could very well succeed in a career in public affairs. Our list includes such notables as the King of Sweden, the Princess of Monaco, the King of Laos, Prince Charles, Nehru, Indira Gandhi, Robert Kennedy, Charles de Gaulle, the mayor of New York, the president of Czechoslovakia, Sir Winston Churchill, the president of Brazil, and four Presidents of the United States. These are people who have used their empathy—their ability to see the other person's point of view—to good advantage in rising to positions of great public eminence.

Most Scorpios have this quality to an even greater degree than the children of Libra. It is borne out as much in their personal lives as on the public stage of world affairs. This quality, although it makes you a marvelous spouse or friend, can also lead to trouble because it makes it difficult for you to recognize your enemies. The typical Scorpio—especially the more introverted types—is so sensitive to feelings, both his own and others', that it always comes as a rude shock to him to discover that there are people in the world who are perfectly willing to ride roughshod over *his* feelings. Alas, there is no shortage of such in the world. You would be wise, then, to build some kind of psychic wall to protect yourself. In myths and fairy tales, the sleeping princess is always protected by the stout walls of a castle or by a ring of magic fire. Such tales are about *ourselves* —they represent the state of our psyche (or soul). As the Bible admonishes, "He that hath an ear, let him hear."

If you are a more introverted Scorpio, preferring the arts to politics and private to public life, you probably have a talent for poetry, idealistic philosophy, or mysticism. Your ear is sensitive to the depths of hidden nuance in such writings—the essence, the "still, small voice" that is often unheard by the hurried scanning of the "modern" reader, who seems to have time for everything except the very things that are most important for his own self-realization and growth. A career as a writer or critic might be indicated for you. If not, then at least you have the great gift of true appreciation for the finest and most subtle thought and art created by the most gifted of mankind.

Your genuine desire to benefit your fellow man makes you a natural philanthropist. The world is in a bad way—as, apparently, it always has been—and there are ample opportunities on every hand to help your suffering fellow man. But are these opportunities real or illusory? Scorpio can easily be caught in a conflict between the sensitivity of his own feelings and the temptation to "give himself away" in the service of others. Can the well-protected sleeping princess also be the bold knight who sallies forth to slay the dragon of injustice? You must find the answer to this question in your own heart, of course. I would only remind you of the old saying, "Charity begins at home." This is not a statement of simple selfishness. Society is made up of individuals, and if each individual were to try sincerely to improve *himself*, the level of all mankind would be raised accordingly. Do-gooders seldom do any real good; they would be wiser to look to the cultivation of their own gardens. And as a wry Jewish joke puts it, "Why are you so mad at me, Sol? I haven't done you any favors lately."

Scorpio, then, is a sign of sensitive feelings, empathy, and philanthropy, in both public and personal spheres, and is often accompained by poetic, mystic, or religious sensibility. It is a wonderful sign for friends, spouses, and benefactors of mankind. The danger is that in your desire to help others, you may hurt yourself more than you can aid them. Keep your ring of magic fire burning! In extreme cases, this tendency to rush in where angels hesitate can lead to martyrdom. It *is* possible to reach your ideal in personal relationships, however, where there is sympathy and flexibility on both sides. It must be remembered, however, that this is only the basic interpretation of your sun sign. It must be compared with your rising sign (Chapter 1) and with all the other elements in your horoscope, which will be described in the chapters to follow.

RELATIONSHIP OF SCORPIO TO OTHER SIGNS

Compatible	Incompatible	Neutral
Scorpio*	Cetus	Aries
Pisces	Cancer	Taurus
Gemini	Leo	Libra
Virgo	Capricorn	Ophiuchus
Sagittarius	Aquarius	

SCORPIO

(November 10 to December 5)

November

10	Richard Burton (actor)
10	Claude Rains (actor)
11	Fyodor Dostoyevski (writer)
11	Gustavus VI (king of Sweden)
12	Kim Hunter (actress)
12	Grace Kelly, princess of Monaco (actress)
13	Alexander King (writer)
13	Sri Savang Vatthana (king of Laos)
14	Prince Charles
14	Aaron Copland (composer)
14	Jawaharlal Nehru (Indian Nationalist leader)
15	Barbara Hutton (socialite)
15	Marianne Moore (poet)
15	Erwin Rommel (field marshal)
16	Jean le Rond d'Alembert (mathematician/philosopher)
16	Burgess Meredith (actor)
17	Rock Hudson (actor)
17	Pat Verduce (singer)
18	Alan Shepard (astronaut)
18	George Shultz (writer)
19	Roy Campanella (baseball player)
19	Indira Gandhi (stateswoman)
19	James Garfield (20th U.S. President)
20	Robert F. Kennedy (politician)
20	Josiah Royce (philosopher)
20	Mitzi Schmidt (painter/poet)
21	André Gide (writer)
21	Ralph Meeker (actor)
22	Charles de Gaulle (statesman/general)
22	Lisa Villaseñor (student)
23	Franklin Pierce (14th U.S. President)

* If born within 10 days of own birthdate.

24 John Lindsay (mayor of New York City)
24 Zachary Taylor (12th U.S. President)
25 Ludvik Svoboda (president of Czechoslovakia)
26 James McGuigan (Cardinal)
27 David Merrick (producer)
28 Brooks Atkinson (drama critic)
29 Edward Hulton (publisher)
30 Sir Winston Churchill (statesman)

December

1 Mary Martin (actress/singer)
2 June Clyde (actress)
2 George Seurat (painter)
2 Lucy Verduce (housewife)
3 Shari Brown (student)
3 John Marin (painter)
4 General Emilio Garrastazu Medici (president of Brazil)
5 Walt Disney (filmmaker)
5 Martin Van Buren (8th U.S. President)

Ophiuchus
(December 6 to December 31)

Ophiuchus, the Serpent-Slayer, is the eleventh sign of the Zodiac. It is one of the two "new" signs introduced by Astrology 14. Ophiuchus is no newer than any of the other constellations, of course, but it is new to astrology, as it entered the Zodiac later than the traditional 12 signs. It occupies the position between Scorpio and Sagittarius in the zodiacal belt, and the sun is in this constellation at the winter solstice.

Until the publication of my earlier book, *Astrology 14*, Ophiuchus had not been recognized by astrologers as a zodiacal constellation. However, it was not completely ignored. In traditional astrology, Ophiuchus ruled the sex-decanate of Scorpio, through which the sun once passed from October 23 to November 2. The old astrology considered Ophiuchus to be representative of *resourcefulness*, and identified him with Jacob. According to the story in Genesis, Jacob wrestled with an angel and would not let go until the angel had blessed him, but in the struggle Jacob's thighbone was thrown out of joint. Astrological symbolism replaced the angel with a serpent (the constellation Serpens), which represents generation, and so Ophiuchus came to symbolize sex and marriage as the interlocking of an inseparable pair. However, a new interpretation is necessary in this Age of Aquarius, especially since Ophiuchus has been "promoted" from a mere decanate-ruler to a full-fledged sun sign.

The ruling planet of Ophiuchus is Pluto, which some astrologers also associate with Scorpio. Farthest out of the nine known planets, it was named for an ancient god of the underworld (also known as Hades). Pluto is a small planet, and is so far away that, from its orbit, the sun would appear to be only another large star. It was discovered so recently (1930) that not much is known about it, and it will probably be a long time before our astronauts will be able to venture that far into outer space. However, since the sun is in the constellation Ophiuchus at the winter solstice (December 22), fast-frozen Pluto seems an appropriate ruler for this sign.

Astrologers usually associate Pluto with death and such disasters as World Wars I and II and the atomic bomb. However, it is worth noting Pluto's mythological association with *Plutus*, which is a personification of *wealth*. Also, the old key word for Ophiuchus, *resourcefulness*, seems to be borne out, as we shall see below. Therefore, it is safe to assume that Pluto's influence is not necessarily malefic, depending on its relation to other elements of your chart. This planet is of particular importance if Ophiuchus is your sun sign (see Chapter 11).

In *Astrology* 14, with no previous characteristics to compare for this sun sign, I provided some information on Ophiuchus as a constellation and as a mythical figure. This material will not be repeated here; the interested reader is referred to my previous book (pp. 87–88).

My preliminary findings as to the children of Ophiuchus were based on a study of 21 persons born under this sign. I have enlarged this list to 45 individuals, and the interpretation that follows is based on this extended list. It must be stressed that, except for the few known to me personally, these people were chosen at random—I made no attempt to "load the dice" to favor my interpretation.

My initial study found Ophiuchans to be *versatile* individuals, with a special penchant for the performing arts. Both talent and sensitivity are definitely indicated and should be developed, if only as a hobby. Politics, however, does not seem to be their strong suit. Further research has not shown anything false in these preliminary interpretations. The influence of the ruling planet, however, must always be kept in mind. Pluto *can* cast a baleful influence, depending on its aspects to other elements. For example, Stalin (December 21) was apparently a "success" as a dictator. He ruled the Soviet Union with an iron hand for many years and was responsible for the death of millions in the infamous purges. After his death, his statues were toppled, and he will be remembered, along with Hitler, as one of history's bloodiest tyrants. He would have been better off behind a plow or driving a tractor!

Your versatility can serve you well in any walk of life, of course. We live in a complex world—a technological society that does not become simpler as its population increases—and most of us need to be "quick-change artists" whether we wish to or not. Whatever situation they find themselves in, Ophiuchans (like cats) can generally manage to land on their feet.

The tendency of your talent is probably toward the limelight. Many Ophiuchans are fine entertainers and are very versatile when on stage. If you have that sort of talent and are not afraid of the footlights or the camera, you have excellent prospects for success in the field of public entertainment. Here your versatility can serve you well. If an Ophiuchan comedian should literally break his leg, he will probably pop up on another show as a pianist—or playing the role of a man confined to a wheelchair. If he should lose his voice, an Ophiuchan singer will take up dancing or high-wire performing.

If your talent is specifically musical, you have the ability to master several instruments, and you can probably sing and compose as well.

Whether or not you consider yourself an entertainer, you have a good deal of personal charm. You like people, especially at a party or other joyful occasion, and may very well be the "life" of every party you attend. You are not one to stay in the background and observe rather than partake, as the children of Taurus are wont to do.

Your ability to entertain, however, does not usually extend to swaying voters or members of a political party to your way of thinking. As mentioned above, a career in politics does not seem advisable. There are different kinds of charisma, and that of Ophiuchus seems better suited for the stage or screen than the political platform.

Talent and sensitivity are so strongly indicated that, unless other elements in your horoscope tend to neutralize them, you will probably feel badly frustrated by what is considered a "normal" life in home, office, or factory. Talent is not rare in human beings. A psychologist has stated that all children are artists of genius up to the age of three. Nursery school, kindergarten, and public school seem to snuff out this original talent more effectively than they teach the child the three R's and "social adjustment." We all have to adjust to the society in which we live, to some extent, or there would be no society—but something precious is often lost in the process. The pressure to conform may make for law and order, but it represses individuality—and without individuality there is no art.

Ophiuchans tend to feel this loss more keenly than do people born under most of the other signs. The urge to create is there, and it is usually not satisfied by "creating" children or a substantial paycheck. Not all of you can be professional entertainers, of course, but all of you can find an outlet—a means of expression for your creative talent and energy. I strongly advise you to look for such an outlet if you have not already found one. Its results can only be positive, whether you are destined for a quiet, private life or a career on the world's stages and screens.

Ophiuchus, then, is a sign of versatility and resourcefulness, with talent and sensitivity strongly indicated, especially in the field of entertainment. It is not a strong sign for a political career, however. The demand for good entertainers is ever-increasing, and awards are awaiting you, whether your "stage" is network TV or your own living room. If you don't let your talent be frustrated, yours can be the greatest satisfaction of all—that of the creator. It must be remembered, however, that this is only the basic interpretation of your sun sign. It must be compared with the rising sign (Chapter 1) and with all the other elements in your horoscope, which will be described in the chapters to follow.

RELATIONSHIP OF OPHIUCHUS TO OTHER SIGNS

Compatible	Incompatible	Neutral
Ophiuchus*	Pisces	Cetus
Aries	Taurus	Gemini
Cancer	Leo	Scorpio
Libra	Virgo	Sagittarius
Capricorn	Aquarius	

OPHIUCHUS

(December 6 to December 31)

December

6	Ira Gershwin (lyricist)
7	Theodor Schwann (physiologist)
8	Sammy Davis, Jr. (entertainer)
8	Jean Sibelius (composer)
9	Maximilian Schell (actor)
10	Emily Dickinson (poet)
10	Dorothy Lamour (actress)
11	Regina Fonseca (dancer)
11	Victor McLaglen (actor)
12	Karl von Rundstedt (field marshal)
12	Anna Schmidt (housewife)
12	Frank Sinatra (singer/actor)
13	Drew Pearson (news columnist)
14	Louis Bausset (writer)
15	Joseph Halévy (orientalist)
16	Noel Coward (dramatist)
16	Norma Petersen (housewife)
16	George Santayana (philosopher)
17	Alexander Agassiz (zoologist/geologist)
18	Willy Brandt (politician)
18	Abe Burrows (comedian)
19	Ralph Richardson (actor)
19	Sue Schmidt (housewife)
20	Max Lerner (news columnist)
21	Jane Fonda (actress)
21	Mike Schmidt (engineer)
21	Josef Stalin (dictator)
22	Gary Bridges (musician)
22	David Brown (musician)
22	André Kostelanetz (musician)
23	Esther Dooling (housewife)

* If born within 10 days of own birthdate.

23 J. Arthur Rank (producer)
24 Ava Gardner (actress)
25 Cab Calloway (musician)
25 Tony Martin (singer)
26 Steve Allen (comedian/musician)
27 Marlene Dietrich (actress)
27 Sandy Jessup (model)
27 Otto Schmidt (Lutheran minister)
28 Woodrow Wilson (28th U.S. President)
29 Pablo Casals (musician)
29 Andrew Johnson (17th U.S. President)
30 Albert Bernard Bongo (president of Gabon Republic)
31 George Marshall (general/statesman)
31 Thomas Macdonough (naval officer)

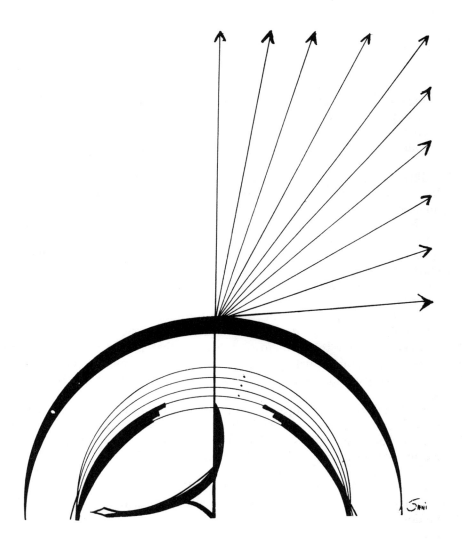

Sagittarius
(January 1 to January 26)

Sagittarius, the Archer, is the twelfth sign of the Zodiac. In traditional astrology, it was the ninth sun sign, following Scorpio. With Pisces at the beginning of the zodiacal year, and with Cetus inserted after Taurus and Ophiuchus after Scorpio, Astrology 14 places Sagittarius in its correct place as the twelfth of the zodiacal constellations.

The ruling planet of Sagittarius is Jupiter, which also rules Cetus. Jupiter is the largest of all the planets that circle the sun. Fifth of the nine known planets, it was named for the chief god of the ancients (called Zeus by the Greeks), befitting its great size. Jupiter has no less than 12 moons, one of which (Titan) is large enough to have an atmosphere. Men will probably not be able to explore Jupiter directly—its gravity would crush a human being—so these moons will most likely be the bases for our astronauts when they have ventured beyond Mars and the asteroid belt.

Astrologically, Jupiter is the "greater fortune"—a powerful and beneficent influence in any horoscope. We derive the adjective "jovial" from another name for this god, Jove, indicating that people with a strongly placed Jupiter are usually good-natured, expansive, and generous. This planet is of particular importance if Sagittarius is your sun sign (see Chapter 7).

In *Astrology 14*, I compared the traditional interpretation of the Sagittarian personality with my preliminary findings based on a study of 22 persons born under this sign. This material will not be repeated here; the interested reader is referred to my previous book (pp. 92–96).

I have enlarged the list of Sagittarians to 42 individuals. The interpretation that follows is based on this extended list. It must be stressed that, except for the few known to me personally, these people were chosen at random—I made no attempt to "load the dice" to favor my interpretation.

My initial study found Sagittarians to be outgoing, usually extraverted types, with a definite humanitarian streak. Like Scorpio, Sagittarius is deeply concerned with the lot of his fellow man; unlike Scorpios, however, Sagittarians are inclined to act on their beliefs. They are doers, not theorists, and there is little of the poet or mystic philosopher in their highly active makeup. Nothing in my further research has indicated these preliminary findings to be wrong. The influence of the ruling planet, Jupiter, intensifies the power and benevolence of this type of person and also tends to make him lucky. If well aspected to other elements in your chart, Jupiter tends to strengthen your ability to perceive what is really going on around you at all times. You are alert to the external world in all of its manifestations, and it is very hard to deceive you on this level.

Jung has divided all of humanity into two general types—extraverts and introverts. When I say that Sagittarians *tend* to be extraverted, I do not mean to imply that it is impossible to be an introvert if you were born under Sagittarius. I mean only that the *majority* of people born under this sign are extraverts, just as the majority of Scorpios are introverts. So many factors, astrological and otherwise, go into the making of personality that it would be ridiculous to assert that one-fourteenth of the human race are all extraverts simply because they were born between January 1 and 26. Such a statement would fall back into the tendency of the old astrology to shove people into predetermined niches. ("All children of Taurus are bull-headed," etc.), which is one of the very things Astrology 14 strives to correct.

With that proviso always in mind, it is safe to state that the typical Sagittarian *is* extraverted, which means that he is more interested in events outside his skin than those within. People, places, and exterior events make up your "real" world; dreams, fantasies, and "visions" are correspondingly "unreal," and you pay them little heed. If you think about it at all, it probably seems very strange to you that introverted types find such fascination in the interior realm, almost to the exclusion of what is going on all around them. The truth is, of course, that *both* realms— outer and inner—are equally real and important. It is also true that we are all mixtures; no one is a "pure" extravert or introvert. Sagittarians dream, too, and Scorpios pursue active careers in the world of the senses.

This energy and interest in the world of affairs, coupled with your active conscience as concerns humanity, would seem to bode well for a career in politics or statesmanship. Although President Nixon (January 9) is a Sagittarian, as was Millard Fillmore (January 7), the political arena may not be the best sphere for you. You tend to have strong and definite ideas about the best way to serve your fellow man, and would probably chafe against the restrictions of following the official "line" of any political party. You probably prefer to see the *direct* results of your labors, and would be happier as a social worker, or in the Peace Corps, or working for a nonprofit foundation with humanitarian ideals.

If you are a typical Sagittarian, you like people and enjoy being in the thick of events. Such an attitude can serve you well in many spheres of human activity—as an actor, salesman, teacher, trial lawyer, or soldier, to mention only a few. Whatever career you choose, rewards may come easily to you. We live in a society that still places a premium on the values of a frontier, although the last frontier (if we exclude outer space and the depths of the sea) vanished many years ago. That is, "outer" accomplishments are recognized and rewarded much more quickly than are those of the spirit. A shift is already in evidence, at the dawning of this Age of Aquarius, from materialistic to more spiritual values—but today it is still obvious that a man is more respected for what he owns than what he is. I do not mean to imply that all Sagittarians are crass materialists, of course; only that their energy and outgoing attitude make it easier for them to survive and prosper in a society whose members still like to see results. Sagittarians are usually well endowed with conscience. If you find it easy to amass riches, you are also willing to share these gains with your less fortunate fellow men.

Any one-sided attitude can be not only limiting but dangerous. If you are so extraverted that only the outer world has meaning for you, to the complete neglect of the inner world of the psyche, you will eventually have to pay a heavy price for this neglect. Mother Nature will see to that. The ideal of personality development is the equal growth of both our inner and outer natures, so that neither is neglected or overemphasized. If you are naturally extraverted, and live in a society like ours that places such a premium on material success (money, possessions, and "status"), it is only too easy to accept these values as the only values, later to find—too late—that your riches and possessions are so much dust blown by the wind. Strive always for balance, and pay attention to your dreams and intuitions; they are as real as anything "out there."

Sagittarius, then, is a sign of extraversion, energy, and humanitarianism of an active sort: a sincere desire to act on your impulses to benefit your fellow man. Success (often early) is strongly indicated in nearly any career that involves outer activity and direct contact with people. You may become too successful, in a materialistic sense, to the detriment of spiritual values; proper attention should also be paid to affairs of the spirit. It must be remembered, however, that this is only the basic interpretation of your sun sign. It must be compared with the rising sign (Chapter 1) and with all the other elements in your horoscope, which will be described in the chapters to follow.

RELATIONSHIP OF SAGITTARIUS TO OTHER SIGNS

Compatible	Incompatible	Neutral
Sagittarius*	Pisces	Taurus

* If born within 10 days of own birthdate.

Cetus	Aries	Cancer
Leo	Gemini	Ophiuchus
Scorpio	Virgo	Capricorn
Aquarius	Libra	

SAGITTARIUS
(January 1 to January 26)

January

1	Barry Goldwater (politician)
1	J. Edgar Hoover (FBI Director)
2	Julius La Rosa (singer)
2	Renata Tebaldi (singer)
3	Victor Borge (comedian/pianist)
4	Everett Dirksen (politician)
5	Gamal Nasser (Egyptian leader/soldier)
6	Carl Sandburg (writer)
6	Danny Thomas (entertainer)
6	Loretta Young (actress)
7	Millard Fillmore (13th U.S. President)
8	Richard Fonseca (insurance agent)
8	Elvis Presley (singer)
9	Richard M. Nixon (37th U.S. President)
10	Ray Bolger (dancer)
11	Eva Le Gallienne (actress)
12	Melissa Benares (painter)
12	Jack London (writer)
13	Vittorio De Sica (actor)
14	John Dos Passos (writer)
14	Albert Schweitzer (humanitarian)
15	Martin Luther King, Jr. (civil rights leader)
15	Maria Schell (actress)
16	Ethel Merman (singer)
17	Moira Shearer (dancer/actress)
18	Cary Grant (actor)
18	Danny Kaye (entertainer)
19	Anton Chekhov (writer)
20	Edwin Aldrin (astronaut)
20	Mischa Elman (musician)
21	John Batman (Australian pioneer)
22	Douglas Bridges (music student)
22	Hugo Schmidt (lumberman)
22	U Thant (statesman)
23	Dorothy Burns (housewife)
24	Maria Tallchief (dancer)

25 Emil Ludwig (writer)
25 Louis Mann (rabbi)
26 Peggy Jessup (music student)
26 Eartha Kitt (singer/actress)
26 Douglas MacArthur (general)
26 Paul Newman (actor)

Capricorn
(January 27 to February 21)

$V\mathcal{S}$

Capricorn, the Goat, is the thirteenth sign of the Zodiac. In traditional astrology, it was the tenth sun sign, following Sagittarius. With Pisces at the beginning of the zodiacal year, and with Cetus inserted after Taurus and Ophiuchus after Scorpio, Astrology 14 places Capricorn in its correct place as the thirteenth of the zodiacal constellations.

The ruling planet of Capricorn is Saturn, which is distinguished by its famous and beautiful rings. Saturn is another giant among the planets, second in size only to mighty Jupiter. Sixth of the nine known planets, it was named for the ancient god of the underworld (the Greek Kronos), and was also identified with Cronus—Father Time. Saturn was long thought to have nine moons, but a tenth (Janus) was discovered as recently as 1966, when the "edge-on" appearance of the rings made it visible. Men will probably not be able to explore Saturn directly—its gravity, like Jupiter's, would crush a human being—so these moons will most likely be the bases for our astronauts when they have ventured beyond Jupiter.

Astrologically, Saturn is traditionally considered the exact opposite of Jupiter. It is thought to be as negative as Jupiter is positive, as malefic as Jupiter is beneficent. It is the governor of old age, its keyword being *limitation*. Gloomy, cold, taciturn, the traditional portrait of the individual ruled by Saturn is that of a bitter old miser, desperately clutching his few remaining shreds of life. But, in Gershwin's words, "It ain't necessarily so!" The influence of Saturn depends upon its relation to other elements of your chart, and its intrinsic "evil" can be neutralized by other planets that are well aspected. Conservatism is not a bad trait in itself; in our flamboyant and reckless age, it could be considered a virtue. Nor does Saturn's influence rule out a sense of humor. Just as the adjective "jovial" is derived from Jupiter (Jove), the adjective "saturnine" is derived from Saturn—and, although it means "heavy, grave, sullen," saturnine *humor* is a type that has become highly popular in recent years. This is, of course, "black" humor, and is well exemplified by the writings of Norman Mailer (January 31) in books such as *Advertisements for Myself* and *Why Are We in Vietnam?* This planet is of particular importance if Capricorn is your sun sign (see Chapter 8).

In *Astrology 14*, I compared the traditional interpretation of the Capricornian personality with my preliminary findings based on a study of 20 persons born under this sign. This material will not be repeated here; the interested reader is referred to my previous book (pp. 97–101).

I have enlarged the list of Capricornians to 41 individuals. The interpretation that follows is based on this extended list. It must be stressed that, except for the few known to me personally, these people were chosen at random—I made no attempt to "load the dice" to favor my interpretation.

My initial study found Capricornians to be realistic and dryly witty, with tendencies for both creative genius and childishness or immaturity in their development. The symbol of their sign (half-goat, half-fish) is apt, for they often do exhibit a split in their personality: the higher the goat may climb (conscious achievement), the farther behind he leaves the fish (in the waters of the unconscious). Since we cannot cut ourselves off from our roots (instincts) any more than a tree can live without the sap rising from its roots, the Capricornian who ignores the sources of his energy and creativity in his eagerness to scale the heights does so at his peril. A rootless tree will atrophy, and a human, genius or not, who sacrifices his instinctual life to pour all of himself into his work is in equally bad straits. Nothing in my further research has indicated these preliminary findings to be wrong. The influence of the ruling planet, however, must always be kept in mind. Ruling Saturn strengthens your sense of conservatism. You are strongly realistic, and tend to make full use of whatever comes your way, be it spiritual or material.

Conservatism and a strong sense of reality would seem to bode well for a career in politics. Such great Presidents of the United States as Abraham Lincoln (February 12) and Franklin D. Roosevelt (January 30) were born under Capricorn, as were McKinley (January 29) and Harrison (February 9), as well as Lord Salisbury (February 3), Adlai Stevenson (February 5), and Elihu Root (February 15). Capricorn does indeed seem a "natural" sign for politicians. But here (as in any other field) the negative potential can overcome the positive. This is well illustrated by another Capricornian, Farouk (February 11), former king of Egypt. The childishness that threatens those born under this sign held full sway with Farouk, who much preferred playing on the Riviera to affairs of state, which he left to his subordinates. While many of his people were starving, he gambled and gamboled in luxury—and died as he had lived, with his face in the remains of a gourmet meal. To contrast such a "ruler" with Lincoln is to see the extremes of the above-mentioned split in the Capricornian personality.

Genius may appear in any of the 14 signs, of course, but Capricorn often seems to beat the odds in this department. Perhaps the greatest actor and the greatest writer thus far produced by our time were born under this sign: John Barrymore (February 14) and James Joyce (February 2). But they, too, paid a heavy price for their well-deserved fame. Barrymore fell prey to alcoholism; Joyce also had a drinking problem—and was so frightened of thunder and lightning that, to the end of his days, he would panic when there was a storm.

The lesson seems clear. As a Capricornian, you probably have great ability (even genius) in your chosen field, but you should be especially alert to the danger of one-sided development. The better you are at your work, the easier it is to "lose" yourself in it—and this can be a real and terrible loss. There seems to be no doubt that the aim of human development is *wholeness*. The goal of nature is not to develop either absent-minded professors or athletes who never read a book once school is out, neither mad scientists nor crazy artists starving in a garret—but whole and well-balanced human beings, with no part of the self (mental, physical, or spiritual) developed at the expense of another. In education, the ancient Greeks laid equal stress on music, philosophy, and gymnastics; *Mens sana in corpore sano*, said the Roman Juvenal—A sound mind in a sound body. Our own time—torn by war, rebellion, and every kind of unrest, as expressed in the philosophy of existentialism and the fragmented forms of modern art—especially needs to follow such old and sage advice. And Capricorn, of all the signs, most needs to be on guard against loss of contact with his roots.

You have a real asset in your ability to remain objective, though this may make you seem cold to your friends and associates. Let them think what they will. Your feelings are as strong as anyone's, and your ability to keep your head and to see clearly what is going on is a distinct advantage in a world where emotional extravagance is often considered a virtue. Such indulgence is sometimes tempting, but morning always brings the hangover; the piper must be paid.

You have all the traits that usually indicate success and material prosperity. If you can check a tendency to throw yourself into your work to the exclusion of other important phases of your life, which means immaturity, there is nothing to stop you from reaching great heights in both your profession and in personal fulfillment and happiness.

Capricorn, then, is a sign of realism, dry wit, and (often) creative genius in many fields. If the danger of the split between the "goat" half of your personality (your conscious aspirations) and the "fish" (the deeper knowledge of the unconscious) is avoided by constantly striving for *balance*, tendencies to immature, one-sided development can be avoided—and then the sky, as the astronauts have shown, is no limit! It must be remembered, however, that this is only the basic interpretation of your sun sign. It must be compared with the rising sign (Chapter 1) and with all the other elements in your horoscope, which will be described in the chapters to follow.

RELATIONSHIP OF CAPRICORN TO OTHER SIGNS

Compatible	Incompatible	Neutral
Capricorn*	Aries	Gemini
Pisces	Cetus	Leo
Taurus	Cancer	Sagittarius
Virgo	Libra	Aquarius
Ophiuchus	Scorpio	

CAPRICORN

(January 27 to February 21)

January

27 George Scheuchenpflug (businessman)
28 Artur Rubinstein (pianist)
29 William McKinley (25th U.S. President)
30 Franklin D. Roosevelt (32nd U.S. President)
31 Norman Mailer (writer)

February

1 Clark Gable (actor)
2 Jascha Heifetz (musician)
2 James Joyce (writer)
3 James A. Michener (writer)
3 Lord Salisbury (statesman)
3 Rick Wagner (Lutheran vicar)
4 Charles Lindbergh (aviator)
5 Adlai Stevenson (statesman)
6 Babe Ruth (baseball player)
7 Charles Dickens (writer)
8 Charles Funck, Jr. (businessman)
8 John Ruskin (art critic/writer)
8 William T. Sherman (general)
8 Jules Verne (writer)
9 William Henry Harrison (9th U.S. President)
10 General Lemuel Shepherd, Jr. (Marine Corps commandant)
11 Farouk (king of Egypt)
11 Carolyn Schmidt (housewife)
12 Abraham Lincoln (16th U.S. President)
13 Kim Novak (actress)

* If born within 10 days of own birthdate.

14 John Barrymore (actor)
14 Jack Benny (comedian)
14 Joyce Carr Jessup (housewife)
14 George Jean Nathan (critic)
15 Cyrus McCormick (inventor)
15 Elihu Root (statesman)
16 Van Wyck Brooks (critic)
17 Andrés Segovia (musician)
17 Mel Welles (actor)
18 Lewis Armistead (Confederate general)
19 Merle Oberon (actress)
20 Sidney Poitier (actor)
21 W. H. Auden (poet)
21 Ann Sheridan (actress)
21 Daniel Villaseñor (art student)

Aquarius
(February 22 to March 20)

Aquarius, the Water-Bearer, is the fourteenth and last sign of the Zodiac. In traditional astrology, it was the eleventh sun sign, following Capricorn. With Pisces at the beginning of the zodiacal year, and with Cetus inserted after Taurus and Ophiuchus after Scorpio, Astrology 14 places Aquarius in its correct place as the fourteenth of the zodiacal constellations.

The ruling planet of Aquarius is Uranus, which has an eccentric orbit. Although it is one of the four giant planets of the solar system, Uranus is so far away that a large telescope is necessary to study its details. Seventh of the nine known planets, it was named for the ancient sky god. Uranus is so far away that it will probably be a long time before our astronauts will be able to explore it at close range. It has five moons.

Astrologically, Uranus is an object of dispute. Some astrologers claim that its influence is beneficent, especially where science, mechanics, and invention are concerned; others have nicknamed this planet "the disruptor" (because of its eccentric orbit), and say that Aquarian types tend to have disruptive personalities because of this planet's rule. Both of these viewpoints seem to be borne out—in part, at least—by studies of people born under Aquarius. It must be remembered, however, that the influence of any planet can be strengthened or lessened by its relationship to other elements of your chart—and even people born under Aquarius are not necessarily Aquarian types. However, this planet is of particular importance if Aquarius is your sun sign (see Chapter 9).

In *Astrology 14*, I compared the traditional interpretation of the Aquarian personality with my preliminary findings based on a study of 21 persons born under this sign. This material will not be repeated here; the interested reader is referred to my previous book (pp. 102–106).

I have enlarged the list of Aquarians to 39 individuals. The interpretation that follows is based on this extended list. It must be stressed that, except for the few known to me personally, these people were chosen at random—I made no attempt to "load the dice" to favor my interpretation.

My initial study found Aquarians to be persons who are not strong politically, but who have a decided penchant for the world of entertainment. Like the children of Ophiuchus, many of them seem to be born for center stage (although usually without the versatility of Ophiuchans). However, they also tend to be finely balanced and, if they don't keep in top condition, physically and mentally, may give way to attacks of "nerves" or "artistic temperament." I also mentioned that they are usually good conversationalists and are attracted by the new and different—sometimes to the extent of being regarded as "characters" by their friends. So far, so good. However, I would like to amend and enlarge upon my initial interpretation. On the first list, 15 of the 21 (or nearly 75 percent) were active in the entertainment world. On the extended list of 39 Aquarians, only 20 (a little more than 50 percent) have careers in the limelight. This is still a striking percentage, of course, and bears out my first attempts to interpret the Aquarian *as an entertainer.* However, that he can also be successful in public life is shown by the addition of several individuals active and successful in the political arena, including the president of Finland (March 9), Emperor Alexander III of Russia (March 10), and Chief Justice Earl Warren of the Supreme Court (March 19). It would seem, then, that Aquarius *can* perform on the political platform as well as the stages and screens of the entertainment world.

My initial interpretation found nothing to confirm the traditional view of the influence of the ruling planet, Uranus, as affecting mechanical science and invention. The new list includes two notable names in these fields—Alexander Graham Bell (March 3) and Albert Einstein (March 14). These are only two out of 39, but their influence can hardly be overstated. The telephone has become so common, in home and office, that it is sometimes hard to remember that there was a time when no such implement existed to expedite our communications a thousandfold. As for Einstein, his theories have not only revolutionized mathematics and physical science, but have altered our basic outlook on the universe. Before him, we lived in a tidy, mechanical, "clockwork" cosmos; no one suspected that time is the fourth dimension of space, or that the fabric of space itself is curved. With such men born under Aquarius, it is necessary to add that there is certainly a *possibility* that Uranus tends to increase your ability to acquire knowledge in scientific and technical fields.

Whether or not you are attracted to the fields of entertainment, politics, science, or invention, you probably have a well-developed analytical ability—a trait you share with the children of Virgo. Analysis (which literally means "taking apart") is indispensable to a scientist or technician, of course. A politician, too, must be able to analyze—not only the complex world of public affairs, but also the strengths and weaknesses of his opposition. Art, on the other hand, is usually achieved by *synthesis*—a bringing-together of many existing things to create something new. What, then, of the many Aquarian artists (our list includes writers and painters as well as entertainers)? Is their Uranian ability to analyze a help or hindrance to the synthesis of their art? In fact, the Aquarian artist usually brings *both* methods into play. He or she *analyzes* the present state of that art, as well as the styles of its practitioners, and is then able to *synthesize* a new and original approach or style.

Aquarius, then, is a sign for entertainers—and also for politicians, scientists, technicians, and inventors. Born under this sign, you have a strong analytical ability that will help you in many other fields besides these. You are probably mechanically inclined, and have the ability to make things work. Also, you are attracted to the odd, the unusual and the paradoxical—a proclivity that may make your friends consider you "a bohemian." Although you are at home in the limelight, you are probably less versatile than Ophiuchans, and more inclined to be nervous and temperamental. There is a definite need for you to stay in top condition, mentally as well as physically, if you are to achieve success as an entertainer or in any other field. You should also be careful to temper your tendency to analyze everything. Very little could be accomplished without analysis, of course, but the habit of overanalysis can destroy the pleasure of simple acceptance and enjoyment. You are a good conversationalist and tend to take an active part in discussions. Try to be a little less analytical and critical, and keep yourself in good condition, and your chances of success and happiness are excellent. For social harmony, always bear in mind that the best habit is that of trying to see the other person's point of view. It must be remembered, however, that this is only the basic interpretation of your sun sign. It must be compared with the rising sign (Chapter 1) and with all the other elements in your horoscope, which will be described in the chapters to follow.

RELATIONSHIP OF AQUARIUS TO OTHER SIGNS

Compatible	Incompatible	Neutral
Aquarius*	Cetus	Pisces
Aries	Taurus	Cancer
Gemini	Leo	Virgo
Libra	Ophiuchus	Capricorn
Sagittarius	Scorpio	

AQUARIUS
(February 22 to March 20)

February

22	Regina Crook (housewife)
22	George Washington (1st U.S. President)
23	Peter Fonda (actor)

* If born within 10 days of own birthdate.

24   Samuel Lover (writer/painter)
25   George Harrison (musician)
26   Jackie Gleason (entertainer)
26   Betty Hutton (entertainer)
26   Teri Schmidt (artist/musician)
27   John Steinbeck (writer)
27   Elizabeth Taylor (actress)
27   Joanne Woodward (actress)
28   Ida Masters Schmidt (housewife)
29   Gioacchino Rossini (composer)

March

1   Harry Belafonte (singer)
1   Dinah Shore (singer)
2   Jennifer Jones (actress)
3   Alexander Graham Bell (inventor)
4   Joan Greenwood (actress)
5   Rex Harrison (actor)
6   Charles Barbaroux (politician)
7   Lord Strabolgi (politician)
8   Gene Fowler (writer)
9   Dr. Urbo Kekkonen (president of Finland)
10   Alexander III (emperor of Russia)
11   Lawrence Welk (musician)
12   Edward Albee (dramatist)
12   Gordon MacRae (singer)
12   Liza Minnelli (entertainer)
13   Sammy Kaye (musician)
13   Martha Schmidt (housewife)
14   Albert Einstein (scientist)
15   Harry James (musician)
16   Jerry Lewis (entertainer)
16   James Madison (4th U.S. President)
17   Nat "King" Cole (singer)
18   Grover Cleveland (22nd U.S. President)
19   Ursula Andress (actress)
19   Earl Warren (Supreme Court chief justice)
20   Henrik Ibsen (dramatist)

THE AGE OF AQUARIUS

Since this chapter on the sun signs concludes with Aquarius, I would like to make a few comments on the larger or more general meaning of this sign. Aquarius not only rules the fourteenth House, it is the ruling sign of the new age that is dawning. No one seems to be able to agree on the exact date, but it is clear that the Age of Pisces the Fish is ending. Both Pisces and Aquarius are signs concerned with water. This is, of course, the natural element of fish and other aquatic creatures—and the symbol of Aquarius is that of a man bearing water in a vessel.

Does this indicate progress? Let us hope so. Pisces is an *animal* sign; Aquarius is a *human* sign. The two fish of Pisces are pulling in opposite directions, whereas the Water-Bearer is single; moreover, his water is *contained* in a vessel, and he has a definite purpose for it. Thus, simply from an evolutionary point of view, progress is apparent.

Astrology is not only a science, but is concerned with spiritual values—as has been pointed out in an excellent recent book*—and this is what "hard" science is never able to understand about it. So we must not think of the water in these symbolic signs as *literal* water—the wet stuff we wash our hands and pots in every day—but, on a deeper level, as representative of spiritual value. In all sacred writings and esoteric teaching, meaning is expressed on two levels—literal and psychological. We all know the literal meaning of water, but what is its esoteric (or "inner") meaning? In the ancient language of symbolism, water means *truth*. And this truth is psychological; it refers to the inner development of man, leading to his spiritual rebirth. I will take an example from the Bible, which is the sacred book most familiar to us. In the Book of Jeremiah, we read:

For my people have committed two evils; they have forsaken me the fountain of living waters, and hewed them out cisterns, broken cisterns, that can hold no water.

The living water is the inner truth that leads to psychological self-development; the broken cisterns symbolize the "death" of people who are unaware of this truth. As William Blake wrote, "The cistern contains: the fountain overflows."

We may be sure that the water borne upon the shoulder of Aquarius is this living water. Many astrologers have prophesied that the Age of Aquarius will bring peace and the development of man's higher spiritual faculties. I do not think it possible to predict that this will either happen or fail to happen. The world today is in a state of chaos, and chaos can lead either to the creation of order or simply to further chaos. There is already a strong revolt, especially among the young, against the materialism of our society. This revolt is a healthy sign, but so far it has been mostly directionless. Materialism is a natural outgrowth of taking everything literally—by appearances only. For spiritual values to replace materialism,

* *The Case for Astrology,* by John Anthony West and Jan Gerhard Toonder, Coward-McCann, Inc., 1970.

we must begin to look for the hidden meaning in words and things. It is a delusion to think that spiritual enlightenment can be acquired through the use of drugs or other "mind-blowing" experiences. It is an individual task, and a difficult one, but it is the only task truly worthy of a human being. The stars are right for such a spiritual reawakening of mankind, but such a transformation never comes about automatically. Nor is it achieved through group action. The poor are not enriched by giving them money, and individuals are not led to illumination by dropping out or joining a commune. The goal of a higher, richer, truly *human* life can be reached only through great individual effort; by looking within yourself; by seeking the waters of truth beneath the distracting glitter of surface appearances. The *tao*, the Way, is rocky. "Know yourself," the Greeks said centuries ago—and it is still the only way to spiritual enlightenment. Until enough individuals follow this path, wars, poverty, and all the other evils so familiar to us will continue, and the Age of Aquarius will then be no better than was the Age of Pisces.

3: The Moon

$$\mathbb{D}$$

O, swear not by the moon, the inconstant moon,
That monthly changes in her circled orb . . .
                                    Romeo and Juliet

MEANING OF MOON IN HOROSCOPE

JULIET'S COMPLAINT has been echoed, in essence, by many an astrologer, before and after Shakespeare's time. However, the "circled orb" she refers to is the *phase* of the moon, and what concerns astrologers is the *position* of the moon, especially at the moment of the subject's birth. Along with the sun and rising sign, the moon is one of the most important elements in your horoscope, and in this chapter you will learn how to place it properly on your chart.

As mentioned in Chapter 2, the moon is the ruling planet of Cancer. Our nearest neighbor in the sky has always been important in the eyes and thoughts of men, but our generation has had a closer look at it than any previous one, thanks to our space program. Astronauts Armstrong and Aldrin, of *Apollo* 11, were the first men to walk on the surface of our satellite, in 1969; other successful *Apollo* flights have been made since. Our lunar astronauts found no traces of life on the airless moon, but the rocks and soil samples they brought back have already yielded important information. The moon was apparently created at the same time as the earth, and was not born out of the "mother" planet; also, the old controversy as to the origin of the craters has been settled—they were caused by both volcanic *and* meteoric activity.

The moon is smaller than the earth and the other planets, but it is relatively large when compared to the size of other satellites as related to their planets. It has always exerted a strong effect upon mankind—an inspiration to lovers and poets, an "impossible" goal for explorers and scientists, a white lamp in the sky for night people. Its influence on the tides has been noted since early times, and its influence on the human psyche—though still only dimly understood—is just as strong. The term "lunatic" was coined in the Middle Ages because the full moon was thought to bring on madness; legends of werewolves and other "change-lings" are still with us. Until recently, science has pooh-poohed such stories, but experiments in asylums have proved that inmates are affected by lunar influence, even when locked away from "the glimpses of the moon."

The moon has always been represented by goddesses, such as Diana and Selene, reflecting the feminine principle. It is opposite to the masculine sun just as feminine Venus is opposite to masculine Mars. Astrologically, the moon represents not only the feminine, but the unconscious in general, the emotions, birth, and growth, and it has always been associated with water. (The spiritual meaning of water as *truth* was noted at the end of Chapter 2.)

The influence of the moon is as variable as its phases. It circles the earth every 28 days, "pulling" on first one continent, then another (actually, the moon and the earth revolve about a common center of gravity, but from our point of view the moon rises and sets like the sun). An obvious fact, but one that is easily overlooked, is that the moon generates no light of its own. Whether white, bluish, or silvery, the light of the moon is *reflected* from the sun, just as a mirror reflects light without being the source of it. This simple physical fact has great *spiritual* importance. The association of the moon with the unconscious has already been noted; its function as a reflector of light makes it symbolic of the *mind*. This may seem surprising at first, for we are accustomed to thinking of our minds as the source of our thoughts. However, it is not the mind, but the spirit, that *creates* consciousness—and this activity is *reflected* by the mind in conscious terms. Or, in psychological language, the unconscious is the source of all psychic energy; this energy is reflected by the conscious mind (ego) in recognizable forms, such as words, images, mathematical symbols, etc. It is easy to see, then, why the moon is of great importance in a horoscope.

Because it is so close to the earth, the moon's apparent motion is much faster than that of the sun and the other planets. From our viewpoint, the moon moves 12 degrees every 24 hours and enters a new sign in a little less than two days. It makes 13 complete orbits a year. That is, it travels 4,680 degrees a year, as compared with the 360 degrees traversed by the sun. Far Pluto, by contrast, is the "slowest" of the planets, moving only about 1.5 degrees a year.

To place the moon symbol (☽) on your chart, turn to Table 4 at the end of this chapter. Here the positions of the moon are listed for each

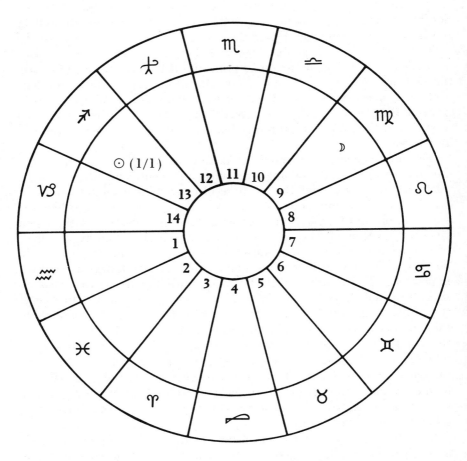

Figure 4. Placement of moon on chart ·of subject born on January 1, 1940, with
Aquarius rising

year from 1890 to 1975. Turn to the year of your birth, and find the date closest to your birthdate. It should be noted that Table 4 lists the dates when the moon *enters* each sign. If your birthdate is not listed in the table, use the *preceding* sign, not the one following your birthdate. That is, if you were born on the twelfth and the table lists Cetus for the eleventh and Taurus for the thirteenth, the moon was still in Cetus on your birthdate, since it did not enter Tarurus until the thirteenth. As a reminder, the symbols of the 14 signs are given in a key at the beginning of Table 4.

To continue our example of someone born on January 1, 1940, with Aquarius rising, Figure 4 shows his chart with the moon symbol entered. In Table 4, it is shown that the moon was in Virgo on January 1, 1940; therefore, the symbol of the moon is entered in the House occupied by Virgo, which (on his chart) is the ninth House.

INTERPRETATION

General interpretations of the meaning of the moon in each of the 14 signs are given below. In reading these, it should be remembered that the moon principally affects the *personality*. Also, the House occupied by your moon affects its interpretation. Our imaginary subject (Figure 4) was born with Aquarius rising; the sun in Sagittarius, which is his thirteenth House; and the moon in Virgo, which is his ninth House. After reading the interpretation of the moon in Virgo, he should turn back to Table 1 (p. 4), which lists the basic meanings of the Houses. The life activity governed by that particular House will be enhanced by the presence of the moon. This is also true of the sun, of course, and of the planets, which we will be placing in the chapters to follow.

MOON IN PISCES ☽ ♓

The moon in Pisces on your chart tends to enhance your belief, especially as concerns your belief in yourself (or lack of it). The ruling planet of Pisces is Neptune, which is often concerned with spiritual affairs. Since the moon primarily affects your personality, its position in Pisces will probably serve to strengthen your feelings about yourself and your relationship with others. This can be positive if the moon is well aspected to other elements of your chart, resulting in a strong personality with pronounced will power, courage, and determination to succeed. On the other hand, if poorly aspected, the moon in Pisces can increase your doubts about yourself and weaken your sense of personal integrity as an individual. You have strong spiritual inclinations. This does not necessarily mean that you are a churchgoer or even that you could define your belief; but you know intuitively that materialism is finally unsatisfactory as a way of life—that man has a higher purpose than coming out first in the rat race. The meaning of the aspects will be taken up in Chapter 12. In the meantime, check the life activity governed by the House occupied by Pisces on your chart (see Table 1) for a clearer picture of the moon's influence on your belief and spiritual drive.

MOON IN ARIES ☽ ♈

The moon in Aries on your chart probably enhances that part of your personality that is concerned with the *will*. A philosopher once noted that we all have the knowledge to lead perfect lives; it is the will that is lacking. Your moon in Aries, if well aspected to other elements of your chart, can add iron to your will power; it can well lead to the development of a powerful, magnetic personality—the stuff of which the "movers and shakers" are made. If your moon is poorly aspected, however, your will may fluctuate in an irregular pattern, making you unsure of your decisions and—in extreme cases—unable to make a decision at all! Following Nietzsche, Alfred Adler based his psychology on man's will to power. It would be foolish to deny this element in human nature; too great a reliance on raw will power, however, can be disastrous. Many of the most important events in our lives cannot be *forced*—they must simply be allowed to happen. You may find this hard to understand and, your will power failing you, fall into a brooding or dogmatic stance, becoming unreasonably stubborn in your beliefs. Aries is ruled by warlike Mars, which often leads to the development of belligerence in your personality. Guard against this tendency, and your strong will can help bring success, prosperity, and happiness.

MOON IN CETUS ☽ ♎

The moon in Cetus on your chart has a direct effect on your personality where you probably feel it most—in your self-regard, your relations with others, and your career. It has been noted that the children of Cetus are often successful in the performing and graphic arts, and have a good deal of personal charm. Cetus is ruled by Jupiter, the "greater fortune," which usually has a beneficent effect in the horoscope. Therefore, in most cases, placement of the moon in Cetus at the moment of your birth will tend to the development of a colorful, individualistic personality— the type that finds it easy to attract friends and is a real boost toward success—especially in the performing arts, salesmanship, and other positions involving direct contact with other people. However, this requires that your moon be favorably aspected to other elements in your chart. If it is poorly aspected, the moon in Cetus may actually have a *repressive* effect on your personality, which results in shyness, a feeling of awkwardness in dealing with others, or even a sense of worthlessness. If this is the case, you can overcome such traits by stressing the strong points in your chart (no horoscope is wholly good or wholly bad). The meaning of the aspects will be taken up in Chapter 12. Check the life activity governed by the House occupied by Cetus on your chart (see Table 1) for a clearer picture of the moon's influence on your personality.

MOON IN TAURUS ☽ ♉

The moon in Taurus on your chart will have a direct—and probably favorable—influence on your love life. The "feminine" moon has always played an important part in affairs of the heart, and Taurus is ruled by Venus, named for the goddess of love. Venus is also associated with music and—to a lesser extent—with mathematics and the physical sciences. If your talent and interests lie in these fields, your moon in Taurus usually bodes well for success. As for romance and marriage, this position for your moon is nearly always indicative of popularity and happiness. If well aspected to other elements in your chart, the moon in Taurus enhances your attraction for the opposite sex and makes it easier for you to understand and get along with them. If poorly aspected, however, it may stress shyness and difficulty in feeling at ease on social occasions. It may also bring out the Taurine trait of *possessiveness*, so beware of clinging too closely to those who are so easily attracted to you. The meaning of the aspects will be taken up in Chapter 12. Check the life activity governed by the House occupied by Taurus on your chart (see Table 1) for a clearer picture of the moon's influence on your love life.

MOON IN GEMINI ☽ ♊

The moon in Gemini on your chart enhances the quality and speed of your thought and your ability to communicate, both orally and in writing. Gemini is ruled by fast-moving Mercury, and it has been noted that the children of Gemini stand out for the strength and agility of their intellect. This aspect of your personality—your nimbleness of mind, ability to grasp quickly complex matters, versatility and variety of interests and talents, and ability to communicate with facility—will be enhanced if your moon in Gemini is well aspected to other elements in your chart. Whatever your sun sign, this position of the moon will help round out your personality and make you a more interesting and colorful friend and a double-valued employee. If poorly aspected, however, the moon in Gemini may bring out more negative traits of the "mercurial" personality: fickleness, a reputation for being two-faced with friends and lovers, and too-easy changes of mind, jobs, and associates. These negative traits can be offset, of course, by concentrating on the strong points in your horoscope. The meaning of the aspects will be taken up in Chapter 12. Check the life activity governed by the House occupied by Gemini on your chart (see Table 1) for a clearer picture of the moon's influence on your intellectual and communicative traits.

MOON IN CANCER ☽ ♋

The moon in Cancer on your chart is bound to have a powerful influence on your personality, especially your emotional sensitivity, as Cancer is the only sign *ruled* by the moon. The strength of its effect in this position is, therefore, approximately doubled. This influence can, of course, be in either a positive or negative direction. If your moon in Cancer is well aspected to other elements in your chart, its effect will be to increase the quality of your emotions, strengthen your conservatism and sense of responsibility (although at heart you may be as changeable as Gemini), and stiffen your sense of duty to family and associates. Barring accidents, you will probably live a long life and remain youthful in your outlook; you will also tend to be a daredevil in your choice of sports, feel at ease in social situations, and have a well-developed sense of humor. If your moon is poorly aspected, however, your conservatism may make you pass up favorable opportunities; also, you may become withdrawn in social situations and too shy to assert yourself, and your participation in sports may be dangerously reckless. The meaning of the aspects will be taken up in Chapter 12. Check the life activity governed by the House occupied by Cancer on your chart (see Table 1) for a clearer picture of the moon's (double) influence on the sensitivity of your emotions and other of the above traits.

MOON IN LEO ☽ ♌

The moon in Leo on your chart enhances the quality of independence in your thought and action. Leo is ruled by the sun, which represents the "masculine" principle—the exact opposite of the "feminine" moon. Psychologically, the joining of these two is a union of opposites or *hieros gamos*—"sacred marriage"—in the heavens. But marriages, of course, can be made in hell as well as in heaven! If well aspected to other elements in your chart, the moon in Leo can lead to a nice balance between activity and passivity, between the independence of Leo and the conservatism of Cancer, and make for a strong, colorful personality with nothing wishy-washy or hesitant about you. You will forge strong friendships and be as fiercely loyal to your loved ones as they are to you. And your enmities will be equally strong. Such a personality is well suited to leaders and pace-setters in politics, business, the arts, and social affairs. If your moon is badly aspected, however, you may develop the trait of independence to the point where you will find it difficult to cooperate with others in any group endeavor—and this applies to marriage and friendship as well as more general affairs. The meaning of the aspects will be taken up in Chapter 12. Check the life activity governed by the House occupied by Leo on your chart (see Table 1) for a clearer picture of the moon's influence on the independence of your personality.

MOON IN VIRGO ☽ ♍

The moon in Virgo on your chart tends to stress the individualism of your personality. This is the quality that makes you stand out in a crowd and be familiar to those around you, whether they have actually met you or not. Virgo is ruled by Mercury, and its influence with the moon in this position usually makes itself felt in your analytical ability. This can be a definite asset to your career, whatever your field. You are able to size up people, situations, and products with a quickness and accuracy that make you an extremely valuable employee. This analytical ability can also be an advantage in your personal life, as you quickly see through bogus offers of friendship and insincere declarations of love. Because of your individualism, your friends may regard you as a "character," but they will do so affectionately, and will usually bestow a nickname on you. If your moon is not well aspected, however, your "one of a kind" quality may be so extreme that it will be hard for you to relate to others. Also, if overdeveloped, your analytical ability may lead you to misapply it in areas where it is inappropriate, such as affairs of the heart. The meaning of the aspects will be taken up in Chapter 12. Check the life activity governed by the House occupied by Virgo on your chart (see Table 1) for a clearer picture of the moon's influence on the individualistic and analytical sides of your personality.

MOON IN LIBRA ☽ ♎

The moon in Libra on your chart tends to enhance the quality of your judgment. That part of your personality that is able to stand aside from emotional attachments—to weigh opposing factors without bias or prejudice—is affected by your moon in this position. If well aspected to other elements in your chart, your moon in Libra can thus be a real aid, in the law and many other careers, as well as in your personal relationships. Like Taurus, Libra is ruled by Venus, the planet of love, and the moon/Libra combination can mean success and happiness in romantic affairs and marriage. Often it also signifies musical talent, especially in the vocal arts; chances are that you have a fine natural singing voice. If badly aspected, however, your moon in Libra can lead to lack of self-confidence, a too-ready willingness to *doubt* your ability to judge. On the other hand, it can lead to a dogmatic insistence that you are *always* right in your judgments. The meaning of the aspects will be taken up in Chapter 12. Check the life activity governed by the House occupied by Libra on your chart (see Table 1) for a clearer picture of the moon's influence on your ability to judge rightly or wrongly.

MOON IN SCORPIO ☽ ♏

The moon in Scorpio on your chart affects your sensitivity, especially where the feelings of others are concerned (empathy). It enhances your interest in human affairs, your idealistic desire to make the world a better place for mankind. If well aspected to other elements in your chart, your moon in Scorpio can help to develop a wonderfully warm, sensitive, and sympathetic personality. Needless to say, many kinds of people are attracted to such a personality. The problem is not how to find friends and lovers, but how to choose among the many who offer themselves. If poorly aspected, however, your moon in Scorpio can lead you into positions where too great a demand is made on your emotional and physical energies, to the detriment of your health and prevention of the development of your own potential and talents—and there is a streak of the poet or mystic in many of you that *should* be developed. Also, your idealistic desire to see only the good in others can blind you to the presence and machinations of those who, through envy, consider you their enemy. The meaning of the aspects will be taken up in Chapter 12. Check the life activity governed by the House occupied by Scorpio on your chart (see Table 1) for a clearer picture of the moon's influence on the sensitive, empathic, and idealistic side of your personality.

MOON IN OPHIUCHUS ☽ ⚕

The moon in Ophiuchus on your chart tends to enhance your resourcefulness—your ability to land catlike on your feet in any situation into which life thrusts you. If well aspected to other elements in your chart, your moon in Ophiuchus can mean not only resourcefulness, but talent, versatility, and sensitivity. Like Cetus types, you have personal charm in no small measure. These qualities bode well for a career in the entertainment field, especially the performing arts. Whether or not you are destined to have a star pinned to your door, you are the type that is popular at parties, and the employee the boss can count on to be able to switch tasks—or do two things at once—without loss of poise. If your moon in Ophiuchus is badly aspected, however, you may choose the wrong field for the exploitation of your talent and ability; politics, for example, would usually be a bad choice. Or you may find yourself in a position making it impossible to develop your talent, which would be extremely frustrating for you. The meaning of the aspects will be taken up in Chapter 12. Check the life activity governed by the House occupied by Ophiuchus on your chart (see Table 1) for a clearer picture of the moon's influence on the resourcefulness and versatility of your personality.

MOON IN SAGITTARIUS ☽ ♐

The moon in Sagittarius on your chart affects your conscience and the side of your personality that tends to make you an extravert. Sagittarius is ruled by Jupiter, the "greater fortune," which is usually a beneficent planet. If well aspected to other elements in your chart, your moon in Sagittarius can lead to the development of an expansive, generous personality. You have a clear-eyed view of the world, and are willing and able to act on your ideals and beliefs. You are probably as sensitive as Scorpio to the needs of mankind, but there is nothing poetic or mystic in your outlook; you want to do something to right these wrongs, and you have the ability and energy to make a positive contribution. Rewards may come quickly to you, and you will be well deserving of them. If your moon in Sagittarius is not well aspected, however, you may develop your extraverted side at the expense of your inner, intuitive nature. This is the position of the successful businessman, say, who has staked everything on his career; he "makes it"—and then finds life strangely empty and unsatisfying. A well-rounded personality demands development of both our inner and outer selves. The meaning of the aspects will be taken up in Chapter 12. Check the life activity governed by the House occupied by Sagittarius on your chart (see Table 1) for a clearer picture of the moon's influence on the extraverted, "realistic," and outwardly active side of your personality.

MOON IN CAPRICORN ☽ ♑

The moon in Capricorn on your chart tends to strengthen your sense of conservatism. You hate to see anything wasted—be it mental, physical, or spiritual—and make full use of everything that comes your way. Capricorn is ruled by Saturn, which is usually considered a malevolent planet. This does not mean that your moon in this position is necessarily bad, however; as with all the other elements of the horoscope, it is the *aspect* that counts most heavily in interpretation. If your moon is well aspected, you can develop a truly realistic, objective view of the world that bodes well for success in many fields, including politics. It should be remembered that not a few great creative geniuses were Capricorn types. You probably also have an excellent sense of humor that expresses itself in dry, subtle wit. If poorly aspected, however, your moon in Capricorn may lead to a too one-sided development of your personality. Like Sagittarius types, you must beware of developing the outward aspects of your life and career to the point of ignoring the inner realm of dreams and intuition. A certain emotional childishness may result, which will continue through life no matter how "mature" you may appear outwardly. The meaning of the aspects will be taken up in Chapter 12. Check the life activity governed by the House occupied by Capricorn on your chart (see Table 1) for a clearer picture of the moon's influence on the conservative side of your personality.

MOON IN AQUARIUS ☽ ♒

The moon in Aquarius on your chart aids in the acquirement of knowledge, especially of the scientific or technical type. Aquarius is ruled by Uranus, which is called "the disruptor" by some astrologers because of its eccentric orbit. This may or may not mean a disruptive streak in your personality, depending upon the aspects of other elements in your chart. In any case, you are probably attracted to the odd and paradoxical, and are willing to try the new and unusual. If well aspected, your moon in Aquarius can lead to the development of a colorful personality and the ability to make things work. You would probably do very well in a scientific or technical career. Or, if the arts are your forte, you could probably succeed in the performing arts (though you may not be as versatile as Ophiuchus types). If your moon is badly aspected, however, a tendency to nervousness and temperament may develop to a point damaging to your career and personal happiness. There is a strong need for you to keep in top condition, both physically and mentally. Your analytical ability is strong, but—like Libra types—you must beware of becoming overly analytical and critical, especially where friends, family, and lovers are concerned. The meaning of the aspects will be taken up in Chapter 12. Check the life activity governed by the House occupied by Aquarius on your chart (see Table 1) for a clearer picture of the moon's influence on your scientific/technical practicality, your temperament, and the "disruptive" elements in your personality.

Table 4

POSITIONS OF MOON BY
YEAR (1890 TO 1975)

Key

♓	Pisces	♍	Virgo
♈	Aries	♎	Libra
⌒	Cetus	♏	Scorpio
♉	Taurus	⚕	Ophiuchus
♊	Gemini	♐	Sagittarius
♋	Cancer	♑	Capricorn
♌	Leo	♒	Aquarius

TABLE 4 127

1890

January	February	March	April	May	June
2 ♉	1 ♊	2 ♋	1 ♌	2 ♎	1 ♏
4 ♊	3 ♋	4 ♌	3 ♍	4 ♏	2 ⛎
6 ♋	5 ♌	6 ♍	5 ♎	6 ⛎	4 ♐
8 ♌	7 ♍	8 ♎	7 ♏	8 ♐	6 ♑
10 ♍	9 ♎	10 ♏	9 ⛎	10 ♑	8 ♒
12 ♎	11 ♏	12 ⛎	11 ♐	12 ♒	10 ♓
14 ♏	13 ⛎	14 ♐	13 ♑	14 ♓	12 ♈
16 ⛎	15 ♐	16 ♑	15 ♒	16 ♈	14 ♈
18 ♐	17 ♑	18 ♒	17 ♓	18 ♈	16 ♉
20 ♑	19 ♒	20 ♓	19 ♈	20 ♉	18 ♊
22 ♒	21 ♓	22 ♈	21 ♈	22 ♊	20 ♋
24 ♓	23 ♈	24 ♈	23 ♉	24 ♋	22 ♌
26 ♈	25 ♈	26 ♉	25 ♊	26 ♌	24 ♍
28 ♈	27 ♉	28 ♊	27 ♋	28 ♍	26 ♎
30 ♉	28 ♊	30 ♋	29 ♌	30 ♎	28 ♏
			30 ♍		30 ⛎

July	August	September	October	November	December
1 ♐	2 ♒	2 ♈	1 ♈	2 ♊	1 ♋
3 ♑	4 ♓	4 ♈	3 ♉	4 ♋	3 ♌
5 ♒	6 ♈	6 ♉	5 ♊	6 ♌	5 ♍
7 ♓	8 ♈	8 ♊	7 ♋	8 ♍	7 ♎
9 ♈	10 ♉	10 ♋	9 ♌	10 ♎	9 ♏
11 ♈	12 ♊	12 ♌	11 ♍	11 ♏	11 ⛎
13 ♉	14 ♋	14 ♍	13 ♎	13 ⛎	13 ♐
15 ♊	16 ♌	16 ♎	15 ♏	15 ♐	15 ♑
17 ♋	17 ♍	18 ♏	17 ⛎	17 ♑	17 ♒
19 ♌	19 ♎	20 ⛎	19 ♐	19 ♒	19 ♓
21 ♍	21 ♏	22 ♐	21 ♑	21 ♓	21 ♈
23 ♎	23 ⛎	24 ♑	23 ♒	23 ♈	23 ♈
25 ♏	25 ♐	26 ♒	25 ♓	25 ♈	25 ♉
27 ⛎	27 ♑	28 ♓	27 ♈	27 ♉	27 ♊
29 ♐	29 ♒	30 ♈	29 ♈	29 ♊	29 ♋
31 ♑	31 ♓		31 ♉		31 ♌

1891

January		February		March		April		May		June	
1	♍	1	♏	1	♏	1	♐	2	♒	1	♓
3	♎	3	⚷	3	⚷	3	♑	4	♓	3	♈
5	♏	5	♐	5	♐	5	♒	6	♈	5	⟋
7	⚷	7	♑	7	♑	7	♓	8	⟋	7	♉
9	♐	9	♒	9	♒	9	♈	10	♉	9	♊
11	♑	11	♓	11	♓	11	⟋	12	♊	11	♋
13	♒	13	♈	13	♈	13	♉	14	♋	13	♌
15	♓	15	⟋	15	⟋	15	♊	16	♌	15	♍
17	♈	17	♉	17	♉	17	♋	18	♍	16	♎
19	⟋	19	♊	19	♊	19	♌	20	♎	18	♏
21	♉	21	♋	21	♋	21	♍	22	♏	20	⚷
23	♊	23	♌	23	♌	22	♎	24	⚷	22	♐
25	♋	25	♍	25	♍	24	♏	26	♐	24	♑
27	♌	27	♎	26	♎	26	⚷	28	♑	26	♒
29	♍			28	♏	28	♐	30	♒	28	♓
31	♎			30	⚷	30	♑			30	♈

July		August		September		October		November		December	
2	⟋	1	♉	1	♋	1	♍	2	♏	1	⚷
4	♉	3	♊	3	♌	3	♎	4	⚷	3	♐
6	♊	5	♋	5	♍	5	♏	6	♐	5	♑
8	♋	7	♌	7	♎	7	⚷	8	♑	7	♒
10	♌	9	♍	8	♏	9	♐	10	♒	9	♓
12	♍	11	♎	10	⚷	11	♑	12	♓	11	♈
13	♎	12	♏	12	♐	13	♒	14	♈	13	⟋
15	♏	14	⚷	14	♑	15	♓	16	⟋	15	♉
17	⚷	16	♐	16	♒	17	♈	18	♉	17	♊
19	♐	18	♑	18	♓	19	⟋	20	♊	19	♋
21	♑	20	♒	20	♈	21	♉	22	♋	21	♌
23	♒	22	♓	22	⟋	23	♊	24	♌	23	♍
25	♓	24	♈	24	♉	25	♋	25	♍	24	♎
27	♈	26	⟋	26	♊	27	♌	27	♎	26	♏
29	⟋	28	♉	28	♋	29	♍	29	♏	28	⚷
		30	♊	30	♌	31	♎			30	♐

4-2

TABLE 4 129

1892

January	February	March	April	May	June
1 ♑	2 ♓	2 ♈	1 ♈	2 ♊	2 ♌
3 ♒	4 ♈	4 ♈	3 ♉	4 ♋	4 ♍
5 ♓	6 ♈	6 ♉	5 ♊	6 ♌	6 ♎
7 ♈	8 ♉	8 ♊	7 ♋	8 ♍	8 ♏
9 ♈	10 ♊	10 ♋	9 ♌	9 ♎	10 ♐
11 ♉	12 ♋	12 ♌	11 ♍	11 ♏	12 ♐
13 ♊	14 ♌	14 ♍	12 ♎	13 ♐	14 ♑
15 ♋	16 ♍	16 ♎	14 ♏	15 ♐	16 ♒
17 ♌	17 ♎	18 ♏	16 ♐	17 ♑	18 ♓
19 ♍	19 ♏	20 ♐	18 ♐	19 ♒	20 ♈
21 ♎	21 ♐	22 ♐	20 ♑	21 ♓	22 ♈
23 ♏	23 ♐	24 ♑	22 ♒	23 ♈	24 ♉
25 ♐	25 ♑	26 ♒	24 ♓	25 ♈	26 ♊
27 ♐	27 ♒	28 ♓	26 ♈	27 ♉	28 ♋
29 ♑	29 ♓	30 ♈	28 ♈	29 ♊	30 ♌
31 ♒			30 ♉	31 ♋	

July	August	September	October	November	December
1 ♍	1 ♏	1 ♐	1 ♑	1 ♓	1 ♈
3 ♎	3 ♐	3 ♑	3 ♒	3 ♈	3 ♈
5 ♏	5 ♐	5 ♒	5 ♓	5 ♈	5 ♉
7 ♐	7 ♑	7 ♓	7 ♈	7 ♉	7 ♊
9 ♐	9 ♒	9 ♈	9 ♈	9 ♊	9 ♋
11 ♑	11 ♓	11 ♈	11 ♉	11 ♋	11 ♌
13 ♒	13 ♈	13 ♉	13 ♊	13 ♌	12 ♍
15 ♓	15 ♈	15 ♊	15 ♋	15 ♍	14 ♎
17 ♈	17 ♉	17 ♋	17 ♌	17 ♎	16 ♏
19 ♈	19 ♊	19 ♌	18 ♍	19 ♏	18 ♐
21 ♉	21 ♋	21 ♍	20 ♎	21 ♐	20 ♐
23 ♊	23 ♌	23 ♎	22 ♏	23 ♐	22 ♑
25 ♋	24 ♍	25 ♏	24 ♐	25 ♑	24 ♒
27 ♌	26 ♎	27 ♐	26 ♐	27 ♒	26 ♓
29 ♍	28 ♏	29 ♐	28 ♑	29 ♓	28 ♈
31 ♎	30 ♐		30 ♒		30 ♈

1893

January		February		March		April		May		June	
1	♉	1	♋	2	♌	1	♍	2	♏	1	⛎
3	♊	3	♌	4	♍	2	♎	4	⛎	3	♐
5	♋	5	♍	6	♎	4	♏	6	♐	4	♑
7	♌	7	♎	8	♏	6	⛎	8	♑	6	♒
9	♍	9	♏	10	⛎	8	♐	10	♒	8	♓
10	♎	11	⛎	12	♐	10	♑	12	♓	10	♈
12	♏	12	♐	14	♑	12	♒	14	♈	12	⟿
14	⛎	14	♑	16	♒	14	♓	16	⟿	14	♉
16	♐	16	♒	18	♓	16	♈	18	♉	16	♊
18	♑	18	♓	20	♈	18	⟿	20	♊	18	♋
20	♒	20	♈	22	⟿	20	♉	22	♋	20	♌
22	♓	22	⟿	24	♉	22	♊	24	♌	22	♍
24	♈	24	♉	26	♊	24	♋	26	♍	24	♎
26	⟿	26	♊	28	♋	26	♌	28	♎	26	♏
28	♉	28	♋	30	♌	28	♍	30	♏	28	⛎
30	♊					30	♎			30	♐

July		August		September		October		November		December	
1	♑	2	♓	2	⟿	1	♉	2	♋	1	♌
3	♒	4	♈	4	♉	3	♊	4	♌	3	♍
5	♓	6	⟿	6	♊	5	♋	6	♍	4	♎
7	♈	8	♉	8	♋	7	♌	7	♎	6	♏
9	⟿	10	♊	10	♌	9	♍	9	♏	8	⛎
11	♉	12	♋	12	♍	11	♎	11	⛎	10	♐
13	♊	14	♌	14	♎	13	♏	13	♐	12	♑
15	♋	16	♍	15	♏	15	⛎	15	♑	14	♒
17	♌	17	♎	17	⛎	17	♐	17	♒	16	♓
19	♍	19	♏	19	♐	19	♑	19	♓	18	♈
21	♎	21	⛎	21	♑	21	♒	21	♈	20	⟿
23	♏	23	♐	23	♒	23	♓	23	⟿	22	♉
25	⛎	25	♑	25	♓	25	♈	25	♉	24	♊
27	♐	27	♒	27	♈	27	⟿	27	♊	26	♋
29	♑	29	♓	29	⟿	29	♉	29	♋	28	♌
31	♒	31	♈			31	♊			30	♍

TABLE 4 131

1894

January	February	March	April	May	June
1 ♎	2 ⊹	2 ⊹	1 ♑	2 ♓	2 ⌐
3 ♏	3 ♐	4 ♐	2 ♒	4 ♈	4 ♉
5 ⊹	5 ♑	5 ♑	4 ♓	6 ⌐	6 ♊
7 ♐	7 ♒	6 ♒	6 ♈	8 ♉	8 ♋
9 ♑	9 ♓	8 ♓	8 ⌐	10 ♊	10 ♌
11 ♒	11 ♈	10 ♈	10 ♉	12 ♋	12 ♍
13 ♓	13 ⌐	12 ⌐	12 ♊	14 ♌	14 ♎
15 ♈	15 ♉	14 ♉	14 ♋	15 ♍	16 ♏
17 ⌐	17 ♊	16 ♊	16 ♌	17 ♎	18 ⊹
19 ♉	19 ♋	18 ♋	18 ♍	19 ♏	20 ♐
21 ♊	21 ♌	20 ♌	20 ♎	21 ⊹	22 ♑
23 ♋	23 ♍	22 ♍	22 ♏	23 ♐	24 ♒
25 ♌	25 ♎	24 ♎	24 ⊹	25 ♑	26 ♓
27 ♍	28 ♏	26 ♏	26 ♐	27 ♒	28 ♈
29 ♎		28 ⊹	28 ♑	29 ♓	30 ⌐
31 ♏		30 ♐	30 ♒	31 ♈	

July	August	September	October	November	December
2 ♉	2 ♋	2 ♍	1 ♎	2 ⊹	1 ♐
4 ♊	4 ♌	3 ♎	3 ♏	4 ♐	3 ♑
6 ♋	5 ♍	5 ♏	5 ⊹	6 ♑	4 ♒
8 ♌	7 ♎	7 ⊹	7 ♐	8 ♒	6 ♓
10 ♍	9 ♏	9 ♐	9 ♑	9 ♓	8 ♈
12 ♎	11 ⊹	11 ♑	11 ♒	11 ♈	10 ⌐
13 ♏	13 ♐	13 ♒	13 ♓	13 ⌐	12 ♉
15 ⊹	15 ♑	15 ♓	15 ♈	15 ♉	14 ♊
17 ♐	17 ♒	17 ♈	17 ⌐	17 ♊	16 ♋
19 ♑	19 ♓	19 ⌐	19 ♉	19 ♋	18 ♌
21 ♒	21 ♈	21 ♉	21 ♊	21 ♌	20 ♍
23 ♓	23 ⌐	23 ♊	23 ♋	23 ♍	22 ♎
25 ♈	25 ♉	25 ♋	25 ♌	25 ♎	24 ♏
27 ⌐	27 ♊	27 ♌	27 ♍	27 ♏	26 ⊹
29 ♉	29 ♋	29 ♍	29 ♎	29 ⊹	28 ♐
31 ♊	31 ♌		31 ♏		30 ♑

1895

January	February	March	April	May	June
1 ♒	1 ♈	2 ↝	2 ♊	2 ♋	2 ♍
3 ♓	3 ↝	4 ♉	4 ♋	4 ♌	3 ♎
5 ♈	5 ♉	6 ♊	6 ♌	5 ♍	5 ♏
7 ↝	7 ♊	8 ♋	8 ♍	7 ♎	7 ⛎
9 ♉	9 ♋	10 ♌	10 ♎	9 ♏	9 ♐
11 ♊	11 ♌	12 ♍	12 ♏	11 ⛎	11 ♑
13 ♋	12 ♍	13 ♎	14 ⛎	13 ♐	13 ♒
15 ♌	14 ♎	15 ♏	16 ♐	15 ♑	15 ♓
16 ♍	16 ♏	17 ⛎	18 ♑	17 ♒	17 ♈
18 ♎	18 ⛎	19 ♐	20 ♒	19 ♓	19 ↝
20 ♏	20 ♐	21 ♑	22 ♓	21 ♈	21 ♉
22 ⛎	22 ♑	23 ♒	24 ♈	23 ↝	23 ♊
24 ♐	24 ♒	25 ♓	26 ↝	25 ♉	25 ♋
26 ♑	26 ♓	27 ♈	28 ♉	27 ♊	27 ♌
28 ♒	28 ♈	29 ↝	30 ♊	29 ♋	29 ♍
30 ♓		31 ♉		31 ♌	

July	August	September	October	November	December
1 ♎	1 ⛎	1 ♑	1 ♒	1 ♈	2 ♉
3 ♏	3 ♐	3 ♒	3 ♓	3 ↝	4 ♊
5 ⛎	5 ♑	5 ♓	5 ♈	5 ♉	6 ♋
7 ♐	7 ♒	7 ♈	7 ↝	7 ♊	8 ♌
9 ♑	9 ♓	9 ↝	9 ♉	9 ♋	10 ♍
11 ♒	11 ♈	11 ♉	11 ♊	11 ♌	12 ♎
13 ♓	13 ↝	13 ♊	13 ♋	12 ♍	14 ♏
15 ♈	15 ♉	15 ♋	15 ♌	14 ♎	16 ⛎
17 ↝	17 ♊	17 ♌	16 ♍	16 ♏	18 ♐
19 ♉	19 ♋	19 ♍	18 ♎	18 ⛎	20 ♑
21 ♊	21 ♌	21 ♎	20 ♏	20 ♐	22 ♒
23 ♋	22 ♍	23 ♏	22 ⛎	22 ♑	24 ♓
25 ♌	24 ♎	25 ⛎	24 ♐	24 ♒	26 ♈
26 ♍	26 ♏	27 ♐	26 ♑	26 ♓	28 ↝
28 ♎	28 ⛎	29 ♑	28 ♒	28 ♈	30 ♉
30 ♏	30 ♐		30 ♓	30 ↝	

TABLE 4 133

1896

January	February	March	April	May	June
1 ♊	1 ♌	1 ♍	1 ♏	1 ♐	1 ♑
3 ♋	3 ♍	3 ♎	3 ♐	3 ♐	2 ♒
5 ♌	4 ♎	5 ♏	5 ♐	4 ♑	4 ♓
7 ♍	6 ♏	6 ♐	7 ♑	6 ♒	6 ♈
8 ♎	8 ♐	8 ♐	9 ♒	8 ♓	8 ♈
10 ♏	10 ♐	10 ♑	11 ♓	10 ♈	10 ♉
12 ♐	12 ♑	12 ♒	13 ♈	12 ♈	12 ♊
14 ♐	14 ♒	14 ♓	15 ♈	14 ♉	14 ♋
16 ♑	16 ♓	16 ♈	17 ♉	16 ♊	16 ♌
18 ♒	18 ♈	18 ♈	19 ♊	18 ♋	18 ♍
20 ♓	20 ♈	20 ♉	21 ♋	20 ♌	20 ♎
22 ♈	22 ♉	22 ♊	23 ♌	22 ♍	22 ♏
24 ♈	24 ♊	24 ♋	25 ♍	24 ♎	24 ♐
26 ♉	26 ♋	26 ♌	27 ♎	26 ♏	26 ♐
28 ♊	28 ♌	28 ♍	29 ♏	28 ♐	28 ♑
30 ♋		30 ♎		30 ♐	30 ♒

July	August	September	October	November	December
2 ♓	2 ♈	2 ♊	1 ♋	2 ♍	1 ♎
4 ♈	4 ♉	4 ♋	3 ♌	3 ♎	3 ♏
6 ♈	6 ♊	6 ♌	5 ♍	5 ♏	5 ♐
8 ♉	8 ♋	8 ♍	7 ♎	7 ♐	6 ♐
10 ♊	10 ♌	10 ♎	9 ♏	9 ♐	8 ♑
12 ♋	11 ♍	12 ♏	11 ♐	11 ♑	10 ♒
14 ♌	13 ♎	14 ♐	13 ♐	13 ♒	12 ♓
16 ♍	15 ♏	16 ♐	15 ♑	15 ♓	14 ♈
17 ♎	17 ♐	18 ♑	17 ♒	17 ♈	16 ♈
19 ♏	19 ♐	20 ♒	19 ♓	19 ♈	18 ♉
21 ♐	21 ♑	22 ♓	21 ♈	21 ♉	20 ♊
23 ♐	23 ♒	24 ♈	23 ♈	23 ♊	22 ♋
25 ♑	25 ♓	26 ♈	25 ♉	25 ♋	24 ♌
27 ♒	27 ♈	28 ♉	27 ♊	27 ♌	26 ♍
29 ♓	29 ♈	30 ♊	29 ♋	29 ♍	28 ♎
31 ♈	31 ♉		31 ♌		30 ♏

1897

January		February		March		April		May		June	
1	⛎	1	♑	2	♒	1	♓	2	☋	2	♊
3	♐	3	♒	4	♓	3	♈	4	♉	4	♋
5	♑	5	♓	6	♈	5	☋	6	♊	6	♌
7	♒	7	♈	8	☋	7	♉	8	♋	8	♍
9	♓	9	☋	10	♉	9	♊	10	♌	9	♎
11	♈	11	♉	12	♊	11	♋	12	♍	11	♏
13	☋	13	♊	14	♋	13	♌	13	♎	13	⛎
15	♉	15	♋	16	♌	15	♍	15	♏	15	♐
17	♊	17	♌	18	♍	16	♎	17	⛎	17	♑
19	♋	18	♍	20	♎	18	♏	19	♐	19	♒
21	♌	20	♎	22	♏	20	⛎	21	♑	21	♓
23	♍	22	♏	24	⛎	22	♐	23	♒	23	♈
25	♎	24	⛎	26	♐	24	♑	25	♓	25	☋
27	♏	26	♐	28	♑	26	♒	27	♈	27	♉
29	⛎	28	♑	30	♒	28	♓	29	☋	29	♊
31	♐					30	♈	31	♉		

July		August		September		October		November		December	
1	♋	1	♍	1	♏	2	⛎	1	♑	2	♓
3	♌	3	♎	3	⛎	4	♐	3	♒	4	♈
5	♍	5	♏	5	♐	5	♑	5	♓	6	☋
7	♎	7	⛎	7	♑	7	♒	7	♈	8	♉
9	♏	9	♐	9	♒	9	♓	9	☋	10	♊
11	⛎	11	♑	11	♓	11	♈	11	♉	12	♋
13	♐	13	♒	13	♈	13	☋	13	♊	14	♌
15	♑	15	♓	15	☋	15	♉	15	♋	16	♍
17	♒	17	♈	17	♉	17	♊	17	♌	18	♎
19	♓	19	☋	19	♊	19	♋	18	♍	20	♏
21	♈	21	♉	21	♋	21	♌	20	♎	22	⛎
23	☋	23	♊	23	♌	23	♍	22	♏	24	♐
25	♉	25	♋	25	♍	25	♎	24	⛎	26	♑
27	♊	27	♌	27	♎	27	♏	26	♐	28	♒
29	♋	29	♍	29	♏	29	⛎	28	♑	30	♓
31	♌	30	♎			31	♐	30	♒		

TABLE 4 135

1898

January	February	March	April	May	June
1 ♈	1 ♉	2 ♊	1 ♋	1 ♍	2 ♏
3 ♉	3 ♊	4 ♋	3 ♌	3 ♎	4 ♐
5 ♉	5 ♋	6 ♌	5 ♍	5 ♏	5 ♐
7 ♊	7 ♌	8 ♍	6 ♎	7 ♐	7 ♑
9 ♋	8 ♍	10 ♎	8 ♏	9 ♐	9 ♒
11 ♌	10 ♎	12 ♏	10 ♐	11 ♑	11 ♓
12 ♍	12 ♏	14 ♐	12 ♐	13 ♒	13 ♈
14 ♎	14 ♐	16 ♐	14 ♑	15 ♓	15 ♉
16 ♏	16 ♐	18 ♑	16 ♒	17 ♈	17 ♉
18 ♐	18 ♑	20 ♒	18 ♓	19 ♉	19 ♊
20 ♐	20 ♒	22 ♓	20 ♈	21 ♉	21 ♋
22 ♑	22 ♓	24 ♈	22 ♉	23 ♊	23 ♌
24 ♒	24 ♈	26 ♉	24 ♉	25 ♋	25 ♍
26 ♓	26 ♉	28 ♉	26 ♊	27 ♌	27 ♎
28 ♈	28 ♉	30 ♊	28 ♋	29 ♍	29 ♏
30 ♉			30 ♌	31 ♎	

July	August	September	October	November	December
1 ♐	1 ♑	2 ♓	1 ♈	1 ♉	1 ♊
3 ♐	3 ♒	4 ♈	3 ♉	3 ♊	3 ♋
5 ♑	5 ♓	6 ♉	5 ♉	5 ♋	5 ♌
7 ♒	7 ♈	8 ♉	7 ♊	7 ♌	6 ♍
9 ♓	9 ♉	10 ♊	9 ♋	9 ♍	8 ♎
11 ♈	11 ♉	12 ♋	11 ♌	11 ♎	10 ♏
13 ♉	13 ♊	14 ♌	13 ♍	13 ♏	12 ♐
15 ♉	15 ♋	16 ♍	14 ♎	15 ♐	14 ♐
17 ♊	17 ♌	17 ♎	16 ♏	17 ♐	16 ♑
19 ♋	19 ♍	19 ♏	18 ♐	19 ♑	18 ♒
21 ♌	21 ♎	21 ♐	20 ♐	21 ♒	20 ♓
23 ♍	23 ♏	23 ♐	22 ♑	23 ♓	22 ♈
25 ♎	25 ♐	25 ♑	24 ♒	25 ♈	24 ♉
27 ♏	27 ♐	27 ♒	26 ♓	27 ♉	26 ♉
29 ♐	29 ♑	29 ♓	28 ♈	29 ♉	28 ♊
30 ♐	31 ♒		30 ♉		30 ♋

1899

January		February		March		April		May		June	
1	♌	1	♎	2	♏	2	♐	2	♑	2	♓
3	♍	3	♏	4	⛎	4	♑	4	♒	4	♈
4	♎	5	⛎	6	♐	6	♒	6	♓	6	🐋
6	♏	7	♐	8	♑	8	♓	8	♈	8	♉
8	⛎	9	♑	10	♒	10	♈	10	🐋	10	♊
10	♐	10	♒	12	♓	12	🐋	12	♉	12	♋
12	♑	12	♓	14	♈	14	♉	14	♊	14	♌
14	♒	14	♈	16	🐋	16	♊	16	♋	15	♍
16	♓	16	🐋	18	♉	18	♋	18	♌	17	♎
18	♈	18	♉	20	♊	20	♌	19	♍	19	♏
20	🐋	20	♊	22	♋	22	♍	21	♎	21	⛎
22	♉	22	♋	24	♌	24	♎	23	♏	23	♐
24	♊	24	♌	26	♍	26	♏	25	⛎	25	♑
26	♋	26	♍	28	♎	28	⛎	27	♐	27	♒
28	♌	28	♎	30	♏	30	♐	29	♑	29	♓
30	♍			31	⛎			31	♒		

July		August		September		October		November		December	
1	♈	1	♉	2	♋	1	♌	2	♎	1	♏
3	🐋	3	♊	4	♌	3	♍	4	♏	2	⛎
5	♉	5	♋	6	♍	5	♎	6	⛎	4	♐
7	♊	7	♌	7	♎	7	♏	7	♐	6	♑
9	♋	9	♍	9	♏	9	⛎	9	♑	8	♒
11	♌	11	♎	11	⛎	11	♐	11	♒	10	♓
13	♍	13	♏	13	♐	13	♑	13	♓	12	♈
14	♎	15	⛎	15	♑	15	♒	15	♈	14	🐋
16	♏	17	♐	17	♒	17	♓	17	🐋	16	♉
18	⛎	19	♑	19	♓	19	♈	19	♉	18	♊
20	♐	21	♒	21	♈	21	🐋	21	♊	20	♋
22	♑	23	♓	23	🐋	23	♉	23	♋	22	♌
24	♒	25	♈	25	♉	25	♊	25	♌	24	♍
26	♓	27	🐋	27	♊	27	♋	27	♍	26	♎
28	♈	29	♉	29	♋	29	♌	29	♎	28	♏
30	🐋	31	♊			31	♍			30	⛎

TABLE 4 137

1900

January	February	March	April	May	June
1 ♐	1 ♒	2 ♓	1 ♈	2 ♉	2 ♋
3 ♑	3 ♓	4 ♈	3 ♈	4 ♊	4 ♌
5 ♒	5 ♈	6 ♈	5 ♉	6 ♋	6 ♍
6 ♓	7 ♈	8 ♉	7 ♊	8 ♌	8 ♎
8 ♈	9 ♉	10 ♊	9 ♋	9 ♍	10 ♏
10 ♈	11 ♊	12 ♋	11 ♌	11 ♎	12 ♐
12 ♉	13 ♋	14 ♌	13 ♍	13 ♏	14 ♐
14 ♊	15 ♌	16 ♍	14 ♎	15 ♐	16 ♑
16 ♋	17 ♍	18 ♎	16 ♏	17 ♐	18 ♒
18 ♌	19 ♎	20 ♏	18 ♐	19 ♑	20 ♓
20 ♍	21 ♏	22 ♐	20 ♐	21 ♒	22 ♈
22 ♎	23 ♐	24 ♐	22 ♑	23 ♓	24 ♈
24 ♏	25 ♐	26 ♑	24 ♒	25 ♈	26 ♉
26 ♐	27 ♑	28 ♒	26 ♓	27 ♈	28 ♊
28 ♐	29 ♒	30 ♓	28 ♈	29 ♉	30 ♋
30 ♑			30 ♈	31 ♊	

July	August	September	October	November	December
2 ♌	1 ♎	2 ♐	1 ♐	2 ♒	1 ♓
4 ♍	3 ♏	4 ♐	3 ♑	4 ♓	3 ♈
6 ♎	5 ♐	6 ♑	5 ♒	6 ♈	5 ♈
8 ♏	7 ♐	8 ♒	7 ♓	8 ♈	7 ♉
10 ♐	9 ♑	10 ♓	9 ♈	10 ♉	9 ♊
11 ♐	11 ♒	12 ♈	11 ♈	12 ♊	11 ♋
13 ♑	13 ♓	14 ♈	13 ♉	14 ♋	13 ♌
15 ♒	15 ♈	16 ♉	15 ♊	16 ♌	15 ♍
17 ♓	17 ♈	18 ♊	17 ♋	18 ♍	17 ♎
19 ♈	19 ♉	20 ♋	19 ♌	19 ♎	18 ♏
21 ♈	21 ♊	22 ♌	21 ♍	21 ♏	20 ♐
23 ♉	23 ♋	24 ♍	23 ♎	23 ♐	22 ♐
25 ♊	25 ♌	26 ♎	25 ♏	25 ♐	24 ♑
27 ♋	27 ♍	27 ♏	27 ♐	27 ♑	26 ♒
29 ♌	28 ♎	29 ♐	29 ♐	29 ♒	28 ♓
31 ♍	30 ♏		31 ♑		30 ♈

1901

January		February		March		April		May		June	
1	⟿	1	♊	1	♊	1	♌	2	♎	1	♏
3	♉	3	♋	3	♋	3	♍	4	♏	3	⛎
5	♊	5	♌	5	♌	5	♎	6	⛎	5	♐
7	♋	7	♍	6	♍	7	♏	8	♐	6	♑
9	♌	9	♎	8	♎	9	⛎	10	♑	8	♒
10	♍	11	♏	10	♏	11	♐	12	♒	10	♓
12	♎	13	⛎	12	⛎	13	♑	14	♓	12	♈
14	♏	15	♐	14	♐	15	♒	16	♈	14	⟿
16	⛎	17	♑	16	♑	17	♓	18	⟿	16	♉
18	♐	19	♒	18	♒	19	♈	20	♉	18	♊
20	♑	21	♓	20	♓	21	⟿	22	♊	20	♋
22	♒	23	♈	22	♈	23	♉	24	♋	22	♌
24	♓	25	⟿	24	⟿	25	♊	26	♌	24	♍
26	♈	27	♉	26	♉	27	♋	28	♍	26	♎
28	⟿			28	♊	29	♌	30	♎	28	♏
30	♉			30	♋	30	♍			30	⛎

July		August		September		October		November		December	
1	♐	2	♒	2	♈	1	⟿	2	♊	1	♋
3	♑	4	♓	4	⟿	3	♉	4	♋	3	♌
5	♒	6	♈	6	♉	5	♊	6	♌	5	♍
7	♓	8	⟿	8	♊	7	♋	8	♍	7	♎
9	♈	10	♉	10	♋	9	♌	9	♎	9	♏
11	⟿	12	♊	12	♌	11	♍	11	♏	11	⛎
13	♉	14	♋	13	♍	13	♎	13	⛎	13	♐
15	♊	16	♌	15	♎	15	♏	15	♐	15	♑
17	♋	18	♍	17	♏	17	⛎	17	♑	17	♒
19	♌	19	♎	19	⛎	19	♐	19	♒	19	♓
21	♍	21	♏	21	♐	21	♑	21	♓	21	♈
23	♎	23	⛎	23	♑	23	♒	23	♈	23	⟿
25	♏	25	♐	25	♒	25	♓	25	⟿	25	♉
27	⛎	27	♑	27	♓	27	♈	27	♉	27	♊
29	♐	29	♒	29	♈	29	⟿	29	♊	29	♋
31	♑	31	♓			31	♉			31	♌

TABLE 4 139

1902

January		February		March		April		May		June	
2	♍	2	♏	1	♏	1	♐	1	♑	1	♓
3	♎	4	♐	3	♐	3	♑	2	♒	3	♈
5	♏	6	♐	5	♐	5	♒	4	♓	5	♈
7	♐	7	♑	6	♑	7	♓	6	♈	7	♉
9	♐	9	♒	8	♒	9	♈	8	♈	9	♊
11	♑	11	♓	10	♓	11	♈	10	♉	11	♋
13	♒	13	♈	12	♈	13	♉	12	♊	13	♌
15	♓	15	♈	14	♈	15	♊	14	♋	15	♍
17	♈	17	♉	16	♉	17	♋	16	♌	16	♎
19	♈	19	♊	18	♊	19	♌	18	♍	18	♏
21	♉	21	♋	20	♋	21	♍	20	♎	20	♐
23	♊	23	♌	22	♌	23	♎	22	♏	22	♐
25	♋	25	♍	24	♍	25	♏	24	♐	24	♑
27	♌	27	♎	26	♎	27	♐	26	♐	26	♒
29	♍			28	♏	29	♐	28	♑	28	♓
31	♎			30	♐			30	♒	30	♈

July		August		September		October		November		December	
2	♈	2	♊	2	♌	1	♍	2	♏	2	♐
4	♉	4	♋	4	♍	3	♎	4	♐	3	♐
6	♊	6	♌	6	♎	5	♏	6	♐	5	♑
8	♋	7	♍	8	♏	7	♐	8	♑	7	♒
10	♌	9	♎	10	♐	9	♐	10	♒	9	♓
11	♍	11	♏	12	♐	11	♑	12	♓	11	♈
13	♎	13	♐	14	♑	13	♒	14	♈	13	♈
15	♏	15	♐	16	♒	15	♓	16	♈	15	♉
17	♐	17	♑	18	♓	17	♈	18	♉	17	♊
19	♐	19	♒	20	♈	19	♈	20	♊	19	♋
21	♑	21	♓	22	♈	21	♉	22	♋	21	♌
23	♒	23	♈	24	♉	23	♊	24	♌	23	♍
25	♓	25	♈	26	♊	25	♋	26	♍	24	♎
27	♈	27	♉	28	♋	27	♌	28	♎	26	♏
29	♈	29	♊	30	♌	29	♍	30	♏	28	♐
31	♉	31	♋			31	♎			30	♐

1903

January	February	March	April	May	June
1 ♑	1 ♓	1 ♓	1 ⌒	2 ♊	1 ♋
3 ♒	3 ♈	3 ♈	3 ♉	4 ♋	3 ♌
5 ♓	5 ⌒	5 ⌒	4 ♊	6 ♌	5 ♍
7 ♈	7 ♉	7 ♉	6 ♋	8 ♍	6 ♎
9 ⌒	9 ♊	9 ♊	8 ♌	10 ♎	8 ♏
11 ♉	11 ♋	11 ♋	10 ♍	12 ♏	10 ⛎
13 ♊	13 ♌	13 ♌	12 ♎	14 ⛎	12 ♐
15 ♋	15 ♍	14 ♍	14 ♏	16 ♐	14 ♑
17 ♌	17 ♎	16 ♎	16 ⛎	18 ♑	16 ♒
18 ♍	19 ♏	18 ♏	18 ♐	20 ♒	18 ♓
20 ♎	21 ⛎	20 ⛎	20 ♑	22 ♓	20 ♈
22 ♏	23 ♐	22 ♐	22 ♒	24 ♈	22 ⌒
24 ⛎	25 ♑	24 ♑	24 ♓	26 ⌒	24 ♉
26 ♐	27 ♒	26 ♒	26 ♈	28 ♉	26 ♊
28 ♑		28 ♓	28 ⌒	30 ♊	28 ♋
30 ♒		30 ♈	30 ♉		30 ♌

July	August	September	October	November	December
2 ♍	2 ♏	2 ⛎	2 ♑	2 ♓	1 ♈
4 ♎	4 ⛎	3 ♐	4 ♒·	4 ♈	3 ⌒
5 ♏	6 ♐	4 ♑	5 ♓	6 ⌒	5 ♉
7 ⛎	8 ♑	6 ♒	7 ♈	8 ♉	7 ♊
9 ♐	10 ♒	8 ♓	9 ⌒	10 ♊	9 ♋
11 ♑	12 ♓	10 ♈	11 ♉	12 ♋	11 ♌
13 ♒	14 ♈	12 ⌒	13 ♊	14 ♌	13 ♍
15 ♓	16 ⌒	14 ♉	15 ♋	16 ♍	14 ♎
17 ♈	18 ♉	16 ♊	17 ♌	17 ♎	16 ♏
19 ⌒	20 ♊	18 ♋	19 ♍	19 ♏	18 ⛎
21 ♉	22 ♋	20 ♌	21 ♎	21 ⛎	20 ♐
23 ♊	24 ♌	22 ♍	23 ♏	23 ♐	22 ♑
25 ♋	26 ♍	24 ♎	25 ⛎	25 ♑	24 ♒
27 ♌	28 ♎	26 ♏	27 ♐	27 ♒	26 ♓
29 ♍	30 ♏	28 ⛎	29 ♑	29 ♓	28 ♈
31 ♎		30 ♐	31 ♒		30 ⌒

TABLE 4 141

1904

January	February	March	April	May	June
1 ♉	2 ♋	2 ♌	2 ♎	1 ♏	1 ♐
3 ♊	4 ♌	4 ♍	4 ♏	3 ♐	3 ♑
5 ♋	6 ♍	6 ♎	6 ♐	5 ♐	5 ♒
7 ♌	7 ♎	8 ♏	8 ♐	7 ♑	7 ♓
9 ♍	9 ♏	10 ♐	10 ♑	9 ♒	9 ♈
11 ♎	11 ♐	11 ♐	12 ♒	11 ♓	11 ♈
13 ♏	13 ♐	13 ♑	13 ♓	13 ♈	13 ♉
15 ♐	15 ♑	15 ♒	15 ♈	14 ♈	15 ♊
17 ♐	17 ♒	17 ♓	17 ♈	16 ♉	17 ♋
19 ♑	19 ♓	19 ♈	19 ♉	18 ♊	19 ♌
21 ♒	21 ♈	21 ♈	21 ♊	20 ♋	21 ♍
23 ♓	23 ♈	23 ♉	23 ♋	22 ♌	23 ♎
25 ♈	25 ♉	25 ♊	25 ♌	24 ♍	25 ♏
27 ♈	27 ♊	27 ♋	27 ♍	26 ♎	27 ♐
29 ♉	29 ♋	29 ♌	29 ♎	28 ♏	29 ♐
31 ♊		31 ♍		30 ♐	

July	August	September	October	November	December
1 ♑	1 ♓	1 ♈	2 ♊	2 ♌	2 ♍
2 ♒	3 ♈	3 ♉	4 ♋	4 ♍	3 ♎
4 ♓	5 ♈	5 ♊	6 ♌	6 ♎	5 ♏
6 ♈	7 ♉	7 ♋	8 ♍	8 ♏	7 ♐
8 ♈	9 ♊	9 ♌	9 ♎	10 ♐	9 ♐
10 ♉	11 ♋	11 ♍	11 ♏	12 ♐	11 ♑
12 ♊	13 ♌	13 ♎	13 ♐	14 ♑	13 ♒
14 ♋	15 ♍	15 ♏	15 ♐	16 ♒	15 ♓
16 ♌	16 ♎	17 ♐	17 ♑	18 ♓	17 ♈
18 ♍	18 ♏	18 ♐	19 ♒	20 ♈	19 ♈
20 ♎	20 ♐	20 ♑	21 ♓	22 ♈	21 ♉
22 ♏	22 ♐	22 ♒	23 ♈	24 ♉	23 ♊
24 ♐	24 ♑	24 ♓	25 ♈	26 ♊	25 ♋
26 ♐	26 ♒	26 ♈	27 ♉	28 ♋	27 ♌
28 ♑	28 ♓	28 ♈	29 ♊	30 ♌	29 ♍
30 ♒	30 ♈	30 ♉	31 ♋		31 ♎

1905

January		February		March		April		May		June	
1	♏	2	♐	1	♐	1	♒	1	♓	1	⌐
3	⛎	4	♑	3	♑	3	♓	3	♈	3	♉
5	♐	6	♒	5	♒	5	♈	5	⌐	5	♊
7	♑	8	♓	7	♓	7	⌐	7	♉	7	♋
9	♒	10	♈	9	♈	9	♉	9	♊	9	♌
11	♓	12	⌐	11	⌐	11	♊	11	♋	11	♍
13	♈	14	♉	13	♉	13	♋	13	♌	12	♎
15	⌐	16	♊	14	♊	15	♌	15	♍	14	♏
17	♉	18	♋	16	♋	17	♍	16	♎	16	⛎
19	♊	20	♌	18	♌	19	♎	18	♏	18	♐
21	♋	22	♍	20	♍	21	♏	20	⛎	20	♑
23	♌	23	♎	22	♎	23	⛎	22	♐	22	♒
25	♍	25	♏	24	♏	25	♐	24	♑	24	♓
27	♎	27	⛎	26	⛎	27	♑	26	♒	26	♈
29	♏			28	♐	29	♒	28	♓	28	⌐
31	⛎			30	♑			30	♈	30	♉

July		August		September		October		November		December	
2	♊	2	♌	1	♍	1	♏	2	♐	1	♑
4	♋	4	♍	3	♎	3	⛎	4	♑	3	♒
6	♌	6	♎	5	♏	5	♐	6	♒	5	♓
8	♍	8	♏	7	⛎	7	♑	8	♓	7	♈
10	♎	10	⛎	8	♐	9	♒	10	♈	8	⌐
12	♏	12	♐	10	♑	11	♓	12	⌐	10	♉
14	⛎	14	♑	12	♒	13	♈	14	♉	12	♊
16	♐	16	♒	14	♓	15	⌐	16	♊	14	♋
17	♑	18	♓	16	♈	17	♉	18	♋	16	♌
19	♒	20	♈	18	⌐	19	♊	20	♌	18	♍
21	♓	22	⌐	20	♉	21	♋	22	♍	20	♎
23	♈	24	♉	22	♊	23	♌	23	♎	22	♏
25	⌐	26	♊	24	♋	25	♍	25	♏	24	⛎
27	♉	28	♋	26	♌	27	♎	27	⛎	26	♐
29	♊	30	♌	28	♍	29	♏	29	♐	28	♑
31	♋			29	♎	31	⛎			30	♒

TABLE 4 143

1906

January	February	March	April	May	June
1 ♓	2 ♈	1 ♈	1 ♊	2 ♌	2 ♎
3 ♈	4 ♉	3 ♉	3 ♋	4 ♍	4 ♏
5 ♈	6 ♊	5 ♊	5 ♌	6 ♎	6 ♐
7 ♉	7 ♋	7 ♋	6 ♍	8 ♏	8 ♐
9 ♊	9 ♌	9 ♌	8 ♎	10 ♐	10 ♑
11 ♋	11 ♍	10 ♍	10 ♏	12 ♐	12 ♒
13 ♌	13 ♎	12 ♎	12 ♐	14 ♑	14 ♓
15 ♍	15 ♏	14 ♏	14 ♐	16 ♒	16 ♈
17 ♎	17 ♐	16 ♐	16 ♑	18 ♓	18 ♈
19 ♏	19 ♐	18 ♐	18 ♒	20 ♈	20 ♉
21 ♐	21 ♑	20 ♑	20 ♓	22 ♈	22 ♊
23 ♐	23 ♒	22 ♒	22 ♈	24 ♉	24 ♋
25 ♑	25 ♓	24 ♓	24 ♈	26 ♊	26 ♌
27 ♒	27 ♈	26 ♈	26 ♉	28 ♋	28 ♍
29 ♓		28 ♈	28 ♊	30 ♌	30 ♎
31 ♈		30 ♉	30 ♋	31 ♍	

July	August	September	October	November	December
2 ♏	2 ♐	1 ♑	1 ♓	2 ♈	1 ♉
4 ♐	4 ♑	2 ♒	3 ♈	4 ♉	3 ♊
5 ♐	6 ♒	4 ♓	5 ♈	6 ♊	4 ♋
7 ♑	8 ♓	6 ♈	7 ♉	8 ♋	6 ♌
9 ♒	10 ♈	8 ♈	9 ♊	10 ♌	8 ♍
11 ♓	12 ♈	10 ♉	11 ♋	11 ♍	10 ♎
13 ♈	14 ♉	12 ♊	13 ♌	13 ♎	12 ♏
15 ♈	16 ♊	14 ♋	15 ♍	15 ♏	14 ♐
17 ♉	18 ♋	16 ♌	17 ♎	17 ♐	16 ♐
19 ♊	20 ♌	18 ♍	19 ♏	19 ♐	18 ♑
21 ♋	22 ♍	19 ♎	21 ♐	21 ♑	20 ♒
23 ♌	24 ♎	21 ♏	23 ♐	23 ♒	22 ♓
25 ♍	26 ♏	23 ♐	25 ♑	25 ♓	24 ♈
27 ♎	28 ♐	25 ♐	27 ♒	27 ♈	26 ♈
29 ♏	30 ♐	27 ♑	29 ♓	29 ♈	28 ♉
31 ♐		29 ♒	31 ♈		30 ♊

1907

(Sign symbols: ♈ Aries, Ↄ Cetus, ♉ Taurus, ♊ Gemini, ♋ Cancer, ♌ Leo, ♍ Virgo, ♎ Libra, ♏ Scorpio, ⛎ Ophiuchus, ♐ Sagittarius, ♑ Capricorn, ♒ Aquarius, ♓ Pisces)

January	February	March	April	May	June
1 ♋	1 ♍	1 ♍	1 ♏	2 ♐	2 ♒
3 ♌	3 ♎	2 ♎	3 ⛎	4 ♑	4 ♓
5 ♍	5 ♏	4 ♏	5 ♐	6 ♒	6 ♈
6 ♎	7 ⛎	6 ⛎	7 ♑	8 ♓	8 Ↄ
8 ♏	9 ♐	8 ♐	9 ♒	10 ♈	10 ♉
10 ⛎	11 ♑	10 ♑	11 ♓	12 Ↄ	12 ♊
12 ♐	13 ♒	12 ♒	13 ♈	14 ♉	14 ♋
14 ♑	15 ♓	14 ♓	15 Ↄ	16 ♊	16 ♌
16 ♒	17 ♈	16 ♈	17 ♉	18 ♋	18 ♍
18 ♓	19 Ↄ	18 Ↄ	19 ♊	21 ♌	20 ♎
20 ♈	21 ♉	20 ♉	21 ♋	22 ♍	22 ♏
22 Ↄ	23 ♊	22 ♊	23 ♌	23 ♎	24 ⛎
24 ♉	25 ♋	24 ♋	25 ♍	25 ♏	25 ♐
26 ♊	27 ♌	26 ♌	26 ♎	27 ⛎	27 ♑
28 ♋		28 ♍	28 ♏	29 ♐	29 ♒
30 ♌		30 ♎	30 ⛎	31 ♑	

July	August	September	October	November	December
1 ♓	2 Ↄ	2 ♊	2 ♋	1 ♍	1 ♎
3 ♈	4 ♉	4 ♋	4 ♌	3 ♎	3 ♏
5 Ↄ	6 ♊	6 ♌	6 ♍	5 ♏	4 ⛎
7 ♉	8 ♋	8 ♍	7 ♎	7 ⛎	6 ♐
9 ♊	10 ♌	10 ♎	9 ♏	9 ♐	8 ♑
11 ♋	12 ♍	12 ♏	11 ⛎	11 ♑	10 ♒
13 ♌	14 ♎	14 ⛎	13 ♐	13 ♒	12 ♓
15 ♍	16 ♏	16 ♐	15 ♑	15 ♓	14 ♈
17 ♎	17 ⛎	18 ♑	17 ♒	17 ♈	16 Ↄ
19 ♏	19 ♐	20 ♒	19 ♓	19 Ↄ	18 ♉
21 ⛎	21 ♑	22 ♓	21 ♈	21 ♉	20 ♊
23 ♐	23 ♒	24 ♈	23 Ↄ	23 ♊	22 ♋
25 ♑	25 ♓	26 Ↄ	25 ♉	25 ♋	24 ♌
27 ♒	27 ♈	28 ♉	27 ♊	27 ♌	26 ♍
29 ♓	29 Ↄ	30 ♊	29 ♋	29 ♍	28 ♎
31 ♈	31 ♉		31 ♌		30 ♏

TABLE 4 145

1908

January		February		March		April		May		June	
1	♐	1	♑	2	♒	2	♈	1	♉	2	♊
3	♐	3	♒	4	♓	4	♉	3	♉	4	♋
5	♑	5	♓	6	♈	6	♉	5	♊	6	♌
7	♒	7	♈	8	♉	7	♊	7	♋	8	♍
9	♓	9	♉	10	♉	9	♋	9	♌	10	♎
11	♈	11	♉	12	♊	11	♌	11	♍	12	♏
13	♉	13	♊	14	♋	13	♍	13	♎	13	♐
15	♉	15	♋	16	♌	15	♎	15	♏	15	♐
17	♊	17	♌	18	♍	17	♏	17	♐	17	♑
19	♋	19	♍	19	♎	19	♐	19	♐	19	♒
21	♌	21	♎	21	♏	21	♐	21	♑	21	♓
23	♍	23	♏	23	♐	23	♑	23	♒	23	♈
24	♎	25	♐	25	♐	25	♒	25	♓	25	♉
26	♏	27	♐	27	♑	27	♓	27	♈	27	♉
28	♐	29	♑	29	♒	29	♈	29	♉	29	♊
30	♐			31	♓			31	♉		

July		August		September		October		November		December	
1	♋	1	♍	1	♏	2	♐	1	♑	2	♓
3	♌	3	♎	3	♐	4	♑	3	♒	4	♈
5	♍	4	♏	5	♐	6	♒	5	♓	6	♉
7	♎	6	♐	7	♑	8	♓	7	♈	8	♉
9	♏	8	♐	9	♒	10	♈	8	♉	10	♊
11	♐	10	♑	11	♓	12	♉	10	♉	12	♋
13	♐	12	♒	13	♈	14	♉	12	♊	14	♌
14	♑	14	♓	15	♉	16	♊	14	♋	16	♍
16	♒	16	♈	17	♉	18	♋	16	♌	18	♎
18	♓	18	♉	19	♊	20	♌	18	♍	20	♏
20	♈	20	♉	21	♋	22	♍	20	♎	21	♐
22	♉	22	♊	23	♌	24	♎	22	♏	23	♐
24	♉	24	♋	25	♍	26	♏	24	♐	25	♑
26	♊	26	♌	27	♎	28	♐	26	♐	27	♒
28	♋	28	♍	28	♏	30	♐	28	♑	29	♓
30	♌	30	♎	30	♐			30	♒	31	♈

1909

January		February		March		April		May		June	
2	⟋	2	♊	2	♊	2	♌	2	♍	1	♏
4	♉	4	♋	3	♋	4	♍	4	♎	3	⛎
6	♊	6	♌	5	♌	6	♎	6	♏	5	♐
8	♋	8	♍	7	♍	8	♏	7	⛎	7	♑
10	♌	10	♎	9	♎	10	⛎	9	♐	9	♒
12	♍	12	♏	11	♏	12	♐	11	♑	11	♓
13	♎	14	⛎	13	⛎	14	♑	13	♒	13	♈
15	♏	16	♐	15	♐	16	♒	15	♓	15	⟋
17	⛎	18	♑	17	♑	18	♓	17	♈	17	♉
19	♐	20	♒	19	♒	20	♈	19	⟋	19	♊
21	♑	22	♓	21	♓	22	⟋	21	♉	21	♋
23	♒	24	♈	23	♈	24	♉	23	♊	23	♌
25	♓	26	⟋	25	⟋	26	♊	25	♋	25	♍
27	♈	28	♉	27	♉	28	♋	27	♌	27	♎
29	⟋			29	♊	30	♌	29	♍	29	♏
31	♉			31	♋			30	♎		

July		August		September		October		November		December	
1	⛎	1	♑	1	♓	1	♈	1	♉	2	♋
3	♐	3	♒	3	♈	3	⟋	3	♊	4	♌
5	♑	5	♓	5	⟋	5	♉	5	♋	6	♍
7	♒	7	♈	7	♉	7	♊	7	♌	8	♎
9	♓	9	⟋	9	♊	9	♋	9	♍	10	♏
11	♈	11	♉	11	♋	11	♌	11	♎	12	⛎
13	⟋	13	♊	13	♌	13	♍	13	♏	14	♐
15	♉	14	♋	15	♍	15	♎	15	⛎	16	♑
17	♊	16	♌	17	♎	17	♏	17	♐	18	♒
19	♋	18	♍	19	♏	19	⛎	19	♑	20	♓
21	♌	20	♎	21	⛎	20	♐	21	♒	22	♈
23	♍	22	♏	23	♐	22	♑	23	♓	24	⟋
25	♎	24	⛎	25	♑	24	♒	25	♈	26	♉
27	♏	26	♐	27	♒	26	♓	27	⟋	28	♊
29	⛎	28	♑	29	♓	28	♈	29	♉	30	♋
31	♐	30	♒			30	⟋	30	♊		

TABLE 4 147

1910

January		February		March		April		May		June	
1	♌	1	♎	2	♏	2	♐	2	♑	2	♓
3	♍	3	♏	4	♐	4	♑	4	♒	4	♈
5	♎	5	♐	6	♐	6	♒	6	♓	6	♈
6	♏	7	♐	8	♑	8	♓	8	♈	8	♉
8	♐	9	♑	10	♒	10	♈	10	♈	10	♊
10	♐	10	♒	12	♓	12	♈	12	♉	12	♋
12	♑	12	♓	13	♈	14	♉	13	♊	14	♌
14	♒	14	♈	15	♈	16	♊	15	♋	16	♍
16	♓	16	♈	17	♉	18	♋	17	♌	18	♎
18	♈	18	♉	19	♊	20	♌	19	♍	20	♏
20	♈	20	♊	21	♋	22	♍	21	♎	21	♐
22	♉	22	♋	23	♌	24	♎	23	♏	23	♐
24	♊	24	♌	25	♍	26	♏	25	♐	25	♑
26	♋	26	♍	27	♎	28	♐	27	♐	27	♒
28	♌	28	♎	29	♏	30	♐	29	♑	29	♓
30	♍			31	♐			31	♒		

July		August		September		October		November		December	
1	♈	1	♉	2	♋	1	♌	1	♎	2	♐
3	♈	3	♊	4	♌	3	♍	3	♏	4	♐
5	♉	5	♋	6	♍	4	♎	5	♐	6	♑
7	♊	7	♌	8	♎	6	♏	7	♐	8	♒
9	♋	9	♍	10	♏	8	♐	9	♑	10	♓
11	♌	11	♎	12	♐	10	♐	11	♒	12	♈
13	♍	13	♏	14	♐	12	♑	13	♓	14	♈
14	♎	15	♐	16	♑	14	♒	14	♈	16	♉
16	♏	17	♐	17	♒	16	♓	16	♈	18	♊
18	♐	19	♑	19	♓	18	♈	18	♉	20	♋
20	♐	21	♒	21	♈	20	♈	20	♊	22	♌
22	♑	23	♓	23	♈	22	♉	22	♋	24	♍
24	♒	25	♈	25	♉	24	♊	24	♌	26	♎
26	♓	27	♈	27	♊	26	♋	26	♍	27	♏
28	♈	29	♉	29	♋	28	♌	28	♎	29	♐
30	♈	31	♊			30	♍	30	♏	31	♐

1911

January	February	March	April	May	June
2 ♑	1 ♒	2 ♓	2 ↩	2 ♉	2 ♋
4 ♒	3 ♓	4 ♈	4 ♉	4 ♊	4 ♌
6 ♓	5 ♈	6 ↩	6 ♊	6 ♋	6 ♍
8 ♈	7 ↩	7 ♉	8 ♋	8 ♌	8 ♎
10 ↩	9 ♉	9 ♊	10 ♌	10 ♍	10 ♏
12 ♉	11 ♊	11 ♋	12 ♍	11 ♎	12 ⛎
14 ♊	13 ♋	13 ♌	14 ♎	13 ♏	14 ♐
16 ♋	15 ♌	15 ♍	16 ♏	15 ⛎	16 ♑
18 ♌	17 ♍	17 ♎	18 ⛎	17 ♐	18 ♒
20 ♍	18 ♎	19 ♏	20 ♐	19 ♑	20 ♓
22 ♎	20 ♏	21 ⛎	22 ♑	21 ♒	21 ♈
24 ♏	22 ⛎	23 ♐	24 ♒	23 ♓	23 ↩
26 ⛎	24 ♐	25 ♑	26 ♓	25 ♈	25 ♉
28 ♐	26 ♑	27 ♒	28 ♈	27 ↩	27 ♊
30 ♑	28 ♒	29 ♓	30 ↩	29 ♉	29 ♋
		31 ♈		31 ♊	

July	August	September	October	November	December
1 ♌	1 ♎	1 ⛎	1 ♐	1 ♒	2 ♈
3 ♍	3 ♏	3 ♐	3 ♑	3 ♓	4 ↩
5 ♎	5 ⛎	5 ♑	5 ♒	5 ♈	6 ♉
7 ♏	7 ♐	7 ♒	7 ♓	6 ↩	8 ♊
9 ⛎	9 ♑	9 ♓	9 ♈	8 ♉	10 ♋
11 ♐	11 ♒	11 ♈	11 ↩	10 ♊	12 ♌
13 ♑	13 ♓	13 ↩	13 ♉	12 ♋	14 ♍
15 ♒	15 ♈	15 ♉	15 ♊	14 ♌	16 ♎
17 ♓	16 ↩	17 ♊	17 ♋	16 ♍	18 ♏
19 ♈	18 ♉	19 ♋	19 ♌	18 ♎	20 ⛎
21 ↩	20 ♊	21 ♌	21 ♍	20 ♏	22 ♐
23 ♉	22 ♋	23 ♍	22 ♎	22 ⛎	24 ♑
25 ♊	24 ♌	25 ♎	24 ♏	24 ♐	26 ♒
27 ♋	26 ♍	27 ♏	26 ⛎	26 ♑	28 ♓
29 ♌	28 ♎	29 ⛎	28 ♐	28 ♒	30 ♈
30 ♍	30 ♏		30 ♑	30 ♓	

TABLE 4 149

1912

January		February		March		April		May		June	
1	♈	1	♊	1	♋	2	♍	1	♎	1	♐
3	♉	2	♋	3	♌	4	♎	3	♏	3	♐
5	♊	4	♌	5	♍	6	♏	5	♐	5	♑
7	♋	6	♍	7	♎	8	♐	7	♐	7	♒
9	♌	8	♎	9	♏	10	♐	8	♑	9	♓
11	♍	10	♏	11	♐	11	♑	10	♒	11	♈
12	♎	12	♐	13	♐	13	♒	12	♓	13	♈
14	♏	14	♐	15	♑	15	♓	14	♈	15	♉
16	♐	16	♑	17	♒	17	♈	16	♈	17	♊
18	♐	18	♒	19	♓	19	♈	18	♉	19	♋
20	♑	20	♓	21	♈	21	♉	20	♊	21	♌
22	♒	22	♈	23	♈	23	♊	22	♋	23	♍
24	♓	24	♈	25	♉	25	♋	24	♌	24	♎
26	♈	26	♉	27	♊	27	♌	26	♍	26	♏
28	♈	28	♊	29	♋	29	♍	28	♎	28	♐
30	♉			31	♌			30	♏	30	♐

July		August		September		October		November		December	
2	♑	2	♓	2	♈	1	♉	2	♋	1	♌
4	♒	4	♈	4	♉	3	♊	4	♌	3	♍
6	♓	6	♈	6	♊	5	♋	6	♍	5	♎
8	♈	8	♉	8	♋	7	♌	8	♎	7	♏
9	♈	10	♊	10	♌	9	♍	10	♏	9	♐
11	♉	12	♋	12	♍	11	♎	11	♐	11	♐
13	♊	14	♌	14	♎	13	♏	13	♐	13	♑
15	♋	16	♍	16	♏	15	♐	15	♑	15	♒
17	♌	18	♎	18	♐	17	♐	17	♒	17	♓
19	♍	20	♏	20	♐	19	♑	19	♓	19	♈
21	♎	22	♐	22	♑	21	♒	21	♈	21	♈
23	♏	23	♐	24	♒	23	♓	23	♈	23	♉
25	♐	25	♑	26	♓	25	♈	25	♉	25	♊
27	♐	27	♒	28	♈	27	♈	27	♊	27	♋
29	♑	29	♓	30	♈	29	♉	29	♋	29	♌
31	♒	31	♈			31	♊			31	♍

1913

January		February		March		April		May		June	
2	♎	2	♇	1	♇	1	♑	2	♓	1	♈
4	♏	3	♐	3	♐	3	♒	4	♈	3	⟓
6	♇	5	♑	5	♑	5	♓	6	⟓	5	♉
8	♐	7	♒	7	♒	7	♈	8	♉	7	♊
10	♑	9	♓	9	♓	9	⟓	10	♊	9	♋
12	♒	11	♈	11	♈	11	♉	12	♋	11	♌
13	♓	13	⟓	13	⟓	13	♊	14	♌	13	♍
15	♈	15	♉	14	♉	15	♋	16	♍	15	♎
17	⟓	17	♊	16	♊	16	♌	18	♎	17	♏
19	♉	19	♋	18	♋	18	♍	20	♏	19	♇
21	♊	21	♌	20	♌	20	♎	22	♇	21	♐
23	♋	23	♍	22	♍	22	♏	24	♐	23	♑
25	♌	25	♎	24	♎	24	♇	26	♑	25	♒
27	♍	27	♏	26	♏	26	♐	28	♒	26	♓
29	♎			28	♇	28	♑	30	♓	28	♈
31	♏			30	♐	30	♒			30	⟓

July		August		September		October		November		December	
2	♉	2	♋	2	♍	1	♎	1	♇	1	♐
4	♊	3	♌	4	♎	3	♏	3	♐	3	♑
6	♋	5	♍	6	♏	5	♇	5	♑	5	♒
8	♌	7	♎	8	♇	7	♐	7	♒	7	♓
10	♍	9	♏	10	♐	9	♑	9	♓	9	♈
12	♎	11	♇	12	♑	11	♒	11	♈	11	⟓
13	♏	13	♐	14	♒	13	♓	13	⟓	13	♉
15	♇	15	♑	16	♓	14	♈	15	♉	15	♊
17	♐	17	♒	18	♈	16	⟓	17	♊	17	♋
19	♑	19	♓	20	⟓	18	♉	19	♋	19	♌
21	♒	21	♈	22	♉	20	♊	21	♌	21	♍
23	♓	23	⟓	24	♊	22	♋	23	♍	23	♎
25	♈	25	♉	26	♋	24	♌	25	♎	25	♏
27	⟓	27	♊	28	♌	26	♍	27	♏	27	♇
29	♉	29	♋	30	♍	28	♎	29	♇	28	♐
31	♊	31	♌			30	♏			30	♑

TABLE 4 151

1914

January	February	March	April	May	June
1 ♒	1 ♈	1 ♈	1 ♉	2 ♋	2 ♍
3 ♓	3 ♈	3 ♈	2 ♊	4 ♌	4 ♎
5 ♈	5 ♉	5 ♉	4 ♋	6 ♍	6 ♏
7 ♈	7 ♊	7 ♊	6 ♌	8 ♎	8 ♐
9 ♉	9 ♋	9 ♋	8 ♍	10 ♏	10 ♐
10 ♊	11 ♌	11 ♌	10 ♎	11 ♐	12 ♑
12 ♋	13 ♍	13 ♍	12 ♏	13 ♐	14 ♒
14 ♌	15 ♎	15 ♎	14 ♐	15 ♑	16 ♓
16 ♍	17 ♏	17 ♏	16 ♐	17 ♒	18 ♈
18 ♎	19 ♐	19 ♐	18 ♑	19 ♓	20 ♈
20 ♏	21 ♐	20 ♐	20 ♒	21 ♈	22 ♉
22 ♐	23 ♑	22 ♑	22 ♓	23 ♈	24 ♊
24 ♐	25 ♒	24 ♒	24 ♈	25 ♉	26 ♋
26 ♑	27 ♓	26 ♓	26 ♈	27 ♊	28 ♌
28 ♒		28 ♈	28 ♉	29 ♋	30 ♍
30 ♓		30 ♈	30 ♊	31 ♌	

July	August	September	October	November	December
2 ♎	1 ♐	2 ♑	1 ♒	1 ♈	2 ♉
3 ♏	3 ♐	4 ♒	3 ♓	3 ♈	4 ♊
5 ♐	5 ♑	6 ♓	5 ♈	5 ♉	6 ♋
7 ♐	7 ♒	8 ♈	7 ♈	7 ♊	8 ♌
9 ♑	9 ♓	9 ♈	9 ♉	8 ♋	10 ♍
11 ♒	11 ♈	11 ♉	11 ♊	10 ♌	12 ♎
13 ♓	13 ♈	13 ♊	13 ♋	12 ♍	14 ♏
15 ♈	15 ♉	15 ♋	15 ♌	14 ♎	16 ♐
17 ♈	17 ♊	17 ♌	17 ♍	16 ♏	18 ♐
19 ♉	19 ♋	19 ♍	19 ♎	18 ♐	20 ♑
21 ♊	21 ♌	21 ♎	20 ♏	20 ♐	22 ♒
23 ♋	23 ♍	23 ♏	22 ♐	22 ♑	24 ♓
25 ♌	25 ♎	25 ♐	24 ♐	24 ♒	26 ♈
27 ♍	27 ♏	27 ♐	26 ♑	26 ♓	28 ♈
29 ♎	29 ♐	29 ♑	28 ♒	28 ♈	30 ♉
31 ♏	31 ♐		30 ♓	30 ♈	

1915

January	February	March	April	May	June
1 ♊	1 ♌	2 ♍	1 ♎	1 ⛎	2 ♑
3 ♋	2 ♍	4 ♎	3 ♏	3 ♐	4 ♒
5 ♌	4 ♎	6 ♏	5 ⛎	5 ♑	6 ♓
7 ♍	6 ♏	8 ⛎	7 ♐	7 ♒	8 ♈
9 ♎	8 ⛎	10 ♐	9 ♑	9 ♓	10 ↄ
11 ♏	10 ♐	12 ♑	11 ♒	11 ♈	11 ♉
13 ⛎	12 ♑	14 ♒	12 ♓	13 ↄ	13 ♊
15 ♐	14 ♒	16 ♓	14 ♈	15 ♉	15 ♋
17 ♑	16 ♓	18 ♈	16 ↄ	17 ♊	17 ♌
18 ♒	18 ♈	20 ↄ	18 ♉	19 ♋	19 ♍
20 ♓	20 ↄ	22 ♉	20 ♊	21 ♌	21 ♎
22 ♈	22 ♉	24 ♊	22 ♋	23 ♍	23 ♏
24 ↄ	24 ♊	26 ♋	24 ♌	25 ♎	25 ⛎
26 ♉	26 ♋	28 ♌	26 ♍	27 ♏	27 ♐
28 ♊	28 ♌	30 ♍	28 ♎	29 ⛎	29 ♑
30 ♋			30 ♏	31 ♐	

July	August	September	October	November	December
1 ♒	1 ♈	2 ♉	1 ♊	1 ♌	2 ♎
3 ♓	3 ↄ	4 ♊	3 ♋	3 ♍	4 ♏
5 ♈	5 ♉	6 ♋	4 ♌	5 ♎	6 ⛎
7 ↄ	7 ♊	8 ♌	6 ♍	7 ♏	8 ♐
9 ♉	9 ♋	10 ♍	8 ♎	8 ⛎	10 ♑
11 ♊	11 ♌	12 ♎	10 ♏	10 ♐	12 ♒
13 ♋	13 ♍	14 ♏	12 ⛎	12 ♑	14 ♓
15 ♌	15 ♎	16 ⛎	14 ♐	14 ♒	16 ♈
17 ♍	17 ♏	18 ♐	16 ♑	16 ♓	17 ↄ
18 ♎	19 ⛎	20 ♑	18 ♒	18 ♈	19 ♉
20 ♏	21 ♐	22 ♒	20 ♓	20 ↄ	21 ♊
22 ⛎	23 ♑	23 ♓	22 ♈	22 ♉	23 ♋
24 ♐	25 ♒	25 ♈	24 ↄ	24 ♊	25 ♌
26 ♑	27 ♓	27 ↄ	26 ♉	26 ♋	27 ♍
28 ♒	29 ♈	29 ♉	28 ♊	28 ♌	29 ♎
30 ♓	31 ↄ		30 ♋	30 ♍	31 ♏

TABLE 4 153

1916

January	February	March	April	May	June
2 ♐	2 ♑	1 ♑	1 ♓	1 ♈	1 ♉
4 ♐	4 ♒	3 ♒	3 ♈	3 ♈	3 ♊
6 ♑	6 ♓	5 ♓	5 ♈	5 ♉	5 ♋
8 ♒	8 ♈	7 ♈	7 ♉	7 ♊	7 ♌
10 ♓	10 ♈	8 ♈	9 ♊	9 ♋	9 ♍
12 ♈	12 ♉	10 ♉	11 ♋	11 ♌	11 ♎
14 ♈	14 ♊	12 ♊	13 ♌	13 ♍	13 ♏
16 ♉	16 ♋	14 ♋	15 ♍	14 ♎	15 ♐
18 ♊	18 ♌	16 ♌	17 ♎	16 ♏	17 ♐
20 ♋	20 ♍	18 ♍	19 ♏	18 ♐	19 ♑
22 ♌	22 ♎	20 ♎	21 ♐	20 ♐	21 ♒
24 ♍	24 ♏	22 ♏	23 ♐	22 ♑	22 ♓
26 ♎	26 ♐	24 ♐	25 ♑	24 ♒	24 ♈
27 ♏	28 ♐	26 ♐	27 ♒	26 ♓	26 ♈
29 ♐		28 ♑	29 ♓	28 ♈	28 ♉
31 ♐		30 ♒		30 ♈	30 ♊

July	August	September	October	November	December
2 ♋	2 ♍	2 ♏	2 ♐	2 ♑	1 ♒
4 ♌	4 ♎	4 ♐	4 ♐	4 ♒	3 ♓
5 ♍	6 ♏	6 ♐	6 ♑	6 ♓	5 ♈
7 ♎	8 ♐	8 ♑	8 ♒	7 ♈	7 ♈
9 ♏	10 ♐	10 ♒	10 ♓	9 ♈	9 ♉
11 ♐	12 ♑	12 ♓	12 ♈	11 ♉	11 ♊
13 ♐	14 ♒	14 ♈	14 ♈	13 ♊	13 ♋
15 ♑	16 ♓	16 ♈	16 ♉	15 ♋	15 ♌
17 ♒	17 ♈	18 ♉	18 ♊	17 ♌	17 ♍
19 ♓	19 ♈	20 ♊	19 ♋	19 ♍	19 ♎
21 ♈	21 ♉	22 ♋	21 ♌	21 ♎	20 ♏
23 ♈	23 ♊	24 ♌	23 ♍	23 ♏	22 ♐
25 ♉	25 ♋	26 ♍	25 ♎	25 ♐	24 ♐
27 ♊	27 ♌	28 ♎	27 ♏	27 ♐	26 ♑
29 ♋	29 ♍	30 ♏	29 ♐	29 ♑	28 ♒
31 ♌	31 ♎		31 ♐		30 ♓

1917

January	February	March	April	May	June
1 ♈	2 ♉	1 ♉	1 ♋	1 ♌	1 ♎
3 ⌐	4 ♊	3 ♊	3 ♌	3 ♍	2 ♏
5 ♉	6 ♋	5 ♋	5 ♍	5 ♎	4 ⛎
7 ♊	8 ♌	7 ♌	7 ♎	7 ♏	6 ♐
9 ♋	10 ♍	9 ♍	9 ♏	8 ⛎	8 ♑
11 ♌	11 ♎	11 ♎	11 ⛎	10 ♐	10 ♒
13 ♍	13 ♏	13 ♏	13 ♐	12 ♑	12 ♓
15 ♎	15 ⛎	15 ⛎	15 ♑	14 ♒	14 ♈
17 ♏	17 ♐	17 ♐	17 ♒	16 ♓	16 ⌐
19 ⛎	19 ♑	19 ♑	19 ♓	18 ♈	18 ♉
21 ♐	21 ♒	21 ♒	21 ♈	20 ⌐	20 ♊
23 ♑	23 ♓	23 ♓	23 ⌐	22 ♉	22 ♋
25 ♒	25 ♈	25 ♈	25 ♉	24 ♊	24 ♌
27 ♓	27 ⌐	26 ⌐	27 ♊	26 ♋	26 ♍
29 ♈		28 ♉	29 ♋	28 ♌	28 ♎
31 ⌐		30 ♊		30 ♍	30 ♏

July	August	September	October	November	December
2 ⛎	2 ♑	2 ♓	2 ♈	2 ♉	1 ♊
4 ♐	4 ♒	4 ♈	4 ⌐	4 ♊	3 ♋
6 ♑	6 ♓	6 ⌐	6 ♉	6 ♋	5 ♌
8 ♒	8 ♈	8 ♉	8 ♊	8 ♌	7 ♍
10 ♓	10 ⌐	10 ♊	9 ♋	10 ♍	9 ♎
12 ♈	12 ♉	12 ♋	11 ♌	12 ♎	11 ♏
13 ⌐	14 ♊	14 ♌	13 ♍	14 ♏	13 ⛎
15 ♉	16 ♋	16 ♍	15 ♎	16 ⛎	15 ♐
17 ♊	18 ♌	18 ♎	17 ♏	18 ♐	17 ♑
19 ♋	20 ♍	20 ♏	19 ⛎	19 ♑	19 ♒
21 ♌	22 ♎	22 ⛎	21 ♐	21 ♒	21 ♓
23 ♍	24 ♏	24 ♐	23 ♑	23 ♓	23 ♈
25 ♎	26 ⛎	26 ♑	25 ♒	25 ♈	25 ⌐
27 ♏	28 ♐	28 ♒	27 ♓	27 ⌐	27 ♉
29 ⛎	29 ♑	30 ♓	29 ♈	29 ♉	29 ♊
31 ♐	31 ♒		31 ⌐		31 ♋

TABLE 4 155

1918

January	February	March	April	May	June
2 ♌	2 ♎	1 ♎	1 ♐	1 ♐	1 ♒
3 ♍	4 ♏	3 ♏	3 ♐	3 ♑	3 ♓
5 ♎	6 ♐	5 ♐	5 ♑	5 ♒	5 ♈
7 ♏	8 ♐	7 ♐	7 ♒	7 ♓	7 ♉
9 ♐	10 ♑	9 ♑	9 ♓	8 ♈	9 ♉
11 ♐	12 ♒	11 ♒	11 ♈	10 ♉	11 ♊
13 ♑	13 ♓	13 ♓	13 ♉	12 ♉	13 ♋
15 ♒	15 ♈	15 ♈	15 ♉	14 ♊	15 ♌
17 ♓	17 ♉	17 ♉	17 ♊	16 ♋	17 ♍
19 ♈	19 ♉	19 ♉	19 ♋	18 ♌	18 ♎
21 ♉	21 ♊	21 ♊	21 ♌	20 ♍	20 ♏
23 ♉	23 ♋	23 ♋	23 ♍	22 ♎	22 ♐
25 ♊	25 ♌	25 ♌	25 ♎	24 ♏	24 ♐
27 ♋	27 ♍	27 ♍	27 ♏	26 ♐	26 ♑
29 ♌		29 ♎	29 ♐	28 ♐	28 ♒
31 ♍		30 ♏		30 ♑	30 ♓

July	August	September	October	November	December
2 ♈	2 ♉	1 ♊	2 ♌	2 ♎	1 ♏
4 ♉	4 ♊	3 ♋	4 ♍	4 ♏	3 ♐
6 ♉	6 ♋	5 ♌	6 ♎	6 ♐	5 ♐
8 ♊	8 ♌	6 ♍	8 ♏	8 ♐	7 ♑
10 ♋	10 ♍	8 ♎	10 ♐	10 ♑	9 ♒
12 ♌	12 ♎	10 ♏	12 ♐	12 ♒	11 ♓
14 ♍	14 ♏	12 ♐	14 ♑	14 ♓	13 ♈
16 ♎	16 ♐	14 ♐	16 ♒	16 ♈	15 ♉
18 ♏	18 ♐	16 ♑	18 ♓	18 ♉	17 ♉
20 ♐	20 ♑	18 ♒	20 ♈	19 ♉	19 ♊
22 ♐	22 ♒	20 ♓	22 ♉	21 ♊	21 ♋
24 ♑	24 ♓	22 ♈	23 ♉	23 ♋	23 ♌
26 ♒	26 ♈	24 ♉	25 ♊	25 ♌	25 ♍
27 ♓	28 ♉	26 ♉	27 ♋	27 ♍	27 ♎
29 ♈	30 ♉	28 ♊	29 ♌	29 ♎	29 ♏
31 ♉		30 ♋	31 ♍		31 ♐

1919

January	February	March	April	May	June
2 ♐	2 ♒	1 ♒	2 ♈	1 ↄ	2 ♊
4 ♑	4 ♓	3 ♓	4 ↄ	3 ♉	3 ♋
6 ♒	6 ♈	5 ♈	6 ♉	5 ♊	5 ♌
8 ♓	8 ↄ	7 ↄ	8 ♊	7 ♋	7 ♍
10 ♈	10 ♉	9 ♉	10 ♋	9 ♌	9 ♎
12 ↄ	11 ♊	11 ♊	12 ♌	11 ♍	11 ♏
14 ♉	13 ♋	13 ♋	14 ♍	13 ♎	13 ⛎
16 ♊	15 ♌	15 ♌	16 ♎	15 ♏	15 ♐
18 ♋	17 ♍	17 ♍	18 ♏	17 ⛎	17 ♑
20 ♌	19 ♎	19 ♎	20 ⛎	19 ♐	19 ♒
22 ♍	21 ♏	21 ♏	22 ♐	21 ♑	21 ♓
24 ♎	23 ⛎	23 ⛎	23 ♑	23 ♒	23 ♈
26 ♏	25 ♐	25 ♐	25 ♒	25 ♓	25 ↄ
27 ⛎	27 ♑	27 ♑	27 ♓	27 ♈	27 ♉
29 ♐		29 ♒	29 ♈	29 ↄ	29 ♊
31 ♑		31 ♓		31 ♉	

July	August	September	October	November	December
1 ♋	1 ♍	1 ♏	2 ♐	2 ♒	2 ♓
3 ♌	2 ♎	3 ⛎	4 ♑	4 ♓	4 ♈
5 ♍	4 ♏	5 ♐	6 ♒	6 ♈	6 ↄ
7 ♎	6 ⛎	7 ♑	8 ♓	8 ↄ	8 ♉
8 ♏	8 ♐	9 ♒	9 ♈	10 ♉	10 ♊
10 ⛎	10 ♑	11 ♓	11 ↄ	12 ♊	12 ♋
12 ♐	12 ♒	13 ♈	13 ♉	14 ♋	14 ♌
14 ♑	14 ♓	15 ↄ	15 ♊	16 ♌	15 ♍
16 ♒	16 ♈	17 ♉	17 ♋	18 ♍	17 ♎
18 ♓	18 ↄ	19 ♊	19 ♌	20 ♎	19 ♏
20 ♈	20 ♉	21 ♋	21 ♍	22 ♏	21 ⛎
22 ↄ	22 ♊	23 ♌	23 ♎	24 ⛎	23 ♐
24 ♉	24 ♋	25 ♍	25 ♏	26 ♐	25 ♑
26 ♊	26 ♌	27 ♎	27 ⛎	28 ♑	27 ♒
28 ♋	28 ♍	28 ♏	29 ♐	30 ♒	29 ♓
30 ♌	30 ♎	30 ⛎	31 ♑		31 ♈

TABLE 4 157

1920

January	February	March	April	May	June
2 ♈	2 ♊	1 ♊	1 ♌	2 ♎	2 ♐
4 ♉	4 ♋	2 ♋	3 ♍	4 ♏	4 ♐
6 ♊	6 ♌	4 ♌	5 ♎	6 ♐	6 ♑
8 ♋	8 ♍	6 ♍	7 ♏	8 ♐	8 ♒
10 ♌	10 ♎	8 ♎	9 ♐	10 ♑	10 ♓
12 ♍	12 ♏	10 ♏	11 ♐	12 ♒	12 ♈
14 ♎	14 ♐	12 ♐	12 ♑	14 ♓	14 ♈
16 ♏	16 ♐	14 ♐	14 ♒	16 ♈	16 ♉
18 ♐	18 ♑	16 ♑	16 ♓	18 ♈	18 ♊
20 ♐	20 ♒	18 ♒	18 ♈	20 ♉	20 ♋
22 ♑	22 ♓	20 ♓	20 ♈	22 ♊	22 ♌
23 ♒	24 ♈	22 ♈	22 ♉	24 ♋	24 ♍
25 ♓	26 ♈	24 ♈	24 ♊	25 ♌	26 ♎
27 ♈	28 ♉	26 ♉	26 ♋	27 ♍	28 ♏
29 ♈		28 ♊	28 ♌	29 ♎	29 ♐
31 ♉		30 ♋	30 ♍	31 ♏	

July	August	September	October	November	December
1 ♐	2 ♒	2 ♈	1 ♈	2 ♊	1 ♋
3 ♑	4 ♓	4 ♈	3 ♉	3 ♋	3 ♌
5 ♒	6 ♈	6 ♉	5 ♊	5 ♌	5 ♍
7 ♓	8 ♈	8 ♊	7 ♋	7 ♍	7 ♎
9 ♈	9 ♉	10 ♋	9 ♌	9 ♎	9 ♏
11 ♈	11 ♊	12 ♌	11 ♍	11 ♏	11 ♐
13 ♉	13 ♋	14 ♍	13 ♎	13 ♐	13 ♐
15 ♊	15 ♌	16 ♎	15 ♏	15 ♐	15 ♑
17 ♋	17 ♍	18 ♏	17 ♐	17 ♑	16 ♒
19 ♌	19 ♎	20 ♐	19 ♐	19 ♒	18 ♓
21 ♍	21 ♏	21 ♐	21 ♑	21 ♓	20 ♈
23 ♎	23 ♐	23 ♑	23 ♒	23 ♈	22 ♈
25 ♏	25 ♐	25 ♒	25 ♓	25 ♈	24 ♉
27 ♐	27 ♑	27 ♓	27 ♈	27 ♉	26 ♊
29 ♐	29 ♒	29 ♈	29 ♈	29 ♊	28 ♋
31 ♑	31 ♓		31 ♉		30 ♌

1921

Note: ⛎ = Ophiuchus, ↩ = Cetus (the two additional signs of the 14-sign zodiac).

January		February		March		April		May		June	
1	♍	1	♏	2	⛎	2	♑	2	♒	2	♈
3	♎	3	⛎	4	♐	4	♒	4	♓	4	↩
5	♏	5	♐	6	♑	6	♓	6	♈	6	♉
7	⛎	7	♑	8	♒	8	♈	8	↩	8	♊
9	♐	9	♒	10	♓	10	↩	10	♉	10	♋
11	♑	11	♓	12	♈	12	♉	12	♊	12	♌
13	♒	12	♈	14	↩	14	♊	14	♋	14	♍
15	♓	14	↩	16	♉	16	♋	16	♌	16	♎
17	♈	16	♉	17	♊	18	♌	18	♍	18	♏
19	↩	18	♊	19	♋	20	♍	20	♎	20	⛎
21	♉	20	♋	21	♌	22	♎	22	♏	22	♐
23	♊	22	♌	23	♍	24	♏	24	⛎	24	♑
25	♋	24	♍	25	♎	26	⛎	26	♐	26	♒
27	♌	26	♎	27	♏	28	♐	27	♑	28	♓
29	♍	28	♏	29	⛎	30	♑	29	♒	30	♈
31	♎			31	♐			31	♓		

July		August		September		October		November		December	
2	↩	1	♊	2	♌	1	♍	1	♏	2	♐
4	♉	3	♋	4	♍	3	♎	3	⛎	4	♑
6	♊	5	♌	6	♎	5	♏	5	♐	6	♒
8	♋	7	♍	8	♏	7	⛎	7	♑	8	♓
10	♌	9	♎	9	⛎	9	♐	9	♒	10	♈
11	♍	11	♏	11	♐	11	♑	11	♓	12	↩
13	♎	13	⛎	13	♑	13	♒	13	♈	14	♉
15	♏	15	♐	15	♒	15	♓	15	↩	16	♊
17	⛎	17	♑	17	♓	17	♈	17	♉	18	♋
19	♐	19	♒	19	♈	19	↩	19	♊	20	♌
21	♑	21	♓	21	↩	20	♉	21	♋	22	♍
23	♒	23	♈	23	♉	22	♊	22	♌	24	♎
25	♓	25	↩	25	♊	24	♋	24	♍	26	♏
27	♈	27	♉	27	♋	26	♌	26	♎	28	⛎
29	↩	29	♊	29	♌	28	♍	28	♏	30	♐
31	♉	31	♋			30	♎	30	⛎		

TABLE 4 159

1922

January	February	March	April	May	June
1 ♑	1 ♓	2 ♈	2 ♉	2 ♊	2 ♌
3 ♒	3 ♈	4 ♉	4 ♊	3 ♋	4 ♍
5 ♓	5 ♉	6 ♉	6 ♋	5 ♌	6 ♎
7 ♈	7 ♉	8 ♊	8 ♌	7 ♍	8 ♏
9 ♉	9 ♊	10 ♋	10 ♍	9 ♎	10 ♐
11 ♉	11 ♋	12 ♌	12 ♎	11 ♏	12 ♐
13 ♊	12 ♌	14 ♍	14 ♏	13 ♐	13 ♑
15 ♋	14 ♍	16 ♎	16 ♐	15 ♐	15 ♒
17 ♌	16 ♎	17 ♏	18 ♐	17 ♑	17 ♓
19 ♍	18 ♏	19 ♐	20 ♑	19 ♒	19 ♈
21 ♎	20 ♐	21 ♐	22 ♒	21 ♓	21 ♉
23 ♏	22 ♐	23 ♑	24 ♓	23 ♈	23 ♉
25 ♐	24 ♑	25 ♒	26 ♈	25 ♉	25 ♊
27 ♐	26 ♒	27 ♓	28 ♉	27 ♉	27 ♋
29 ♑	28 ♓	29 ♈	30 ♉	29 ♊	29 ♌
30 ♒		31 ♉		31 ♋	

July	August	September	October	November	December
1 ♍	1 ♏	1 ♐	1 ♑	1 ♓	2 ♉
3 ♎	3 ♐	3 ♑	3 ♒	3 ♈	4 ♉
5 ♏	5 ♐	5 ♒	5 ♓	5 ♉	6 ♊
7 ♐	7 ♑	7 ♓	7 ♈	7 ♉	8 ♋
9 ♐	9 ♒	9 ♈	9 ♉	9 ♊	10 ♌
11 ♑	11 ♓	11 ♉	11 ♉	11 ♋	12 ♍
13 ♒	13 ♈	13 ♉	13 ♊	12 ♌	14 ♎
15 ♓	14 ♉	15 ♊	15 ♋	14 ♍	16 ♏
17 ♈	16 ♉	17 ♋	17 ♌	16 ♎	18 ♐
19 ♉	18 ♊	19 ♌	19 ♍	18 ♏	20 ♐
21 ♉	20 ♋	21 ♍	21 ♎	20 ♐	22 ♑
23 ♊	22 ♌	23 ♎	22 ♏	22 ♐	24 ♒
24 ♋	24 ♍	25 ♏	24 ♐	24 ♑	25 ♓
26 ♌	26 ♎	27 ♐	26 ♐	26 ♒	27 ♈
28 ♍	28 ♏	29 ♐	28 ♑	28 ♓	29 ♉
30 ♎	30 ♐		30 ♒	30 ♈	31 ♉

1923

January		February		March		April		May		June	
2	♊	1	♋	2	♌	2	♎	1	♏	1	♐
4	♋	3	♌	4	♍	4	♏	3	⛎	3	♑
6	♌	4	♍	6	♎	6	⛎	5	♐	5	♒
8	♍	6	♎	8	♏	8	♐	7	♑	7	♓
10	♎	8	♏	9	⛎	10	♑	9	♒	8	♈
12	♏	10	⛎	11	♐	12	♒	11	♓	10	↫
14	⛎	12	♐	13	♑	14	♓	13	♈	12	♉
16	♐	14	♑	15	♒	16	♈	15	↫	14	♊
18	♑	16	♒	17	♓	18	↫	17	♉	16	♋
20	♒	18	♓	19	♈	19	♉	19	♊	18	♌
22	♓	20	♈	21	↫	21	♊	21	♋	20	♍
24	♈	22	↫	23	♉	23	♋	22	♌	22	♎
26	↫	24	♉	25	♊	25	♌	24	♍	24	♏
28	♉	26	♊	27	♋	27	♍	26	♎	26	⛎
30	♊	28	♋	29	♌	29	♎	28	♏	28	♐
				31	♍			30	⛎	30	♑

July		August		September		October		November		December	
2	♒	1	♓	1	↫	2	♊	1	♋	2	♍
4	♓	3	♈	3	♉	4	♋	3	♌	4	♎
6	♈	5	↫	5	♊	6	♌	5	♍	5	♏
8	↫	7	♉	6	♋	8	♍	7	♎	7	⛎
10	♉	9	♊	8	♌	10	♎	9	♏	9	♐
12	♊	11	♋	10	♍	12	♏	11	⛎	11	♑
14	♋	13	♌	12	♎	14	⛎	13	♐	13	♒
16	♌	15	♍	14	♏	16	♐	14	♑	15	♓
18	♍	16	♎	16	⛎	18	♑	16	♒	17	♈
20	♎	18	♏	18	♐	20	♒	18	♓	19	↫
22	♏	20	⛎	20	♑	22	♓	20	♈	21	♉
24	⛎	22	♐	22	♒	24	♈	22	↫	23	♊
26	♐	24	♑	24	♓	26	↫	24	♉	25	♋
28	♑	26	♒	26	♈	28	♉	26	♊	27	♌
30	♒	28	♓	28	↫	30	♊	28	♋	29	♍
		30	♈	30	♉			30	♌	31	♎

TABLE 4 161

1924

January	February	March	April	May	June
2 ♏	2 ♐	2 ♑	1 ♒	2 ♈	2 ♉
4 ♐	4 ♑	4 ♒	3 ♓	4 ♉	3 ♊
6 ♐	6 ♒	6 ♓	5 ♈	6 ♉	5 ♋
8 ♑	8 ♓	8 ♈	7 ♉	8 ♊	7 ♌
10 ♒	10 ♈	10 ♉	9 ♉	10 ♋	9 ♍
12 ♓	12 ♉	12 ♉	11 ♊	12 ♌	11 ♎
14 ♈	14 ♉	14 ♊	13 ♋	13 ♍	13 ♏
15 ♉	16 ♊	16 ♋	15 ♌	15 ♎	15 ♐
17 ♉	18 ♋	18 ♌	17 ♍	17 ♏	17 ♐
19 ♊	19 ♌	20 ♍	19 ♎	19 ♐	19 ♑
21 ♋	21 ♍	22 ♎	21 ♏	21 ♐	21 ♒
23 ♌	23 ♎	24 ♏	23 ♐	23 ♑	23 ♓
25 ♍	25 ♏	26 ♐	25 ♐	25 ♒	25 ♈
27 ♎	27 ♐	28 ♐	27 ♑	27 ♓	27 ♉
29 ♏	29 ♐	30 ♑	29 ♒	29 ♈	29 ♉
31 ♐			30 ♓	31 ♉	

July	August	September	October	November	December
1 ♊	2 ♌	2 ♎	1 ♏	1 ♐	2 ♒
3 ♋	4 ♍	4 ♏	3 ♐	3 ♑	4 ♓
5 ♌	6 ♎	6 ♐	5 ♐	5 ♒	6 ♈
7 ♍	8 ♏	8 ♐	7 ♑	7 ♓	8 ♉
9 ♎	10 ♏	10 ♑	9 ♒	9 ♈	10 ♉
11 ♏	11 ♐	12 ♒	11 ♓	11 ♉	12 ♊
13 ♐	13 ♑	14 ♓	13 ♈	13 ♉	14 ♋
15 ♐	15 ♒	15 ♈	15 ♉	14 ♊	16 ♌
17 ♑	17 ♓	17 ♉	17 ♉	16 ♋	18 ♍
19 ♒	19 ♈	19 ♉	19 ♊	18 ♌	20 ♎
21 ♓	21 ♉	21 ♊	21 ♋	20 ♍	22 ♏
23 ♈	23 ♉	23 ♋	23 ♌	22 ♎	24 ♐
25 ♉	25 ♊	25 ♌	25 ♍	24 ♏	26 ♐
27 ♉	27 ♋	27 ♍	26 ♎	26 ♐	28 ♑
29 ♊	29 ♌	29 ♎	28 ♏	28 ♐	30 ♒
31 ♋	31 ♍		30 ♐	30 ♑	

1925

January		February		March		April		May		June	
1	♓	1	♎	2	♉	2	♋	1	♌	2	♎
3	♈	3	♉	4	♊	4	♌	3	♍	4	♏
5	♎	5	♊	6	♋	6	♍	5	♎	6	♐
7	♉	7	♋	8	♌	8	♎	7	♏	8	♐
9	♊	9	♌	10	♍	10	♏	9	♐	10	♑
11	♋	11	♍	12	♎	12	♐	11	♐	12	♒
13	♌	12	♎	14	♏	14	♐	13	♑	14	♓
15	♍	14	♏	16	♐	16	♑	15	♒	16	♈
17	♎	16	♐	18	♐	18	♒	17	♓	18	♎
19	♏	18	♐	20	♑	20	♓	19	♈	20	♉
21	♐	20	♑	22	♒	22	♈	21	♎	22	♊
22	♐	22	♒	24	♓	24	♎	23	♉	23	♋
24	♑	24	♓	25	♈	26	♉	25	♊	25	♌
26	♒	26	♈	27	♎	28	♊	27	♋	27	♍
28	♓	28	♎	29	♉	30	♋	29	♌	29	♎
30	♈			31	♊			31	♍		

July		August		September		October		November		December	
1	♏	2	♐	2	♒	1	♓	1	♎	1	♉
3	♐	3	♑	4	♓	3	♈	3	♉	3	♊
5	♐	5	♒	6	♈	5	♎	5	♊	5	♋
7	♑	7	♓	7	♎	7	♉	7	♋	6	♌
9	♒	9	♈	9	♉	9	♊	9	♌	8	♍
11	♓	11	♎	11	♊	11	♋	11	♍	10	♎
13	♈	13	♉	13	♋	13	♌	13	♎	12	♏
15	♎	15	♊	15	♌	15	♍	15	♏	14	♐
17	♉	17	♋	17	♍	17	♎	17	♐	16	♐
19	♊	19	♌	19	♎	18	♏	19	♐	18	♑
21	♋	21	♍	21	♏	20	♐	21	♑	20	♒
23	♌	23	♎	23	♐	22	♐	23	♒	22	♓
25	♍	25	♏	25	♐	24	♑	25	♓	24	♈
27	♎	27	♐	27	♑	26	♒	27	♈	26	♎
29	♏	29	♐	29	♒	28	♓	29	♎	28	♉
31	♐	31	♑			30	♈			30	♊

TABLE 4 163

1926

January	February	March	April	May	June
1 ♋	1 ♍	1 ♍	1 ♏	2 ♐	2 ♒
3 ♌	3 ♎	3 ♎	3 ☋	4 ♑	4 ♓
5 ♍	5 ♏	4 ♏	5 ♐	6 ♒	6 ♈
7 ♎	7 ☋	6 ☋	7 ♑	8 ♓	8 ☊
9 ♏	9 ♐	8 ♐	9 ♒	10 ♈	10 ♉
11 ☋	11 ♑	10 ♑	11 ♓	12 ☊	12 ♊
13 ♐	13 ♒	12 ♒	13 ♈	14 ♉	14 ♋
15 ♑	15 ♓	14 ♓	14 ☊	16 ♊	16 ♌
16 ♒	17 ♈	16 ♈	16 ♉	18 ♋	18 ♍
18 ♓	19 ☊	18 ☊	18 ♊	19 ♌	20 ♎
20 ♈	21 ♉	20 ♉	20 ♋	21 ♍	22 ♏
22 ☊	23 ♊	22 ♊	22 ♌	23 ♎	24 ☋
24 ♉	25 ♋	24 ♋	24 ♍	25 ♏	26 ♐
26 ♊	27 ♌	26 ♌	26 ♎	27 ☋	28 ♑
28 ♋		28 ♍	28 ♏	29 ♐	29 ♒
30 ♌		30 ♎	30 ☋	31 ♑	

July	August	September	October	November	December
1 ♓	2 ☊	2 ♊	1 ♋	2 ♍	1 ♎
3 ♈	4 ♉	3 ♋	3 ♌	4 ♎	3 ♏
5 ☊	6 ♊	5 ♌	5 ♍	6 ♏	5 ☋
7 ♉	8 ♋	7 ♍	7 ♎	8 ☋	7 ♐
9 ♊	10 ♌	9 ♎	9 ♏	10 ♐	9 ♑
11 ♋	12 ♍	11 ♏	11 ☋	11 ♑	11 ♒
13 ♌	14 ♎	13 ☋	13 ♐	13 ♒	13 ♓
15 ♍	16 ♏	15 ♐	15 ♑	15 ♓	14 ♈
17 ♎	17 ☋	17 ♑	17 ♒	17 ♈	16 ☊
19 ♏	19 ♐	19 ♒	19 ♓	19 ☊	18 ♉
21 ☋	21 ♑	21 ♓	21 ♈	21 ♉	20 ♊
23 ♐	23 ♒	23 ♈	23 ☊	23 ♊	22 ♋
25 ♑	25 ♓	25 ☊	25 ♉	25 ♋	24 ♌
27 ♒	27 ♈	27 ♉	27 ♊	27 ♌	26 ♍
29 ♓	29 ☊	29 ♊	29 ♋	29 ♍	28 ♎
31 ♈	31 ♉		31 ♌		30 ♏

1927

January	February	March	April	May	June
1 ⚷	1 ♑	2 ♒	1 ♓	2 ↝	1 ♉
3 ♐	3 ♒	4 ♓	3 ♈	4 ♉	3 ♊
5 ♑	5 ♓	6 ♈	5 ↝	6 ♊	5 ♋
7 ♒	6 ♈	8 ↝	7 ♉	8 ♋	7 ♌
9 ♓	8 ↝	10 ♉	9 ♊	10 ♌	9 ♍
11 ♈	10 ♉	12 ♊	10 ♋	12 ♍	11 ♎
13 ↝	12 ♊	14 ♋	12 ♌	14 ♎	13 ♏
15 ♉	14 ♋	16 ♌	14 ♍	16 ♏	15 ⚷
17 ♊	16 ♌	18 ♍	16 ♎	18 ⚷	17 ♐
19 ♋	18 ♍	20 ♎	18 ♏	20 ♐	18 ♑
21 ♌	20 ♎	22 ♏	20 ⚷	22 ♑	20 ♒
23 ♍	22 ♏	24 ⚷	22 ♐	24 ♒	22 ♓
24 ♎	24 ⚷	26 ♐	24 ♑	26 ♓	24 ♈
26 ♏	26 ♐	28 ♑	26 ♒	28 ♈	26 ↝
28 ⚷	28 ♑	30 ♒	28 ♓	30 ↝	28 ♉
30 ♐			30 ♈		30 ♊

July	August	September	October	November	December
2 ♋	2 ♍	2 ♏	1 ⚷	2 ♑	1 ♒
4 ♌	4 ♎	4 ⚷	3 ♐	4 ♒	3 ♓
6 ♍	6 ♏	6 ♐	5 ♑	6 ♓	5 ♈
7 ♎	8 ⚷	8 ♑	7 ♒	8 ♈	7 ↝
9 ♏	10 ♐	10 ♒	9 ♓	10 ↝	8 ♉
11 ⚷	12 ♑	12 ♓	11 ♈	12 ♉	10 ♊
13 ♐	13 ♒	14 ♈	13 ↝	14 ♊	12 ♋
15 ♑	15 ♓	16 ↝	15 ♉	16 ♋	14 ♌
17 ♒	17 ♈	18 ♉	17 ♊	18 ♌	16 ♍
19 ♓	19 ↝	20 ♊	19 ♋	20 ♍	18 ♎
21 ♈	21 ♉	22 ♋	21 ♌	22 ♎	20 ♏
23 ↝	23 ♊	23 ♌	23 ♍	24 ♏	22 ⚷
25 ♉	25 ♋	25 ♍	25 ♎	25 ⚷	24 ♐
27 ♊	27 ♌	27 ♎	27 ♏	27 ♐	26 ♑
29 ♋	29 ♍	29 ♏	29 ⚷	29 ♑	28 ♒
31 ♌	31 ♎		31 ♐		30 ♓

TABLE 4 165

1928

January	February	March	April	May	June
1 ♈	1 ♉	2 ♊	2 ♌	1 ♍	2 ♏
3 ♈	3 ♊	4 ♋	4 ♍	3 ♎	4 ♐
5 ♉	5 ♋	6 ♌	6 ♎	5 ♏	6 ♐
7 ♊	7 ♌	8 ♍	8 ♏	7 ♐	7 ♑
9 ♋	9 ♍	9 ♎	10 ♐	9 ♐	9 ♒
11 ♌	11 ♎	11 ♏	12 ♐	11 ♑	11 ♓
13 ♍	13 ♏	13 ♐	14 ♑	13 ♒	13 ♈
15 ♎	15 ♐	15 ♐	16 ♒	15 ♓	15 ♈
17 ♏	17 ♐	17 ♑	18 ♓	17 ♈	17 ♉
19 ♐	19 ♑	19 ♒	20 ♈	19 ♈	19 ♊
21 ♐	21 ♒	21 ♓	22 ♈	21 ♉	21 ♋
23 ♑	23 ♓	23 ♈	24 ♉	23 ♊	23 ♌
25 ♒	25 ♈	25 ♈	26 ♊	25 ♋	25 ♍
27 ♓	27 ♈	27 ♉	27 ♋	27 ♌	27 ♎
28 ♈	29 ♉	29 ♊	29 ♌	29 ♍	29 ♏
30 ♈		31 ♋		31 ♎	

July	August	September	October	November	December
1 ♐	1 ♑	1 ♓	1 ♈	1 ♉	2 ♋
3 ♐	3 ♒	3 ♈	3 ♈	3 ♊	4 ♌
5 ♑	5 ♓	5 ♈	4 ♉	5 ♋	6 ♍
7 ♒	7 ♈	7 ♉	6 ♊	7 ♌	8 ♎
9 ♓	9 ♈	9 ♊	8 ♋	9 ♍	10 ♏
10 ♈	11 ♉	11 ♋	10 ♌	11 ♎	12 ♐
12 ♈	13 ♊	13 ♌	12 ♍	13 ♏	14 ♐
14 ♉	15 ♋	15 ♍	14 ♎	14 ♐	16 ♑
16 ♊	17 ♌	17 ♎	16 ♏	16 ♐	18 ♒
18 ♋	19 ♍	19 ♏	18 ♐	18 ♑	20 ♓
20 ♌	20 ♎	21 ♐	20 ♐	20 ♒	22 ♈
22 ♍	22 ♏	23 ♐	22 ♑	22 ♓	24 ♈
24 ♎	24 ♐	25 ♑	24 ♒	24 ♈	26 ♉
26 ♏	26 ♐	27 ♒	26 ♓	26 ♈	28 ♊
28 ♐	28 ♑	29 ♓	28 ♈	28 ♉	30 ♋
30 ♐	30 ♒		30 ♈	30 ♊	31 ♌

1929

January	February	March	April	May	June
2 ♍	1 ♎	2 ♏	2 ♐	1 ♑	2 ♓
4 ♎	3 ♏	4 ⛎	4 ♑	3 ♒	4 ♈
6 ♏	5 ⛎	6 ♐	6 ♒	5 ♓	6 Ↄ
8 ⛎	7 ♐	8 ♑	8 ♓	7 ♈	8 ♉
10 ♐	9 ♑	10 ♒	10 ♈	9 Ↄ	10 ♊
12 ♑	10 ♒	12 ♓	12 Ↄ	11 ♉	12 ♋
14 ♒	12 ♓	14 ♈	14 ♉	13 ♊	14 ♌
16 ♓	14 ♈	16 Ↄ	16 ♊	15 ♋	15 ♍
18 ♈	16 Ↄ	17 ♉	18 ♋	17 ♌	17 ♎
20 Ↄ	18 ♉	19 ♊	20 ♌	19 ♍	19 ♏
22 ♉	20 ♊	21 ♋	22 ♍	21 ♎	21 ⛎
24 ♊	22 ♋	23 ♌	24 ♎	23 ♏	23 ♐
26 ♋	24 ♌	25 ♍	26 ♏	25 ⛎	25 ♑
28 ♌	26 ♍	27 ♎	27 ⛎	27 ♐	27 ♒
30 ♍	28 ♎	29 ♏	29 ♐	29 ♑	29 ♓
		31 ⛎		31 ♒	

July	August	September	October	November	December
1 ♈	1 ♉	2 ♋	1 ♌	1 ♎	2 ⛎
3 Ↄ	3 ♊	4 ♌	3 ♍	3 ♏	4 ♐
4 ♉	5 ♋	6 ♍	4 ♎	5 ⛎	6 ♑
6 ♊	7 ♌	8 ♎	6 ♏	7 ♐	8 ♒
8 ♋	9 ♍	10 ♏	8 ⛎	9 ♑	10 ♓
10 ♌	11 ♎	11 ⛎	10 ♐	11 ♒	12 ♈
12 ♍	13 ♏	13 ♐	12 ♑	13 ♓	14 Ↄ
14 ♎	15 ⛎	15 ♑	14 ♒	14 ♈	16 ♉
16 ♏	17 ♐	17 ♒	16 ♓	16 Ↄ	17 ♊
18 ⛎	19 ♑	19 ♓	18 ♈	18 ♉	19 ♋
20 ♐	21 ♒	21 ♈	20 Ↄ	20 ♊	21 ♌
22 ♑	23 ♓	23 Ↄ	22 ♉	22 ♋	23 ♍
24 ♒	25 ♈	25 ♉	24 ♊	24 ♌	25 ♎
26 ♓	27 Ↄ	27 ♊	26 ♋	26 ♍	27 ♏
28 ♈	29 ♉	29 ♋	28 ♌	28 ♎	29 ⛎
30 Ↄ	31 ♊		30 ♍	30 ♏	31 ♐

TABLE 4 167

1930

January	February	March	April	May	June
2 ♑	1 ♒	2 ♓	1 ♈	1 ♉	2 ♋
4 ♒	3 ♓	4 ♈	3 ♉	3 ♊	4 ♌
6 ♓	5 ♈	6 ♈	5 ♊	5 ♋	6 ♍
8 ♈	7 ♈	8 ♉	7 ♋	7 ♌	8 ♎
10 ♈	9 ♉	10 ♊	9 ♌	9 ♍	10 ♏
12 ♉	11 ♊	12 ♋	11 ♍	11 ♎	12 ♐
14 ♊	13 ♋	14 ♌	13 ♎	13 ♏	14 ♐
16 ♋	15 ♌	16 ♍	15 ♏	15 ♐	15 ♑
18 ♌	17 ♍	17 ♎	17 ♐	17 ♐	17 ♒
20 ♍	19 ♎	19 ♏	19 ♐	19 ♑	19 ♓
22 ♎	21 ♏	21 ♐	21 ♑	21 ♒	21 ♈
24 ♏	23 ♐	23 ♐	23 ♒	23 ♓	23 ♈
26 ♐	24 ♐	25 ♑	25 ♓	25 ♈	25 ♉
28 ♐	26 ♑	27 ♒	27 ♈	27 ♈	27 ♊
30 ♑	28 ♒	29 ♓	29 ♈	29 ♉	29 ♋
		30 ♈		31 ♊	

July	August	September	October	November	December
1 ♌	1 ♎	1 ♐	2 ♑	2 ♓	2 ♈
3 ♍	3 ♏	3 ♐	4 ♒	4 ♈	4 ♈
5 ♎	5 ♐	5 ♑	6 ♓	6 ♈	6 ♉
6 ♏	7 ♐	7 ♒	8 ♈	8 ♉	8 ♊
8 ♐	9 ♑	9 ♓	10 ♈	10 ♊	10 ♋
10 ♐	11 ♒	11 ♈	12 ♉	12 ♋	11 ♌
12 ♑	13 ♓	13 ♈	14 ♊	14 ♌	13 ♍
14 ♒	15 ♈	15 ♉	16 ♋	16 ♍	15 ♎
16 ♓	16 ♈	17 ♊	18 ♌	18 ♎	17 ♏
18 ♈	18 ♉	18 ♋	20 ♍	20 ♏	19 ♐
20 ♈	20 ♊	20 ♌	22 ♎	22 ♐	21 ♐
22 ♉	22 ♋	22 ♍	24 ♏	24 ♐	23 ♑
24 ♊	24 ♌	24 ♎	26 ♐	26 ♑	25 ♒
26 ♋	26 ♍	26 ♏	28 ♐	28 ♒	27 ♓
28 ♌	28 ♎	28 ♐	30 ♑	30 ♓	29 ♈
30 ♍	30 ♏	30 ♐	31 ♒		31 ♈

1931

January		February		March		April		May		June	
2	♉	2	♋	2	♋	2	♍	1	♎	1	⛎
4	♊	4	♌	3	♌	4	♎	3	♏	3	♐
6	♋	6	♍	5	♍	5	♏	5	⛎	5	♑
8	♌	8	♎	7	♎	7	⛎	7	♐	7	♒
10	♍	10	♏	9	♏	9	♐	9	♑	9	♓
12	♎	12	⛎	11	⛎	11	♑	11	♒	11	♈
14	♏	14	♐	13	♐	13	♒	13	♓	13	ↄ
16	⛎	16	♑	15	♑	15	♓	15	♈	15	♉
18	♐	18	♒	17	♒	17	♈	16	ↄ	17	♊
20	♑	20	♓	19	♓	19	ↄ	18	♉	18	♋
21	♒	22	♈	21	♈	21	♉	20	♊	20	♌
23	♓	24	ↄ	23	ↄ	23	♊	22	♋	22	♍
25	♈	26	♉	25	♉	25	♋	24	♌	24	♎
27	ↄ	28	♊	27	♊	27	♌	26	♍	26	♏
29	♉			29	♋	29	♍	28	♎	28	⛎
31	♊			31	♌			30	♏	30	♐

July		August		September		October		November		December	
2	♑	1	♒	1	♈	2	♉	2	♋	1	♌
4	♒	3	♓	3	ↄ	4	♊	4	♌	3	♍
6	♓	5	♈	5	♉	5	♋	6	♍	5	♎
8	♈	7	ↄ	7	♊	7	♌	8	♎	7	♏
10	ↄ	9	♉	9	♋	9	♍	10	♏	9	⛎
12	♉	11	♊	11	♌	11	♎	12	⛎	11	♐
14	♊	13	♋	13	♍	13	♏	14	♐	13	♑
16	♋	15	♌	14	♎	15	⛎	16	♑	15	♒
18	♌	17	♍	16	♏	17	♐	18	♒	17	♓
20	♍	19	♎	18	⛎	19	♑	20	♓	19	♈
22	♎	21	♏	20	♐	21	♒	21	♈	21	ↄ
24	♏	23	⛎	22	♑	23	♓	23	ↄ	23	♉
26	⛎	25	♐	24	♒	25	♈	25	♉	25	♊
28	♐	26	♑	26	♓	27	ↄ	27	♊	27	♋
30	♑	28	♒	28	♈	29	♉	29	♋	29	♌
		30	♓	30	ↄ	31	♊			31	♍

TABLE 4 169

1932

January	February	March	April	May	June
2 ♎	2 ⛎	2 ♐	2 ♒	1 ♓	2 ☋
4 ♏	4 ♐	4 ♑	4 ♓	3 ♈	4 ♉
6 ⛎	6 ♑	6 ♒	6 ♈	5 ☋	6 ♊
8 ♐	8 ♒	8 ♓	8 ☋	7 ♉	8 ♋
9 ♑	10 ♓	9 ♈	10 ♉	9 ♊	10 ♌
11 ♒	12 ♈	11 ☋	12 ♊	11 ♋	12 ♍
13 ♓	14 ☋	13 ♉	14 ♋	13 ♌	14 ♎
15 ♈	16 ♉	15 ♊	16 ♌	15 ♍	16 ♏
17 ☋	18 ♊	17 ♋	18 ♍	17 ♎	17 ⛎
19 ♉	19 ♋	19 ♌	19 ♎	19 ♏	19 ♐
21 ♊	21 ♌	21 ♍	21 ♏	21 ⛎	21 ♑
23 ♋	23 ♍	23 ♎	23 ⛎	23 ♐	23 ♒
25 ♌	25 ♎	25 ♏	25 ♐	25 ♑	25 ♓
27 ♍	27 ♏	27 ⛎	27 ♑	27 ♒	27 ♈
29 ♎	29 ⛎	29 ♐	29 ♒	29 ♓	29 ☋
31 ♏		31 ♑		31 ♈	

July	August	September	October	November	December
1 ♉	1 ♋	2 ♍	1 ♎	1 ⛎	2 ♑
2 ♊	3 ♌	4 ♎	3 ♏	3 ♐	4 ♒
4 ♋	5 ♍	6 ♏	4 ⛎	5 ♑	6 ♓
6 ♌	7 ♎	8 ⛎	6 ♐	7 ♒	7 ♈
8 ♍	9 ♏	10 ♐	8 ♑	9 ♓	9 ☋
10 ♎	11 ⛎	11 ♑	10 ♒	11 ♈	11 ♉
12 ♏	13 ♐	13 ♒	12 ♓	13 ☋	13 ♊
14 ⛎	15 ♑	15 ♓	14 ♈	14 ♉	15 ♋
16 ♐	17 ♒	17 ♈	16 ☋	16 ♊	17 ♌
18 ♑	19 ♓	19 ☋	18 ♉	18 ♋	19 ♍
20 ♒	21 ♈	21 ♉	20 ♊	20 ♌	21 ♎
22 ♓	23 ☋	23 ♊	22 ♋	22 ♍	23 ♏
24 ♈	25 ♉	25 ♋	24 ♌	24 ♎	25 ⛎
26 ☋	27 ♊	27 ♌	26 ♍	26 ♏	27 ♐
28 ♉	29 ♋	29 ♍	28 ♎	28 ⛎	29 ♑
30 ♊	31 ♌		30 ♏	30 ♐	31 ♒

1933

January		February		March		April		May		June	
2	♓	1	♈	2	⌐	2	♊	2	♋	2	♍
4	♈	3	⌐	4	♉	4	♋	4	♌	4	♎
6	⌐	5	♉	6	♊	6	♌	6	♍	6	♏
8	♉	7	♊	8	♋	8	♍	8	♎	8	⊬
10	♊	8	♋	10	♌	10	♎	9	♏	9	♐
12	♋	10	♌	11	♍	12	♏	11	⊬	11	♑
14	♌	12	♍	13	♎	14	⊬	13	♐	13	♒
16	♍	14	♎	15	♏	16	♐	15	♑	15	♓
18	♎	16	♏	17	⊬	18	♑	17	♒	17	♈
20	♏	18	⊬	19	♐	20	♒	19	♓	19	⌐
22	⊬	20	♐	21	♑	22	♓	21	♈	21	♉
24	♐	22	♑	23	♒	24	♈	23	⌐	23	♊
26	♑	24	♒	25	♓	26	⌐	25	♉	25	♋
28	♒	26	♓	27	♈	28	♉	27	♊	27	♌
30	♓	28	♈	29	⌐	30	♊	29	♋	29	♍
				31	♉			31	♌		

July		August		September		October		November		December	
1	♎	1	⊬	1	♑	2	♓	1	♈	2	♉
3	♏	3	♐	3	♒	4	♈	3	⌐	4	♊
5	⊬	5	♑	5	♓	6	⌐	5	♉	6	♋
7	♐	7	♒	7	♈	8	♉	7	♊	8	♌
9	♑	9	♓	9	⌐	10	♊	8	♋	9	♍
10	♒	10	♈	10	♉	12	♋	10	♌	11	♎
12	♓	12	⌐	12	♊	14	♌	12	♍	13	♏
14	♈	14	♉	14	♋	16	♍	14	♎	15	⊬
16	⌐	16	♊	16	♌	18	♎	16	♏	17	♐
18	♉	18	♋	18	♍	20	♏	18	⊬	19	♑
20	♊	20	♌	20	♎	22	⊬	20	♐	21	♒
22	♋	22	♍	22	♏	24	♐	22	♑	23	♓
24	♌	24	♎	24	⊬	26	♑	24	♒	25	♈
26	♍	26	♏	26	♐	28	♒	26	♓	27	⌐
28	♎	28	⊬	28	♑	30	♓	28	♈	29	♉
30	♏	30	♐	30	♒			30	⌐	31	♊

TABLE 4 171

1934

January	February	March	April	May	June
2 ♋	1 ♌	2 ♍	2 ♏	2 ♐	2 ♑
4 ♌	3 ♍	4 ♎	4 ♐	4 ♐	4 ♒
6 ♍	4 ♎	6 ♏	6 ♐	5 ♑	5 ♓
8 ♎	6 ♏	7 ♐	8 ♑	7 ♒	7 ♈
10 ♏	8 ♐	9 ♐	10 ♒	9 ♓	9 ♈
12 ♐	10 ♐	11 ♑	12 ♓	11 ♈	11 ♉
14 ♐	12 ♑	13 ♒	14 ♈	13 ♈	13 ♊
16 ♑	14 ♒	15 ♓	16 ♈	15 ♉	15 ♋
18 ♒	16 ♓	17 ♈	18 ♉	17 ♊	17 ♌
20 ♓	18 ♈	19 ♈	20 ♊	19 ♋	19 ♍
22 ♈	20 ♈	21 ♉	22 ♋	21 ♌	21 ♎
24 ♈	22 ♉	23 ♊	24 ♌	23 ♍	23 ♏
26 ♉	24 ♊	25 ♋	26 ♍	25 ♎	25 ♐
28 ♊	26 ♋	27 ♌	28 ♎	27 ♏	27 ♐
30 ♋	28 ♌	29 ♍	30 ♏	29 ♐	29 ♑
		31 ♎		31 ♐	

July	August	September	October	November	December
1 ♒	1 ♈	1 ♉	1 ♊	1 ♌	2 ♎
3 ♓	3 ♈	3 ♊	3 ♋	3 ♍	4 ♏
5 ♈	5 ♉	5 ♋	4 ♌	4 ♎	6 ♐
6 ♈	6 ♊	7 ♌	6 ♍	6 ♏	8 ♐
8 ♉	8 ♋	9 ♍	8 ♎	8 ♐	10 ♑
10 ♊	10 ♌	11 ♎	10 ♏	10 ♐	12 ♒
12 ♋	12 ♍	13 ♏	12 ♐	12 ♑	14 ♓
14 ♌	14 ♎	15 ♐	14 ♐	14 ♒	16 ♈
16 ♍	16 ♏	17 ♐	16 ♑	16 ♓	18 ♈
18 ♎	18 ♐	19 ♑	18 ♒	18 ♈	20 ♉
20 ♏	20 ♐	21 ♒	20 ♓	20 ♈	22 ♊
22 ♐	22 ♑	23 ♓	22 ♈	22 ♉	24 ♋
24 ♐	24 ♒	25 ♈	24 ♈	24 ♊	26 ♌
26 ♑	26 ♓	27 ♈	26 ♉	26 ♋	28 ♍
28 ♒	28 ♈	29 ♉	28 ♊	28 ♌	30 ♎
30 ♓	30 ♈		30 ♋	30 ♍	

1935

January		February		March		April		May		June	
1	♏	1	♐	2	♑	2	♓	1	♈	1	♉
2	⛎	2	♑	4	♒	4	♈	3	⟿	3	♊
4	♐	4	♒	6	♓	6	⟿	5	♉	5	♋
6	♑	6	♓	8	♈	8	♉	7	♊	7	♌
8	♒	8	♈	10	⟿	10	♊	9	♋	9	♍
10	♓	10	⟿	12	♉	12	♋	11	♌	11	♎
12	♈	12	♉	14	♊	14	♌	13	♍	13	♏
14	⟿	14	♊	16	♋	16	♍	15	♎	15	⛎
16	♉	16	♋	18	♌	18	♎	17	♏	17	♐
18	♊	18	♌	20	♍	20	♏	19	⛎	19	♑
20	♋	20	♍	22	♎	22	⛎	21	♐	21	♒
22	♌	22	♎	24	♏	24	♐	23	♑	23	♓
24	♍	24	♏	26	⛎	26	♑	25	♒	25	♈
26	♎	26	⛎	28	♐	28	♒	27	♓	27	⟿
28	♏	28	♐	30	♑	30	♓	29	♈	29	♉
30	⛎			31	♒			31	⟿		

July		August		September		October		November		December	
1	♊	1	♌	1	♎	1	♏	1	♐	2	♒
2	♋	3	♍	3	♏	3	⛎	3	♑	4	♓
4	♌	5	♎	5	⛎	5	♐	5	♒	6	♈
6	♍	7	♏	7	♐	7	♑	7	♓	8	⟿
8	♎	9	⛎	9	♑	9	♒	9	♈	10	♉
10	♏	11	♐	11	♒	11	♓	11	⟿	12	♊
12	⛎	13	♑	13	♓	13	♈	13	♉	14	♋
14	♐	15	♒	15	♈	15	⟿	15	♊	16	♌
16	♑	17	♓	17	⟿	17	♉	17	♋	18	♍
18	♒	19	♈	19	♉	19	♊	19	♌	20	♎
20	♓	21	⟿	21	♊	21	♋	21	♍	22	♏
22	♈	23	♉	23	♋	23	♌	23	♎	24	⛎
24	⟿	25	♊	25	♌	25	♍	25	♏	26	♐
26	♉	27	♋	27	♍	27	♎	27	⛎	28	♑
28	♊	29	♌	29	♎	28	♏	28	♐	29	♒
30	♋	30	♍			30	⛎	30	♑	31	♓

TABLE 4 173

1936

January	February	March	April	May	June
2 ♈	2 ♉	1 ♉	1 ♋	2 ♍	1 ♎
4 ♈	4 ♊	3 ♊	3 ♌	4 ♎	3 ♏
6 ♉	6 ♋	5 ♋	5 ♍	6 ♏	5 ♐
8 ♊	8 ♌	7 ♌	7 ♎	8 ♐	7 ♐
10 ♋	10 ♍	9 ♍	9 ♏	10 ♐	9 ♑
12 ♌	12 ♎	11 ♎	11 ♐	12 ♑	11 ♒
14 ♍	14 ♏	13 ♏	13 ♐	14 ♒	13 ♓
16 ♎	16 ♐	15 ♐	15 ♑	16 ♓	15 ♈
18 ♏	18 ♐	17 ♐	17 ♒	18 ♈	17 ♈
20 ♐	20 ♑	19 ♑	19 ♓	20 ♈	19 ♉
22 ♐	22 ♒	21 ♒	21 ♈	22 ♉	21 ♊
24 ♑	24 ♓	23 ♓	23 ♈	24 ♊	23 ♋
26 ♒	26 ♈	25 ♈	25 ♉	26 ♋	25 ♌
28 ♓	28 ♈	27 ♈	27 ♊	28 ♌	26 ♍
29 ♈		28 ♉	28 ♋	30 ♍	28 ♎
31 ♈		30 ♊	30 ♌		30 ♏

July	August	September	October	November	December
2 ♐	2 ♑	2 ♓	2 ♈	2 ♉	1 ♊
4 ♐	4 ♒	4 ♈	4 ♈	4 ♊	3 ♋
6 ♑	6 ♓	6 ♈	6 ♉	6 ♋	5 ♌
8 ♒	8 ♈	8 ♉	8 ♊	8 ♌	7 ♍
10 ♓	10 ♈	10 ♊	10 ♋	10 ♍	9 ♎
12 ♈	12 ♉	12 ♋	12 ♌	12 ♎	11 ♏
14 ♈	14 ♊	14 ♌	14 ♍	14 ♏	13 ♐
16 ♉	16 ♋	16 ♍	16 ♎	16 ♐	15 ♐
18 ♊	18 ♌	18 ♎	18 ♏	18 ♐	17 ♑
20 ♋	20 ♍	20 ♏	20 ♐	20 ♑	19 ♒
22 ♌	22 ♎	22 ♐	22 ♐	22 ♒	21 ♓
24 ♍	24 ♏	24 ♐	24 ♑	24 ♓	23 ♈
26 ♎	26 ♐	26 ♑	25 ♒	25 ♈	25 ♈
27 ♏	27 ♐	28 ♒	27 ♓	27 ♈	26 ♉
29 ♐	29 ♑	30 ♓	29 ♈	29 ♉	28 ♊
31 ♐	31 ♒		31 ♈		30 ♋

1937

January	February	March	April	May	June
1 ♌	2 ♎	1 ♎	1 ⛎	1 ♐	1 ♒
3 ♍	4 ♏	3 ♏	3 ♐	3 ♑	3 ♓
5 ♎	6 ⛎	5 ⛎	5 ♑	5 ♒	5 ♈
7 ♏	8 ♐	7 ♐	7 ♒	7 ♓	7 Cetus
9 ⛎	10 ♑	9 ♑	9 ♓	9 ♈	9 ♉
11 ♐	12 ♒	11 ♒	11 ♈	11 Cetus	11 ♊
13 ♑	14 ♓	13 ♓	13 Cetus	13 ♉	13 ♋
15 ♒	16 ♈	15 ♈	15 ♉	15 ♊	15 ♌
17 ♓	18 Cetus	17 Cetus	17 ♊	17 ♋	17 ♍
19 ♈	20 ♉	19 ♉	19 ♋	19 ♌	19 ♎
21 Cetus	22 ♊	21 ♊	21 ♌	21 ♍	21 ♏
23 ♉	23 ♋	23 ♋	23 ♍	23 ♎	23 ⛎
25 ♊	25 ♌	25 ♌	25 ♎	24 ♏	24 ♐
27 ♋	27 ♍	26 ♍	27 ♏	26 ⛎	26 ♑
29 ♌		28 ♎	29 ⛎	28 ♐	28 ♒
31 ♍		30 ♏		30 ♑	30 ♓

July	August	September	October	November	December
2 ♈	1 Cetus	1 ♊	2 ♌	1 ♍	2 ♏
4 Cetus	3 ♉	3 ♋	4 ♍	3 ♎	4 ⛎
6 ♉	5 ♊	5 ♌	6 ♎	5 ♏	6 ♐
8 ♊	7 ♋	7 ♍	8 ♏	6 ⛎	7 ♑
10 ♋	9 ♌	8 ♎	10 ⛎	8 ♐	9 ♒
12 ♌	11 ♍	10 ♏	12 ♐	10 ♑	11 ♓
14 ♍	13 ♎	12 ⛎	14 ♑	12 ♒	13 ♈
16 ♎	15 ♏	14 ♐	16 ♒	14 ♓	15 Cetus
18 ♏	17 ⛎	16 ♑	18 ♓	16 ♈	17 ♉
20 ⛎	19 ♐	18 ♒	20 ♈	18 Cetus	19 ♊
22 ♐	21 ♑	20 ♓	22 Cetus	20 ♉	21 ♋
24 ♑	22 ♒	22 ♈	24 ♉	22 ♊	23 ♌
26 ♒	24 ♓	24 Cetus	26 ♊	24 ♋	25 ♍
28 ♓	26 ♈	26 ♉	28 ♋	26 ♌	27 ♎
30 ♈	28 Cetus	28 ♊	30 ♌	28 ♍	29 ♏
	30 ♉	30 ♋		30 ♎	31 ⛎

TABLE 4 175

1938

January		February		March		April		May		June	
2	♐	2	♒	1	♒	2	♈	1	♈	1	♊
4	♑	4	♓	3	♓	4	♈	3	♉	3	♋
6	♒	6	♈	5	♈	6	♉	5	♊	5	♌
8	♓	8	♈	7	♈	8	♊	7	♋	7	♍
9	♈	9	♉	9	♉	9	♋	9	♌	9	♎
11	♈	11	♊	11	♊	11	♌	10	♍	11	♏
13	♉	13	♋	13	♋	13	♍	12	♎	13	♏
15	♊	15	♌	15	♌	15	♎	14	♏	15	♐
17	♋	17	♍	17	♍	17	♏	16	♏	17	♑
19	♌	19	♎	19	♎	19	♏	18	♐	19	♒
21	♍	21	♏	21	♏	21	♐	20	♑	21	♓
23	♎	23	♏	23	♏	23	♑	22	♒	23	♈
25	♏	25	♐	25	♐	25	♒	24	♓	25	♈
27	♏	27	♑	27	♑	27	♓	26	♈	27	♉
29	♐			29	♒	29	♈	28	♈	29	♊
31	♑			31	♓			30	♉		

July		August		September		October		November		December	
1	♋	1	♍	1	♏	2	♐	2	♒	1	♓
3	♌	3	♎	3	♏	4	♑	4	♓	3	♈
5	♍	5	♏	5	♐	6	♒	6	♈	5	♈
7	♎	7	♏	7	♑	8	♓	8	♈	7	♉
8	♏	8	♐	8	♒	9	♈	9	♉	9	♊
10	♏	10	♑	10	♓	11	♈	11	♊	11	♋
12	♐	12	♒	12	♈	13	♉	13	♋	13	♌
14	♑	14	♓	14	♈	15	♊	15	♌	15	♍
16	♒	16	♈	16	♉	17	♋	17	♍	17	♎
18	♓	18	♈	18	♊	19	♌	19	♎	19	♏
20	♈	20	♉	20	♋	21	♍	21	♏	21	♏
22	♈	22	♊	22	♌	23	♎	23	♏	23	♐
24	♉	24	♋	24	♍	25	♏	25	♐	25	♑
26	♊	26	♌	26	♎	27	♏	27	♑	27	♒
28	♋	28	♍	28	♏	29	♐	29	♒	29	♓
30	♌	30	♎	30	♐	31	♑			31	♈

1939

January		February		March		April		May		June	
2	♎	2	♊	1	♊	2	♌	1	♍	1	♏
4	♉	4	♋	3	♋	4	♍	3	♎	3	✝
6	♊	6	♌	5	♌	6	♎	5	♏	5	♐
7	♋	7	♍	7	♍	7	♏	7	✝	7	♑
9	♌	9	♎	9	♎	9	✝	8	♐	9	♒
11	♍	11	♏	11	♏	11	♐	10	♑	11	♓
13	♎	13	✝	13	✝	13	♑	12	♒	13	♈
15	♏	15	♐	15	♐	15	♒	14	♓	15	♎
17	✝	17	♑	17	♑	17	♓	16	♈	17	♉
19	♐	19	♒	19	♒	19	♈	18	♎	19	♊
21	♑	21	♓	21	♓	21	♎	20	♉	21	♋
23	♒	23	♈	23	♈	23	♉	22	♊	23	♌
25	♓	25	♎	25	♎	25	♊	24	♋	25	♍
27	♈	27	♉	27	♉	27	♋	26	♌	27	♎
29	♎			29	♊	29	♌	28	♍	29	♏
31	♉			31	♋			30	♎	30	✝

July		August		September		October		November		December	
2	♐	2	♒	2	♈	2	♎	2	♊	1	♋
4	♑	4	♓	4	♎	3	♉	3	♋	3	♌
6	♒	5	♈	6	♉	5	♊	5	♌	5	♍
8	♓	7	♎	8	♊	7	♋	7	♍	7	♎
10	♈	9	♉	10	♋	9	♌	9	♎	9	♏
12	♎	11	♊	12	♌	11	♍	11	♏	11	✝
14	♉	13	♋	14	♍	13	♎	13	✝	13	♐
16	♊	15	♌	16	♎	15	♏	15	♐	15	♑
18	♋	17	♍	18	♏	17	✝	17	♑	17	♒
20	♌	19	♎	20	✝	19	♐	19	♒	19	♓
22	♍	21	♏	22	♐	21	♑	21	♓	21	♈
24	♎	23	✝	24	♑	23	♒	23	♈	23	♎
26	♏	25	♐	26	♒	25	♓	25	♎	25	♉
28	✝	27	♑	28	♓	27	♈	27	♉	27	♊
30	♐	29	♒	30	♈	29	♎	29	♊	29	♋
31	♑	31	♓			31	♉			31	♌

TABLE 4 177

1940

January	February	March	April	May	June
1 ♍	1 ♏	2 ♐	2 ♑	1 ♒	1 ♈
3 ♎	3 ♐	4 ♐	4 ♒	3 ♓	3 ♈
5 ♏	5 ♐	6 ♑	6 ♓	4 ♈	5 ♉
7 ♐	7 ♑	8 ♒	8 ♈	6 ♈	7 ♊
9 ♐	9 ♒	10 ♓	10 ♈	8 ♉	9 ♋
11 ♑	11 ♓	12 ♈	12 ♉	10 ♊	11 ♌
13 ♒	13 ♈	14 ♈	14 ♊	12 ♋	13 ♍
15 ♓	15 ♈	16 ♉	16 ♋	14 ♌	15 ♎
17 ♈	17 ♉	18 ♊	18 ♌	16 ♍	17 ♏
19 ♈	19 ♊	20 ♋	20 ♍	18 ♎	19 ♐
21 ♉	21 ♋	22 ♌	22 ♎	20 ♏	21 ♐
23 ♊	23 ♌	24 ♍	24 ♏	22 ♐	23 ♑
25 ♋	25 ♍	26 ♎	26 ♐	24 ♐	25 ♒
27 ♌	27 ♎	28 ♏	28 ♐	26 ♑	27 ♓
29 ♍	29 ♏	30 ♐	30 ♑	28 ♒	29 ♈
31 ♎		31 ♐		30 ♓	

July	August	September	October	November	December
1 ♈	1 ♊	1 ♌	1 ♍	1 ♏	2 ♐
2 ♉	2 ♋	3 ♍	2 ♎	2 ♐	3 ♑
4 ♊	4 ♌	5 ♎	4 ♏	4 ♐	5 ♒
6 ♋	6 ♍	7 ♏	6 ♐	6 ♑	7 ♓
8 ♌	8 ♎	9 ♐	8 ♐	8 ♒	9 ♈
10 ♍	10 ♏	11 ♐	10 ♑	10 ♓	11 ♈
12 ♎	12 ♐	13 ♑	12 ♒	12 ♈	13 ♉
14 ♏	14 ♐	15 ♒	14 ♓	14 ♈	15 ♊
16 ♐	16 ♑	17 ♓	16 ♈	16 ♉	17 ♋
18 ♐	18 ♒	19 ♈	18 ♈	18 ♊	19 ♌
20 ♑	20 ♓	21 ♈	20 ♉	20 ♋	21 ♍
22 ♒	22 ♈	23 ♉	22 ♊	22 ♌	23 ♎
24 ♓	24 ♈	25 ♊	24 ♋	24 ♍	25 ♏
26 ♈	26 ♉	27 ♋	26 ♌	26 ♎	27 ♐
28 ♈	28 ♊	29 ♌	28 ♍	28 ♏	29 ♐
30 ♉	30 ♋		30 ♎	30 ♐	31 ♑

1941

January		February		March		April		May		June	
2	♒	2	♈	1	♈	1	♉	2	♋	1	♌
4	♓	4	⌐	3	⌐	3	♊	4	♌	3	♍
6	♈	6	♉	5	♉	5	♋	6	♍	5	♎
8	⌐	8	♊	7	♊	7	♌	8	♎	7	♏
10	♉	10	♋	9	♋	9	♍	10	♏	9	⛎
12	♊	12	♌	11	♌	11	♎	12	⛎	11	♐
14	♋	14	♍	13	♍	13	♏	14	♐	13	♑
16	♌	16	♎	15	♎	15	⛎	16	♑	15	♒
18	♍	18	♏	17	♏	17	♐	18	♒	17	♓
20	♎	20	⛎	10	⛎	19	♑	20	♓	19	♈
22	♏	22	♐	21	♐	21	♒	22	♈	21	⌐
24	⛎	24	♑	23	♑	23	♓	24	⌐	22	♉
26	♐	26	♒	25	♒	25	♈	26	♉	24	♊
28	♑	27	♓	27	♓	26	⌐	28	♊	26	♋
29	♒			28	♈	28	♉	30	♋	28	♌
31	♓			30	⌐	30	♊			30	♍

July		August		September		October		November		December	
2	♎	2	⛎	1	♐	2	♒	2	♈	1	⌐
4	♏	4	♐	3	♑	4	♓	4	⌐	3	♉
6	⛎	6	♑	5	♒	6	♈	6	♉	5	♊
8	♐	8	♒	7	♓	8	⌐	8	♊	7	♋
10	♑	10	♓	9	♈	10	♉	10	♋	9	♌
12	♒	12	♈	11	⌐	12	♊	12	♌	11	♍
14	♓	14	⌐	13	♉	14	♋	13	♍	13	♎
16	♈	16	♉	15	♊	15	♌	15	♎	15	♏
18	⌐	18	♊	16	♋	17	♍	17	♏	17	⛎
20	♉	20	♋	18	♌	19	♎	19	⛎	19	♐
21	♊	22	♌	20	♍	21	♏	21	♐	21	♑
23	♋	24	♍	22	♎	23	⛎	23	♑	23	♒
25	♌	26	♎	24	♏	25	♐	25	♒	25	♓
27	♍	28	♏	26	⛎	27	♑	27	♓	27	♈
29	♎	30	⛎	28	♐	29	♒	29	♈	29	⌐
31	♏			30	♑	31	♓			31	♉

TABLE 4 179

1942

January		February		March		April		May		June	
2	♊	2	♌	1	♌	2	♎	1	♏	1	♐
4	♋	4	♍	3	♍	4	♏	3	♐	3	♑
6	♌	6	♎	5	♎	5	♐	4	♐	5	♒
8	♍	7	♏	7	♏	7	♐	6	♑	7	♓
9	♎	9	♐	9	♐	9	♑	8	♒	9	♈
11	♏	11	♐	11	♐	11	♒	10	♓	11	♈
13	♐	13	♑	13	♑	13	♓	12	♈	13	♉
15	♐	15	♒	15	♒	15	♈	14	♈	15	♊
17	♑	17	♓	17	♓	17	♈	16	♉	17	♋
19	♒	19	♈	19	♈	19	♉	18	♊	19	♌
21	♓	21	♈	21	♈	21	♊	20	♋	21	♍
23	♈	23	♉	23	♉	23	♋	22	♌	23	♎
25	♈	25	♊	25	♊	25	♌	24	♍	25	♏
27	♉	27	♋	27	♋	27	♍	26	♎	27	♐
29	♊			29	♌	29	♎	28	♏	29	♐
31	♋			31	♍			30	♐	30	♑

July		August		September		October		November		December	
2	♒	2	♈	1	♈	1	♊	2	♌	1	♍
4	♓	4	♈	3	♉	3	♋	4	♍	3	♎
6	♈	6	♉	5	♊	5	♌	6	♎	5	♏
8	♈	8	♊	7	♋	7	♍	8	♏	7	♐
10	♉	10	♋	9	♌	9	♎	10	♐	9	♐
12	♊	12	♌	11	♍	11	♏	12	♐	11	♑
14	♋	14	♍	13	♎	13	♐	14	♑	13	♒
16	♌	16	♎	15	♏	15	♐	16	♒	15	♓
18	♍	18	♏	17	♐	17	♑	18	♓	17	♈
20	♎	20	♐	19	♐	19	♒	20	♈	19	♈
22	♏	22	♐	21	♑	21	♓	22	♈	21	♉
24	♐	24	♑	23	♒	23	♈	24	♉	23	♊
26	♐	26	♒	24	♓	25	♈	26	♊	25	♋
28	♑	28	♓	26	♈	27	♉	27	♋	26	♌
29	♒	30	♈	28	♈	29	♊	29	♌	28	♍
31	♓			30	♉	31	♋			30	♎

1943

January	February	March	April	May	June
1 ♏	2 ♐	1 ♐	1 ♒	1 ♓	1 ♈
3 ⛎	4 ♑	3 ♑	3 ♓	3 ϒ	3 ♉
5 ♐	6 ♒	5 ♒	5 ϒ	5 ♈	5 ♊
7 ♑	8 ♓	7 ♓	7 ♈	7 ♉	7 ♋
9 ♒	10 ϒ	9 ϒ	9 ♉	9 ♊	9 ♌
11 ♓	12 ♈	11 ♈	11 ♊	11 ♋	11 ♍
13 ϒ	14 ♉	13 ♉	13 ♋	13 ♌	13 ♎
15 ♈	16 ♊	15 ♊	15 ♌	15 ♍	15 ♏
17 ♉	18 ♋	17 ♋	17 ♍	17 ♎	16 ⛎
19 ♊	20 ♌	19 ♌	19 ♎	18 ♏	18 ♐
21 ♋	21 ♍	21 ♍	21 ♏	20 ⛎	20 ♑
23 ♌	23 ♎	22 ♎	23 ⛎	22 ♐	22 ♒
25 ♍	25 ♏	24 ♏	25 ♐	24 ♑	24 ♓
27 ♎	27 ⛎	26 ⛎	27 ♑	26 ♒	26 ϒ
29 ♏		28 ♐	29 ♒	28 ♓	28 ♈
31 ⛎		30 ♑		30 ϒ	30 ♉

July	August	September	October	November	December
2 ♊	2 ♌	1 ♍	2 ♏	1 ⛎	2 ♑
4 ♋	4 ♍	3 ♎	4 ⛎	3 ♐	4 ♒
6 ♌	6 ♎	5 ♏	6 ♐	5 ♑	5 ♓
8 ♍	8 ♏	7 ⛎	8 ♑	6 ♒	7 ϒ
10 ♎	10 ⛎	9 ♐	10 ♒	8 ♓	9 ♈
12 ♏	12 ♐	10 ♑	12 ♓	10 ϒ	11 ♉
14 ⛎	14 ♑	12 ♒	14 ϒ	12 ♈	13 ♊
15 ♐	16 ♒	14 ♓	16 ♈	14 ♉	15 ♋
17 ♑	18 ♓	16 ϒ	18 ♉	16 ♊	17 ♌
19 ♒	20 ϒ	18 ♈	20 ♊	18 ♋	19 ♍
21 ♓	22 ♈	20 ♉	22 ♋	20 ♌	21 ♎
23 ϒ	24 ♉	22 ♊	24 ♌	22 ♍	23 ♏
25 ♈	26 ♊	24 ♋	26 ♍	24 ♎	25 ⛎
27 ♉	28 ♋	26 ♌	28 ♎	26 ♏	27 ♐
29 ♊	30 ♌	28 ♍	30 ♏	28 ⛎	29 ♑
31 ♋		30 ♎		30 ♐	31 ♒

TABLE 4 181

1944

January	February	March	April	May	June
2 ♓	1 ♉	2 ♉	2 ♋	1 ♌	2 ♎
3 ♈	3 ♉	4 ♊	4 ♌	3 ♍	4 ♏
5 ♉	5 ♊	6 ♋	6 ♍	5 ♎	6 ♐
7 ♉	7 ♋	8 ♌	8 ♎	7 ♏	8 ♐
9 ♊	9 ♌	10 ♍	10 ♏	9 ♐	10 ♑
11 ♋	11 ♍	12 ♎	12 ♐	11 ♐	12 ♒
13 ♌	13 ♎	14 ♏	14 ♐	13 ♑	14 ♓
15 ♍	15 ♏	16 ♐	16 ♑	15 ♒	16 ♈
17 ♎	17 ♐	18 ♐	18 ♒	17 ♓	18 ♉
19 ♏	19 ♐	20 ♑	20 ♓	19 ♈	20 ♉
21 ♐	21 ♑	22 ♒	22 ♈	21 ♉	22 ♊
23 ♐	23 ♒	24 ♓	24 ♉	23 ♉	23 ♋
25 ♑	25 ♓	26 ♈	26 ♉	25 ♊	25 ♌
27 ♒	27 ♈	28 ♉	27 ♊	27 ♋	27 ♍
29 ♓	29 ♉	29 ♉	29 ♋	29 ♌	29 ♎
31 ♈		31 ♊		31 ♍	

July	August	September	October	November	December
1 ♏	1 ♐	2 ♒	1 ♓	2 ♉	1 ♉
3 ♐	3 ♑	4 ♓	3 ♈	4 ♉	3 ♊
5 ♐	5 ♒	6 ♈	5 ♉	6 ♊	5 ♋
7 ♑	7 ♓	8 ♉	7 ♉	8 ♋	7 ♌
9 ♒	9 ♈	10 ♉	9 ♊	10 ♌	9 ♍
11 ♓	11 ♉	12 ♊	11 ♋	11 ♍	10 ♎
13 ♈	13 ♉	14 ♋	13 ♌	13 ♎	12 ♏
15 ♉	15 ♊	15 ♌	15 ♍	15 ♏	14 ♐
17 ♉	17 ♋	17 ♍	17 ♎	17 ♐	16 ♐
19 ♊	19 ♌	19 ♎	19 ♏	19 ♐	18 ♑
21 ♋	21 ♍	21 ♏	21 ♐	21 ♑	20 ♒
22 ♌	23 ♎	23 ♐	23 ♐	23 ♒	22 ♓
24 ♍	25 ♏	25 ♐	25 ♑	25 ♓	24 ♈
26 ♎	27 ♐	27 ♑	27 ♒	27 ♈	26 ♉
28 ♏	29 ♐	29 ♒	29 ♓	29 ♉	28 ♉
30 ♐	31 ♑		31 ♈		30 ♊

1945

January		February		March		April		May		June	
1	♋	1	♍	1	♍	1	♏	1	♐	1	♑
3	♌	3	♎	3	♎	3	⚷	2	♐	2	♒
5	♍	5	♏	5	♏	5	♐	4	♑	4	♓
7	♎	7	⚷	6	⚷	7	♑	6	♒	6	♈
8	♏	9	♐	8	♐	9	♒	8	♓	8	⟝
10	⚷	11	♑	10	♑	11	♓	10	♈	10	♉
12	♐	13	♒	12	♒	13	♈	12	⟝	12	♊
14	♑	15	♓	14	♓	15	⟝	14	♉	14	♋
16	♒	17	♈	16	♈	17	♉	16	♊	16	♌
18	♓	19	⟝	18	⟝	19	♊	18	♋	18	♍
20	♈	21	♉	20	♉	21	♋	20	♌	20	♎
22	⟝	23	♊	22	♊	23	♌	22	♍	22	♏
24	♉	25	♋	24	♋	25	♍	24	♎	24	⚷
26	♊	27	♌	26	♌	27	♎	26	♏	26	♐
28	♋			28	♍	29	♏	28	⚷	28	♑
30	♌			30	♎			30	♐	30	♒

July		August		September		October		November		December	
2	♓	2	⟝	2	♊	1	♋	2	♍	1	♎
4	♈	4	♉	4	♋	3	♌	4	♎	3	♏
6	⟝	6	♊	6	♌	5	♍	6	♏	5	⚷
8	♉	8	♋	8	♍	7	♎	7	⚷	7	♐
10	♊	10	♌	10	♎	9	♏	9	♐	9	♑
12	♋	12	♍	12	♏	11	⚷	11	♑	11	♒
14	♌	14	♎	14	⚷	13	♐	13	♒	13	♓
16	♍	16	♏	15	♐	15	♑	15	♓	15	♈
18	♎	18	⚷	17	♑	17	♒	17	♈	17	⟝
20	♏	20	♐	19	♒	19	♓	19	⟝	19	♉
22	⚷	21	♑	21	♓	21	♈	21	♉	21	♊
24	♐	23	♒	23	♈	23	⟝	23	♊	23	♋
26	♑	25	♓	25	⟝	25	♉	25	♋	25	♌
28	♒	27	♈	27	♉	27	♊	27	♌	27	♍
29	♓	29	⟝	29	♊	29	♋	29	♍	29	♎
31	♈	31	♉			31	♌			30	♏

TABLE 4 183

1946

January		February		March		April		May		June	
1	♐	1	♑	2	♒	1	♓	2	♉	1	♉
3	♐	3	♒	4	♓	3	♈	4	♉	3	♊
5	♑	5	♓	6	♈	5	♉	6	♊	4	♋
7	♒	7	♈	8	♉	7	♉	8	♋	6	♌
9	♓	9	♉	10	♉	9	♊	10	♌	8	♍
11	♈	11	♉	12	♊	11	♋	12	♍	10	♎
13	♉	13	♊	14	♋	12	♌	14	♎	12	♏
15	♉	15	♋	16	♌	14	♍	16	♏	14	♐
17	♊	17	♌	18	♍	16	♎	18	♐	16	♐
19	♋	18	♍	20	♎	18	♏	20	♐	18	♑
21	♌	20	♎	22	♏	20	♐	22	♑	20	♒
23	♍	22	♏	24	♐	22	♐	24	♒	22	♓
24	♎	24	♐	26	♐	24	♑	26	♓	24	♈
26	♏	26	♐	28	♑	26	♒	28	♈	26	♉
28	♐	28	♑	30	♒	28	♓	30	♉	28	♉
30	♐					30	♈			30	♊

July		August		September		October		November		December	
1	♋	1	♍	2	♏	1	♐	2	♑	1	♒
3	♌	3	♎	4	♐	3	♐	4	♒	3	♓
5	♍	5	♏	6	♐	5	♑	6	♓	4	♈
7	♎	7	♐	8	♑	7	♒	7	♈	6	♉
9	♏	9	♐	10	♒	9	♓	9	♉	8	♉
11	♐	11	♑	12	♓	11	♈	11	♉	10	♊
13	♐	13	♒	14	♈	13	♉	13	♊	12	♋
15	♑	15	♓	15	♉	15	♉	15	♋	14	♌
17	♒	17	♈	17	♉	17	♊	17	♌	16	♍
19	♓	19	♉	19	♊	19	♋	19	♍	18	♎
21	♈	21	♉	21	♋	21	♌	21	♎	20	♏
23	♉	23	♊	23	♌	23	♍	23	♏	22	♐
24	♉	25	♋	25	♍	25	♎	25	♐	24	♐
26	♊	27	♌	27	♎	27	♏	27	♐	26	♑
28	♋	29	♍	29	♏	29	♐	29	♑	28	♒
30	♌	31	♎			31	♐			30	♓

1947

January	February	March	April	May	June
1 ♈	2 ♉	1 ♉	1 ♋	2 ♍	1 ♎
3 Cet	4 ♊	3 ♊	3 ♌	4 ♎	3 ♏
5 ♉	6 ♋	5 ♋	5 ♍	6 ♏	4 ⛎
7 ♊	8 ♌	7 ♌	7 ♎	8 ⛎	6 ♐
9 ♋	10 ♍	9 ♍	9 ♏	10 ♐	8 ♑
11 ♌	12 ♎	11 ♎	11 ⛎	12 ♑	10 ♒
13 ♍	14 ♏	13 ♏	12 ♐	14 ♒	12 ♓
15 ♎	16 ⛎	15 ⛎	14 ♑	16 ♓	14 ♈
17 ♏	18 ♐	17 ♐	16 ♒	18 ♈	16 Cet
19 ⛎	20 ♑	18 ♑	18 ♓	20 Cet	18 ♉
21 ♐	21 ♒	20 ♒	20 ♈	22 ♉	20 ♊
23 ♑	23 ♓	22 ♓	22 Cet	24 ♊	22 ♋
25 ♒	25 ♈	24 ♈	24 ♉	26 ♋	24 ♌
27 ♓	27 Cet	26 Cet	26 ♊	28 ♌	26 ♍
29 ♈		28 ♉	28 ♋	30 ♍	28 ♎
31 Cet		30 ♊	30 ♌		30 ♏

July	August	September	October	November	December
2 ⛎	2 ♑	2 ♓	1 ♈	2 ♉	1 ♊
4 ♐	4 ♒	4 ♈	3 Cet	4 ♊	2 ♋
6 ♑	6 ♓	6 Cet	5 ♉	6 ♋	4 ♌
8 ♒	8 ♈	8 ♉	7 ♊	7 ♌	6 ♍
10 ♓	10 Cet	10 ♊	9 ♋	9 ♍	8 ♎
12 ♈	12 ♉	12 ♋	11 ♌	11 ♎	10 ♏
14 Cet	14 ♊	14 ♌	13 ♍	13 ♏	12 ⛎
16 ♉	16 ♋	15 ♍	15 ♎	15 ⛎	14 ♐
18 ♊	18 ♌	17 ♎	17 ♏	17 ♐	16 ♑
20 ♋	20 ♍	19 ♏	19 ⛎	19 ♑	18 ♒
22 ♌	21 ♎	21 ⛎	21 ♐	21 ♒	20 ♓
24 ♍	23 ♏	23 ♐	23 ♑	23 ♓	22 ♈
26 ♎	25 ⛎	25 ♑	25 ♒	25 ♈	24 Cet
27 ♏	27 ♐	27 ♒	27 ♓	27 Cet	26 ♉
29 ⛎	29 ♑	29 ♓	29 ♈	29 ♉	28 ♊
31 ♐	31 ♒		31 Cet		30 ♋

TABLE 4 185

1948

January	February	March	April	May	June
1 ♌	1 ♎	1 ♏	1 ♐	1 ♑	1 ♓
3 ♍	3 ♏	3 ♐	3 ♑	3 ♒	2 ♈
5 ♎	5 ♐	5 ♐	5 ♒	5 ♓	4 ♈
7 ♏	7 ♐	7 ♑	7 ♓	6 ♈	6 ♉
9 ♐	9 ♑	9 ♒	9 ♈	8 ♈	8 ♊
11 ♐	11 ♒	11 ♓	11 ♈	10 ♉	10 ♋
13 ♑	13 ♓	13 ♈	13 ♉	12 ♊	12 ♌
15 ♒	15 ♈	14 ♈	15 ♊	14 ♋	14 ♍
17 ♓	17 ♈	16 ♉	17 ♋	16 ♌	16 ♎
19 ♈	18 ♉	18 ♊	19 ♌	18 ♍	18 ♏
21 ♈	20 ♊	20 ♋	21 ♍	20 ♎	20 ♐
23 ♉	22 ♋	22 ♌	23 ♎	22 ♏	22 ♐
24 ♊	24 ♌	24 ♍	25 ♏	24 ♐	24 ♑
26 ♋	26 ♍	26 ♎	27 ♐	26 ♐	26 ♒
28 ♌	28 ♎	28 ♏	29 ♐	28 ♑	28 ♓
30 ♍		30 ♐		30 ♒	30 ♈

July	August	September	October	November	December
2 ♈	1 ♉	1 ♋	2 ♍	1 ♎	2 ♐
4 ♉	3 ♊	3 ♌	4 ♎	3 ♏	3 ♐
6 ♊	5 ♋	5 ♍	6 ♏	5 ♐	5 ♑
8 ♋	7 ♌	7 ♎	8 ♐	7 ♐	7 ♒
10 ♌	9 ♍	9 ♏	10 ♐	8 ♑	9 ♓
12 ♍	11 ♎	11 ♐	12 ♑	10 ♒	11 ♈
14 ♎	13 ♏	13 ♐	14 ♒	12 ♓	13 ♈
16 ♏	15 ♐	15 ♑	16 ♓	14 ♈	15 ♉
18 ♐	17 ♐	16 ♒	18 ♈	16 ♈	17 ♊
20 ♐	19 ♑	18 ♓	20 ♈	18 ♉	19 ♋
22 ♑	21 ♒	20 ♈	22 ♉	20 ♊	21 ♌
24 ♒	22 ♓	22 ♈	24 ♊	22 ♋	23 ♍
26 ♓	24 ♈	24 ♉	26 ♋	24 ♌	25 ♎
28 ♈	26 ♈	26 ♊	28 ♌	26 ♍	27 ♏
30 ♈	28 ♉	28 ♋	30 ♍	28 ♎	29 ♐
	30 ♊	30 ♌		30 ♏	31 ♐

1949

January		February		March		April		May		June	
2	♑	2	♓	1	♓	1	↩	1	♉	1	♋
4	♒	4	♈	3	♈	3	♉	3	♊	2	♌
6	♓	6	↩	5	↩	5	♊	5	♋	4	♍
8	♈	8	♉	7	♉	7	♋	7	♌	6	♎
10	↩	10	♊	9	♊	9	♌	8	♍	8	♏
12	♉	12	♋	11	♋	11	♍	10	♎	10	⛎
14	♊	14	♌	13	♌	13	♎	12	♏	12	♐
16	♋	16	♍	15	♍	15	♏	14	⛎	14	♑
18	♌	18	♎	16	♎	17	⛎	16	♐	16	♒
20	♍	19	♏	18	♏	19	♐	18	♑	18	♓
22	♎	21	⛎	20	⛎	21	♑	20	♒	20	♈
24	♏	23	♐	22	♐	23	♒	22	♓	22	↩
25	⛎	25	♑	24	♑	25	♓	24	♈	24	♉
27	♐	27	♒	26	♒	27	♈	26	↩	26	♊
29	♑			28	♓	29	↩	28	♉	28	♋
31	♒			30	♈			30	♊	30	♌

July		August		September		October		November		December	
2	♍	2	♏	2	♐	1	♑	2	♓	2	↩
4	♎	4	⛎	4	♑	3	♒	4	♈	4	♉
6	♏	6	♐	6	♒	5	♓	5	↩	6	♊
8	⛎	8	♑	8	♓	7	♈	7	♉	8	♋
10	♐	10	♒	10	♈	9	↩	9	♊	10	♌
12	♑	12	♓	12	↩	11	♉	11	♋	12	♍
14	♒	14	♈	13	♉	13	♊	13	♌	14	♎
16	♓	16	↩	15	♊	15	♋	15	♍	16	♏
18	♈	18	♉	17	♋	17	♌	17	♎	18	⛎
20	↩	19	♊	19	♌	19	♍	19	♏	20	♐
22	♉	21	♋	21	♍	21	♎	21	⛎	22	♑
24	♊	23	♌	23	♎	23	♏	23	♐	24	♒
25	♋	25	♍	25	♏	25	⛎	25	♑	26	♓
27	♌	27	♎	27	⛎	27	♐	27	♒	28	♈
29	♍	29	♏	29	♐	29	♑	29	♓	30	↩
31	♎	31	⛎			31	♒	30	♈		

TABLE 4 187

1950

January		February		March		April		May		June	
1	♉	2	♋	1	♋	1	♍	1	♎	1	⛎
3	♊	4	♌	3	♌	3	♎	3	♏	2	♐
5	♋	6	♍	5	♍	5	♏	5	⛎	4	♑
7	♌	8	♎	7	♎	7	⛎	7	♐	6	♒
9	♍	10	♏	9	♏	9	♐	8	♑	8	♓
11	♎	12	⛎	11	⛎	11	♑	10	♒	10	♈
13	♏	14	♐	13	♐	13	♒	12	♓	12	⌐
15	⛎	16	♑	15	♑	15	♓	14	♈	14	♉
17	♐	18	♒	16	♒	17	♈	16	⌐	16	♊
19	♑	19	♓	18	♓	19	⌐	18	♉	18	♋
21	♒	21	♈	20	♈	21	♉	20	♊	20	♌
23	♓	23	⌐	22	⌐	23	♊	22	♋	22	♍
25	♈	25	♉	24	♉	25	♋	24	♌	24	♎
27	⌐	27	♊	26	♊	27	♌	26	♍	26	♏
29	♉			28	♋	29	♍	28	♎	27	⛎
31	♊			30	♌			30	♏	29	♐

July		August		September		October		November		December	
1	♑	2	♓	2	⌐	1	♉	2	♋	2	♍
3	♒	4	♈	4	♉	3	♊	4	♌	4	♎
5	♓	6	⌐	6	♊	5	♋	5	♍	6	♏
7	♈	8	♉	8	♋	7	♌	7	♎	8	⛎
9	⌐	10	♊	10	♌	9	♍	9	♏	10	♐
11	♉	12	♋	12	♍	11	♎	11	⛎	12	♑
13	♊	14	♌	13	♎	13	♏	13	♐	14	♒
15	♋	16	♍	15	♏	15	⛎	15	♑	16	♓
17	♌	18	♎	17	⛎	17	♐	17	♒	18	♈
19	♍	19	♏	19	♐	19	♑	19	♓	20	⌐
21	♎	21	⛎	21	♑	21	♒	21	♈	22	♉
23	♏	23	♐	23	♒	23	♓	23	⌐	24	♊
25	⛎	25	♑	25	♓	25	♈	25	♉	26	♋
27	♐	27	♒	27	♈	27	⌐	27	♊	28	♌
29	♑	29	♓	29	⌐	29	♉	29	♋	30	♍
31	♒	31	♈			31	♊	30	♌		

1951

January		February		March		April		May		June	
1	♎	1	⛎	2	♐	1	♑	2	♓	2	⌐
3	♏	3	♐	4	♑	3	♒	4	♈	4	♉
5	⛎	5	♑	6	♒	5	♓	6	⌐	6	♊
7	♐	7	♒	8	♓	7	♈	8	♉	8	♋
9	♑	9	♓	10	♈	9	⌐	10	♊	10	♌
11	♒	11	♈	12	⌐	11	♉	12	♋	12	♍
13	♓	13	⌐	14	♉	13	♊	14	♌	14	♎
15	♈	15	♉	16	♊	15	♋	16	♍	16	♏
17	⌐	17	♊	18	♋	17	♌	18	♎	18	⛎
19	♉	19	♋	20	♌	19	♍	20	♏	20	♐
21	♊	21	♌	22	♍	21	♎	22	⛎	22	♑
23	♋	23	♍	24	♎	23	♏	24	♐	23	♒
25	♌	25	♎	26	♏	25	⛎	25	♑	25	♓
27	♍	27	♏	28	⛎	26	♐	27	♒	27	♈
29	♎	28	⛎	30	♐	28	♑	29	♓	29	⌐
30	♏					30	♒	31	♈		

July		August		September		October		November		December	
1	♉	2	♋	2	♍	1	♎	1	⛎	2	♑
3	♊	4	♌	4	♎	3	♏	3	♐	4	♒
5	♋	6	♍	6	♏	5	⛎	5	♑	6	♓
7	♌	8	♎	8	⛎	7	♐	7	♒	8	♈
9	♍	10	♏	10	♐	9	♑	9	♓	10	⌐
11	♎	12	⛎	12	♑	11	♒	11	♈	12	♉
13	♏	14	♐	14	♒	13	♓	13	⌐	14	♊
15	⛎	16	♑	16	♓	15	♈	14	♉	16	♋
17	♐	18	♒	17	♈	16	⌐	16	♊	18	♌
19	♑	19	♓	19	⌐	18	♉	18	♋	20	♍
21	♒	21	♈	21	♉	20	♊	20	♌	22	♎
23	♓	23	⌐	23	♊	22	♋	22	♍	24	♏
25	♈	25	♉	25	♋	24	♌	24	♎	26	⛎
27	⌐	27	♊	27	♌	26	♍	26	♏	28	♐
29	♉	29	♋	29	♍	28	♎	28	⛎	30	♑
31	♊	31	♌			30	♏	30	♐		

TABLE 4 189

1952

January	February	March	April	May	June
1 ♒	1 ♈	2 ♈	2 ♊	1 ♋	1 ♍
3 ♓	3 ♈	4 ♉	4 ♋	3 ♌	3 ♎
5 ♈	5 ♉	6 ♊	5 ♌	5 ♍	5 ♏
7 ♈	7 ♊	7 ♋	7 ♍	7 ♎	7 ♐
9 ♉	9 ♋	9 ♌	9 ♎	9 ♏	9 ♐
10 ♊	11 ♌	11 ♍	11 ♏	11 ♐	11 ♑
12 ♋	13 ♍	13 ♎	13 ♐	13 ♐	13 ♒
14 ♌	15 ♎	15 ♏	15 ♐	15 ♑	15 ♓
16 ♍	17 ♏	17 ♐	17 ♑	17 ♒	17 ♈
18 ♎	19 ♐	19 ♐	19 ♒	19 ♓	19 ♈
20 ♏	21 ♐	21 ♑	21 ♓	21 ♈	21 ♉
22 ♐	23 ♑	23 ♒	23 ♈	23 ♈	23 ♊
24 ♐	25 ♒	25 ♓	25 ♈	25 ♉	25 ♋
26 ♑	27 ♓	27 ♈	27 ♉	27 ♊	27 ♌
28 ♒	29 ♈	29 ♈	29 ♊	29 ♋	29 ♍
30 ♓		31 ♉		31 ♌	30 ♎

July	August	September	October	November	December
2 ♏	2 ♐	1 ♑	2 ♓	1 ♈	2 ♉
4 ♐	4 ♑	3 ♒	4 ♈	3 ♈	4 ♊
6 ♐	6 ♒	5 ♓	6 ♈	5 ♉	6 ♋
8 ♑	8 ♓	7 ♈	8 ♉	7 ♊	8 ♌
10 ♒	10 ♈	9 ♈	10 ♊	9 ♋	10 ♍
12 ♓	12 ♈	11 ♉	12 ♋	11 ♌	12 ♎
14 ♈	14 ♉	13 ♊	14 ♌	13 ♍	14 ♏
16 ♈	16 ♊	15 ♋	16 ♍	15 ♎	16 ♐
18 ♉	18 ♋	17 ♌	18 ♎	17 ♏	18 ♐
20 ♊	20 ♌	19 ♍	20 ♏	19 ♐	19 ♑
22 ♋	22 ♍	21 ♎	22 ♐	20 ♐	21 ♒
24 ♌	24 ♎	23 ♏	24 ♐	22 ♑	23 ♓
26 ♍	26 ♏	24 ♐	26 ♑	24 ♒	25 ♈
28 ♎	28 ♐	26 ♐	28 ♒	26 ♓	27 ♈
29 ♏	30 ♐	28 ♑	30 ♓	28 ♈	29 ♉
31 ♐		30 ♒		30 ♈	31 ♊

1953

January		February		March		April		May		June	
2	♋	2	♍	2	♍	2	♏	1	⛎	1	♑
4	♌	4	♎	4	♎	4	⛎	3	♐	3	♒
6	♍	6	♏	6	♏	6	♐	5	♑	5	♓
8	♎	8	⛎	8	⛎	8	♑	7	♒	7	♈
10	♏	10	♐	10	♐	10	♒	9	♓	9	∿
12	⛎	12	♑	12	♑	12	♓	11	♈	11	♉
14	♐	14	♒	14	♒	13	♈	12	∿	13	♊
16	♑	16	♓	15	♓	15	∿	14	♉	15	♋
17	♒	18	♈	17	♈	17	♉	16	♊	17	♌
19	♓	20	∿	19	∿	19	♊	18	♋	19	♍
21	♈	22	♉	21	♉	21	♋	20	♌	21	♎
23	∿	24	♊	23	♊	23	♌	22	♍	23	♏
25	♉	26	♋	25	♋	25	♍	24	♎	25	⛎
27	♊	28	♌	27	♌	27	♎	26	♏	27	♐
29	♋			29	♍	29	♏	28	⛎	29	♑
31	♌			31	♎			30	♐		

July		August		September		October		November		December	
1	♒	1	♈	1	♉	1	♊	1	♌	2	♎
3	♓	3	∿	3	♊	2	♋	3	♍	4	♏
5	♈	5	♉	5	♋	4	♌	5	♎	6	⛎
7	∿	6	♊	7	♌	6	♍	7	♏	8	♐
8	♉	8	♋	9	♍	8	♎	9	⛎	10	♑
10	♊	10	♌	11	♎	10	♏	11	♐	12	♒
12	♋	12	♍	13	♏	12	⛎	13	♑	14	♓
14	♌	14	♎	15	⛎	14	♐	15	♒	16	♈
16	♍	16	♏	17	♐	16	♑	17	♓	18	∿
18	♎	18	⛎	19	♑	18	♒	19	♈	20	♉
20	♏	20	♐	21	♒	20	♓	21	∿	22	♊
22	⛎	22	♑	23	♓	22	♈	23	♉	24	♋
24	♐	24	♒	25	♈	24	∿	25	♊	25	♌
26	♑	26	♓	27	∿	26	♉	27	♋	27	♍
28	♒	28	♈	29	♉	28	♊	28	♌	29	♎
30	♓	30	∿			30	♋	30	♍	31	♏

TABLE 4 191

1954

January	February	March	April	May	June
2 ♏	2 ♑	2 ♑	2 ♓	2 ♈	2 ♉
4 ♐	4 ♒	4 ♒	4 ♈	4 ♉	4 ♊
6 ♑	6 ♓	6 ♓	6 ♉	6 ♉	6 ♋
8 ♒	8 ♈	8 ♈	8 ♉	8 ♊	8 ♌
10 ♓	10 ♉	10 ♉	10 ♊	10 ♋	10 ♍
12 ♈	12 ♉	12 ♉	12 ♋	12 ♌	12 ♎
14 ♉	14 ♊	14 ♊	14 ♌	14 ♍	14 ♏
16 ♉	16 ♋	16 ♋	16 ♍	16 ♎	15 ♐
18 ♊	18 ♌	18 ♌	18 ♎	17 ♏	17 ♐
20 ♋	20 ♍	20 ♍	20 ♏	19 ♐	19 ♑
22 ♌	22 ♎	21 ♎	22 ♐	21 ♐	21 ♒
23 ♍	24 ♏	23 ♏	24 ♐	23 ♑	23 ♓
25 ♎	26 ♐	25 ♐	26 ♑	25 ♒	25 ♈
27 ♏	28 ♐	27 ♐	28 ♒	27 ♓	27 ♉
29 ♐		29 ♑	30 ♓	29 ♈	29 ♉
31 ♐		31 ♒		31 ♉	

July	August	September	October	November	December
1 ♊	2 ♌	2 ♎	1 ♏	2 ♐	1 ♑
3 ♋	4 ♍	4 ♏	3 ♐	4 ♑	3 ♒
5 ♌	6 ♎	6 ♐	5 ♐	5 ♒	4 ♓
7 ♍	8 ♏	8 ♐	7 ♑	7 ♓	6 ♈
9 ♎	10 ♐	9 ♑	9 ♒	9 ♈	8 ♉
11 ♏	11 ♐	11 ♒	11 ♓	11 ♉	10 ♉
13 ♐	13 ♑	13 ♓	13 ♈	13 ♉	12 ♊
15 ♐	15 ♒	15 ♈	15 ♉	15 ♊	14 ♋
17 ♑	17 ♓	17 ♉	17 ♉	17 ♋	16 ♌
19 ♒	19 ♈	19 ♉	19 ♊	19 ♌	18 ♍
21 ♓	21 ♉	21 ♊	21 ♋	21 ♍	20 ♎
23 ♈	23 ♉	23 ♋	23 ♌	23 ♎	22 ♏
25 ♉	25 ♊	25 ♌	25 ♍	25 ♏	24 ♐
27 ♉	27 ♋	27 ♍	27 ♎	27 ♐	26 ♐
29 ♊	29 ♌	29 ♎	29 ♏	29 ♐	28 ♑
31 ♋	31 ♍		31 ♐		30 ♒

1955

January		February		March		April		May		June	
1	♓	1	ↄ	1	♉	2	♋	1	♌	2	♎
2	♈	2	♉	3	♊	4	♌	3	♍	4	♏
4	ↄ	4	♊	5	♋	6	♍	5	♎	6	⛎
6	♉	6	♋	7	♌	8	♎	7	♏	8	♐
8	♊	8	♌	9	♍	10	♏	9	⛎	10	♑
10	♋	10	♍	11	♎	12	⛎	11	♐	12	♒
12	♌	12	♎	13	♏	14	♐	13	♑	14	♓
14	♍	14	♏	15	⛎	16	♑	15	♒	16	♈
16	♎	16	⛎	17	♐	18	♒	17	♓	18	ↄ
18	♏	18	♐	19	♑	20	♓	19	♈	20	♉
20	⛎	20	♑	21	♒	22	♈	21	ↄ	22	♊
22	♐	22	♒	23	♓	24	ↄ	23	♉	23	♋
24	♑	24	♓	25	♈	26	♉	25	♊	25	♌
26	♒	26	♈	27	ↄ	27	♊	27	♋	27	♍
28	♓	28	ↄ	29	♉	29	♋	29	♌	29	♎
30	♈			31	♊			31	♍		

July		August		September		October		November		December	
1	♏	1	♐	1	♒	1	♓	1	ↄ	1	♉
3	⛎	3	♑	3	♓	3	♈	3	♉	3	♊
5	♐	5	♒	5	♈	5	ↄ	5	♊	5	♋
7	♑	7	♓	7	ↄ	7	♉	7	♋	7	♌
9	♒	9	♈	9	♉	9	♊	9	♌	9	♍
11	♓	11	ↄ	11	♊	11	♋	11	♍	11	♎
13	♈	13	♉	13	♋	13	♌	13	♎	12	♏
15	ↄ	15	♊	15	♌	15	♍	15	♏	14	⛎
17	♉	17	♋	17	♍	16	♎	17	⛎	16	♐
19	♊	19	♌	19	♎	18	♏	19	♐	18	♑
21	♋	20	♍	21	♏	20	⛎	21	♑	20	♒
22	♌	22	♎	23	⛎	22	♐	23	♒	22	♓
24	♍	24	♏	25	♐	24	♑	25	♓	24	♈
26	♎	26	⛎	27	♑	26	♒	27	♈	26	ↄ
28	♏	28	♐	29	♒	28	♓	29	ↄ	28	♉
30	⛎	30	♑			30	♈			30	♊

TABLE 4 193

1956

January		February		March		April		May		June	
1	♋	1	♍	1	♎	2	⛎	1	♐	1	♒
3	♌	3	♎	3	♏	4	♐	3	♑	3	♓
5	♍	5	♏	5	⛎	5	♑	4	♒	5	♈
7	♎	7	⛎	7	♐	7	♒	6	♓	7	⟜
9	♏	8	♐	9	♑	9	♓	8	♈	9	♉
10	⛎	10	♑	11	♒	11	♈	10	⟜	11	♊
12	♐	12	♒	13	♓	13	⟜	12	♉	13	♋
14	♑	14	♓	15	♈	15	♉	14	♊	15	♌
16	♒	16	♈	17	⟜	17	♊	16	♋	17	♍
18	♓	18	⟜	19	♉	19	♋	18	♌	19	♎
20	♈	20	♉	21	♊	21	♌	20	♍	21	♏
22	⟜	22	♊	23	♋	23	♍	22	♎	23	⛎
24	♉	24	♋	25	♌	25	♎	24	♏	25	♐
26	♊	26	♌	27	♍	27	♏	26	⛎	27	♑
28	♋	28	♍	29	♎	29	⛎	28	♐	29	♒
30	♌			31	♏			30	♑	30	♓

July		August		September		October		November		December	
1	♈	2	♉	2	♋	1	♌	2	♎	1	♏
3	⟜	4	♊	4	♌	3	♍	4	♏	3	⛎
5	♉	6	♋	6	♍	5	♎	6	⛎	5	♐
7	♊	8	♌	8	♎	7	♏	8	♐	7	♑
9	♋	10	♍	10	♏	9	⛎	10	♑	9	♒
11	♌	12	♎	12	⛎	11	♐	12	♒	11	♓
13	♍	14	♏	14	♐	13	♑	14	♓	13	♈
15	♎	16	⛎	16	♑	15	♒	16	♈	15	⟜
17	♏	18	♐	18	♒	17	♓	18	⟜	17	♉
19	⛎	20	♑	20	♓	19	♈	20	♉	19	♊
21	♐	22	♒	22	♈	21	⟜	21	♊	20	♋
23	♑	24	♓	24	⟜	23	♉	23	♋	22	♌
25	♒	26	♈	25	♉	25	♊	25	♌	24	♍
27	♓	27	⟜	27	♊	27	♋	27	♍	26	♎
29	♈	29	♉	29	♋	29	♌	29	♎	28	♏
31	⟜	31	♊			31	♍			30	⛎

1957

January		February		March		April		May		June	
1	♐	2	♒	1	♒	1	♈	2	♉	1	♊
3	♑	4	♓	3	♓	3	⚲	4	♊	3	♋
5	♒	6	♈	5	♈	5	♉	6	♋	5	♌
7	♓	8	⚲	7	⚲	7	♊	8	♌	7	♍
9	♈	10	♉	9	♉	9	♋	10	♍	9	♎
11	⚲	12	♊	11	♊	11	♌	12	♎	10	♏
13	♉	14	♋	13	♋	13	♍	14	♏	12	⛎
15	♊	15	♌	15	♌	14	♎	16	⛎	14	♐
17	♋	17	♍	16	♍	16	♏	18	♐	16	♑
19	♌	19	♎	18	♎	18	⛎	20	♑	18	♒
21	♍	21	♏	20	♏	20	♐	22	♒	20	♓
23	♎	23	⛎	22	⛎	22	♑	24	♓	22	♈
25	♏	25	♐	24	♐	24	♒	26	♈	24	⚲
27	⛎	27	♑	26	♑	26	♓	28	⚲	26	♉
29	♐			28	♒	28	♈	30	♉	28	♊
31	♑			30	♓	30	⚲			30	♋

July		August		September		October		November		December	
2	♌	2	♎	1	♏	2	♐	1	♒	1	♓
4	♍	4	♏	3	⛎	3	♑	3	♓	3	♈
6	♎	6	⛎	4	♐	5	♒	5	♈	5	⚲
8	♏	8	♐	6	♑	7	♓	7	⚲	7	♉
9	⛎	10	♑	8	♒	9	♈	9	♉	9	♊
11	♐	12	♒	10	♓	11	⚲	11	♊	11	♋
13	♑	14	♓	12	♈	13	♉	13	♋	13	♌
15	♒	16	♈	14	⚲	15	♊	15	♌	15	♍
17	♓	18	⚲	16	♉	17	♋	17	♍	17	♎
19	♈	20	♉	18	♊	19	♌	19	♎	19	♏
21	⚲	22	♊	20	♋	21	♍	21	♏	21	⛎
23	♉	24	♋	22	♌	23	♎	23	⛎	23	♐
25	♊	26	♌	24	♍	25	♏	25	♐	25	♑
27	♋	28	♍	26	♎	27	⛎	27	♑	27	♒
29	♌	30	♎	28	♏	29	♐	29	♒	28	♓
31	♍			30	⛎	31	♑			30	♈

TABLE 4 195

1958

January		February		March		April		May		June	
1	♈	1	♊	2	♋	2	♍	2	♎	2	♏
2	♉	3	♋	4	♌	4	♎	4	♏	4	♐
4	♊	5	♌	6	♍	6	♏	6	♏	6	♑
6	♋	7	♍	8	♎	8	♏	8	♐	8	♒
8	♌	9	♎	10	♏	10	♐	10	♑	10	♓
10	♍	11	♏	12	♏	12	♑	12	♒	12	♈
12	♎	13	♏	14	♐	14	♒	14	♓	14	♈
14	♏	15	♐	16	♑	16	♓	16	♈	16	♉
16	♏	17	♑	18	♒	18	♈	18	♈	18	♊
18	♐	19	♒	20	♓	20	♈	20	♉	20	♋
20	♑	21	♓	22	♈	22	♉	22	♊	22	♌
22	♒	23	♈	24	♈	24	♊	24	♋	23	♍
24	♓	25	♈	26	♉	26	♋	25	♌	25	♎
26	♈	27	♉	28	♊	28	♌	27	♍	27	♏
28	♈	28	♊	29	♋	30	♍	29	♎	29	♏
30	♉			31	♌			31	♏		

July		August		September		October		November		December	
1	♐	1	♒	2	♈	1	♈	1	♊	1	♋
3	♑	3	♓	4	♈	3	♉	3	♋	3	♌
5	♒	5	♈	6	♉	5	♊	5	♌	5	♍
7	♓	7	♈	8	♊	7	♋	7	♍	7	♎
9	♈	9	♉	10	♋	9	♌	9	♎	9	♏
11	♈	11	♊	12	♌	11	♍	11	♏	11	♏
13	♉	13	♋	14	♍	13	♎	13	♏	12	♐
15	♊	15	♌	16	♎	15	♏	15	♐	14	♑
17	♋	17	♍	17	♏	16	♏	17	♑	16	♒
19	♌	19	♎	19	♏	18	♐	19	♒	18	♓
21	♍	21	♏	21	♐	20	♑	21	♓	20	♈
22	♎	23	♏	23	♑	22	♒	23	♈	22	♈
24	♏	25	♐	25	♒	24	♓	25	♈	24	♉
26	♏	27	♑	27	♓	26	♈	27	♉	26	♊
28	♐	29	♒	29	♈	28	♈	29	♊	28	♋
30	♑	31	♓			30	♉			30	♌

1959

January	February	March	April	May	June
1 ♍	1 ♏	1 ♏	1 ♐	1 ♒	2 ♈
3 ♎	3 ⛎	3 ⛎	3 ♑	3 ♓	3 ↩
5 ♏	5 ♐	5 ♐	5 ♒	5 ♈	5 ♉
7 ⛎	7 ♑	7 ♑	6 ♓	7 ↩	7 ♊
9 ♐	9 ♒	8 ♒	8 ♈	9 ♉	9 ♋
10 ♑	11 ♓	10 ♓	10 ↩	11 ♊	11 ♌
12 ♒	13 ♈	12 ♈	12 ♉	13 ♋	13 ♍
14 ♓	15 ↩	14 ↩	14 ♊	15 ♌	15 ♎
16 ♈	17 ♉	16 ♉	16 ♋	17 ♍	17 ♏
18 ↩	19 ♊	18 ♊	18 ♌	19 ♎	19 ⛎
20 ♉	21 ♋	20 ♋	20 ♍	21 ♏	21 ♐
22 ♊	23 ♌	22 ♌	22 ♎	23 ⛎	23 ♑
24 ♋	25 ♍	24 ♍	24 ♏	25 ♐	25 ♒
26 ♌	27 ♎	26 ♎	26 ⛎	27 ♑	27 ♓
28 ♍		28 ♏	28 ♐	29 ♒	29 ♈
30 ♎		30 ⛎	30 ♑	31 ♓	

July	August	September	October	November	December
1 ↩	1 ♊	1 ♌	2 ♎	1 ♏	2 ♐
2 ♉	3 ♋	3 ♍	4 ♏	3 ⛎	4 ♑
4 ♊	5 ♌	5 ♎	6 ⛎	5 ♐	6 ♒
6 ♋	7 ♍	7 ♏	8 ♐	7 ♑	8 ♓
8 ♌	9 ♎	9 ⛎	10 ♑	9 ♒	10 ♈
10 ♍	11 ♏	11 ♐	12 ♒	11 ♓	12 ↩
12 ♎	13 ⛎	13 ♑	14 ♓	13 ♈	14 ♉
14 ♏	15 ♐	15 ♒	16 ♈	15 ↩	16 ♊
16 ⛎	17 ♑	17 ♓	18 ↩	17 ♉	18 ♋
18 ♐	19 ♒	19 ♈	20 ♉	19 ♊	20 ♌
20 ♑	21 ♓	21 ↩	22 ♊	21 ♋	21 ♍
22 ♒	23 ♈	23 ♉	24 ♋	22 ♌	23 ♎
24 ♓	25 ↩	25 ♊	26 ♌	24 ♍	25 ♏
26 ♈	27 ♉	26 ♋	28 ♍	26 ♎	27 ⛎
28 ↩	28 ♊	28 ♌	30 ♎	28 ♏	29 ♐
30 ♉	30 ♋	30 ♍		30 ⛎	31 ♑

TABLE 4 197

1960

January		February		March		April		May		June	
2	♒	1	♓	1	♈	1	♉	1	♊	1	♌
4	♓	3	♈	3	♈	3	♊	3	♋	3	♍
6	♈	5	♈	5	♉	5	♋	5	♌	5	♎
8	♉	7	♉	7	♊	7	♌	7	♍	7	♏
10	♉	9	♊	9	♋	9	♍	9	♎	9	♐
12	♊	11	♋	11	♌	11	♎	11	♏	10	♐
14	♋	13	♌	13	♍	13	♏	12	♐	12	♑
16	♌	15	♍	15	♎	15	♐	14	♐	14	♒
18	♍	16	♎	16	♏	17	♐	16	♑	16	♓
20	♎	18	♏	18	♐	19	♑	18	♒	18	♈
22	♏	20	♐	20	♐	21	♒	20	♓	20	♉
24	♐	22	♐	22	♑	23	♓	22	♈	22	♉
26	♐	24	♑	24	♒	25	♈	24	♉	24	♊
28	♑	26	♒	26	♓	27	♉	26	♉	26	♋
30	♒	28	♓	28	♈	29	♉	28	♊	28	♌
				30	♉			30	♋	30	♍

July		August		September		October		November		December	
2	♎	2	♐	1	♐	2	♒	2	♈	1	♉
4	♏	4	♐	3	♑	4	♓	4	♉	3	♉
6	♐	6	♑	4	♒	6	♈	6	♉	5	♊
8	♐	8	♒	6	♓	8	♉	8	♊	7	♋
9	♑	10	♓	8	♈	10	♉	10	♋	9	♌
11	♒	12	♈	10	♉	12	♊	12	♌	11	♍
13	♓	14	♉	12	♉	14	♋	14	♍	13	♎
15	♈	16	♉	14	♊	16	♌	16	♎	15	♏
17	♉	18	♊	16	♋	18	♍	18	♏	17	♐
19	♉	20	♋	18	♌	20	♎	20	♐	19	♐
21	♊	22	♌	20	♍	22	♏	22	♐	20	♑
23	♋	24	♍	22	♎	24	♐	24	♑	22	♒
25	♌	26	♎	24	♏	26	♐	26	♒	24	♓
27	♍	28	♏	26	♐	28	♑	27	♓	26	♈
29	♎	30	♐	28	♐	30	♒	29	♈	28	♉
31	♏			30	♑	31	♓			30	♉

1961

January	February	March	April	May	June
1 ♊	2 ♌	1 ♌	2 ♎	1 ♏	1 ♐
3 ♋	4 ♍	3 ♍	4 ♏	3 ⛎	2 ♑
5 ♌	6 ♎	5 ♎	6 ⛎	5 ♐	4 ♒
7 ♍	8 ♏	7 ♏	8 ♐	7 ♑	6 ♓
9 ♎	10 ⛎	9 ⛎	10 ♑	8 ♒	8 ♈
11 ♏	12 ♐	11 ♐	12 ♒	10 ♓	10 ⟿
13 ⛎	14 ♑	13 ♑	13 ♓	12 ♈	12 ♉
15 ♐	15 ♒	15 ♒	15 ♈	14 ⟿	14 ♊
17 ♑	17 ♓	17 ♓	17 ⟿	16 ♉	16 ♋
19 ♒	19 ♈	19 ♈	19 ♉	18 ♊	18 ♌
21 ♓	21 ⟿	21 ⟿	21 ♊	20 ♋	20 ♍
23 ♈	23 ♉	23 ♉	23 ♋	22 ♌	22 ♎
25 ⟿	25 ♊	25 ♊	25 ♌	24 ♍	24 ♏
27 ♉	27 ♋	27 ♋	27 ♍	26 ♎	26 ⛎
29 ♊		29 ♌	29 ♎	28 ♏	28 ♐
31 ♋		31 ♍		30 ⛎	30 ♑

July	August	September	October	November	December
2 ♒	2 ♈	2 ♉	2 ♊	2 ♌	2 ♍
4 ♓	4 ⟿	4 ♊	4 ♋	4 ♍	3 ♎
6 ♈	6 ♉	6 ♋	6 ♌	6 ♎	5 ♏
8 ⟿	8 ♊	8 ♌	8 ♍	8 ♏	7 ⛎
10 ♉	10 ♋	10 ♍	10 ♎	10 ⛎	9 ♐
12 ♊	12 ♌	12 ♎	11 ♏	12 ♐	11 ♑
14 ♋	14 ♍	14 ♏	13 ⛎	14 ♑	13 ♒
16 ♌	16 ♎	16 ⛎	15 ♐	16 ♒	15 ♓
18 ♍	18 ♏	18 ♐	17 ♑	18 ♓	17 ♈
20 ♎	19 ⛎	20 ♑	19 ♒	20 ♈	19 ⟿
22 ♏	21 ♐	22 ♒	21 ♓	22 ⟿	21 ♉
24 ⛎	23 ♑	24 ♓	23 ♈	24 ♉	23 ♊
25 ♐	25 ♒	26 ♈	25 ⟿	26 ♊	25 ♋
27 ♑	27 ♓	28 ⟿	27 ♉	28 ♋	27 ♌
29 ♒	29 ♈	30 ♉	29 ♊	30 ♌	29 ♍
31 ♓	31 ⟿		31 ♋		31 ♎

TABLE 4 199

1962

January	February	March	April	May	June
1 ♏	1 ♐	1 ♐	1 ♒	1 ♓	1 ♉
3 ♐	3 ♑	3 ♐	3 ♓	3 ♈	3 ♉
5 ♐	5 ♒	5 ♒	5 ♈	5 ♉	4 ♊
7 ♑	7 ♓	7 ♓	7 ♉	7 ♉	6 ♋
9 ♒	9 ♈	9 ♈	9 ♉	9 ♊	8 ♌
11 ♓	11 ♉	11 ♉	11 ♊	10 ♋	10 ♍
13 ♈	13 ♉	13 ♉	13 ♋	12 ♌	12 ♎
15 ♉	15 ♊	15 ♊	15 ♌	14 ♍	14 ♏
17 ♉	17 ♋	17 ♋	17 ♍	16 ♎	16 ♐
19 ♊	19 ♌	18 ♌	19 ♎	18 ♏	18 ♐
21 ♋	21 ♍	20 ♍	21 ♏	20 ♐	20 ♑
23 ♌	23 ♎	22 ♎	23 ♐	22 ♐	22 ♒
24 ♍	25 ♏	24 ♏	25 ♐	24 ♑	24 ♓
26 ♎	27 ♐	26 ♐	27 ♑	26 ♒	26 ♈
28 ♏		28 ♐	29 ♒	28 ♓	28 ♉
30 ♐		30 ♑		30 ♈	30 ♉

July	August	September	October	November	December
2 ♊	2 ♌	2 ♎	2 ♏	2 ♐	2 ♑
4 ♋	4 ♍	4 ♏	4 ♐	4 ♑	4 ♒
6 ♌	6 ♎	6 ♐	6 ♐	6 ♒	5 ♓
8 ♍	8 ♏	8 ♐	8 ♑	8 ♓	7 ♈
10 ♎	10 ♐	10 ♑	10 ♒	10 ♈	9 ♉
12 ♏	12 ♐	12 ♒	12 ♓	12 ♉	11 ♉
14 ♐	14 ♑	14 ♓	13 ♈	14 ♉	13 ♊
16 ♐	16 ♒	16 ♈	15 ♉	16 ♊	15 ♋
18 ♑	18 ♓	18 ♉	17 ♉	18 ♋	17 ♌
20 ♒	20 ♈	20 ♉	19 ♊	20 ♌	19 ♍
22 ♓	21 ♉	22 ♊	21 ♋	22 ♍	21 ♎
24 ♈	23 ♉	24 ♋	23 ♌	24 ♎	23 ♏
26 ♉	25 ♊	26 ♌	25 ♍	26 ♏	25 ♐
27 ♉	27 ♋	28 ♍	27 ♎	28 ♐	27 ♐
29 ♊	29 ♌	30 ♎	29 ♏	30 ♐	29 ♑
31 ♋	31 ♍		31 ♐		31 ♒

1963

January		February		March		April		May		June	
2	♓	2	↼	1	↼	2	♊	1	♋	2	♍
4	♈	4	♉	3	♉	4	♋	3	♌	4	♎
6	↼	6	♊	5	♊	6	♌	5	♍	6	♏
8	♉	8	♋	7	♋	8	♍	7	♎	7	⛎
10	♊	10	♌	9	♌	10	♎	9	♏	9	♐
12	♋	12	♍	11	♍	12	♏	11	⛎	11	♑
14	♌	14	♎	13	♎	14	⛎	13	♐	13	♒
16	♍	16	♏	15	♏	15	♐	15	♑	15	♓
18	♎	18	⛎	17	⛎	17	♑	17	♒	17	♈
20	♏	20	♐	19	♐	19	♒	19	♓	19	↼
22	⛎	21	♑	21	♑	21	♓	21	♈	21	♉
24	♐	23	♒	23	♒	23	♈	23	↼	23	♊
26	♑	25	♓	25	♓	25	↼	25	♉	25	♋
27	♒	27	♈	27	♈	27	♉	27	♊	27	♌
29	♓			29	↼	29	♊	29	♋	29	♍
31	♈			31	♉			31	♌		

July		August		September		October		November		December	
1	♎	1	⛎	1	♑	2	♓	1	♈	2	♉
2	♏	3	♐	3	♒	4	♈	3	↼	4	♊
4	⛎	4	♑	5	♓	6	↼	5	♉	6	♋
6	♐	6	♒	7	♈	8	♉	7	♊	7	♌
8	♑	8	♓	9	↼	10	♊	9	♋	9	♍
10	♒	10	♈	11	♉	12	♋	11	♌	11	♎
12	♓	12	↼	13	♊	14	♌	12	♍	13	♏
14	♈	14	♉	15	♋	16	♍	14	♎	15	⛎
16	↼	16	♊	17	♌	18	♎	16	♏	17	♐
18	♉	18	♋	19	♍	20	♏	18	⛎	19	♑
20	♊	20	♌	20	♎	22	⛎	20	♐	21	♒
22	♋	22	♍	22	♏	24	♐	22	♑	23	♓
24	♌	24	♎	24	⛎	26	♑	24	♒	25	♈
26	♍	26	♏	26	♐	28	♒	26	♓	27	↼
28	♎	28	⛎	28	♑	30	♊	28	♈	29	♉
30	♏	30	♐	30	♒			30	↼	31	♊

TABLE 4 201

1964

January		February		March		April		May		June	
1	♋	2	♍	2	♎	2	⛎	2	♐	2	♒
3	♌	4	♎	4	♏	4	♐	4	♑	4	♓
5	♍	6	♏	6	⛎	6	♑	6	♒	6	♈
7	♎	8	⛎	8	♐	8	♒	8	♓	8	⟜
9	♏	10	♐	10	♑	10	♓	10	♈	10	♉
11	⛎	12	♑	12	♒	12	♈	11	⟜	12	♊
13	♐	14	♒	14	♓	14	⟜	13	♉	14	♋
15	♑	16	♓	16	♈	16	♉	15	♊	16	♌
17	♒	18	♈	18	⟜	18	♊	17	♋	18	♍
19	♓	20	⟜	19	♉	20	♋	19	♌	20	♎
21	♈	22	♉	21	♊	22	♌	21	♍	22	♏
23	⟜	23	♊	23	♋	24	♍	23	♎	24	⛎
25	♉	25	♋	25	♌	26	♎	25	♏	26	♐
27	♊	27	♌	27	♍	28	♏	27	⛎	28	♑
29	♋	29	♍	29	♎	30	⛎	29	♐	30	♒
31	♌			31	♏			31	♑		

July		August		September		October		November		December	
2	♓	2	⟜	2	♊	1	♋	2	♍	1	♎
3	♈	4	♉	4	♋	3	♌	4	♎	3	♏
5	⟜	6	♊	6	♌	5	♍	6	♏	5	⛎
7	♉	8	♋	8	♍	7	♎	8	⛎	7	♐
9	♊	10	♌	10	♎	9	♏	10	♐	9	♑
11	♋	12	♍	12	♏	11	⛎	11	♑	11	♒
13	♌	14	♎	14	⛎	13	♐	13	♒	13	♓
15	♍	16	♏	16	♐	15	♑	15	♓	15	♈
17	♎	18	⛎	18	♑	17	♒	17	♈	17	⟜
19	♏	20	♐	19	♒	19	♓	19	⟜	19	♉
21	⛎	22	♑	21	♓	21	♈	21	♉	21	♊
23	♐	24	♒	23	♈	23	⟜	23	♊	23	♋
25	♑	25	♓	25	⟜	25	♉	25	♋	25	♌
27	♒	27	♈	27	♉	27	♊	27	♌	27	♍
29	♓	29	⟜	29	♊	29	♋	29	♍	29	♎
31	♈	31	♉			31	♌			31	♏

1965

Note: ⛎ = Ophiuchus (cross-shaped glyph); ♆ here denotes the Cetus glyph (the hook-shaped symbol).

January	February	March	April	May	June
2 ⛎	2 ♑	2 ♒	1 ♓	2 ♆	2 ♊
3 ♐	3 ♒	4 ♓	3 ♈	4 ♉	4 ♋
5 ♑	5 ♓	6 ♈	5 ♆	6 ♊	6 ♌
7 ♒	7 ♈	8 ♆	7 ♉	8 ♋	8 ♍
9 ♓	9 ♆	10 ♉	9 ♊	10 ♌	10 ♎
11 ♈	11 ♉	12 ♊	11 ♋	12 ♍	12 ♏
13 ♆	13 ♊	14 ♋	13 ♌	14 ♎	14 ⛎
15 ♉	15 ♋	16 ♌	15 ♍	16 ♏	16 ♐
17 ♊	17 ♌	18 ♍	17 ♎	18 ⛎	18 ♑
19 ♋	19 ♍	20 ♎	19 ♏	19 ♐	20 ♒
21 ♌	21 ♎	22 ♏	21 ⛎	21 ♑	22 ♓
23 ♍	23 ♏	24 ⛎	23 ♐	23 ♒	24 ♈
25 ♎	24 ⛎	26 ♐	24 ♑	25 ♓	26 ♆
27 ♏	26 ♐	28 ♑	26 ♒	27 ♈	28 ♉
29 ⛎	28 ♑	30 ♒	28 ♓	29 ♆	30 ♊
31 ♐			30 ♈	31 ♉	

July	August	September	October	November	December
2 ♋	2 ♍	1 ♏	1 ⛎	1 ♑	2 ♓
4 ♌	4 ♎	3 ⛎	3 ♐	3 ♒	4 ♈
6 ♍	5 ♏	5 ♐	5 ♑	5 ♓	6 ♆
8 ♎	7 ⛎	7 ♑	7 ♒	7 ♈	8 ♉
10 ♏	9 ♐	9 ♒	9 ♓	9 ♆	10 ♊
11 ⛎	11 ♑	11 ♓	11 ♈	11 ♉	12 ♋
13 ♐	13 ♒	13 ♈	13 ♆	13 ♊	14 ♌
15 ♑	15 ♓	15 ♆	15 ♉	15 ♋	16 ♍
17 ♒	17 ♈	17 ♉	17 ♊	16 ♌	18 ♎
19 ♓	19 ♆	19 ♊	19 ♋	18 ♍	20 ♏
21 ♈	21 ♉	21 ♋	21 ♌	20 ♎	22 ⛎
23 ♆	23 ♊	23 ♌	22 ♍	22 ♏	24 ♐
25 ♉	25 ♋	25 ♍	24 ♎	24 ⛎	26 ♑
27 ♊	27 ♌	27 ♎	26 ♏	26 ♐	28 ♒
29 ♋	29 ♍	29 ♏	28 ⛎	28 ♑	30 ♓
31 ♌	30 ♎		30 ♐	30 ♒	

TABLE 4 203

1966

January	February	March	April	May	June
1 ♈	1 ♉	2 ♊	2 ♌	1 ♍	2 ♏
3 ♈	2 ♊	4 ♋	4 ♍	3 ♎	4 ♐
5 ♉	4 ♋	6 ♌	6 ♎	5 ♏	6 ♐
7 ♊	6 ♌	8 ♍	8 ♏	7 ♐	8 ♑
8 ♋	8 ♍	10 ♎	10 ♐	9 ♐	10 ♒
10 ♌	10 ♎	12 ♏	12 ♐	11 ♑	12 ♓
12 ♍	12 ♏	14 ♐	14 ♑	13 ♒	13 ♈
14 ♎	14 ♐	16 ♐	16 ♒	15 ♓	15 ♈
16 ♏	16 ♐	18 ♑	18 ♓	17 ♈	17 ♉
18 ♐	18 ♑	20 ♒	20 ♈	19 ♈	19 ♊
20 ♐	20 ♒	22 ♓	21 ♈	21 ♉	21 ♋
22 ♑	22 ♓	24 ♈	23 ♉	23 ♊	23 ♌
24 ♒	24 ♈	26 ♈	25 ♊	25 ♋	25 ♍
26 ♓	26 ♈	27 ♉	27 ♋	27 ♌	27 ♎
28 ♈	28 ♉	29 ♊	29 ♌	29 ♍	29 ♏
30 ♈		31 ♋		31 ♎	

July	August	September	October	November	December
1 ♐	2 ♑	1 ♓	1 ♈	1 ♉	2 ♋
3 ♐	4 ♒	3 ♈	3 ♈	3 ♊	4 ♌
5 ♑	5 ♓	5 ♈	5 ♉	5 ♋	6 ♍
7 ♒	7 ♈	7 ♉	7 ♊	7 ♌	8 ♎
9 ♓	9 ♈	9 ♊	9 ♋	9 ♍	10 ♏
11 ♈	11 ♉	11 ♋	11 ♌	11 ♎	12 ♐
13 ♈	13 ♊	13 ♌	13 ♍	13 ♏	14 ♐
15 ♉	15 ♋	15 ♍	15 ♎	15 ♐	16 ♑
17 ♊	17 ♌	17 ♎	17 ♏	16 ♐	18 ♒
19 ♋	19 ♍	19 ♏	19 ♐	18 ♑	20 ♓
21 ♌	21 ♎	21 ♐	21 ♐	20 ♒	22 ♈
23 ♍	23 ♏	23 ♐	22 ♑	22 ♓	24 ♈
25 ♎	25 ♐	25 ♑	24 ♒	24 ♈	26 ♉
27 ♏	27 ♐	27 ♒	26 ♓	26 ♈	28 ♊
29 ♐	29 ♑	29 ♓	28 ♈	28 ♉	30 ♋
31 ♐	30 ♒		30 ♈	30 ♊	

1967

January		February		March		April		May		June	
1	♌	1	♎	2	♏	2	♐	1	♑	1	♓
3	♍	2	♏	4	⛎	4	♑	3	♒	3	♈
5	♎	4	⛎	6	♐	6	♒	5	♓	5	↷
7	♏	6	♐	8	♑	8	♓	7	♈	7	♉
8	⛎	8	♑	10	♒	10	♈	9	↷	9	♊
10	♐	10	♒	12	♓	12	↷	11	♉	11	♋
12	♑	12	♓	14	♈	14	♉	13	♊	13	♌
14	♒	14	♈	16	↷	16	♊	15	♋	15	♍
16	♓	16	↷	18	♉	18	♋	16	♌	17	♎
18	♈	18	♉	20	♊	20	♌	18	♍	19	♏
20	↷	20	♊	22	♋	21	♍	20	♎	21	⛎
22	♉	22	♋	24	♌	23	♎	22	♏	23	♐
24	♊	24	♌	26	♍	25	♏	24	⛎	25	♑
26	♋	26	♍	27	♎	27	⛎	26	♐	27	♒
28	♌	28	♎	29	♏	29	♐	28	♑	29	♓
30	♍			31	⛎			30	♒		

July		August		September		October		November		December	
1	♈	1	♉	1	♋	2	♍	2	♏	1	⛎
3	↷	2	♊	3	♌	4	♎	4	⛎	3	♐
5	♉	4	♋	5	♍	6	♏	6	♐	5	♑
7	♊	6	♌	7	♎	8	⛎	8	♑	7	♒
8	♋	8	♍	9	♏	10	♐	10	♒	9	♓
10	♌	10	♎	11	⛎	12	♑	12	♓	11	♈
12	♍	12	♏	13	♐	14	♒	13	♈	13	↷
14	♎	14	⛎	15	♑	16	♓	15	↷	15	♉
16	♏	16	♐	17	♒	18	♈	17	♉	17	♊
18	⛎	18	♑	19	♓	19	↷	19	♊	19	♋
20	♐	20	♒	21	♈	21	♉	21	♋	21	♌
22	♑	22	♓	23	↷	23	♊	23	♌	23	♍
24	♒	24	♈	24	♉	25	♋	25	♍	25	♎
26	♓	26	↷	26	♊	27	♌	27	♎	27	♏
28	♈	28	♉	28	♋	29	♍	29	♏	29	⛎
30	↷	30	♊	30	♌	31	♎			31	♐

TABLE 4 205

1968

January	February	March	April	May	June
2 ♑	1 ♒	2 ♈	1 ♈	2 ♊	2 ♌
4 ♒	2 ♓	4 ♈	3 ♉	4 ♋	4 ♍
6 ♓	4 ♈	6 ♉	5 ♊	6 ♌	6 ♎
8 ♈	6 ♈	8 ♊	7 ♋	8 ♍	8 ♏
10 ♈	8 ♉	10 ♋	9 ♌	10 ♎	10 ♐
12 ♉	10 ♊	12 ♌	11 ♍	12 ♏	12 ♐
14 ♊	12 ♋	14 ♍	13 ♎	14 ♐	14 ♑
16 ♋	14 ♌	16 ♎	15 ♏	15 ♐	16 ♒
18 ♌	16 ♍	18 ♏	17 ♐	17 ♑	18 ♓
20 ♍	18 ♎	20 ♐	19 ♐	19 ♒	20 ♈
22 ♎	20 ♏	22 ♐	20 ♑	21 ♓	22 ♈
24 ♏	22 ♐	24 ♑	22 ♒	23 ♈	24 ♉
26 ♐	24 ♐	26 ♒	24 ♓	25 ♈	26 ♊
28 ♐	26 ♑	28 ♓	26 ♈	27 ♉	28 ♋
30 ♑	27 ♒	30 ♈	28 ♈	29 ♊	30 ♌
	29 ♓		30 ♉	31 ♋	

July	August	September	October	November	December
2 ♍	1 ♏	2 ♐	1 ♑	1 ♓	2 ♈
4 ♎	3 ♐	4 ♑	3 ♒	3 ♈	4 ♉
6 ♏	5 ♐	6 ♒	5 ♓	5 ♈	6 ♊
7 ♐	7 ♑	8 ♓	7 ♈	7 ♉	8 ♋
9 ♐	9 ♒	10 ♈	9 ♈	9 ♊	10 ♌
11 ♑	11 ♓	12 ♈	11 ♉	11 ♋	12 ♍
13 ♒	13 ♈	14 ♉	13 ♊	12 ♌	14 ♎
15 ♓	15 ♈	16 ♊	15 ♋	14 ♍	16 ♏
17 ♈	17 ♉	18 ♋	17 ♌	16 ♎	18 ♐
19 ♈	19 ♊	20 ♌	18 ♍	18 ♏	20 ♐
21 ♉	21 ♋	22 ♍	20 ♎	20 ♐	22 ♑
23 ♊	23 ♌	23 ♎	22 ♏	22 ♐	24 ♒
25 ♋	25 ♍	25 ♏	24 ♐	24 ♑	26 ♓
27 ♌	27 ♎	27 ♐	26 ♐	26 ♒	28 ♈
29 ♍	29 ♏	29 ♐	28 ♑	28 ♓	30 ♈
31 ♎	31 ♐		30 ♒	30 ♈	

1969

January		February		March		April		May		June	
1	♉	1	♋	2	♌	2	♎	1	♏	2	♐
3	♊	2	♌	4	♍	4	♏	3	⛎	4	♑
4	♋	4	♍	6	♎	6	⛎	5	♐	6	♒
6	♌	6	♎	8	♏	8	♐	7	♑	8	♓
8	♍	8	♏	10	⛎	10	♑	9	♒	10	♈
10	♎	10	⛎	12	♐	12	♒	11	♓	11	Cetus
12	♏	12	♐	14	♑	14	♓	13	♈	13	♉
14	⛎	14	♑	16	♒	16	♈	15	Cetus	15	♊
16	♐	16	♒	18	♓	18	Cetus	17	♉	17	♋
18	♑	18	♓	20	♈	19	♉	19	♊	19	♌
20	♒	20	♈	22	Cetus	21	♊	21	♋	21	♍
22	♓	22	Cetus	24	♉	23	♋	23	♌	23	♎
24	♈	24	♉	25	♊	25	♌	25	♍	25	♏
26	Cetus	26	♊	27	♋	27	♍	27	♎	27	⛎
28	♉	28	♋	29	♌	29	♎	29	♏	29	♐
30	♊			31	♍			31	⛎		

July		August		September		October		November		December	
1	♑	1	♓	2	Cetus	1	♉	1	♋	1	♌
3	♒	3	♈	4	♉	3	♊	3	♌	3	♍
5	♓	5	Cetus	6	♊	5	♋	5	♍	5	♎
6	♈	7	♉	8	♋	7	♌	7	♎	7	♏
8	Cetus	9	♊	10	♌	9	♍	9	♏	9	⛎
10	♉	11	♋	12	♍	11	♎	11	⛎	11	♐
12	♊	13	♌	14	♎	13	♏	13	♐	12	♑
14	♋	15	♍	16	♏	15	⛎	15	♑	14	♒
16	♌	17	♎	18	⛎	17	♐	17	♒	16	♓
18	♍	19	♏	20	♐	19	♑	19	♓	18	♈
20	♎	21	⛎	22	♑	20	♒	21	♈	20	Cetus
22	♏	23	♐	24	♒	22	♓	23	Cetus	22	♉
24	⛎	25	♑	25	♓	24	♈	25	♉	24	♊
26	♐	27	♒	27	♈	26	Cetus	27	♊	26	♋
28	♑	29	♓	29	Cetus	28	♉	29	♋	28	♌
30	♒	31	♈			30	♊			30	♍

TABLE 4 207

1970

January		February		March		April		May		June	
1	♎	1	♐	2	♐	1	♑	2	♓	2	♈
3	♏	3	♐	4	♑	3	♒	4	♈	4	♉
5	♐	5	♑	6	♒	5	♓	6	♈	6	♊
6	♐	7	♒	8	♓	7	♈	8	♉	8	♋
8	♑	9	♓	10	♈	9	♈	10	♊	10	♌
10	♒	11	♈	12	♈	11	♉	12	♋	11	♍
12	♓	13	♈	14	♉	13	♊	14	♌	13	♎
14	♈	15	♉	16	♊	15	♋	16	♍	15	♏
16	♈	17	♊	18	♋	17	♌	17	♎	17	♐
18	♉	19	♋	20	♌	19	♍	19	♏	19	♐
20	♊	21	♌	22	♍	21	♎	21	♐	21	♑
22	♋	23	♍	24	♎	22	♏	23	♐	23	♒
24	♌	25	♎	26	♏	24	♐	25	♑	25	♓
26	♍	27	♏	28	♐	26	♐	27	♒	27	♈
28	♎	28	♐	30	♐	28	♑	29	♓	29	♈
30	♏					30	♒	31	♈		

July		August		September		October		November		December	
1	♉	2	♋	1	♍	1	♎	1	♐	1	♐
3	♊	3	♌	3	♎	3	♏	3	♐	3	♑
5	♋	5	♍	5	♏	5	♐	5	♑	5	♒
7	♌	7	♎	7	♐	7	♐	7	♒	7	♓
9	♍	9	♏	9	♐	9	♑	9	♓	9	♈
11	♎	11	♐	11	♑	11	♒	11	♈	11	♈
13	♏	13	♐	13	♒	13	♓	13	♈	13	♉
15	♐	15	♑	15	♓	15	♈	15	♉	14	♊
17	♐	17	♒	17	♈	17	♈	17	♊	16	♋
19	♑	19	♓	19	♈	19	♉	19	♋	18	♌
21	♒	21	♈	21	♉	21	♊	21	♌	20	♍
23	♓	23	♈	23	♊	22	♋	23	♍	22	♎
25	♈	25	♉	25	♋	24	♌	25	♎	24	♏
27	♈	27	♊	27	♌	26	♍	27	♏	26	♐
29	♉	28	♋	29	♍	28	♎	29	♐	28	♐
31	♊	30	♌			30	♏			30	♑

1971

January		February		March		April		May		June	
1	♒	1	♈	2	⟿	2	♊	2	♋	1	♌
3	♓	2	⟿	4	♉	4	♋	4	♌	3	♍
5	♈	4	♉	6	♊	6	♌	6	♍	5	♎
7	⟿	6	♊	8	♋	8	♍	8	♎	7	♏
8	♉	8	♋	10	♌	10	♎	10	♏	9	⛎
10	♊	10	♌	12	♍	12	♏	12	⛎	11	♐
12	♋	12	♍	14	♎	14	⛎	14	♐	13	♑
14	♌	14	♎	16	♏	16	♐	16	♑	15	♒
16	♍	16	♏	18	⛎	18	♑	18	♒	16	♓
18	♎	18	⛎	20	♐	20	♒	20	♓	18	♈
20	♏	20	♐	22	♑	22	♓	22	♈	20	⟿
22	⛎	22	♑	24	♒	24	♈	24	⟿	22	♉
24	♐	24	♒	26	♓	26	⟿	26	♉	24	♊
26	♑	26	♓	27	♈	28	♉	28	♊	26	♋
28	♒	28	♈	29	⟿	30	♊	30	♋	28	♌
30	♓			31	♉					30	♍

July		August		September		October		November		December	
2	♎	2	⛎	2	♑	1	♒	2	♈	1	⟿
4	♏	4	♐	4	♒	3	♓	4	⟿	3	♉
6	⛎	5	♑	6	♓	5	♈	6	♉	5	♊
8	♐	7	♒	8	♈	7	⟿	8	♊	7	♋
10	♑	9	♓	10	⟿	9	♉	10	♋	9	♌
11	♒	11	♈	12	♉	11	♊	12	♌	11	♍
13	♓	13	⟿	14	♊	13	♋	14	♍	13	♎
15	♈	15	♉	16	♋	15	♌	16	♎	14	♏
17	⟿	17	♊	18	♌	17	♍	18	♏	16	⛎
19	♉	19	♋	20	♍	19	♎	19	⛎	18	♐
21	♊	21	♌	22	♎	21	♏	21	♐	20	♑
23	♋	23	♍	24	♏	23	⛎	23	♑	22	♒
25	♌	25	♎	26	⛎	25	♐	25	♒	24	♓
27	♍	27	♏	27	♐	27	♑	27	♓	26	♈
29	♎	29	⛎	29	♑	29	♒	29	♈	28	⟿
31	♏	31	♐			31	♓			30	♉

TABLE 4 209

1972

January	February	March	April	May	June
2 ♊	2 ♌	1 ♍	2 ♏	1 ♐	2 ♑
4 ♋	3 ♍	3 ♎	4 ♐	3 ♐	4 ♒
6 ♌	5 ♎	5 ♏	6 ♐	5 ♑	6 ♓
8 ♍	7 ♏	7 ♐	8 ♑	7 ♒	8 ♈
9 ♎	9 ♐	9 ♐	10 ♒	9 ♓	10 ♈
11 ♏	11 ♐	11 ♑	12 ♓	11 ♈	12 ♉
13 ♐	13 ♑	13 ♒	14 ♈	13 ♈	13 ♊
15 ♐	15 ♒	15 ♓	16 ♈	15 ♉	15 ♋
17 ♑	17 ♓	17 ♈	18 ♉	17 ♊	17 ♌
19 ♒	19 ♈	19 ♈	20 ♊	19 ♋	19 ♍
21 ♓	21 ♈	21 ♉	21 ♋	21 ♌	21 ♎
23 ♈	23 ♉	23 ♊	23 ♌	23 ♍	23 ♏
25 ♈	25 ♊	25 ♋	25 ♍	25 ♎	25 ♐
27 ♉	27 ♋	27 ♌	27 ♎	27 ♏	27 ♐
29 ♊	28 ♌	29 ♍	29 ♏	29 ♐	29 ♑
31 ♋		31 ♎		31 ♐	

July	August	September	October	November	December
1 ♒	1 ♈	1 ♉	2 ♋	1 ♌	1 ♍
3 ♓	2 ♈	3 ♊	4 ♌	3 ♍	3 ♎
5 ♈	4 ♉	5 ♋	6 ♍	5 ♎	5 ♏
7 ♈	6 ♊	7 ♌	8 ♎	7 ♏	7 ♐
8 ♉	8 ♋	9 ♍	10 ♏	9 ♐	9 ♐
10 ♊	10 ♌	11 ♎	12 ♐	11 ♐	11 ♑
12 ♋	12 ♍	13 ♏	14 ♐	13 ♑	13 ♒
14 ♌	14 ♎	15 ♐	16 ♑	15 ♒	14 ♓
16 ♍	16 ♏	17 ♐	18 ♒	17 ♓	16 ♈
18 ♎	18 ♐	19 ♑	20 ♓	19 ♈	18 ♈
20 ♏	20 ♐	21 ♒	22 ♈	21 ♈	20 ♉
22 ♐	22 ♑	23 ♓	24 ♈	23 ♉	22 ♊
24 ♐	24 ♒	24 ♈	26 ♉	25 ♊	24 ♋
26 ♑	26 ♓	26 ♈	28 ♊	27 ♋	26 ♌
28 ♒	28 ♈	28 ♉	30 ♋	29 ♌	28 ♍
30 ♓	30 ♈	30 ♊			30 ♎

1973

January	February	March	April	May	June
1 ♏	1 ♐	2 ♑	2 ♓	1 ♈	2 ♉
3 ⛎	3 ♑	4 ♒	4 ♈	3 Ↄ	4 ♊
5 ♐	4 ♒	6 ♓	6 Ↄ	5 ♉	6 ♋
7 ♑	6 ♓	8 ♈	8 ♉	7 ♊	8 ♌
8 ♒	8 ♈	10 Ↄ	10 ♊	9 ♋	10 ♍
10 ♓	10 Ↄ	12 ♉	12 ♋	11 ♌	12 ♎
12 ♈	12 ♉	14 ♊	14 ♌	13 ♍	14 ♏
14 Ↄ	14 ♊	16 ♋	16 ♍	15 ♎	15 ⛎
16 ♉	16 ♋	18 ♌	18 ♎	17 ♏	17 ♐
18 ♊	18 ♌	20 ♍	20 ♏	19 ⛎	19 ♑
20 ♋	20 ♍	22 ♎	22 ⛎	21 ♐	21 ♒
22 ♌	22 ♎	24 ♏	23 ♐	23 ♑	23 ♓
24 ♍	24 ♏	26 ⛎	25 ♑	25 ♒	25 ♈
26 ♎	26 ⛎	28 ♐	27 ♒	27 ♓	27 Ↄ
28 ♏	28 ♐	29 ♑	29 ♓	29 ♈	29 ♉
30 ⛎		31 ♒		31 Ↄ	

July	August	September	October	November	December
1 ♊	1 ♌	1 ♎	2 ⛎	1 ♐	2 ♒
3 ♋	3 ♍	3 ♏	4 ♐	3 ♑	4 ♓
5 ♌	5 ♎	5 ⛎	6 ♑	5 ♒	6 ♈
7 ♍	7 ♏	7 ♐	8 ♒	7 ♓	8 Ↄ
9 ♎	9 ⛎	9 ♑	10 ♓	9 ♈	10 ♉
10 ♏	11 ♐	11 ♒	12 ♈	11 Ↄ	12 ♊
12 ⛎	13 ♑	13 ♓	14 Ↄ	13 ♉	13 ♋
14 ♐	15 ♒	15 ♈	16 ♉	15 ♊	15 ♌
16 ♑	17 ♓	17 Ↄ	18 ♊	17 ♋	17 ♍
18 ♒	19 ♈	19 ♉	20 ♋	18 ♌	19 ♎
20 ♓	21 Ↄ	21 ♊	22 ♌	20 ♍	21 ♏
22 ♈	23 ♉	23 ♋	24 ♍	22 ♎	23 ⛎
24 Ↄ	25 ♊	25 ♌	26 ♎	24 ♏	25 ♐
26 ♉	27 ♋	26 ♍	28 ♏	26 ⛎	27 ♑
28 ♊	29 ♌	28 ♎	30 ⛎	28 ♐	29 ♒
30 ♋	31 ♍	30 ♏		30 ♑	31 ♓

(Symbols: ♈ Aries, Ↄ Cetus, ♉ Taurus, ♊ Gemini, ♋ Cancer, ♌ Leo, ♍ Virgo, ♎ Libra, ♏ Scorpio, ⛎ Ophiuchus, ♐ Sagittarius, ♑ Capricorn, ♒ Aquarius, ♓ Pisces)

TABLE 4 211

1974

January	February	March	April	May	June
2 ♈	1 ♈	1 ♉	2 ♋	1 ♌	1 ♎
4 ♈	3 ♉	3 ♊	4 ♌	3 ♍	3 ♏
6 ♉	4 ♊	5 ♋	6 ♍	5 ♎	5 ♐
8 ♊	6 ♋	7 ♌	8 ♎	7 ♏	7 ♐
10 ♋	8 ♌	9 ♍	10 ♏	9 ♐	9 ♑
12 ♌	10 ♍	11 ♎	12 ♐	11 ♐	11 ♒
14 ♍	12 ♎	13 ♏	14 ♐	13 ♑	13 ♓
16 ♎	14 ♏	15 ♐	16 ♑	15 ♒	15 ♈
18 ♏	16 ♐	17 ♐	18 ♒	17 ♓	17 ♈
20 ♐	18 ♐	19 ♑	20 ♓	18 ♈	19 ♉
22 ♐	20 ♑	21 ♒	22 ♈	20 ♈	21 ♊
24 ♑	22 ♒	23 ♓	23 ♈	22 ♉	23 ♋
26 ♒	24 ♓	25 ♈	25 ♉	24 ♊	25 ♌
28 ♓	26 ♈	27 ♈	27 ♊	26 ♋	27 ♍
30 ♈	28 ♈	29 ♉	29 ♋	28 ♌	29 ♎
		31 ♊		30 ♍	

July	August	September	October	November	December
1 ♏	2 ♐	1 ♒	2 ♈	1 ♈	2 ♊
3 ♐	4 ♑	3 ♓	4 ♈	3 ♉	4 ♋
5 ♐	6 ♒	5 ♈	6 ♉	5 ♊	6 ♌
7 ♑	7 ♓	7 ♈	8 ♊	7 ♋	8 ♍
9 ♒	9 ♈	9 ♉	10 ♋	9 ♌	10 ♎
11 ♓	11 ♈	11 ♊	12 ♌	11 ♍	12 ♏
13 ♈	13 ♉	13 ♋	14 ♍	13 ♎	13 ♐
15 ♈	15 ♊	15 ♌	16 ♎	15 ♏	15 ♐
17 ♉	17 ♋	17 ♍	18 ♏	17 ♐	17 ♑
19 ♊	19 ♌	19 ♎	20 ♐	18 ♐	19 ♒
21 ♋	21 ♍	21 ♏	22 ♐	20 ♑	21 ♓
23 ♌	23 ♎	23 ♐	24 ♑	22 ♒	23 ♈
25 ♍	25 ♏	25 ♐	26 ♒	24 ♓	25 ♈
27 ♎	27 ♐	26 ♑	28 ♓	26 ♈	27 ♉
29 ♏	29 ♐	28 ♒	30 ♈	28 ♈	29 ♊
31 ♐	31 ♑	30 ♓		30 ♉	31 ♋

1975

January	February	March	April	May	June
2 ♌	1 ♍	1 ♎	1 ⛎	1 ♐	1 ♒
4 ♍	3 ♎	3 ♏	3 ♐	3 ♑	3 ♓
6 ♎	4 ♏	5 ⛎	5 ♑	5 ♒	5 ♈
8 ♏	6 ⛎	7 ♐	7 ♒	7 ♓	7 ⌒
10 ⛎	8 ♐	9 ♑	9 ♓	9 ♈	9 ♉
12 ♐	10 ♑	11 ♒	11 ♈	11 ⌒	11 ♊
14 ♑	12 ♒	13 ♓	13 ⌒	13 ♉	12 ♋
16 ♒	14 ♓	15 ♈	15 ♉	15 ♊	14 ♌
18 ♓	16 ♈	17 ⌒	17 ♊	17 ♋	16 ♍
20 ♈	18 ⌒	19 ♉	19 ♋	18 ♌	18 ♎
22 ⌒	20 ♉	21 ♊	21 ♌	20 ♍	20 ♏
24 ♉	22 ♊	23 ♋	23 ♍	22 ♎	22 ⛎
26 ♊	24 ♋	25 ♌	25 ♎	24 ♏	24 ♐
28 ♋	26 ♌	26 ♍	27 ♏	26 ⛎	26 ♑
30 ♌	28 ♍	28 ♎	29 ⛎	28 ♐	28 ♒
		30 ♏		30 ♑	30 ♓

July	August	September	October	November	December
2 ♈	1 ⌒	1 ♊	2 ♌	2 ♎	1 ♏
4 ⌒	3 ♉	2 ♋	4 ♍	4 ♏	3 ⛎
6 ♉	4 ♊	4 ♌	6 ♎	6 ⛎	5 ♐
8 ♊	6 ♋	6 ♍	8 ♏	8 ♐	7 ♑
10 ♋	8 ♌	8 ♎	10 ⛎	10 ♑	9 ♒
12 ♌	10 ♍	10 ♏	12 ♐	12 ♒	11 ♓
14 ♍	12 ♎	12 ⛎	14 ♑	14 ♓	13 ♈
16 ♎	14 ♏	14 ♐	16 ♒	16 ♈	15 ⌒
18 ♏	16 ⛎	16 ♑	18 ♓	18 ⌒	17 ♉
20 ⛎	18 ♐	18 ♒	20 ♈	20 ♉	19 ♊
22 ♐	20 ♑	20 ♓	22 ⌒	22 ♊	21 ♋
24 ♑	22 ♒	22 ♈	24 ♉	24 ♋	23 ♌
26 ♒	24 ♓	24 ⌒	26 ♊	26 ♌	25 ♍
28 ♓	26 ♈	26 ♉	28 ♋	27 ♍	26 ♎
30 ♈	28 ⌒	28 ♊	29 ♌	29 ♎	28 ♏
	30 ♉	30 ♋	31 ♍		30 ⛎

4: Mercury

BEFORE WE GO into the astrological meaning of the planet Mercury, a few words on planetary motion are in order. The planets were called "wandering stars" by the ancients because, unlike the "fixed" stars, they seemed to be free to wander about among the constellations. Closer study revealed that their motions, though complex, were regular, and their risings and settings could be predicted.

Of course, the planets revolve around the sun in nearly circular orbits, as does the one we live on, the earth. But since astrology is a *geocentric* science—the view of the universe being that of a fixed earth at the center —the motions of the other planets *seem* more irregular than they actually are; in fact, downright strange! Mercury, for example, occasionally seems to go backward. This is known as *retrograde motion*. The planet does not, of course, slow down and back up, but it seems to from our point of view on earth. Thus, in March 1900, Mercury moved from Aquarius into Pisces; then it moved *back* into Aquarius; finally, in April of the same year, it returned to Pisces and went on into Aries according to its regular forward progression. This phenomenon can be understood if you imagine yourself looking at the sun and being able to see Mercury at the same time. The sun's apparent motion is carrying it forward through the constellations, from Pisces to Aquarius, and Mercury is whirling around it in its rapid orbit. Obviously, as you observe from earth, Mercury will sometimes appear to be ahead of the sun, sometimes even with it, and sometimes *behind* it. It is like a small boy walking forward and whirling a yo-yo around his head. The yo-yo circles the boy's head, but it is part of the *system* that is moving forward. So, when you look up dates and positions in the planetary tables, do not think that you are finding mistakes when the signs are occasionally out of order.

MEANING OF MERCURY IN HOROSCOPE

As mentioned above, Mercury is closer to the sun than is the earth; it is also smaller. It is the first of the nine known planets, and its proximity to the sun gives it a surface temperature of 610°F.; therefore, it is highly unlikely that there is life on this planet. It is fast-moving, its orbit being only 88 earth days, and it moves through 1,494 degrees per year. Also, it is never more than 28 degrees from the sun, so it is highly probable that Mercury on your natal chart will either be in your sun sign or in the sign immediately preceding or following it.

Mercury was named for the wing-footed messenger of the gods, whom the Greeks called Hermes. He is usually pictured as a handsome, swift-moving youth with wings on his helmet and heels, carrying a caduceus, the wand that signified his dual role as divine herald and conductor of souls to the underworld (used today as a symbol of medicine). It is generally agreed by astrologers that Mercury represents the intellect and most forms of mental or physical communication. We derive our adjective "mercurial" from this god's speed, agility, and occasional duplicity and undependability. Having this dual aspect, Mercury is neither beneficent nor malefic in your chart, but a mixture of both, depending upon the other aspects in your horoscope. A well-aspected Mercury usually increases the strength of your intellect, especially where mental agility and analytical ability are concerned. It will also positively affect your ability to do two things at once, or to hold down two jobs simultaneously, as Mercury is one of the "double" signs. If your Mercury is badly aspected, however, it can produce a tendency to be two-faced, fickle, or unstable. As always, one must study the aspects of all the planets, and note their Houses, to interpret one's horoscope properly.

Mercury rules two signs, Gemini and Virgo, so it is a particularly important element in your chart if one of these is your sun sign. It is the intellect of Gemini types that is most strongly affected by the ruling planet; Virgo types usually receive an increase (or decrease) in their analytical ability from the influence of ruling Mercury.

To place the symbol of Mercury (☿) on your chart, turn to Table 5 at the end of this chapter. Here the positions of Mercury are listed for each year from 1890 to 1975. Turn to the year of your birth and find the span of time that includes your birthdate. It should be noted that Table 5 lists inclusive sets of dates. That is, if you were born on the seventh and the table lists Mercury in Ophiuchus from the first to the seventh, Mercury was still in Ophiuchus on your birthdate, since it did not enter Sagittarius until the eighth. As a reminder, the symbols of the 14 signs are given in a key at the beginning of Table 5.

To continue our example of someone born on January 1, 1940, with Aquarius rising, Figure 5 shows his chart with the symbol of Mercury entered. In Table 5, it is shown that Mercury was in Ophiuchus on January 1, 1940; therefore, the symbol of Mercury is entered in the House occupied by Ophiuchus, which (on his chart) is the twelfth House.

INTERPRETATION

General interpretations of the meaning of Mercury in each of the 14 signs are given below. In reading these, it should be remembered that Mercury has no absolute meaning; whether it is a help or a hindrance depends upon its relationship to other elements of your chart. Also, the House occupied by Mercury affects its interpretation. Our imaginary subject (Figure 5) was born with Mercury in Ophiuchus, which is his twelfth House. After reading the interpretation of Mercury in Ophiuchus, he should turn back to Table 1 (p. 4), which lists the basic meanings of the Houses. The life activity governed by that particular House will be enhanced by the presence of Mercury. This is also true of the other planets, of course, which we will be placing in the chapters to follow.

MERCURY IN PISCES ☿ ♓

Mercury in Pisces on your chart will make its effect felt primarily in matters of belief. This includes not only belief in the conventional sense, concerning religion or the choice of a philosophy of life, but your belief in yourself as an individual. Pisces is ruled by Neptune, which is often connected with spiritual affairs. The presence of Mercury—with its effect on intellect, analytical ability, and versatility—in Pisces tends to offset blind faith. If you have strong spiritual convictions, they have probably withstood the test of hard thought and close analysis. People with Mercury in Pisces are of the type that founded Gnosticism in the early centuries of the Christian era. That is, persons whose minds could not be contented with acceptance of the supernatural "on faith"—who had to realize the universe, and its Creator, as a logical structure, something that their minds as well as their hearts could recognize and appreciate. Your spiritual beliefs and inclinations can either be weakened or strengthened by Mercury in this position, depending upon its aspects to other elements of your chart. The meaning of the aspects will be taken up in Chapter 12. In the meantime, check the life activity governed by the House occupied

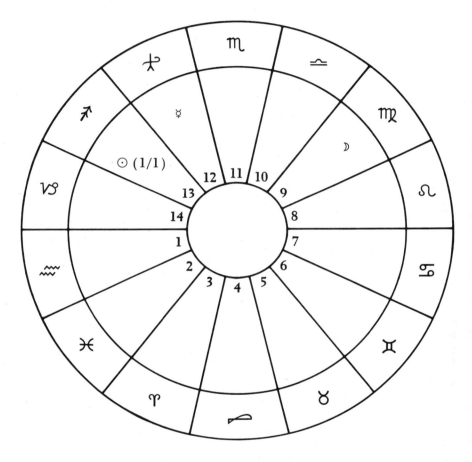

Figure 5. Placement of Mercury on chart of subject born on January 1, 1940, with Aquarius rising

by Pisces on your chart (see Table 1) for a clearer picture of the influence of Mercury on your belief and spiritual drive.

MERCURY IN ARIES ☿ ♈

Mercury in Aries on your chart affects the power of your will. Whatever your position in life, whatever shape your desires and ambitions may take, it is obvious that in almost every case nothing can be achieved without the driving power of will. In an increasingly large and complex society, with tremendous pressure placed on the individual to conform to the accepted norm, it is much harder today to carve out a personal empire than it was, say, in the nineteenth century. You may have intelligence, talent, and singleness of purpose, but these are ineffective without the will to drive them forward and stick to your purpose. Mercury in Aries, if well aspected to other elements in your horoscope, can help you greatly. Where all else fails, the simple will to go on, never to give up despite apparently overwhelming odds, can often lead to success and victory. On the other hand, a poorly aspected Mercury may lead you into a position of rigidity and inflexibility. Strength of will is one thing; dogmatism is quite another. In most cases, however, Mercury, the "dual" and subtle, will enable you to bend when the winds of opposition are of breaking strength. The meaning of the aspects will be taken up in Chapter 12. In the meantime, check the life activity governed by the House occupied by Aries on your chart (see Table 1) for a clearer picture of the influence of Mercury on the strength of your will.

MERCURY IN CETUS ☿ ♎

Mercury in Cetus on your chart will make itself felt at the heart of your being—your self-regard, your relations with others, and your career. Cetus is ruled by Jupiter, the "greater fortune," and a well-aspected Mercury will certainly increase your chances of success and happiness, especially if you are planning or engaging in a career in the performing or graphic arts. Mercury, a charmer himself, will enhance the natural charm and self-confidence associated with Cetus. Moreover, the intellectual and analytical qualities associated with Mercury can balance out a personality that may rely too much on charm, good looks, and personal magnetism. On the other hand, a poorly aspected Mercury can lead to self-doubts and have a repressive effect on your natural exuberance and love of life and people. In some cases, this can tend to increase a sense of personal inferiority and awkwardness in the presence of others. As always, the *total* horoscope must be considered for a complete picture of the individual personality, both actual and potential. The meaning of the aspects will be taken up in Chapter 12. In the meantime, check the life activity governed by the House occupied by Cetus on your chart (see Table 1) for a clearer picture of the influence of Mercury on your estimation of yourself, your personal relations, and your career.

MERCURY IN TAURUS ☿ ♉

Mercury in Taurus on your chart will probably make its influence felt where your affairs of the heart and marriage are concerned. Taurus is ruled by Venus, and a proper balance between masculine Mercury and feminine Venus bodes well for romantic success and happiness. Venus is also associated with music. It has been noted above that Taurus is the strongest sign for musical talent in the Zodiac; also, that music is often allied with mathematics and the physical sciences. So the intellectual and analytical qualities of Mercury, when placed in Taurus, indicate extremely good chances for success in the fields of music and the "hard" sciences, as well as in affairs of the heart. This depends, of course, on its aspects to other elements in your chart. Favorable aspects indicate not only success in these fields, but that you are attractive to the opposite sex, understand and get along well with them; you have great sensitivity of feeling and probably possess uncommon physical strength. A poorly aspected Mercury, however, will increase your innate shyness, making it difficult for you to relax on social occasions; it may also make you possessive beyond reasonable limits. The meaning of the aspects will be taken up in Chapter 12. In the meantime, check the life activity governed by the House occupied by Taurus on your chart (see Table 1) for a clearer picture of the influence of Mercury on your love life and career.

MERCURY IN GEMINI ☿ ♊

Mercury in Gemini on your chart will tend to strengthen or double the intrinsic qualities of both the planet Mercury and the sign Gemini, as Mercury is the ruling planet of this sign. We have noted that Gemini types are outstanding for the strength and agility of their intellect, especially where communication (both written and oral) is concerned. If well aspected to other elements in your chart, therefore, Mercury in Gemini will enhance your versatility, the nimbleness of your mind, and your ability to express yourself clearly and concisely, whether in written form or in conversation. These traits can increase the color and power of your personality, as well as make you a more valuable employee in many fields. On the other hand, should your Mercury be poorly aspected to other elements, the "dark" side of Mercury can be felt in your life. You may earn a reputation for fickleness or untrustworthiness—a "here today, gone tomorrow" person whom others will hesitate to depend on, both in business and in matters of the heart. The meaning of the aspects will be taken up in Chapter 12. In the meantime, check the life activity governed by the House occupied by Gemini on your chart (see Table 1) for a clearer picture of the influence of Mercury on your intellectual traits and powers of communication.

MERCURY IN CANCER ☿ ♋

Mercury in Cancer on your chart will probably enhance the sensitivity of your emotions. Cancer is the only sign ruled by the feminine moon, and the presence of masculine, wing-footed Mercury in this sign will certainly affect your emotional life. Whether this influence is positive or negative depends, of course, on the aspects of Mercury to other elements in your chart. A well-aspected Mercury will increase your emotional sensitivity and your innate sense of conservatism, making you strongly conscious of your duty to your family, friends, and employer. Mercury will help you to analyze your prospects clearly and realistically, and you won't make a move without being sure it is in the right direction. If you can resist a tendency to partake in dangerous sports, you will probably lead a long and successful life, your sensitivity to others and sense of humor making you a social success as well as a solid citizen. If your Mercury is poorly aspected, however, you may plunge recklessly both professionally and socially, "fickle" Mercury overriding your conservative caution. The meaning of the aspects will be taken up in Chapter 12. In the meantime, check the life activity governed by the House occupied by Cancer on your chart (see Table 1) for a clearer picture of the influence of Mercury on your emotional sensitivity and the other traits mentioned above.

MERCURY IN LEO ☿ ♌

Mercury in Leo on your chart makes its effect felt in your sense of personal independence. Leo is the only sign ruled by the sun, the masculine principle in the Zodiac, and the presence of swift-footed Mercury (also masculine) in this sign usually bodes well for strength as well as independence of character. Such a conjunction can, however, be either bad or good, depending on other elements in your chart. If well aspected, Mercury in Leo will enhance your leadership ability, helping to make you a pace-setter rather than a follower of trends established by others. It can strengthen and color your personality, so that the bonds of friendship you forge will be all but unbreakable—and make you equally implacable as an enemy! The Leo/Mercury combination leads to anything but wishy-washy personalities. If your Mercury is badly aspected to other planets, you may have a tendency to carry the trait of independence to extremes—a real maverick who can't adjust to any social norms or conventions may end up as a very lonely man or woman. As always, moderation is the best rule. The meaning of the aspects will be taken up in Chapter 12. In the meantime, check the life activity governed by the House occupied by Leo on your chart (see Table 1) for a clearer picture of the influence of Mercury on your sense of personal independence.

MERCURY IN VIRGO ☿ ♍

Virgo is one of the two signs ruled by Mercury. As is the case with Gemini, then, the presence of ruling Mercury in Virgo will strengthen or double the intrinsic qualities of both the planet Mercury and the sign Virgo. We have noted that Virgo types stand out for their individualism and for their analytical ability—both traits that will ordinarily be enhanced by the presence of Mercury. If this planet is well aspected to other elements in your chart, you will tend to be strongly individualistic, the colorful and slightly off-beat type of personality that usually bears a nickname and is recognized by everyone in your vicinity. The strong, positive effect of Mercury on your intellect will enhance your already considerable analytical ability. This will increase your value as an employee, as you can quickly see newer and better ways of doing things. It will also help your social life, as you can also analyze people's motives, and it would take an excellent actor to fool you. If your Mercury is poorly aspected, however, you may carry the analytical ability too far, so that your friends and family can justly complain that you analyze people and situations to death. The meaning of the aspects will be taken up in Chapter 12. In the meantime, check the life activity governed by the House occupied by Virgo on your chart (see Table 1) for a clearer picture of the influence of Mercury on your individualism and analytical ability.

MERCURY IN LIBRA ☿ ♎

Mercury in Libra on your chart will probably affect the quality of your judgment. The presence of this planet adds quickness and keenness to the Libran intuition for justice—the ability to weigh both sides of an argument dispassionately and without prejudice. Also, Libra (like Taurus) is ruled by Venus, the planet associated with love and musical talent. If your Mercury is well aspected to other elements in your chart, not only your ability to make fair judgments will be enhanced, but also your chances of success and happiness in love and marriage; and it is more than likely that you are gifted in the art of music. (Taurus types usually tend to be instrumentalists, whereas Libra-type musicians often excel in the vocal arts.) A career in politics or any branch of the law or as a singer would seem to be indicated. However, if your Mercury is badly aspected, you may tend to lack confidence in your ability to judge—or, on the other hand, to be too dogmatic in your opinions. And, of course, a singer can hardly afford lack of confidence in his voice! The meaning of the aspects will be taken up in Chapter 12. In the meantime, check the life activity governed by the House occupied by Libra on your chart (see Table 1) for a clearer picture of the influence of Mercury on the quality of your judgment.

MERCURY IN SCORPIO ☿ ♏

Mercury in Scorpio on your chart will probably make its effect felt in your empathy; that is, your sensitivity to the feelings of others. Scorpio is ruled by Mars, which is often associated with warlike traits, but we have noted that Scorpio types tend to be strongly humanistic—sometimes to the point of martyrdom—with an innate passion for justice. If your Mercury is well aspected to other elements in your chart, you are probably deeply sensitive to the moods and feelings of those around you, strongly idealistic, and have a touch of the poet or mystic in your makeup. You are always concerned with the betterment of the human lot, whether or not you take an active part in movements for greater social justice. Your sensitivity, warmth, and genuine concern for others are traits that easily draw friends and lovers to you. If your Mercury is poorly aspected, however, you have probably grown used to the remark that you are *too* sensitive for your own good, suffering needlessly over wrongs that you are powerless to set right. Also, unscrupulous people may take advantage of your desire to help. The meaning of the aspects will be taken up in Chapter 12. In the meantime, check the life activity governed by the House occupied by Scorpio on your chart (see Table 1) for a clearer picture of the influence of Mercury on your empathy and humanistic ideals.

MERCURY IN OPHIUCHUS ☿ ⛎

Mercury in Ophiuchus on your chart will probably enhance your versatility and resourcefulness. The quickness and mental agility associated with Mercury, if it is well aspected to other elements in your chart, can give a positive boost to these traits, which are more and more necessary as the society we live in becomes more and more complex. Ophiuchus is ruled by Pluto, named for the god Plutus, who is a personification of wealth; this is appropriate, for Ophiuchus types are often endowed with a wealth of talents and abilities. Ophiuchus types being noted for their talents, we find many of them in the field of entertainment, so it is more than likely that a well-aspected Mercury in this sign will mean you are endowed as an actor, singer, dancer, mimic, etc. Sensitivity usually accompanies talent, and you also possess personal charm. If your Mercury is poorly aspected, however, you may find yourself in an inappropriate field for the exploitation of your talents; or, even worse, be frustrated in your attempts to express them. The meaning of the aspects will be taken up in Chapter 12. In the meantime, check the life activity governed by the House occupied by Ophiuchus on your chart (see Table 1) for a clearer picture of the influence of Mercury on your versatility, resourcefulness, and talents.

MERCURY IN SAGITTARIUS ☿ ♐

Mercury in Sagittarius on your chart will probably make its effect felt in the areas of your conscience, your extraversion, and your humanitarian activities. Sagittarius is ruled by Jupiter, the "greater fortune," which is why Sagittarius types are often thought to be lucky. If your Mercury is well aspected, its effect on your intellect, combined with the benevolence of Jupiter, can indeed lead to good fortune and success in all areas of life. You are outgoing, sociable, and good natured; moreover, your conscience leads you into fields where you can do something to better the lot of humanity. Unlike Scorpio types, who are also humanitarians, you wish to act on your ideals, there being little of the poet or mystic in your nature. A poorly aspected Mercury, on the other hand, can lead to over-development of your active, extraverted side while you ignore your inner, intuitive nature. In extreme cases, this would lead to a lopsided personality and endanger your psychic health. The meaning of the aspects will be taken up in Chapter 12. In the meantime, check the life activity governed by the House occupied by Sagittarius on your chart (see Table 1) for a clearer picture of the influence of Mercury on your conscience and extraverted tendencies.

MERCURY IN CAPRICORN ☿ ♑

Mercury in Capricorn on your chart will probably enhance your conservatism. Capricorn is ruled by Saturn, a planet often associated with old age, illness, and misfortune. Although Saturn is usually considered malevolent, a well-aspected Mercury in this sign can offset its apparent disadvantages, "youthful" and quick-thinking Mercury balancing the realism and conservatism of Saturn. The traits of conservatism and a dryly realistic approach to life are bad only if carried to extremes. You can avoid waste without being a miser, and a realistic attitude to life's problems is often not only beneficial but necessary for sheer survival! Capricorn types are often gifted with a dry wit and not infrequently with genius. However, a poorly aspected Mercury can lead to a one-sided personality that excludes all dreams as nonsense, and a full life cannot be lived without dreams. It may also mean that emotional childishness will not be outgrown, but can continue through adulthood, making it impossible to develop as a mature and well-rounded human being. The meaning of the aspects will be taken up in Chapter 12. In the meantime, check the life activity governed by the House occupied by Capricorn on your chart (see Table 1) for a clearer picture of the influence of Mercury on your conservatism and realistic approach to life.

MERCURY IN AQUARIUS ☿ ♒

Mercury in Aquarius on your chart strongly affects your intellect and aids in the acquirement of knowledge, especially of the scientific or technical type. Aquarius is ruled by Uranus, sometimes called the "the disruptor" because of its eccentric orbit. A well-aspected Mercury will not only sharpen your wits in areas of technology and science, but will be a positive help if you should go into the field of entertainment (as many Aquarius types have). You have an inquiring mind and are attracted to the odd, the unusual, even the eccentric. Your ability to be practical and creative at the same time bodes well for success in many careers besides those connected with science or entertainment, for which you probably have a particular flair. A poorly aspected Mercury, however, may tend to influence the development of too much temperament and nervousness; you will find it necessary to keep in top physical and mental condition, especially if your forte is one of the performing arts. You have a keen critical and analytical sense, but these can be damaging to your career and personal relationships if they are overdone. The meaning of the aspects will be taken up in Chapter 12. In the meantime, check the life activity governed by the House occupied by Aquarius on your chart (see Table 1) for a clearer picture of the influence of Mercury on your temperament, scientific or technical practicality, and possible "disruptive" elements in your makeup.

Table 5

POSITIONS OF MERCURY BY YEAR (1890 TO 1975)

Key

♓	Pisces	♍	Virgo
♈	Aries	♎	Libra
⤳	Cetus	♏	Scorpio
♉	Taurus	⚕	Ophiuchus
♊	Gemini	♐	Sagittarius
♋	Cancer	♑	Capricorn
♌	Leo	♒	Aquarius

TABLE 5 225

1890		1891		1892	
Dates	*Sign*	*Dates*	*Sign*	*Dates*	*Sign*
Jan. 1–Jan. 8	♐	Jan. 1–Feb. 17	♐	Jan. 1–Jan. 24	♐
Jan. 9–Jan. 31	♑	Feb. 18–Mar. 7	♑	Jan. 25–Feb. 11	♐
Feb. 1–Feb. 21	♐	Mar. 8–Mar. 21	♒	Feb. 12–Feb. 27	♑
Feb. 22–Mar. 13	♑	Mar. 22–Apr. 3	♓	Feb. 28–Mar. 12	♒
Mar. 14–Mar. 30	♒	Apr. 4–Apr. 21	♈	Mar. 13–Mar. 27	♓
Mar. 31–Apr. 11	♓	Apr. 22 –May 7	♎	Mar. 28–Apr. 26	♈
Apr. 12–Apr. 24	♈	May 8–June 4	♈	Apr. 27–May 8	♓
Apr. 25–June 29	♎	June 5–June 23	♎	May 9–May 31	♈
June 30–July 13	♉	June 24–July 4	♉	June 1–June 14	♎
July 14–July 25	♊	July 5–July 16	♊	June 15–June 25	♉
July 26–Aug. 6	♋	July 17–July 30	♋	June 26–July 8	♊
Aug. 7–Aug. 23	♌	July 31–Aug. 21	♌	July 9–July 25	♋
Aug. 24–Oct. 27	♍	Aug. 22–Sept. 6	♍	July 26–Aug. 29	♌
Oct. 28–Nov. 12	♎	Sept. 7–Oct. 4	♌	Aug. 30–Sept. 9	♋
Nov. 13–Nov. 28	♏	Oct. 5–Oct. 19	♍	Sept. 10–Sept. 26	♌
Nov. 29–Dec. 16	♐	Oct. 20–Nov. 4	♎	Sept. 27–Oct. 11	♍
Dec. 17–Dec. 31	♐	Nov. 5–Nov. 21	♏	Oct. 12–Oct. 27	♎
		Nov. 22–Dec. 11	♐	Oct. 28–Nov. 14	♏
		Dec. 12–Dec. 25	♐	Nov. 15–Dec. 18	♐
		Dec. 26–Dec. 31	♐	Dec. 19–Dec. 25	♏
				Dec. 26–Dec. 31	♐

1893		1894		1895	
Dates	*Sign*	*Dates*	*Sign*	*Dates*	*Sign*
Jan. 1–Jan. 17	♐	Jan. 1–Jan. 11	♐	Jan. 1–Jan. 3	♐
Jan. 18–Feb. 3	♐	Jan. 12–Jan. 27	♐	Jan. 4–Jan. 19	♐
Feb. 4–Feb. 18	♑	Jan. 28–Feb. 10	♑	Jan. 20–Feb. 4	♑
Feb. 19–Mar. 5	♒	Feb. 11–Apr. 16	♒	Feb. 5–Feb. 28	♒
Mar. 6–May 9	♓	Apr. 17–May 3	♓	Mar. 1–Mar. 20	♑
May 10–May 24	♈	May 4–May 15	♈	Mar. 21–Apr. 11	♒
May 25–June 5	♎	May 16–May 27	♎	Apr. 12–Apr. 25	♓
June 6–June 16	♉	May 28–June 10	♉	Apr. 26–May 7	♈
June 17–July 2	♊	June 11–Aug. 15	♊	May 8–May 19	♎
July 3–Sept. 5	♋	Aug. 16–Aug. 28	♋	May 20–June 7	♉
Sept. 6–Sept. 18	♌	Aug. 29–Sept. 10	♌	June 8–June 29	♊
Sept. 19–Oct. 3	♍	Sept. 11–Sept. 26	♍	June 30–July 23	♉
Oct. 4–Oct. 20	♎	Sept. 27–Oct. 16	♎	July 24–Aug. 7	♊
Oct. 21–Dec. 23	♏	Oct. 17–Nov. 10	♏	Aug. 8–Aug. 20	♋
Dec. 24–Dec. 31	♐	Nov. 11–Nov. 29	♎	Aug. 21–Sept. 3	♌

continued

1893		1894		1895	
Dates	*Sign*	*Dates*	*Sign*	*Dates*	*Sign*
		Nov. 30–Dec. 17	♏	Sept. 4–Sept. 20	♍
		Dec. 18–Dec. 31	⛎	Sept. 21–Nov. 23	♎
				Nov. 24–Dec. 10	♏
				Dec. 11–Dec. 27	⛎
				Dec. 28–Dec. 31	♐

1896		1897		1898	
Dates	*Sign*	*Dates*	*Sign*	*Dates*	*Sign*
Jan. 1–Jan. 12	♐	Jan. 1–Jan. 7	♐	Jan. 1–Jan. 11	♐
Jan. 13–Mar. 16	♑	Jan. 8–Jan. 18	♑	Jan. 12–Jan. 24	⛎
Mar. 17–Apr. 3	♒	Jan. 19–Feb. 20	♐	Jan. 25–Feb. 15	♐
Apr. 4–Apr. 16	♓	Feb. 21–Mar. 10	♑	Feb. 16–Mar. 3	♑
Apr. 17–Apr. 28	♈	Mar. 11–Mar. 26	♒	Mar. 4–Mar. 18	♒
Apr. 29–May 13	∿	Mar. 27–Apr. 7	♓	Mar. 19–Mar. 31	♓
May 14–June 16	♉	Apr. 8–Apr. 21	♈	Apr. 1–June 3	♈
June 17–June 25	∿	Apr. 22–June 26	∿	June 4–June 19	∿
June 26–July 17	♉	June 27–July 9	♉	June 20–June 30	♉
July 18–July 29	♊	July 10–July 21	♊	July 1–July 13	♊
July 30–Aug. 10	♋	July 22–Aug. 3	♋	July 14–July 27	♋
Aug. 11–Aug. 26	♌	Aug. 4–Aug. 21	♌	July 28–Oct. 1	♌
Aug. 27–Sept. 17	♍	Aug. 22–Sept. 26	♍	Oct. 2–Oct. 16	♍
Sept. 18–Oct. 3	♎	Sept. 27–Oct. 5	♌	Oct. 17–Nov. 1	♎
Oct. 4–Oct. 30	♍	Oct. 6–Oct. 23	♍	Nov. 2–Nov. 18	♏
Oct. 31–Nov. 15	♎	Oct. 24–Nov. 8	♎	Nov. 19–Dec. 31	⛎
Nov. 16–Dec. 2	♏	Nov. 9–Nov. 25	♏		
Dec. 3–Dec. 19	⛎	Nov. 26–Dec. 13	⛎		
Dec. 20–Dec. 31	♐	Dec. 14–Dec. 31	♐		

1899		1900		1901	
Dates	*Sign*	*Dates*	*Sign*	*Dates*	*Sign*
Jan. 1–Jan. 21	⛎	Jan. 1–Jan. 15	⛎	Jan. 1–Jan. 8	⛎
Jan. 22–Feb. 8	♐	Jan. 16–Feb. 1	♐	Jan. 9–Jan. 24	♐
Feb. 9–Feb. 23	♑	Feb. 2–Feb. 15	♑	Jan. 25–Feb. 8	♑
Feb. 24–Mar. 10	♒	Feb. 16–Mar. 3	♒	Feb. 9–Apr. 15	♒
Mar. 11–Mar. 28	♓	Mar. 4–Mar. 29	♓	Apr. 16–Apr. 30	♓
Mar. 29–Apr. 6	♈	Mar. 30–Apr. 16	♒	May 1–May 12	♈
Apr. 7–May 12	∿	Apr. 17–May 7	♓	May 13–May 24	∿
May 13–May 29	♈	May 8–May 21	♈	May 25–June 8	♉

TABLE 5 227

continued

1899		1900		1901	
Dates	*Sign*	*Dates*	*Sign*	*Dates*	*Sign*
May 30–June 10	♈	May 22–June 2	♈	June 9–Aug. 12	♊
June 11–June 22	♉	June 3–June 14	♉	Aug. 13–Aug. 25	♋
June 23–July 6	♊	June 15–July 1	♊	Aug. 26–Sept. 8	♌
July 7–July 26	♋	July 2–Aug. 5	♋	Sept. 9–Sept. 24	♍
July 27–Aug. 14	♌	Aug. 6–Aug. 16	♊	Sept. 25–Oct. 17	♎
Aug. 15–Sept. 9	♋	Aug. 17–Sept. 2	♋	Oct. 18–Oct. 30	♏
Sept. 10–Sept. 23	♌	Sept. 3–Sept. 15	♌	Oct. 31–Nov. 27	♎
Sept. 24–Oct. 8	♍	Sept. 16–Oct. 1	♍	Nov. 28–Dec. 15	♏
Oct. 9–Oct. 25	♎	Oct. 2–Oct. 19	♎	Dec. 16–Dec. 31	♐
Oct. 26–Nov. 13	♏	Oct. 20–Dec. 22	♏		
Nov. 14–Dec. 6	♐	Dec. 23–Dec. 31	♐		
Dec. 7–Dec. 26	♏				
Dec. 27–Dec. 31	♐				

1902		1903		1904	
Dates	*Sign*	*Dates*	*Sign*	*Dates*	*Sign*
Jan. 1	♐	Jan. 1–Jan. 10	♐	Jan. 1–Feb. 20	♐
Jan. 2–Jan. 17	♐	Jan. 11–Feb. 7	♑	Feb. 21–Mar. 8	♑
Jan. 18–Feb. 3	♑	Feb. 8–Feb. 22	♐	Mar. 9–Mar. 23	♒
Feb. 4–Feb. 15	♒	Feb. 23–Mar. 16	♑	Mar. 24–Apr. 5	♓
Feb. 16–Mar. 20	♑	Mar. 17–Apr. 1	♒	Apr. 6–Apr. 20	♈
Mar. 21–Apr. 8	♒	Apr. 2–Apr. 14	♓	Apr. 21–May 15	♈
Apr. 9–Apr. 22	♓	Apr. 15–Apr. 26	♈	May 16–June 4	♈
Apr. 23–May 4	♈	Apr. 27–May 18	♈	June 5–June 24	♈
May 5–May 17	♈	May 19–May 26	♉	June 25–July 6	♉
May 18–July 22	♉	May 27–June 29	♈	July 7–July 18	♊
July 23–Aug. 5	♊	June 30–July 15	♉	July 19–Aug. 1	♋
Aug. 6–Aug. 17	♋	July 16–July 27	♊	Aug. 2–Aug. 21	♌
Aug. 18–Aug. 31	♌	July 28–Aug. 9	♋	Aug. 22–Sept. 12	♍
Sept. 1–Sept. 19	♍	Aug. 10–Aug. 25	♌	Sept. 13–Oct. 5	♌
Sept. 20–Oct. 22	♎	Aug. 26–Oct. 29	♍	Oct. 6–Oct. 21	♍
Oct. 23–Nov. 3	♍	Oct. 30–Nov. 14	♎	Oct. 22–Nov. 6	♎
Nov. 4–Nov. 21	♎	Nov. 15–Nov. 30	♏	Nov. 7–Nov. 22	♏
Nov. 22–Dec. 8	♏	Dec. 1–Dec. 18	♐	Nov. 23–Dec. 12	♐
Dec. 9–Dec. 25	♐	Dec. 19–Dec. 31	♐	Dec. 13–Dec. 30	♐
Dec. 26–Dec. 31	♐			Dec. 31	♐

1905		1906		1907	
Dates	*Sign*	*Dates*	*Sign*	*Dates*	*Sign*
Jan. 1–Jan. 25	⛎	Jan. 1–Jan. 20	⛎	Jan. 1–Jan. 13	⛎
Jan. 26–Feb. 13	♐	Jan. 21–Feb. 6	♐	Jan. 14–Jan. 29	♐
Feb. 14–Feb. 28	♑	Feb. 7–Feb. 21	♑	Jan. 30–Feb. 13	♑
Mar. 1–Mar. 15	♒	Feb. 22–Mar. 7	♒	Feb. 14–Mar. 3	♒
Mar. 16–Mar. 29	♓	Mar. 8–May 11	♓	Mar. 4–Mar. 13	♓
Mar. 30–June 2	♈	May 12–May 26	♈	Mar. 14–Apr. 17	♒
June 3–June 16	↢	May 27–June 7	↢	Apr. 18–May 5	♓
June 17–June 27	♉	June 8–June 19	♉	May 6–May 18	♈
June 28–July 10	♊	June 20–July 4	♊	May 19–May 30	↢
July 11–July 26	♋	July 5–Sept. 7	♋	May 31–June 12	♉
July 27–Sept. 29	♌	Sept. 8–Sept. 21	♌	June 13–July 4	♊
Sept. 30–Oct. 13	♍	Sept. 22–Oct. 6	♍	July 5–July 17	♋
Oct. 14–Oct. 29	♎	Oct. 7–Oct. 23	♎	July 18–Aug. 17	♊
Oct. 30–Nov. 16	♏	Oct. 24–Nov. 14	♏	Aug. 18–Aug. 30	♋
Nov. 17–Dec. 31	⛎	Nov. 15–Nov. 24	⛎	Aug. 31–Sept. 13	♌
		Nov. 25–Dec. 25	♏	Sept. 14–Sept. 29	♍
		Dec. 26–Dec. 31	⛎	Sept. 30–Oct. 17	♎
				Oct. 18–Nov. 16	♏
				Nov. 17–Nov. 30	♎
				Dec. 1–Dec. 19	♏
				Dec. 20–Dec. 31	⛎

1908		1909		1910	
Dates	*Sign*	*Dates*	*Sign*	*Dates*	*Sign*
Jan. 1–Jan. 6	⛎	Jan. 1–Jan. 13	♐	Jan. 1–Jan. 8	♐
Jan. 7–Jan. 22	♐	Jan. 14–Mar. 18	♑	Jan. 9–Jan. 25	♑
Jan. 23–Feb. 6	♑	Mar. 19–Apr. 5	♒	Jan. 26–Feb. 22	♐
Feb. 7–Mar. 6	♒	Apr. 6–Apr. 18	♓	Feb. 23–Mar. 13	♑
Mar. 7–Mar. 19	♑	Apr. 19–Apr. 30	♈	Mar. 14–Mar. 28	♒
Mar. 20–Apr. 12	♒	May 1–May 15	↢	Mar. 29–Apr. 10	♓
Apr. 13–Apr. 27	♓	May 16–July 19	♉	Apr. 11–Apr. 23	♈
Apr. 28–May 9	♈	July 20–Aug. 1	♊	Apr. 24–June 28	↢
May 10–May 21	↢	Aug. 2–Aug. 13	♋	June 29–July 11	♉
May 22–June 7	♉	Aug. 14–Aug. 28	♌	July 12–July 23	♊
June 8–July 7	♊	Aug. 29–Sept. 18	♍	July 24–Aug. 5	♋
July 8–July 22	♉	Sept. 19–Oct. 9	♎	Aug. 6–Aug. 23	♌
July 23–Aug. 9	♊	Oct. 10–Nov. 1	♍	Aug. 24–Oct. 26	♍
Aug. 10–Aug. 21	♋	Nov. 2–Nov. 18	♎	Oct. 27–Nov. 11	♎
Aug. 22–Sept. 4	♌	Nov. 19–Dec. 4	♏	Nov. 12–Nov. 27	♏

TABLE 5 229

continued

1908		1909		1910	
Dates	*Sign*	*Dates*	*Sign*	*Dates*	*Sign*
Sept. 5–Sept. 21	♍	Dec. 5–Dec. 21	♐	Nov. 28–Dec. 15	♐
Sept. 22–Nov. 25	♎	Dec. 22–Dec. 31	♐	Dec. 16–Dec. 31	♐
Nov. 26–Dec. 11	♏				
Dec. 12–Dec. 29	♐				
Dec. 30–Dec. 31	♐				

1911		1912		1913	
Dates	*Sign*	*Dates*	*Sign*	*Dates*	*Sign*
Jan. 1–Jan. 18	♐	Jan. 1–Jan. 23	♐	Jan. 1–Jan. 17	♐
Jan. 19–Jan. 24	♐	Jan. 24–Feb. 10	♐	Jan. 18–Feb. 2	♐
Jan. 25–Feb. 17	♐	Feb. 11–Feb. 26	♑	Feb. 3–Feb. 17	♑
Feb. 18–Mar. 5	♑	Feb. 27–Mar. 11	♒	Feb. 18–Mar. 4	♒
Mar. 6–Mar. 20	♒	Mar. 12–Mar. 27	♓	Mar. 5–Apr. 7	♓
Mar. 21–Apr. 2	♓	Mar. 28–Apr. 14	♈	Apr. 8–Apr. 13	♒
Apr. 3–June 5	♈	Apr. 15–May 12	♓	Apr. 14–May 9	♓
June 6–June 21	♉	May 13–May 30	♈	May 10–May 23	♈
June 22–July 3	♉	May 31–June 12	♉	May 24–June 3	♉
July 4–July 15	♊	June 13–June 23	♉	June 4–June 15	♉
July 16–July 30	♋	June 24–July 7	♊	June 16–July 2	♊
July 31–Oct. 3	♌	July 8–July 25	♋	July 3–Sept. 3	♋
Oct. 4–Oct. 18	♍	July 26–Aug. 20	♌	Sept. 4–Sept. 17	♌
Oct. 19–Nov. 3	♎	Aug. 21–Sept. 10	♋	Sept. 18–Oct. 2	♍
Nov. 4–Nov. 20	♏	Sept. 11–Sept. 25	♌	Oct. 3–Oct. 20	♎
Nov. 21–Dec. 31	♐	Sept. 26–Oct. 10	♍	Oct. 21–Dec. 23	♏
		Oct. 11–Oct. 26	♎	Dec. 24–Dec. 31	♐
		Oct. 27–Nov. 14	♏		
		Nov. 15–Dec. 10	♐		
		Dec. 11–Dec. 27	♏		
		Dec. 28–Dec. 31	♐		

1914		1915		1916	
Dates	*Sign*	*Dates*	*Sign*	*Dates*	*Sign*
Jan. 1–Jan. 10	♐	Jan. 1–Jan. 2	♐	Jan. 1–Jan. 11	♐
Jan. 11–Jan. 26	♐	Jan. 3–Jan. 18	♐	Jan. 12–Feb. 14	♑
Jan. 27–Feb. 9	♑	Jan. 19–Feb. 3	♑	Feb. 15–Feb. 20	♐
Feb. 10–Apr. 16	♒	Feb. 4–Feb. 20	♒	Feb. 21–Mar. 16	♑
Apr. 17–May 2	♓	Feb. 21–Mar. 21	♑	Mar. 17–Apr. 1	♒
May 3–May 14	♈	Mar. 22–Apr. 10	♒	Apr. 2–Apr. 14	♓

continued

1914		1915		1916	
Dates	*Sign*	*Dates*	*Sign*	*Dates*	*Sign*
May 15–May 26	⟋	Apr. 11–Apr. 24	♓	Apr. 15–Apr. 26	♈
May 27–June 9	♉	Apr. 25–May 6	♈	Apr. 27–May 15	⟋
June 10–Aug. 14	♊	May 7–May 18	⟋	May 16–June 2	♉
Aug. 15–Aug. 26	♋	May 19–July 23	♉	June 3–June 28	⟋
Aug. 27–Sept. 9	♌	July 24–Aug. 6	♊	June 29–July 16	♉
Sept. 10–Sept. 25	♍	Aug. 7–Aug. 18	♋	July 17–July 28	♊
Sept. 26–Oct. 16	♎	Aug. 19–Sept. 2	♌	July 29–Aug. 9	♋
Oct. 17–Nov. 4	♏	Sept. 3–Sept. 20	♍	Aug. 10–Aug. 25	♌
Nov. 5–Nov. 29	♎	Sept. 21–Oct. 29	♎	Aug. 26–Oct. 29	♍
Nov. 30–Dec. 16	♏	Oct. 30–Nov. 2	♍	Oct. 30–Nov. 14	♎
Dec. 17–Dec. 31	⛎	Nov. 3–Nov. 23	♎	Nov. 15–Dec. 1	♏
		Nov. 24–Dec. 9	♏	Dec. 2–Dec. 18	⛎
		Dec. 10–Dec. 26	⛎	Dec. 19–Dec. 31	♐
		Dec. 27–Dec. 31	♐		

1917		1918		1919	
Dates	*Sign*	*Dates*	*Sign*	*Dates*	*Sign*
Jan. 1–Feb. 20	♐	Jan. 1–Jan. 4	♐	Jan. 1–Jan. 21	⛎
Feb. 21–Mar. 9	♑	Jan. 5–Jan. 25	⛎	Jan. 22–Feb. 7	♐
Mar. 10–Mar. 24	♒	Jan. 26–Feb. 14	♐	Feb. 8–Feb. 22	♑
Mar. 25–Apr. 6	♓	Feb. 15–Mar. 2	♑	Feb. 23–Mar. 8	♒
Apr. 7–Apr. 21	♈	Mar. 3–Mar. 16	♒	Mar. 9–May 12	♓
Apr. 22–June 25	⟋	Mar. 17–Mar. 30	♓	May 13–May 28	♈
June 26–July 7	♉	Mar. 31–June 3	♈	May 29–June 9	⟋
July 8–July 19	♊	June 4–June 17	⟋	June 10–June 20	♉
July 20–Aug. 2	♋	June 18–June 29	♉	June 21–July 5	♊
Aug. 3–Aug. 21	♌	June 30–July 11	♊	July 6–Sept. 8	♋
Aug. 22–Sept. 18	♍	July 12–July 27	♋	Sept. 9–Sept. 22	♌
Sept. 19–Oct. 6	♌	July 28–Sept. 30	♌	Sept. 23–Oct. 7	♍
Oct. 7–Oct. 22	♍	Oct. 1–Oct. 15	♍	Oct. 8–Oct. 24	♎
Oct. 23–Nov. 7	♎	Oct. 16–Oct. 31	♎	Oct. 25–Nov. 14	♏
Nov. 8–Nov. 24	♏	Nov. 1–Nov. 17	♏	Nov. 15–Nov. 29	⛎
Nov. 25–Dec. 12	⛎	Nov. 18–Dec. 31	⛎	Nov. 30–Dec. 26	♏
Dec. 13–Dec. 31	♐			Dec. 27–Dec. 31	⛎

TABLE 5 231

1920		1921		1922	
Dates	*Sign*	*Dates*	*Sign*	*Dates*	*Sign*
Jan. 1–Jan. 14	♓	Jan. 1–Jan. 6	♓	Jan. 1–Jan 15	♐
Jan. 15–Jan. 31	♐	Jan. 7–Jan. 22	♐	Jan. 16–Mar. 19	♑
Feb. 1–Feb. 14	♑	Jan. 23–Feb. 6	♑	Mar. 20–Apr. 6	♒
Feb. 15–Mar. 2	♒	Feb. 7–Apr. 13	♒	Apr. 7–Apr. 20	♓
Mar. 3–Mar. 19	♓	Apr. 14–Apr. 28	♓	Apr. 21–May 2	♈
Mar. 20–Apr. 17	♒	Apr. 29–May 10	♈	May 3–May 16	♎
Apr. 18–May 5	♓	May 11–May 22	♎	May 17–July 20	♉
May 6–May 19	♈	May 23–June 7	♉	July 21–Aug. 2	♊
May 20–May 30	♎	June 8–Aug. 10	♊	Aug. 3–Aug. 14	♋
May 31–June 12	♉	Aug. 11–Aug. 23	♋	Aug. 15–Aug. 29	♌
June 13–July 1	♊	Aug. 24–Sept. 5	♌	Aug. 30–Sept. 18	♍
July 2–July 24	♋	Sept. 6–Sept. 22	♍	Sept. 19–Oct. 14	♎
July 25–Aug. 16	♊	Sept. 23–Nov. 26	♎	Oct. 15–Nov. 2	♍
Aug. 17–Aug. 31	♋	Nov. 27–Dec. 13	♏	Nov. 3–Nov. 19	♎
Sept. 1–Sept. 13	♌	Dec. 14–Dec. 30	♓	Nov. 20–Dec. 6	♏
Sept. 14–Sept. 29	♍	Dec. 31	♐	Dec. 7–Dec. 23	♓
Sept. 30–Oct. 17	♎			Dec. 24–Dec. 31	♐
Oct. 18–Nov. 21	♏				
Nov. 22–Nov. 29	♎				
Nov. 30–Dec. 20	♏				
Dec. 21–Dec. 31	♓				

1923		1924		1925	
Dates	*Sign*	*Dates*	*Sign*	*Dates*	*Sign*
Jan. 1–Jan. 9	♐	Jan. 1–Feb. 18	♐	Jan. 1–Jan. 23	♓
Jan. 10–Jan. 29	♑	Feb. 19–Mar. 6	♑	Jan. 24–Feb. 11	♐
Jan. 30–Feb. 22	♐	Mar. 7–Mar. 21	♒	Feb. 12–Feb. 26	♑
Feb. 23–Mar. 14	♑	Mar. 22–Apr. 2	♓	Feb. 27–Mar. 13	♒
Mar. 15–Mar. 30	♒	Apr. 3–Apr. 22	♈	Mar. 14–Mar. 27	♓
Mar. 31–Apr. 11	♓	Apr. 23–May 1	♎	Mar. 28–Apr. 21	♈
Apr. 12–Apr. 24	♈	May 2–June 5	♈	Apr. 22–May 11	♓
Apr. 25–June 29	♎	June 6–June 21	♎	May 12–May 31	♈
June 30–July 13	♉	June 22–July 3	♉	June 1–June 13	♎
July 14–July 25	♊	July 4–July 15	♊	June 14–June 25	♉
July 26–Aug. 7	♋	July 16–July 30	♋	June 26–July 8	♊
Aug. 8–Aug. 23	♌	July 31–Aug. 23	♌	July 9–July 25	♋
Aug. 24–Oct. 27	♍	Aug. 24–Sept. 2	♍	July 26–Aug. 26	♌
Oct. 28–Nov. 12	♎	Sept. 3–Oct. 4	♌	Aug. 27–Sept. 10	♋
Nov. 13–Nov. 28	♏	Oct. 5–Oct. 19	♍	Sept. 11–Sept. 26	♌

continued

1923		1924		1925	
Dates	*Sign*	*Dates*	*Sign*	*Dates*	*Sign*
Nov. 29–Dec. 16	⛎	Oct. 20–Nov. 4	♎	Sept. 27–Oct. 11	♍
Dec. 17–Dec. 31	♐	Nov. 5–Nov. 21	♏	Oct. 12–Oct. 27	♎
		Nov. 22–Dec. 12	⛎	Oct. 28–Nov. 15	♏
		Dec. 13–Dec. 22	♐	Nov. 16–Dec. 15	⛎
		Dec. 23–Dec. 31	⛎	Dec. 16–Dec. 27	♏
				Dec. 28–Dec. 31	⛎

1926		1927		1928	
Dates	*Sign*	*Dates*	*Sign*	*Dates*	*Sign*
Jan. 1–Jan. 18	⛎	Jan. 1–Jan. 11	⛎	Jan. 1–Jan. 4	⛎
Jan. 19–Feb. 3	♐	Jan. 12–Jan. 27	♐	Jan. 5–Jan. 19	♐
Feb. 4–Feb. 18	♑	Jan. 28–Feb. 11	♑	Jan. 20–Feb. 4	♑
Feb. 19–Mar. 5	♒	Feb. 12–Apr. 17	♒	Feb. 5–Feb. 26	♒
Mar. 6–May 10	♓	Apr. 18–May 3	♓	Feb. 27–Mar. 20	♑
May 11–May 24	♈	May 4–May 16	♈	Mar. 21–Apr. 10	♒
May 25–June 5	↢	May 17–May 27	↢	Apr. 11–Apr. 24	♓
June 6–June 17	♉	May 28–June 10	♉	Apr. 25–May 6	♈
June 18–July 2	♊	June 11–Aug. 15	♊	May 7–May 19	↢
July 3–Sept. 5	♋	Aug. 16–Aug. 28	♋	May 20–June 9	♉
Sept. 6–Sept. 18	♌	Aug. 29–Sept. 11	♌	June 10–June 23	♊
Sept. 19–Oct. 4	♍	Sept. 12–Sept. 27	♍	June 24–July 23	♉
Oct. 5–Oct. 21	♎	Sept. 28–Oct. 17	♎	July 24–Aug. 7	♊
Oct. 22–Dec. 24	♏	Oct. 18–Nov. 8	♏	Aug. 8–Aug. 19	♋
Dec. 25–Dec. 31	⛎	Nov. 9–Nov. 29	♎	Aug. 20–Sept. 2	♌
		Nov. 30–Dec. 17	♏	Sept. 3–Sept. 20	♍
		Dec. 18–Dec. 31	⛎	Sept. 21–Nov. 23	♎
				Nov. 24–Dec. 9	♏
				Dec. 10–Dec. 26	⛎
				Dec. 27–Dec. 31	♐

1929		1930		1931	
Dates	*Sign*	*Dates*	*Sign*	*Dates*	*Sign*
Jan. 1–Jan. 11	♐	Jan. 1–Jan. 8	♐	Jan. 1–Jan. 8	♐
Jan. 12–Mar. 17	♑	Jan. 9–Jan. 16	♑	Jan. 9–Jan. 25	⛎
Mar. 18–Apr. 3	♒	Jan. 17–Feb. 21	♐	Jan. 26–Feb. 15	♐
Apr. 4–Apr. 16	♓	Feb. 22–Mar. 11	♑	Feb. 16–Mar. 3	♑
Apr. 17–Apr. 28	♈	Mar. 12–Mar. 26	♒	Mar. 4–Mar. 18	♒
Apr. 29–May 14	↢	Mar. 27–Apr. 8	♓	Mar. 19–Mar. 31	♓

TABLE 5 233

continued

1929 Dates	Sign	1930 Dates	Sign	1931 Dates	Sign
May 15–June 11	♉	Apr. 9–Apr. 21	♈	Apr. 1–June 4	♈
June 12–June 27	♎	Apr. 22–June 26	♎	June 5–June 19	♎
June 28–July 17	♉	June 27–July 9	♉	June 20–June 30	♉
July 18–July 29	♊	July 10–July 21	♊	July 1–July 13	♊
July 30–Aug. 11	♋	July 22–Aug. 3	♋	July 14–July 28	♋
Aug. 12–Aug. 26	♌	Aug. 4–Aug. 21	♌	July 29–Oct. 1	♌
Aug. 27–Sept. 19	♍	Aug. 22–Sept. 23	♍	Oct. 2–Oct. 16	♍
Sept. 20–Sept. 30	♎	Sept. 24–Oct. 7	♌	Oct. 17–Nov. 1	♎
Oct. 1–Oct. 30	♍	Oct. 8–Oct. 24	♍	Nov. 2–Nov. 18	♏
Oct. 31–Nov. 16	♎	Oct. 25–Nov. 8	♎	Nov. 19–Dec. 31	♐
Nov. 17–Dec. 2	♏	Nov. 9–Nov. 25	♏		
Dec. 3–Dec. 19	♐	Nov. 26–Dec. 13	♐		
Dec. 20–Dec. 31	♐	Dec. 14–Dec. 31	♐		

1932 Dates	Sign	1933 Dates	Sign	1934 Dates	Sign
Jan. 1–Jan. 22	♐	Jan. 1–Jan. 15	♐	Jan. 1–Jan. 8	♐
Jan. 23–Feb. 8	♐	Jan. 16–Jan. 31	♐	Jan. 9–Jan. 23	♐
Feb. 9–Feb. 23	♑	Feb. 1–Feb. 15	♑	Jan. 24–Feb. 7	♑
Feb. 24–Mar. 9	♒	Feb. 16–Mar. 2	♒	Feb. 8–Apr. 14	♒
Mar. 10–May 11	♓	Mar. 3–Mar. 25	♓	Apr. 15–Apr. 30	♓
May 12–May 28	♈	Mar. 26–Apr. 17	♒	May 1–May 12	♈
May 29–June 9	♎	Apr. 18–May 7	♓	May 13–May 23	♎
June 10–June 21	♉	May 8–May 20	♈	May 24–June 8	♉
June 22–July 5	♊	May 21–June 1	♎	June 9–Aug. 12	♊
July 6–July 27	♋	June 2–June 13	♉	Aug. 13–Aug. 24	♋
July 28–Aug. 9	♌	June 14–July 1	♊	Aug. 25–Sept. 7	♌
Aug. 10–Sept. 8	♋	July 2–July 31	♋	Sept. 8–Sept. 23	♍
Sept. 9–Sept. 23	♌	Aug. 1–Aug. 17	♊	Sept. 24–Oct. 17	♎
Sept. 24–Oct. 8	♍	Aug. 18–Sept. 1	♋	Oct. 18–Oct. 26	♏
Oct. 9–Oct. 24	♎	Sept. 2–Sept. 15	♌	Oct. 27–Nov. 27	♎
Oct. 25–Nov. 13	♏	Sept. 16–Sept. 30	♍	Nov. 28–Dec. 14	♏
Nov. 14–Dec. 3	♐	Oct. 1–Oct. 18	♎	Dec. 15–Dec. 31	♐
Dec. 4–Dec. 26	♏	Oct. 19–Dec. 21	♏		
Dec. 27–Dec. 31	♐	Dec. 22–Dec. 31	♐		

1935 Dates	Sign	1936 Dates	Sign	1937 Dates	Sign
Jan. 1–Jan. 16	♐	Jan. 1–Jan. 10	♐	Jan. 1–Feb. 18	♐
Jan. 17–Feb. 4	♑	Jan. 11–Feb. 4	♑	Feb. 19–Mar. 7	♑
Feb. 5–Feb. 11	♒	Feb. 5–Feb. 22	♐	Mar. 8–Mar. 22	♒
Feb. 12–Mar. 20	♑	Feb. 23–Mar. 14	♑	Mar. 23–Apr. 4	♓
Mar. 21–Apr. 8	♒	Mar. 15–Mar. 30	♒	Apr. 5–Apr. 20	♈
Apr. 9–Apr. 21	♓	Mar. 31–Apr. 12	♓	Apr. 21–May 10	ↄ
Apr. 22–May 3	♈	Apr. 13–Apr. 24	♈	May 11–June 4	♈
May 4–May 17	ↄ	Apr. 25–June 28	ↄ	June 5–June 23	ↄ
May 18–July 22	♉	June 29–July 13	♉	June 24–July 5	♉
July 23–Aug. 4	♊	July 14–July 25	♊	July 6–July 17	♊
Aug. 5–Aug. 16	♋	July 26–Aug. 7	♋	July 18–July 31	♋
Aug. 17–Aug. 31	♌	Aug. 8–Aug. 23	♌	Aug. 1–Aug. 21	♌
Sept. 1–Sept. 19	♍	Aug. 24–Oct. 27	♍	Aug. 22–Sept. 9	♍
Sept. 20–Oct. 19	♎	Oct. 28–Nov. 12	♎	Sept. 10–Oct. 5	♌
Oct. 20–Nov. 3	♍	Nov. 13–Nov. 29	♏	Oct. 6–Oct. 20	♍
Nov. 4–Nov. 20	♎	Nov. 30–Dec. 16	⛎	Oct. 21–Nov. 2	♎
Nov. 21–Dec. 7	♏	Dec. 17–Dec. 31	♐	Nov. 3–Nov. 22	♏
Dec. 8–Dec. 24	⛎			Nov. 23–Dec. 12	⛎
Dec. 25–Dec. 31	♐			Dec. 13–Dec. 27	♐
				Dec. 28–Dec. 31	⛎

1938 Dates	Sign	1939 Dates	Sign	1940 Dates	Sign
Jan. 1–Jan. 24	⛎	Jan. 1–Jan. 19	⛎	Jan. 1–Jan. 12	⛎
Jan. 25–Feb. 12	♐	Jan. 20–Feb. 5	♐	Jan. 13–Jan. 28	♐
Feb. 13–Feb. 28	♑	Feb. 6–Feb. 20	♑	Jan. 29–Feb. 12	♑
Mar. 1–Mar. 14	♒	Feb. 21–Mar. 6	♒	Feb. 13–Mar. 3	♒
Mar. 15–Mar. 28	♓	Mar. 7–May 11	♓	Mar. 4–Mar. 7	♓
Mar. 29–May 1	♈	May 12–May 25	♈	Mar. 8–Apr. 16	♒
May 2–May 8	♓	May 26–June 6	ↄ	Apr. 17–May 3	♓
May 9–June 2	♈	June 7–June 18	♉	May 4–May 16	♈
June 3–June 15	ↄ	June 19–July 3	♊	May 17–May 28	ↄ
June 16–June 26	♉	July 4–Sept. 6	♋	May 29–June 10	♉
June 27–July 9	♊	Sept. 7–Sept. 20	♌	June 11–Aug. 15	♊
July 10–July 26	♋	Sept. 21–Oct. 5	♍	Aug. 16–Aug. 28	♋
July 27–Sept. 2	♌	Oct. 6–Oct. 22	♎	Aug. 29–Sept. 11	♌
Sept. 3–Sept. 10	♋	Oct. 23–Nov. 15	♏	Sept. 12–Sept. 27	♍
Sept. 11–Sept. 28	♌	Nov. 16–Nov. 19	⛎	Sept. 28–Oct. 16	♎
Sept. 29–Oct. 12	♍	Nov. 20–Dec. 25	♏	Oct. 17–Nov. 12	♏

continued

TABLE 5 235

1938 Dates	Sign	1939 Dates	Sign	1940 Dates	Sign
Oct. 13–Oct. 29	♎	Dec. 26–Dec. 31	♐	Nov. 13–Nov. 29	♎
Oct. 30–Nov. 16	♏			Nov. 30–Dec. 18	♏
Nov. 17–Dec. 22	♐			Dec. 19–Dec. 31	♐
Dec. 23–Dec. 25	♏				
Dec. 26–Dec. 31	♐				

1941 Dates	Sign	1942 Dates	Sign	1943 Dates	Sign
Jan. 1–Jan. 4	♐	Jan. 1–Jan. 13	♐	Jan. 1–Jan. 8	♐
Jan. 5–Jan. 20	♐	Jan. 14–Mar. 18	♑	Jan. 9–Jan. 22	♑
Jan. 21–Feb. 4	♑	Mar. 19–Apr. 4	♒	Jan. 23–Feb. 21	♐
Feb. 5–Mar. 2	♒	Apr. 5–Apr. 17	♓	Feb. 22–Mar. 12	♑
Mar. 3–Mar. 20	♑	Apr. 18–Apr. 29	♈	Mar. 13–Mar. 27	♒
Mar. 21–Apr. 11	♒	Apr. 30–May 14	♉	Mar. 28–Apr. 9	♓
Apr. 12–Apr. 26	♓	May 15–July 18	♉	Apr. 10–Apr. 22	♈
Apr. 27–May 8	♈	July 19–July 31	♊	Apr. 23–June 27	♉
May 9–May 20	♉	Aug. 1–Aug. 12	♋	June 28–July 11	♉
May 21–June 7	♉	Aug. 13–Aug. 27	♌	July 12–July 22	♊
June 8–July 2	♊	Aug. 28–Sept. 18	♍	July 23–Aug. 4	♋
July 3–July 23	♉	Sept. 19–Oct. 6	♎	Aug. 5–Aug. 22	♌
July 24–Aug. 8	♊	Oct. 7–Nov. 3	♍	Aug. 23–Sept. 30	♍
Aug. 9–Aug. 20	♋	Nov. 4–Nov. 17	♎	Oct. 1–Oct. 6	♌
Aug. 21–Sept. 3	♌	Nov. 18–Dec. 3	♏	Oct. 7–Oct. 25	♍
Sept. 4–Sept. 21	♍	Dec. 4–Dec. 21	♐	Oct. 26–Nov. 10	♎
Sept. 22–Nov. 24	♎	Dec. 22–Dec. 31	♐	Nov. 11–Nov. 26	♏
Nov. 25–Dec. 11	♏			Nov. 27–Dec. 14	♐
Dec. 12–Dec. 28	♐			Dec. 15–Dec. 31	♐
Dec. 29–Dec. 31	♐				

1944 Dates	Sign	1945 Dates	Sign	1946 Dates	Sign
Jan. 1–Jan. 14	♐	Jan. 1–Jan. 22	♐	Jan. 1–Jan. 16	♐
Jan. 15–Jan. 25	♐	Jan. 23–Feb. 9	♐	Jan. 17–Feb. 1	♐
Jan. 26–Feb. 16	♐	Feb. 10–Feb. 24	♑	Feb. 2–Feb. 16	♑
Feb. 17–Mar. 4	♑	Feb. 25–Mar. 10	♒	Feb. 17–Mar. 3	♒
Mar. 5–Mar. 18	♒	Mar. 11–Mar. 27	♓	Mar. 4–Apr. 1	♓
Mar. 19–Mar. 31	♓	Mar. 28–Apr. 9	♈	Apr. 2–Apr. 16	♒
Apr. 1–June 4	♈	Apr. 10–May 12	♓	Apr. 17–May 8	♓

continued

1944		1945		1946	
Dates	*Sign*	*Dates*	*Sign*	*Dates*	*Sign*
June 5–June 19	⟿	May 13–May 29	♈	May 9–May 22	♈
June 20–July 1	♉	May 30–June 11	⟿	May 23–June 2	⟿
July 2–July 13	♊	June 12–June 22	♉	June 3–June 15	♉
July 14–July 28	♋	June 23–July 6	♊	June 16–July 1	♊
July 29–Oct. 1	♌	July 7–July 26	♋	July 2–Aug. 8	♋
Oct. 2–Oct. 16	♍	July 27–Aug. 16	♌	Aug. 9–Aug. 15	♊
Oct. 17–Nov. 1	♎	Aug. 17–Sept. 9	♋	Aug. 16–Sept. 3	♋
Nov. 2–Nov. 19	♏	Sept. 10–Sept. 24	♌	Sept. 4–Sept. 16	♌
Nov. 20–Dec. 31	⛎	Sept. 25–Oct. 9	♍	Sept. 17–Oct. 1	♍
		Oct. 10–Oct. 25	♎	Oct. 2–Oct. 19	♎
		Oct. 26–Nov. 13	♏	Oct. 20–Dec. 22	♏
		Nov. 14–Dec. 7	⛎	Dec. 23–Dec. 31	⛎
		Dec. 8–Dec. 27	♏		
		Dec. 28–Dec. 31	⛎		

1947		1948		1949	
Dates	*Sign*	*Dates*	*Sign*	*Dates*	*Sign*
Jan. 1–Jan. 9	⛎	Jan. 1–Jan. 2	⛎	Jan. 1–Jan. 10	♐
Jan. 10–Jan. 25	♐	Jan. 3–Jan. 17	♐	Jan. 11–Feb. 8	♑
Jan. 26–Feb. 9	♑	Jan. 18–Feb. 3	♑	Feb. 9–Feb. 20	♐
Feb. 10–Apr. 15	♒	Feb. 4–Feb. 17	♒	Feb. 21–Mar. 15	♑
Apr. 16–May 1	♓	Feb. 18–Mar. 20	♑	Mar. 16–Apr. 1	♒
May 2–May 13	♈	Mar. 21–Apr. 8	♒	Apr. 2–Apr. 14	♓
May 14–May 25	⟿	Apr. 9–Apr. 22	♓	Apr. 15–Apr. 26	♈
May 26–June 8	♉	Apr. 23–May 4	♈	Apr. 27–May 16	⟿
June 9–Aug. 13	♊	May 5–May 17	⟿	May 17–May 26	♉
Aug. 14–Aug. 26	♋	May 18–July 22	♉	May 27–June 29	⟿
Aug. 27–Sept. 8	♌	July 23–Aug. 4	♊	June 30–July 15	♉
Sept. 9–Sept. 25	♍	Aug. 5–Aug. 16	♋	July 16–July 27	♊
Sept. 26–Oct. 16	♎	Aug. 17–Aug. 31	♌	July 28–Aug. 8	♋
Oct. 17–Nov. 1	♏	Sept. 1–Sept. 18	♍	Aug. 9–Aug. 24	♌
Nov. 2–Nov. 28	♎	Sept. 19–Oct. 24	♎	Aug. 25–Oct. 29	♍
Nov. 29–Dec. 15	♏	Oct. 25–Nov. 2	♍	Oct. 30–Nov. 14	♎
Dec. 16–Dec. 31	⛎	Nov. 3–Nov. 21	♎	Nov. 15–Nov. 30	♏
		Nov. 22–Dec. 7	♏	Dec. 1–Dec. 17	⛎
		Dec. 8–Dec. 24	⛎	Dec. 18–Dec. 31	♐
		Dec. 25–Dec. 31	♐		

TABLE 5 237

1950		1951		1952	
Dates	Sign	Dates	Sign	Dates	Sign
Jan. 1–Feb. 19	♐	Jan. 1	♐	Jan. 1–Jan. 20	♑
Feb. 20–Mar. 9	♑	Jan. 2–Jan. 25	♑	Jan. 21–Feb. 6	♐
Mar. 10–Mar. 24	♒	Jan. 26–Feb. 13	♐	Feb. 7–Feb. 21	♑
Mar. 25–Apr. 5	♓	Feb. 14–Mar. 1	♑	Feb. 22–Mar. 7	♒
Apr. 6–Apr. 20	♈	Mar. 2–Mar. 15	♒	Mar. 8–May 10	♓
Apr. 21–May 19	♉	Mar. 16–Mar. 29	♓	May 11–May 26	♈
May 20–June 3	♈	Mar. 30–June 3	♈	May 27–June 7	♉
June 4–June 24	♉	June 4–June 16	♉	June 8–June 19	♉
June 25–July 7	♉	June 17–June 28	♉	June 20–July 3	♊
July 8–July 19	♊	June 29–July 11	♊	July 4–Sept. 6	♋
July 20–Aug. 1	♋	July 12–July 27	♋	Sept. 7–Sept. 20	♌
Aug. 2–Aug. 21	♌	July 28–Sept. 29	♌	Sept. 21–Oct. 5	♍
Aug. 22–Sept. 15	♍	Sept. 30–Oct. 14	♍	Oct. 6–Oct. 22	♎
Sept. 16–Oct. 6	♌	Oct. 15–Oct. 30	♎	Oct. 23–Nov. 13	♏
Oct. 7–Oct. 22	♍	Oct. 31–Nov. 17	♏	Nov. 14–Nov. 25	♐
Oct. 23–Nov. 6	♎	Nov. 18–Dec. 31	♐	Nov. 26–Dec. 25	♏
Nov. 7–Nov. 23	♏			Dec. 26–Dec. 31	♐
Nov. 24–Dec. 12	♐				
Dec. 13–Dec. 31	♐				

1953		1954		1955	
Dates	Sign	Dates	Sign	Dates	Sign
Jan. 1–Jan. 13	♑	Jan. 1–Jan. 5	♑	Jan. 1–Jan. 14	♐
Jan. 14–Jan. 29	♐	Jan. 6–Jan. 21	♐	Jan. 15–Mar. 19	♑
Jan. 30–Feb. 12	♑	Jan. 22–Feb. 5	♑	Mar. 20–Apr. 6	♒
Feb. 13–Mar. 2	♒	Feb. 6–Mar. 9	♒	Apr. 7–Apr. 19	♓
Mar. 3–Mar. 15	♓	Mar. 10–Mar. 18	♑	Apr. 20–May 1	♈
Mar. 16–Apr. 17	♒	Mar. 19–Apr. 12	♒	May 2–May 15	♉
Apr. 18–May 5	♓	Apr. 13–Apr. 27	♓	May 16–July 20	♉
May 6–May 18	♈	Apr. 28–May 9	♈	July 21–Aug. 1	♊
May 19–May 29	♉	May 10–May 21	♉	Aug. 2–Aug. 14	♋
May 30–June 11	♉	May 22–June 7	♉	Aug. 15–Aug. 29	♌
June 12–July 2	♊	June 8–July 11	♊	Aug. 30–Sept. 18	♍
July 3–July 19	♋	July 12–July 22	♉	Sept. 19–Oct. 11	♎
July 20–Aug. 16	♊	July 23–Aug. 10	♊	Oct. 12–Nov. 2	♍
Aug. 17–Aug. 30	♋	Aug. 11–Aug. 22	♋	Nov. 3–Nov. 18	♎
Aug. 31–Sept. 12	♌	Aug. 23–Sept. 5	♌	Nov. 19–Dec. 5	♏
Sept. 13–Sept. 28	♍	Sept. 6–Sept. 22	♍	Dec. 6–Dec. 22	♐
Sept. 29–Oct. 17	♎	Sept. 23–Nov. 25	♎	Dec. 23–Dec. 31	♐

continued

1953		1954		1955	
Dates	*Sign*	*Dates*	*Sign*	*Dates*	*Sign*
Oct. 18–Nov. 17	♏	Nov. 26–Dec. 12	♏		
Nov. 18–Nov. 29	♎	Dec. 13–Dec. 29	⛎		
Nov. 30–Dec. 19	♏	Dec. 30–Dec. 31	♐		
Dec. 20–Dec. 31	⛎				

1956		1957		1958	
Dates	*Sign*	*Dates*	*Sign*	*Dates*	*Sign*
Jan. 1–Jan. 8	♐	Jan. 1–Feb. 16	♐	Jan. 1–Jan. 23	⛎
Jan. 9–Jan. 27	♑	Feb. 17–Mar. 5	♑	Jan. 24–Feb. 10	♐
Jan. 28–Feb. 22	♐	Mar. 6–Mar. 20	♒	Feb. 11–Feb. 25	♑
Feb. 23–Mar. 12	♑	Mar. 21–Apr. 2	♓	Feb. 26–Mar. 12	♒
Mar. 13–Mar. 28	♒	Apr. 3–June 4	♈	Mar. 13–Mar. 27	♓
Mar. 29–Apr. 10	♓	June 5–June 21	🐳	Mar. 28–Apr. 17	♈
Apr. 11–Apr. 22	♈	June 22–July 3	♉	Apr. 18–May 12	♓
Apr. 23–June 27	🐳	July 4–July 15	♊	May 13–May 31	♈
June 28–July 11	♉	July 16–July 29	♋	June 1–June 12	🐳
July 12–July 23	♊	July 30–Oct. 3	♌	June 13–June 24	♉
July 24–Aug. 5	♋	Oct. 4–Oct. 18	♍	June 25–July 7	♊
Aug. 6–Aug. 22	♌	Oct. 19–Nov. 3	♎	July 8–July 25	♋
Aug. 23–Oct. 25	♍	Nov. 4–Nov. 20	♏	July 26–Aug. 23	♌
Oct. 26–Nov. 10	♎	Nov. 21–Dec. 10	⛎	Aug. 24–Sept. 10	♋
Nov. 11–Nov. 27	♏	Dec. 11–Dec. 18	♐	Sept. 11–Sept. 26	♌
Nov. 28–Dec. 14	⛎	Dec. 19–Dec. 31	⛎	Sept. 27–Oct. 10	♍
Dec. 15–Dec. 31	♐			Oct. 11–Oct. 27	♎
				Oct. 28–Nov. 14	♏
				Nov. 15–Dec. 12	⛎
				Dec. 13–Dec. 27	♏
				Dec. 28–Dec. 31	⛎

1959		1960		1961	
Dates	*Sign*	*Dates*	*Sign*	*Dates*	*Sign*
Jan. 1–Jan. 17	⛎	Jan. 1–Jan. 10	⛎	Jan. 1–Jan. 3	⛎
Jan. 18–Feb. 3	♐	Jan. 11–Jan. 26	♐	Jan. 4–Jan. 18	♐
Feb. 4–Feb. 17	♑	Jan. 27–Feb. 10	♑	Jan. 19–Feb. 3	♑
Feb. 18–Mar. 4	♒	Feb. 11–Apr. 15	♒	Feb. 4–Feb. 22	♒
Mar. 5–May 9	♓	Apr. 16–May 1	♓	Feb. 23–Mar. 21	♑
May 10–May 23	♈	May 2–May 14	♈	Mar. 22–Apr. 10	♒
May 24–June 4	🐳	May 15–May 25	🐳	Apr. 11–Apr. 24	♓

TABLE 5 239

continued

1959		1960		1961	
Dates	*Sign*	*Dates*	*Sign*	*Dates*	*Sign*
June 5–June 16	♉	May 26–June 8	♉	Apr. 25–May 6	♈
June 17–July 2	♊	June 9–Aug. 13	♊	May 7–May 18	♈
July 3–Sept. 4	♋	Aug. 14–Aug. 26	♋	May 19–July 23	♉
Sept. 5–Sept. 18	♌	Aug. 27–Sept. 9	♌	July 24–Aug. 6	♊
Sept. 19–Oct. 3	♍	Sept. 10–Sept. 25	♍	Aug. 7–Aug. 18	♋
Oct. 4–Oct. 20	♎	Sept. 26–Oct. 15	♎	Aug. 19–Sept. 2	♌
Oct. 21–Dec. 23	♏	Oct. 16–Nov. 5	♏	Sept. 3–Sept. 20	♍
Dec. 24–Dec. 31	⛎	Nov. 6–Nov. 28	♎	Sept. 21–Nov. 23	♎
		Nov. 29–Dec. 16	♏	Nov. 24–Dec. 9	♏
		Dec. 17–Dec. 31	⛎	Dec. 10–Dec. 26	⛎
				Dec. 27–Dec. 31	♐

1962		1963		1964	
Dates	*Sign*	*Dates*	*Sign*	*Dates*	*Sign*
Jan. 1–Jan. 11	♐	Jan. 1–Jan. 10	♐	Jan. 1–Jan. 6	♐
Jan. 12–Mar. 17	♑	Jan. 11–Jan. 12	♑	Jan. 7–Jan. 26	⛎
Mar. 18–Apr. 3	♒	Jan. 13–Feb. 21	♐	Jan. 27–Feb. 15	♐
Apr. 4–Apr. 16	♓	Feb. 22–Mar. 10	♑	Feb. 16–Mar. 2	♑
Apr. 17–Apr. 28	♈	Mar. 11–Mar. 26	♒	Mar. 3–Mar. 16	♒
Apr. 29–May 15	♈	Mar. 27–Apr. 7	♓	Mar. 17–Mar. 30	♓
May 16–June 6	♉	Apr. 8–Apr. 21	♈	Mar. 31–June 3	♈
June 7–June 29	♈	Apr. 22–June 26	♈	June 4–June 17	♈
June 30–July 17	♉	June 27–July 9	♉	June 18–June 29	♉
July 18–July 29	♊	July 10–July 21	♊	June 30–July 12	♊
July 30–Aug. 10	♋	July 22–Aug. 3	♋	July 13–July 27	♋
Aug. 11–Aug. 26	♌	Aug. 4–Aug. 22	♌	July 28–Sept. 30	♌
Aug. 27–Sept. 22	♍	Aug. 23–Sept. 20	♍	Oct. 1–Oct. 15	♍
Sept. 23–Sept. 26	♎	Sept. 21–Oct. 7	♌	Oct. 16–Oct. 31	♎
Sept. 27–Oct. 30	♍	Oct. 8–Oct. 23	♍	Nov. 1–Nov. 17	♏
Oct. 31–Nov. 15	♎	Oct. 24–Nov. 8	♎	Nov. 18–Dec. 31	⛎
Nov. 16–Dec. 2	♏	Nov. 9–Nov. 25	♏		
Dec. 3–Dec. 19	⛎	Nov. 26–Dec. 13	⛎		
Dec. 20–Dec. 31	♐	Dec. 14–Dec. 31	♐		

1965		1966		1967	
Dates	*Sign*	*Dates*	*Sign*	*Dates*	*Sign*
Jan. 1–Jan. 21	⛎	Jan. 1–Jan. 14	⛎	Jan. 1–Jan. 7	⛎
Jan. 22–Feb. 7	♐	Jan. 15–Jan. 31	♐	Jan. 8–Jan. 23	♐

continued

1965		1966		1967	
Dates	*Sign*	*Dates*	*Sign*	*Dates*	*Sign*
Feb. 8–Feb. 22	♑	Feb. 1–Feb. 14	♑	Jan. 24–Feb. 7	♑
Feb. 23–Mar. 9	♒	Feb. 15–Mar. 3	♒	Feb. 8–Apr. 14	♒
Mar. 10–May 12	♓	Mar. 4–Mar. 22	♓	Apr. 15–Apr. 29	♓
May 13–May 28	♈	Mar. 23–Apr. 17	♒	Apr. 30–May 11	♈
May 29–June 9	♎	Apr. 18–May 7	♓	May 12–May 23	♎
June 10–June 21	♉	May 8–May 20	♈	May 24–June 8	♉
June 22–July 5	♊	May 21–May 31	♎	June 9–Aug. 11	♊
July 6–July 31	♋	June 1–June 13	♉	Aug. 12–Aug. 24	♋
Aug. 1–Aug. 3	♌	June 14–July 2	♊	Aug. 25–Sept. 7	♌
Aug. 4–Sept. 8	♋	July 3–July 27	♋	Sept. 8–Sept. 23	♍
Sept. 9–Sept. 22	♌	July 28–Aug. 17	♊	Sept. 24–Nov. 27	♎
Sept. 23–Oct. 7	♍	Aug. 18–Sept. 1	♋	Nov. 28–Dec. 14	♏
Oct. 8–Oct. 24	♎	Sept. 2–Sept. 14	♌	Dec. 15–Dec. 31	♐
Oct. 25–Nov. 13	♏	Sept. 15–Sept. 30	♍		
Nov. 14–Dec. 1	♐	Oct. 1–Oct. 18	♎		
Dec. 2–Dec. 26	♏	Oct. 19–Nov. 24	♏		
Dec. 27–Dec. 31	♐	Nov. 25–Nov. 29	♎		
		Nov. 30–Dec. 21	♏		
		Dec. 22–Dec. 31	♐		

1968		1969		1970	
Dates	*Sign*	*Dates*	*Sign*	*Dates*	*Sign*
Jan. 1–Jan. 16	♐	Jan. 1–Jan. 9	♐	Jan. 1–Feb. 18	♐
Jan. 17–Mar. 19	♑	Jan. 10–Jan. 31	♑	Feb. 19–Mar. 7	♑
Mar. 20–Apr. 7	♒	Feb. 1–Feb. 22	♐	Mar. 8–Mar. 22	♒
Apr. 8–Apr. 20	♓	Feb. 23–Mar. 14	♑	Mar. 23–Apr. 4	♓
Apr. 21–May 2	♈	Mar. 15–Mar. 30	♒	Apr. 5–Apr. 22	♈
May 3–May 16	♎	Mar. 31–Apr. 12	♓	Apr. 23–May 5	♎
May 17–July 20	♉	Apr. 13–Apr. 24	♈	May 6–June 5	♈
July 21–Aug. 2	♊	Apr. 25–June 28	♎	June 6–June 23	♎
Aug. 3–Aug. 15	♋	June 29–July 13	♉	June 24–July 5	♉
Aug. 16–Aug. 29	♌	July 14–July 25	♊	July 6–July 17	♊
Aug. 30–Sept. 18	♍	July 26–Aug. 7	♋	July 18–July 31	♋
Sept. 19–Oct. 16	♎	Aug. 8–Aug. 23	♌	Aug. 1–Aug. 22	♌
Oct. 17–Nov. 2	♍	Aug. 24–Oct. 27	♍	Aug. 23–Sept. 6	♍
Nov. 3–Nov. 19	♎	Oct. 28–Nov. 12	♎	Sept. 7–Oct. 5	♌
Nov. 20–Dec. 6	♏	Nov. 13–Nov. 28	♏	Oct. 6–Oct. 20	♍
Dec. 7–Dec. 23	♐	Nov. 29–Dec. 16	♐	Oct. 21–Nov. 5	♎
Dec. 24–Dec. 31	♐	Dec. 17–Dec. 31	♐	Nov. 6–Nov. 22	♏

TABLE 5 241

continued

1968		1969		1970	
Dates	*Sign*	*Dates*	*Sign*	*Dates*	*Sign*
				Nov. 23–Dec. 12	♏
				Dec. 13–Dec. 25	♐
				Dec. 26–Dec. 31	♏

1971		1972		1973	
Dates	*Sign*	*Dates*	*Sign*	*Dates*	*Sign*
Jan. 1–Jan. 24	♏	Jan. 1–Jan. 19	♏	Jan. 1–Jan. 11	♏
Jan. 25–Feb. 11	♐	Jan. 20–Feb. 5	♐	Jan. 12–Jan. 27	♐
Feb. 12–Feb. 27	♑	Feb. 6–Feb. 19	♑	Jan. 28–Feb. 11	♑
Feb. 28–Mar. 13	♒	Feb. 20–Mar. 5	♒	Feb. 12–Apr. 16	♒
Mar. 14–Mar. 28	♓	Mar. 6–May 9	♓	Apr. 17–May 3	♓
Mar. 29–Apr. 25	♈	May 10–May 24	♈	May 4–May 16	♈
Apr. 26–May 11	♓	May 25–June 5	♎	May 17–May 27	♎
May 12–June 1	♈	June 6–June 17	♉	May 28–June 10	♉
June 2–June 14	♎	June 18–July 2	♊	June 11–Aug. 15	♊
June 15–June 26	♉	July 3–Sept. 5	♋	Aug. 16–Aug. 28	♋
June 27–July 9	♊	Sept. 6–Sept. 19	♌	Aug. 29–Sept. 11	♌
July 10–July 26	♋	Sept. 20–Oct. 4	♍	Sept. 12–Sept. 27	♍
July 27–Aug. 29	♌	Oct. 5–Oct. 21	♎	Sept. 28–Oct. 16	♎
Aug. 30–Sept. 10	♋	Oct. 22–Dec. 24	♏	Oct. 17–Nov. 10	♏
Sept. 11–Sept. 27	♌	Dec. 25–Dec. 31	♐	Nov. 11–Nov. 29	♎
Sept. 28–Oct. 12	♍			Nov. 30–Dec. 17	♏
Oct. 13–Oct. 28	♎			Dec. 18–Dec. 31	♐
Oct. 29–Nov. 15	♏				
Nov. 16–Dec. 18	♐				
Dec. 19–Dec. 27	♏				
Dec. 28–Dec. 31	♐				

1974		1975	
Dates	*Sign*	*Dates*	*Sign*
Jan. 1–Jan. 4	♇	Jan. 1–Jan. 12	♐
Jan. 5–Jan. 19	♐	Jan. 13–Mar. 18	♑
Jan. 20–Feb. 4	♑	Mar. 19–Apr. 4	♒
Feb. 5–Feb. 27	♒	Apr. 5–Apr. 17	♓
Feb. 28–Mar. 21	♑	Apr. 18–Apr. 29	♈
Mar. 22–Apr. 11	♒	Apr. 30–May 15	♏
Apr. 12–Apr. 25	♓	May 16–June 15	♉
Apr. 26–May 7	♈	June 16–June 27	♏
May 8–May 20	♏	June 28–July 18	♉
May 21–June 9	♉	July 19–July 30	♊
June 10–June 27	♊	July 31–Aug. 12	♋
June 28–July 23	♉	Aug. 13–Aug. 27	♌
July 24–Aug. 8	♊	Aug. 28–Sept. 19	♍
Aug. 9–Aug. 20	♋	Sept. 20–Oct. 3	♎
Aug. 21–Sept. 3	♌	Oct. 4–Oct. 31	♍
Sept. 4–Sept. 21	♍	Nov. 1–Nov. 17	♎
Sept. 22–Nov. 24	♎	Nov. 18–Dec. 3	♏
Nov. 25–Dec. 10	♏	Dec. 4–Dec. 20	♇
Dec. 11–Dec. 28	♇	Dec. 21–Dec. 31	♐
Dec. 29–Dec. 31	♐		

5: Venus

♀

BESIDES THE MOON, earth's nearest neighbor in the heavens is the planet Venus. Venus is not only closer to us than any other planet, but is nearest to terrestrial size of all the members of the solar system. Most of us know this planet as the morning or evening star. Named for the goddess of love (the Greek Aphrodite), Venus has always been a mystery, like the heart of woman to man. Although relatively close to us, it is difficult to observe. One reason for this is that it is closer to the sun, and we all know the difficulty of observing something when a bright light is behind it or when it is on the other side of a bright light. The second reason is that the surface of Venus is always shrouded by a thick layer of clouds, which makes direct observation impossible.

It was thought for many years that Venus might have a civilization similar to ours. This made it a favorite subject of writers of fantasy and science fiction, who usually depicted an idyllic setting of great forests and sunny meadows—the Earthly Paradise that earthmen have lost. But recent explorations by Russian robot spacecraft that have penetrated the veil of clouds indicate that the surface is extremely hot and the atmosphere unbreathable by humans. So much for our dreams of Arcadia! The truth about Venus will probably not be known until our astronauts are able to go there.

Venus is the second of the nine known planets of the solar system. It has no satellites. Being closer to the sun, its orbit (or year) is shorter than the earth's. It takes Venus 225 days to make one circuit of the sun; thus it is slower than Mercury (88 days) and faster than earth (365 days). As might be expected, then, since Mercury and Venus are both closer to the

244 THE ASTROLOGY 14 HOROSCOPE

sun than the earth, Venus also exhibits the *retrograde motion* described for Mercury in Chapter 4. However, it does so less frequently, so that— from our point of view on earth—Venus has a slower and more orderly movement than that of fiery, fast-moving Mercury.

MEANING OF VENUS IN HOROSCOPE

As mentioned above, Venus moves faster than the earth. Its orbit is 225 days, and it moves through 585 degrees per year. The farther a planet is from the sun, the slower its apparent motion. Thus, as we shall see in Chapter 6, Mars, the fourth planet, moves through only 191 degrees per year.

Named for the goddess of love, Venus (like the moon) is principally concerned with the emotions. This planet rules the signs Taurus and Libra, so its placement in your chart is particularly significant if one of these is your sun sign. As we have noted in earlier chapters, Venus is also associated with music. All of us are interested in romance, most of us in marriage, and not a few have musical talent or aspirations in that direction. Therefore, Venus is an important element in *any* horoscope.

The lovely goddess Venus (or Aphrodite) represents the *feminine* principle—the exact opposite of Mars, who is symbolic of the masculine principle. Astrologically, there is a close connection between these two planets, as they complement each other. Venus is known as the "lesser fortune" (Jupiter is the "greater fortune"). It is a beneficent planet in your horoscope (unless adversely aspected by other elements) and, as we have noted, is of particular importance if Taurus or Libra is your sun sign.

In most cases, Venus is a beneficent element in your horoscope, bringing good luck, especially where emotional matters (such as affairs of the heart) are concerned. It will enhance your personal appeal, your attractiveness to the opposite sex; it will tend to counter the powerful effect of masculine Mars, bringing out the gentler and more refined side of your nature. Ideally, Venus and Mars should balance and complement each other, since each of us—man or woman—has masculine and feminine elements in his or her makeup. In a man, his feminine side is mainly unconscious, of course, just as a woman's masculine side is mainly unconscious. But we have learned that the unconscious plays just as great a part in our lives as does the conscious mind, or ego. These two opposite elements were known to the ancients as *logos* ("mind") and *eros* ("love"); we who are interested in astrology can just as well think of them as Mars and Venus. Thus, a man's nature tends to be dominated by his mind, and it is easier for him to be objective about a situation; a woman naturally tends to be dominated by her emotions, and she will react subjectively to most situations. Of course, it would be ridiculous to say that men don't feel and women don't think! I am only pointing up a psychological *fact*: men and women are different not only physically, but in the very nature of their psyches—a fact that the more extreme proponents of women's lib should take to heart.

When the balance between Mars and Venus is very lopsided, we have the unfortunate result of "womanish" men and "mannish" women; and, in extreme cases, homosexuals and lesbians. This does not mean that such people become so merely because Mars or Venus is poorly aspected in their horoscopes; obviously, many other influences—social, familial, etc.— are at work. But I repeat that a horoscope is an excellent tool by which to help you *know yourself*—and knowledge is power. Whether or not you act on the knowledge thus gained is up to you, but at least it is at your disposal.

To place the symbol of Venus (♀) on your chart, turn to Table 6 at the end of this chapter. Here the positions of Venus are listed for each year from 1890 to 1975. Turn to the year of your birth and find the span of time that includes your birthdate. It should be noted that Table 6 lists *inclusive* sets of dates. That is, if you were born on the seventeenth and the table lists Venus in Cetus from the first to the seventeenth, Venus was still in Cetus on your birthdate, since it did not enter Taurus until the eighteenth. As a reminder, the symbols of the 14 signs are given in a key at the beginning of Table 6.

To continue our example of someone born on January 1, 1940, with Aquarius rising, Figure 6 shows his chart with the symbol of Venus entered. In Table 6, it is shown that Venus was in Capricorn on January 1, 1940; therefore, the symbol of Venus is entered in the House occupied by Capricorn, which (on his chart) is the fourteenth House.

INTERPRETATION

General interpretations of the meaning of Venus in each of the 14 signs are given below. In reading these, it should be remembered that Venus, though usually beneficent, has no *absolute* meaning; whether it is a help or a hindrance depends upon its relationship to other elements of your chart. Also, the House occupied by Venus affects its interpretation. Our imaginary subject (Figure 6) was born with Venus in Capricorn, which is his fourteenth House. After reading the interpretation of Venus in Capricorn, he should turn back to Table 1 (p. 4), which lists the basic meanings of the Houses. The life activity governed by that particular House will be enhanced by the presence of Venus. This is also true of the other planets, which we will be placing in the chapters to follow.

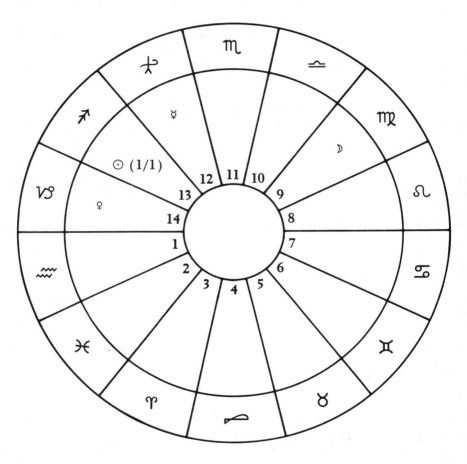

Figure 6. Placement of Venus on chart of subject born on January 1, 1940, with Aquarius rising

VENUS IN PISCES ♀ ♓

Venus in Pisces on your chart affects your emotional attitude toward matters of belief. Pisces is ruled by Neptune, which is often associated with spiritual affairs. But do not limit your definition of *belief* to purely religious or metaphysical concerns: your definition of the good life, spoken or not, is a matter of belief; so is your belief in yourself as an individual (or lack of it). As we have seen, Venus rules the emotions and also is associated with music. Its position in Pisces on your chart, if well aspected to other elements, will increase the emotional intensity of your beliefs, whatever they may be. If you belong to a church or temple, you are probably devout and take your religious life seriously. If interested in politics, you are an ardent supporter of your party. In affairs of the heart, Venus will provide a positive boost, keeping your love life glowing even after many years of marriage. You are almost certain to love music (especially the more romantic composers), and, if this is your field, your talent and audience appeal will be enhanced by Venus. A poorly aspected Venus, on the other hand, may tend to make you overemotional in your reactions to life situations, and you might find yourself passionately defending lost causes. The meaning of the aspects will be taken up in Chapter 12. Meantime, check the life activity governed by the House occupied by Pisces on your chart (see Table 1) for a clearer picture of Venus's influence on your beliefs and love life.

VENUS IN ARIES ♀ ♈

Venus in Aries on your chart adds emotional intensity to the power of your will. Aries is ruled by Mars, and we have noted that Mars and Venus are complementary—the male and female principles, respectively. No personality can mature without a proper balance between these principles. If well aspected, Venus in this sign can be of great benefit in softening the hard edge of the will to power often demonstrated by Aries types. Will is of the mind (*logos*), and in our century we have seen the disastrous results of driving will when it is coldly ruthless. Venus adds the warmth of human concern and thoughtfulness. This Mars/Venus combination can be very fortunate: in proper balance, it leads to a strong, ambitious personality that is also kind and generous. However, if your Venus is poorly aspected to other elements, there may be too much emotionalism in your ambition, as we see in the case of fanatics, who are passionately convinced of the exclusive rightness of their dogma, be it religious, political, or whatever. The meaning of the aspects will be taken up in

Chapter 12. Meanwhile, check the life activity governed by the House occupied by Aries on your chart (see Table 1) for a clearer picture of Venus's influence on the emotional portion of your will.

VENUS IN CETUS ♀ ⤳

Venus in Cetus on your chart enhances your emotional attitude toward yourself, toward others, and toward your career. Since Cetus is ruled by Jupiter, the "greater fortune," its combination with Venus, the "lesser fortune," almost surely signifies good luck and prosperity. Again we have a masculine/feminine (Jupiter/Venus) combination that, if properly balanced, can lead to a well-developed personality: strong but kind, steady and ambitious without loss of sensitivity. These qualities will serve especially well if your field should be the performing or graphic arts (if the former, Venus's connection with music will add an extra benefit). For both men and women, Venus in this sign will enhance your charm, personal magnetism, and attractiveness to the opposite sex. If your Venus is poorly aspected to other elements, however, the intensity of your emotions may lead you to see yourself and others in a bad light, and you may suffer needlessly over slights both real and imagined. The meaning of the aspects will be taken up in Chapter 12. Meantime, check the life activity governed by the House occupied by Cetus on your chart (see Table 1) for a clearer picture of Venus's influence on the emotions connected with your self-regard, your relationships with others, and your career.

VENUS IN TAURUS ♀ ♉

Venus in Taurus on your chart will certainly enhance your emotional life, especially where romance and marriage are concerned. Taurus is ruled by Venus. This means that the qualities of both sign and planet are approximately doubled with Venus in this sign. A well-aspected Venus, then, will greatly improve your chances of success and happiness in love affairs, marriage, parenthood, and other emotional relationships. You are attractive to the opposite sex, and probably find your social calendar fuller than you can easily manage. This planet/sign combination is especially fortunate if your field is music, mathematics, science, or technology. If you are a pianist, for example, your playing will exhibit not only technical proficiency, but the emotional warmth and color without which great music is impossible. If your Venus is poorly aspected, on the other hand, you may be the type of lover who clings too closely, is jealously possessive, and tends to smother the beloved with affection. The meaning of the aspects will be taken up in Chapter 12. Meantime, check the life activity governed by the House occupied by Taurus on your chart (see Table 1) for a clearer picture of Venus's influence on the emotional quality of your personal relationships and its effect on your career.

VENUS IN GEMINI ♀ ♊

Venus in Gemini on your chart adds emotional color and power to your intellect and your communicative skills, be they oral or written. Gemini is ruled by Mercury and, as we noted in the last chapter, the wing-footed god affects versatility and mental agility, as well as powers of communication. If well aspected, feminine Venus can add a beneficent counterpole to masculine Mercury. Keenness of intellect by itself is not enough for a well-balanced personality; neither is emotional sensitivity and warmth. But the two in harmony can lead to a well-rounded, colorful, and sympathetic human being who has everything going for him or her. This position is especially fortunate for writers, announcers, mathematicians, and all of us who have to wear more hats than one in our careers and home lives. If your Venus is poorly aspected to other elements, however, you may spread yourself too thin by taking on too many tasks at once, and your powers of oral communication may develop to the point where you are over-aggressive in conversation. The meaning of the aspects will be taken up in Chapter 12. Meantime, check the life activity governed by the House occupied by Gemini on your chart (see Table 1) for a clearer picture of Venus's influence on your mental agility, versatility, and powers of communication.

VENUS IN CANCER ♀ ♋

Venus in Cancer on your chart will affect the quality and sensitivity of your emotions, and undoubtedly will have an effect on your personality. Cancer is ruled by the feminine moon, which directly affects your personality (the sun, which rules Leo, affects your individuality). If well aspected, Venus in this sign will add warmth and sympathy to your personality, will help you to understand and "feel for" others, and probably make you sought after as a lover, friend, or confidant. It will also help you keep a youthful outlook, whatever your years, and (barring accidents) actually increase your longevity. A poorly aspected Venus, on the other hand, may increase your shyness (which will often be mistaken for aloofness) and tend to make you feel unsure of your ground in emotional relationships. Also, your emotional sensitivity may lead you into situations where others will take advantage of your sensitivity and willingness to give all to help others. The meaning of the aspects will be taken up in Chapter 12. Meantime, check the life activity governed by the House occupied by Cancer on your chart (see Table 1) for a clearer picture of Venus's influence on your emotional sensitivity, youthful outlook, and possibilities of leading a long life.

VENUS IN LEO ♀ ♌

Venus in Leo on your chart affects your attitude toward your sense of personal independence. Kingly Leo is ruled by the sun and is definitely masculine. As noted above, the combination of feminine Venus in a masculine sign can be a very fortunate one. For proper balance, the personality needs approximately equal portions of masculine and feminine elements (mind and emotions, objective and subjective, etc.), and this can be greatly helped if your Venus is well aspected to other elements in your chart. Venus will then temper the more rugged aspects of your independence, showing that "to be is to be related" and that, no matter how self-sufficient you may consider yourself, you cannot live a full and happy life without the love, friendship, and cooperation of your fellow-travelers on this planet. Thus softened, your independence will be expressed in positive gains and a successful career made with the help of others, not at their expense. A poorly aspected Venus, however, can help to make you a maverick instead of a leader, and may make you distrustful of others, which can end in loneliness. The meaning of the aspects will be taken up in Chapter 12. Meantime, check the life activity governed by the House occupied by Leo on your chart (see Table 1) for a clearer picture of Venus's influence on your feeling of personal independence.

VENUS IN VIRGO ♀ ♍

Venus in Virgo on your chart affects your individualism and your analytical ability. Virgo is ruled by Mercury, which, as we have noted, is concerned with your ability to analyze people, products, and situations. The presence of Venus in this sign can add emotional warmth to this primarily intellectual activity. If well aspected to other elements in your chart, Venus can thus add a stabilizing quality both to your individualism and to your powers of analysis. You are probably popular with members of both sexes and have been dubbed with a nickname. Your analytical powers will be used to help others as well as yourself, and your criticism will inevitably be constructive and given in such a way as not to hurt others' feelings. On the other hand, if your Venus is poorly aspected, your individualism may be extreme, so that some will think of you as a crank; also, you may find it hard to resist being overcritical, and a catty tone may creep into your evaluations. The meaning of the aspects will be taken up in Chapter 12. Meantime, check the life activity governed by the House occupied by Virgo on your chart (see Table 1) for a clearer picture of Venus's influence on the emotional quality of your individualism and analytical ability.

VENUS IN LIBRA ♀ ♎

Venus in Libra on your chart will have a powerful effect on the quality of your judgment, especially where emotional matters are concerned. Like Taurus, Libra is ruled by Venus, and the presence of the planetary ruler in this sign approximately doubles the influence of both sign and planet. The association of Venus with the emotions, music, and the "hard" sciences has been noted. If your Venus is well aspected to other elements in your chart, then it is highly probable that all areas of your life involving the emotions will be positively enhanced, which bodes well for your love life, marriage, and friendships. This combination is excellent for musicians (especially singers), mathematicians, and anyone involved in science or technology. You have an intuitive talent for judging any kind of dispute, being able to put your personal feelings aside for the moment. You have a passion for justice (but it may be justice on your own terms rather than according to legal definitions). On the other hand, if your Venus is poorly aspected, you may tend to lack self-confidence in this talent; or you may, like some Aries types, let your opinions harden into dogmatism and feel that you are *never* wrong. The meaning of the aspects will be taken up in Chapter 12. Meanwhile, check the life activity governed by the House occupied by Libra on your chart (see Table 1, page 4) for a clearer picture of Venus's influence on the quality of your judgment.

VENUS IN SCORPIO ♀ ♏

Venus in Scorpio on your chart affects the emotional intensity of your empathy—your sensitivity to the feelings of others. Scorpio is ruled by masculine Mars. If your Venus is well aspected, this can mean an excellent balance between the masculine and feminine principles, as described above. Of course, a mature personality needs both principles in approximately equal balance. Venus will increase the warmth and depth of your sensitivity to the moods and feelings of those around you. It is easy to become callous to others in a technocracy like ours, where the law of the jungle—survival at any cost—seems paramount; you, however, genuinely *feel* for the other fellow, because you can put yourself in his place, and your sympathy flows easily. This is an excellent combination for humanitarians of all sorts, and also for poets and mystics. If your Venus is poorly aspected, however, you may find that your humanitarian ideals can lead you into bad situations—even martyrdom—and there is always the danger of less sensitive people taking advantage of your interest and compassion. The meaning of the aspects will be taken up in Chapter 12. Meantime, check the life activity governed by the House occupied by Scorpio on your chart (see Table 1) for a clearer picture of Venus's influence on your empathy and emotional attachment to humanistic ideals of fair play and justice.

VENUS IN OPHIUCHUS ♀ ⚕

Venus in Ophiuchus on your chart will probably affect your resourcefulness and versatility. Ophiuchus is ruled by Pluto, which is named for a god who is a personification of wealth. Again, feminine Venus in a masculine sign can denote the proper balance of masculine and feminine characteristics in your personality. Ophiuchus types are not only versatile and sensitive, they are often talented, especially in the entertainment field. A well-aspected Venus will increase the emotional depth of your performance, whatever your field—be it center stage or simply telling stories in the family circle. Venus will also enhance your versatility; like Gemini types, you can wear more than one hat or do one thing while thinking about another. You have a good deal of personal charm, and your warmth and sensitivity will usually result in no lack of admirers. If your Venus is poorly aspected, on the other hand, you may find yourself in a situation where your talents cannot be exploited, or your creative drive may be frustrated by an unsuitable life style. The meaning of the aspects will be taken up in Chapter 12. Meantime, check the life activity governed by the House occupied by Ophiuchus on your chart (see Table 1) for a clearer picture of Venus's influence on your versatility, resourcefulness, and emotional outlet via your talents.

VENUS IN SAGITTARIUS ♀ ♐

Venus in Sagittarius on your chart affects your very active conscience, humanitarian activities, and extraversion in many spheres. Sagittarius is ruled by Jupiter, the "greater fortune," so Venus, the "lesser fortune," in this sign ordinarily denotes good luck and the development of a well-rounded, expansive, generous personality. This is further enhanced (if your Venus is well aspected) by the balance between masculine Jupiter and feminine Venus. You are probably the type of person who, in legend, fell down a well and came up unhurt and with a gold watch in his hand!

Success will probably come easily to you, social as well as material, for nearly everyone is attracted to a warm, outgoing personality. You have humanitarian ideals and wish to act on them, having true compassion for your less fortunate fellows and being willing to work long hours to better their condition. If your Venus is poorly aspected, however, you may depend too much on your extraverted side, tending to ignore your inner nature, so that you fail to develop the well-rounded and mature personality that the Jupiter/Venus combination usually promises. The meaning of the aspects will be taken up in Chapter 12. Meantime, check the life activity governed by the House occupied by Sagittarius on your chart (see Table 1) for a clearer picture of Venus's influence on your conscience and humanistic depth.

VENUS IN CAPRICORN ♀ ♑

Venus in Capricorn on your chart affects your conservatism and adds an emotional dimension to your "realistic" approach to life's problems and possibilities. Capricorn is ruled by "gloomy" Saturn, often associated by astrologers with old age, illness, and misfortune. However, Saturn being a masculine deity, the presence of feminine Venus—if well aspected to other elements—can offset this rather forbidding picture. The conservative and dryly realistic, intellectual traits of Saturn can be nicely balanced by the emotional depth and sensitivity of the goddess of love and bringer of music. Good sense dictates that the conservative approach is often the best, and realism is necessary for sheer survival. Also, the dry wit of Saturn is softened by the warmth and sympathy of Venus. On the other hand, if your Venus is badly aspected to other elements, your sense of conservatism and realism may be exaggerated to the point where you feel an emotional dread at the thought of taking any chances at all. This will tend to cripple the development of maturity, and an emotional childishness may result even if you live to the age of Father Time himself! The meaning of the aspects will be taken up in Chapter 12. Meanwhile, check the life activity governed by the House occupied by Capricorn on your chart (see Table 1) for a clearer picture of Venus's influence on your emotional need to be conservative and realistic.

VENUS IN AQUARIUS ♀ ♒

Venus in Aquarius on your chart will affect your temperament, especially where the choice of a career and life style are concerned. This effect will be strongly felt in such areas as the acquisition of knowledge of a scientific or technical type. Aquarius is ruled by Uranus, which is sometimes called "the disruptor" because of its eccentric orbit. If your Venus is well aspected to other elements, it can mean a nice balance between the masculine and feminine elements in your makeup. Venus will be helpful in offsetting the intellectual approach needed in such fields so that it does not become an exclusive preoccupation. If your career should be in the field of entertainment, which is common for Aquarius types, Venus will add warmth and personal charisma to your performance. A poorly aspected Venus, however, can bring out the "disruptive" trait symbolized by the orbit of Uranus, and your otherwise fine analytical and critical abilities may be exaggerated to the point where you are thought of as a "nit-picker." Also, you may tend to be temperamental and nervous, and will find it necessary to keep in top physical and mental condition. The meaning of the aspects will be taken up in Chapter 12. Meantime, check the life activity governed by the House occupied by Aquarius on your chart (see Table 1) for a clearer picture of Venus's influence on the emotional elements of your temperament, analytical and technical ability, and "disruptive" elements in your personality.

Table 6

POSITIONS OF VENUS BY
YEAR (1890 TO 1975)

Key

♓	Pisces	♍	Virgo
♈	Aries	♎	Libra
⬿	Cetus	♏	Scorpio
♉	Taurus	⚕	Ophiuchus
♊	Gemini	♐	Sagittarius
♋	Cancer	♑	Capricorn
♌	Leo	♒	Aquarius

1890	
Dates	*Sign*
Jan. 1–Jan. 9	⛎
Jan. 10–Jan. 30	♐
Jan. 31–Feb. 20	♑
Feb. 21–Mar. 14	♒
Mar. 15–Apr. 3	♓
Apr. 4–Apr. 24	♈
Apr. 25–May 14	⟜
May 15–June 4	♉
June 5–June 24	♊
June 25–July 15	♋
July 16–Aug. 6	♌
Aug. 7–Aug. 29	♍
Aug. 30–Sept. 23	♎
Sept. 24–Oct. 25	♏
Oct. 26–Dec. 1	⛎
Dec. 2–Dec. 31	♏

1891	
Dates	*Sign*
Jan. 1–Jan. 16	♏
Jan. 17–Feb. 15	⛎
Feb. 16–Mar. 11	♐
Mar. 12–Apr. 3	♑
Apr. 4–Apr. 26	♒
Apr. 27–May 18	♓
May 19–June 8	♈
June 9–June 29	⟜
June 30–July 19	♉
July 20–Aug. 8	♊
Aug. 9–Aug. 28	♋
Aug. 29–Sept. 18	♌
Sept. 19–Oct. 9	♍
Oct. 10–Oct. 29	♎
Oct. 30–Nov. 19	♏
Nov. 20–Dec. 11	⛎
Dec. 12–Dec. 31	♐

1892	
Dates	*Sign*
Jan. 1	♐
Jan. 2–Jan 22	♑
Jan. 23–Feb. 13	♒
Feb. 14–Mar. 5	♓
Mar. 6–Mar. 27	♈
Mar. 28–Apr. 19	⟜
Apr. 20–May 16	♉
May 17–July 23	♊
July 24–Aug. 7	♉
Aug. 8–Sept. 13	♊
Sept 14–Oct. 7	♋
Oct. 8–Oct. 30	♌
Oct. 31–Nov. 20	♍
Nov. 21–Dec. 12	♎
Dec. 13–Dec. 31	♏

1893	
Dates	*Sign*
Jan. 1–Jan. 2	♏
Jan. 3–Jan. 24	⛎
Jan. 25–Feb. 13	♐
Feb. 14–Mar. 6	♑
Mar. 7–Mar. 28	♒
Mar. 29–Apr. 18	♓
Apr. 19–May 8	♈
May 9–May 29	⟜
May 30–June 18	♉
June 19–July 8	♊
July 9–July 28	♋
July 29–Aug. 18	♌
Aug. 19–Sept. 9	♍
Sept. 10–Oct. 1	♎
Oct. 2–Oct. 23	♏
Oct. 24–Nov. 16	⛎
Nov. 17–Dec. 10	♐
Dec. 11–Dec. 31	♑

1894	
Dates	*Sign*
Jan. 1–Jan. 13	♑
Jan. 14–Feb. 7	♒
Feb. 8–Apr. 6	♑
Apr. 7–May 5	♒
May 6–May 29	♓
May 30–June 21	♈
June 22–July 12	⟜
July 13–Aug. 2	♉
Aug. 3–Aug. 23	♊
Aug. 24–Sept. 12	♋
Sept. 13–Oct. 3	♌
Oct. 4–Oct. 23	♍
Oct. 24–Nov. 13	♎
Nov. 14–Dec. 4	♏
Dec. 5–Dec. 25	⛎
Dec. 26–Dec. 31	♐

1895	
Dates	*Sign*
Jan. 1–Jan. 15	♐
Jan. 16–Feb. 5	♑
Feb. 6–Feb. 27	♒
Feb. 28–Mar. 19	♓
Mar. 20–Apr. 9	♈
Apr. 10–Apr. 30	⟜
May 2–May 21	♉
May 22–June 13	♊
June 14–July 6	♋
July 7–Aug. 5	♌
Aug. 6–Sept. 19	♍
Sept. 20–Oct. 31	♌
Nov. 1–Nov. 30	♍
Dec. 1–Dec. 24	♎
Dec. 25–Dec. 31	♏

TABLE 6 257

1896		1897		1898	
Dates	*Sign*	*Dates*	*Sign*	*Dates*	*Sign*
Jan. 1–Jan. 15	♏	Jan. 1–Jan. 8	♑	Jan. 1–Jan. 9	♐
Jan. 16–Feb. 7	♐	Jan. 9–Feb. 1	♒	Jan. 10–Jan. 30	♐
Feb. 8–Feb. 28	♐	Feb. 2–Feb. 27	♓	Jan. 31–Feb. 19	♑
Feb. 29–Mar. 20	♑	Feb. 28–June 26	♈	Feb. 20–Mar. 13	♒
Mar. 21–Apr. 12	♒	June 27–July 22	♉	Mar. 14–Apr. 3	♓
Apr. 13–May 3	♓	July 23–Aug. 14	♉	Apr. 4–Apr. 23	♈
May 4–May 23	♈	Aug. 15–Sept. 5	♊	Apr. 24–May 13	♉
May 24–June 12	♉	Sept. 6–Sept. 26	♋	May 14–June 3	♉
June 13–July 3	♉	Sept. 27–Oct. 17	♌	June 4–June 24	♊
July 4–July 23	♊	Oct. 18–Nov. 7	♍	June 25–July 14	♋
July 24–Aug. 12	♋	Nov. 8–Nov. 28	♎	July 15–Aug. 6	♌
Aug. 13–Sept. 2	♌	Nov. 29–Dec. 18	♏	Aug. 7–Aug. 29	♍
Sept. 3–Sept. 23	♍	Dec. 19–Dec. 31	♐	Aug. 30–Sept. 23	♎
Sept. 24–Oct. 14	♎			Sept. 24–Oct. 27	♏
Oct. 15–Nov. 4	♏			Oct. 28–Nov. 24	♐
Nov. 5–Nov. 26	♐			Nov. 25–Dec. 31	♏
Nov. 27–Dec. 17	♐				
Dec. 18–Dec. 31	♑				

1899		1900		1901	
Dates	*Sign*	*Dates*	*Sign*	*Dates*	*Sign*
Jan. 1–Jan. 17	♏	Jan. 1–Jan. 21	♑	Jan. 1–Jan. 2	♏
Jan. 18–Feb. 15	♐	Jan. 22–Feb. 13	♒	Jan. 3–Jan. 24	♐
Feb. 16–Mar. 11	♐	Feb. 14–Mar. 6	♓	Jan. 25–Feb. 14	♐
Mar. 12–Apr. 3	♑	Mar. 7–Mar. 28	♈	Feb. 15–Mar. 7	♑
Apr. 4–Apr. 26	♒	Mar. 29–Apr. 20	♉	Mar. 8–Mar. 29	♒
Apr. 27–May 17	♓	Apr. 21–May 17	♉	Mar. 30–Apr. 18	♓
May 18–June 7	♈	May 18–July 16	♊	Apr. 19–May 9	♈
June 8–June 28	♉	July 17–Aug. 12	♉	May 10–May 29	♉
June 29–July 19	♉	Aug. 13–Sept. 14	♊	May 30–June 18	♉
July 20–Aug. 8	♊	Sept. 15–Oct. 8	♋	June 19–July 9	♊
Aug. 9–Aug. 28	♋	Oct. 9–Oct. 30	♌	July 10–July 29	♋
Aug. 29–Sept. 17	♌	Oct. 31–Nov. 21	♍	July 30–Aug. 19	♌
Sept. 18–Oct. 8	♍	Nov. 22–Dec. 12	♎	Aug. 20–Sept. 9	♍
Oct. 9–Oct. 29	♎	Dec. 13–Dec. 31	♏	Sept. 10–Oct. 1	♎
Oct. 30–Nov. 19	♏			Oct. 2–Oct. 23	♏
Nov. 20–Dec. 10	♐			Oct. 24–Nov. 16	♐
Dec. 11–Dec. 31	♐			Nov. 17–Dec. 11	♐
				Dec. 12–Dec. 31	♑

1902		1903		1904	
Dates	*Sign*	*Dates*	*Sign*	*Dates*	*Sign*
Jan. 1–Jan. 18	♑	Jan. 1–Jan. 15	♐	Jan. 1–Jan. 16	♏
Jan. 19–Jan. 31	♒	Jan. 16–Feb. 5	♑	Jan. 17–Feb. 7	⛎
Feb. 1–Apr. 7	♑	Feb. 6–Feb. 27	♒	Feb. 8–Feb. 29	♐
Apr. 8–May 6	♒	Feb. 28–Mar. 20	♓	Mar. 1–Mar. 21	♑
May 7–May 30	♓	Mar. 21–Apr. 9	♈	Mar. 22–Apr. 12	♒
May 31–June 21	♈	Apr. 10–Apr. 30	⟿	Apr. 13–May 3	♓
June 22–July 13	⟿	May 1–May 22	♉	May 4–May 23	♈
July 14–Aug. 3	♉	May 23–June 13	♊	May 24–June 13	⟿
Aug. 4–Aug. 23	♊	June 14–July 7	♋	June 14–July 3	♉
Aug. 24–Sept. 12	♋	July 8–Aug. 8	♌	July 4–July 24	♊
Sept. 13–Oct. 3	♌	Aug. 9–Sept. 15	♍	July 25–Aug. 12	♋
Oct. 4–Oct. 24	♍	Sept. 16–Nov. 2	♌	Aug. 13–Sept. 2	♌
Oct. 25–Nov. 14	♎	Nov. 3–Dec. 1	♍	Sept. 3–Sept. 23	♍
Nov. 15–Dec. 4	♏	Dec. 2–Dec. 24	♎	Sept. 24–Oct. 14	♎
Dec. 5–Dec. 26	⛎	Dec. 25–Dec. 31	♏	Oct. 15–Nov. 4	♏
Dec. 27–Dec. 31	♐			Nov. 5–Nov. 26	⛎
				Nov. 27–Dec. 18	♐
				Dec. 19–Dec. 31	♑

1905		1906		1907	
Dates	*Sign*	*Dates*	*Sign*	*Dates*	*Sign*
Jan. 1–Jan. 9	♑	Jan. 1–Jan. 9	⛎	Jan. 1–Jan. 19	♏
Jan. 10–Feb. 2	♒	Jan 10–Jan. 30	♐	Jan. 20–Feb. 16	⛎
Feb. 3–Feb. 28	♓	Jan. 31–Feb. 20	♑	Feb. 17–Mar. 12	♐
Mar. 1–June 27	♈	Feb. 21–Mar. 7	♒	Mar. 13–Apr. 3	♑
June 28–July 23	⟿	Mar. 8–Apr. 3	♓	Apr. 4–Apr. 27	♒
July 24–Aug. 15	♉	Apr. 4–Apr. 23	♈	Apr. 28–May 18	♓
Aug. 16–Sept. 6	♊	Apr. 24–May 14	⟿	May 19–June 8	♈
Sept. 7–Sept. 26	♋	May 15–June 4	♉	June 9–June 28	⟿
Sept. 27–Oct. 17	♌	June 5–June 24	♊	June 29–July 19	♉
Oct. 18–Nov. 7	♍	June 25–July 15	♋	July 20–Aug. 8	♊
Nov. 8–Nov. 28	♎	July 16–Aug. 6	♌	Aug. 9–Aug. 28	♋
Nov. 29–Dec. 19	♏	Aug. 7–Aug. 30	♍	Aug. 29–Sept. 18	♌
Dec. 20–Dec. 31	⛎	Aug. 31–Sept. 24	♎	Sept. 19–Oct. 9	♍
		Sept. 25–Nov. 1	♏	Oct. 10–Oct. 29	♎
		Nov. 2–Nov. 16	⛎	Oct. 30–Nov. 19	♏
		Nov. 17–Dec. 31	♏	Nov. 20–Dec. 11	⛎
				Dec. 12–Dec. 31	♐

TABLE 6 259

1908		1909		1910	
Dates	*Sign*	*Dates*	*Sign*	*Dates*	*Sign*
Jan. 1	♐	Jan. 1–Jan. 2	♏	Jan. 1–Apr. 8	♑
Jan. 2–Jan. 22	♑	Jan. 3–Jan. 24	☋	Apr. 9–May 6	♒
Jan. 23–Feb. 13	♒	Jan. 25–Feb. 13	♐	May 7–May 30	♓
Feb. 14–Mar. 6	♓	Feb. 14–Mar. 6	♑	May 31–June 21	♈
Mar. 7–Mar. 27	♈	Mar. 7–Mar. 28	♒	June 22–July 12	☊
Mar. 28–Apr. 20	☊	Mar. 29–Apr. 18	♓	July 13–Aug. 2	♉
Apr. 21–May 18	♉	Apr. 19–May 8	♈	Aug. 3–Aug. 23	♊
May 19–July 10	♊	May 9–May 28	☊	Aug. 24–Sept. 12	♋
July 11–Aug. 14	♉	May 29–June 18	♉	Sept. 13–Oct. 2	♌
Aug. 15–Sept. 14	♊	June 19–July 8	♊	Oct. 3–Oct. 23	♍
Sept. 15–Oct. 7	♋	July 9–July 28	♋	Oct. 24–Nov. 13	♎
Oct. 8–Oct. 30	♌	July 29–Aug. 18	♌	Nov. 14–Dec. 4	♏
Oct. 31–Nov. 21	♍	Aug. 19–Sept. 9	♍	Dec. 5–Dec. 25	☋
Nov. 22–Dec. 12	♎	Sept. 10–Oct. 1	♎	Dec. 26–Dec. 31	♐
Dec. 13–Dec. 31	♏	Oct. 2–Oct. 23	♏		
		Oct. 24–Nov. 16	☋		
		Nov. 17–Dec. 11	♐		
		Dec. 12–Dec. 31	♑		

1911		1912		1913	
Dates	*Sign*	*Dates*	*Sign*	*Dates*	*Sign*
Jan. 1–Jan. 15	♐	Jan. 1–Jan. 15	♏	Jan. 1–Jan. 9	♑
Jan. 16–Feb. 5	♑	Jan. 16–Feb. 7	☋	Jan. 10–Feb. 2	♒
Feb. 6–Feb. 27	♒	Feb. 8–Feb. 28	♐	Feb. 3–Feb. 28	♓
Feb. 28–Mar. 19	♓	Feb. 29–Mar. 20	♑	Mar. 1–June 27	♈
Mar. 20–Apr. 9	♈	Mar. 21–Apr. 12	♒	June 28–July 23	☊
Apr. 10–Apr. 30	☊	Apr. 13–May 3	♓	July 24–Aug. 15	♉
May 1–May 21	♉	May 4–May 23	♈	Aug. 16–Sept. 5	♊
May 22–June 13	♊	May 24–June 12	☊	Sept. 6–Sept. 26	♋
June 14–July 7	♋	June 13–July 3	♉	Sept. 27–Oct. 17	♌
July 8–Aug. 9	♌	July 4–July 23	♊	Oct. 18–Nov. 7	♍
Aug. 10–Sept. 7	♍	July 24–Aug. 12	♋	Nov. 8–Nov. 27	♎
Sept. 8–Nov. 3	♌	Aug. 13–Sept. 2	♌	Nov. 28–Dec. 18	♏
Nov. 4–Dec. 1	♍	Sept. 3–Sept. 23	♍	Dec. 19–Dec. 31	☋
Dec. 2–Dec. 24	♎	Sept. 24–Oct. 14	♎		
Dec. 25–Dec. 31	♏	Oct. 15–Nov. 4	♏		
		Nov. 5–Nov. 26	☋		
		Nov. 27–Dec. 17	♐		
		Dec. 18–Dec. 31	♑		

1914		1915		1916	
Dates	*Sign*	*Dates*	*Sign*	*Dates*	*Sign*
Jan. 1–Jan. 9	♇	Jan. 1–Jan. 19	♏	Jan. 1–Jan. 21	♑
Jan. 10–Jan. 29	♐	Jan. 20–Feb. 16	♇	Jan. 22–Feb. 13	♒
Jan. 30–Feb. 19	♑	Feb. 17–Mar. 11	♐	Feb. 14–Mar. 5	♓
Feb. 20–Mar. 13	♒	Mar. 12–Apr. 3	♑	Mar. 6–Mar. 27	♈
Mar. 14–Apr. 2	♓	Apr. 4–Apr. 26	♒	Mar. 28–Apr. 20	⛎
Apr. 3–Apr. 23	♈	Apr. 27–May 17	♓	Apr. 21–May 19	♉
Apr. 24–May 13	⛎	May 18–June 7	♈	May 20–July 4	♊
May 14–June 3	♉	June 8–June 28	⛎	July 5–Aug. 15	♉
June 4–June 24	♊	June 29–July 18	♉	Aug. 16–Sept. 14	♊
June 25–July 15	♋	July 19–Aug. 8	♊	Sept. 15–Oct. 7	♋
July 16–Aug. 6	♌	Aug. 9–Aug. 28	♋	Oct. 8–Oct. 29	♌
Aug. 7–Aug. 29	♍	Aug. 29–Sept. 17	♌	Oct. 30–Nov. 20	♍
Aug. 30–Sept. 24	♎	Sept. 18–Oct. 8	♍	Nov. 21–Dec. 11	♎
Sept. 25–Dec. 31	♏	Oct. 9–Oct. 29	♎	Dec. 12–Dec. 31	♏
		Oct. 30–Nov. 19	♏		
		Nov. 20–Dec. 10	♇		
		Dec. 11–Dec. 31	♐		

1917		1918		1919	
Dates	*Sign*	*Dates*	*Sign*	*Dates*	*Sign*
Jan. 1	♏	Jan. 1–Apr. 8	♑	Jan. 1–Jan. 14	♐
Jan. 2–Jan. 23	♇	Apr. 9–May 6	♒	Jan. 15–Feb. 4	♑
Jan. 24–Feb. 13	♐	May 7–May 29	♓	Feb. 5–Feb. 26	♒
Feb. 14–Mar. 6	♑	May 30–June 20	♈	Feb. 27–Mar. 19	♓
Mar. 7–Mar. 28	♒	June 21–July 12	⛎	Mar. 20–Apr. 8	♈
Mar. 29–Apr. 17	♓	July 13–Aug. 2	♉	Apr. 9–Apr. 29	⛎
Apr. 18–May 8	♈	Aug. 3–Aug. 22	♊	Apr. 30–May 21	♉
May 9–May 28	⛎	Aug. 23–Sept. 11	♋	May 22–June 13	♊
May 29–June 17	♉	Sept. 12–Oct. 2	♌	June 14–July 7	♋
June 18–July 8	♊	Oct. 3–Oct. 23	♍	July 8–Aug. 13	♌
July 9–July 28	♋	Oct. 24–Nov. 12	♎	Aug. 14–Aug. 31	♍
July 29–Aug. 18	♌	Nov. 13–Dec. 3	♏	Sept. 1–Nov. 3	♌
Aug. 19–Sept. 9	♍	Dec. 4–Dec. 25	♇	Nov. 4–Nov. 30	♍
Sept. 10–Sept. 30	♎	Dec. 26–Dec. 31	♐	Dec. 1–Dec. 24	♎
Oct. 1–Oct. 23	♏			Dec. 25–Dec. 31	♏
Oct. 24–Nov. 16	♇				
Nov. 17–Dec. 12	♐				
Dec. 13–Dec. 31	♑				

TABLE 6 261

1920		1921		1922	
Dates	*Sign*	*Dates*	*Sign*	*Dates*	*Sign*
Jan. 1–Jan. 15	♏	Jan. 1–Jan. 8	♑	Jan. 1–Jan. 8	♑
Jan. 16–Feb. 6	♑	Jan. 9–Feb. 2	♒	Jan. 9–Jan. 29	♐
Feb. 7–Feb. 28	♐	Feb. 3–Mar. 1	♓	Jan. 30–Feb. 19	♑
Feb. 29–Mar. 20	♑	Mar. 2–May 4	♈	Feb. 20–Mar. 12	♒
Mar. 21–Apr. 11	♒	May 5–May 23	♓	Mar. 13–Apr. 2	♓
Apr. 12–May 2	♓	May 24–June 28	♈	Apr. 3–Apr. 22	♈
May 3–May 22	♈	June 29–July 22	♎	Apr. 23–May 13	♎
May 23–June 12	♎	July 23–Aug. 14	♉	May 14–June 3	♉
June 13–July 2	♉	Aug. 15–Sept. 5	♊	June 4–June 23	♊
July 3–July 22	♊	Sept. 6–Sept. 25	♋	June 24–July 14	♋
July 23–Aug. 11	♋	Sept. 26–Oct. 16	♌	July 15–Aug. 5	♌
Aug. 12–Sept. 1	♌	Oct. 17–Nov. 6	♍	Aug. 6–Aug. 29	♍
Sept. 2–Sept. 22	♍	Nov. 7–Nov. 27	♎	Aug. 30–Sept. 25	♎
Sept. 23–Oct. 13	♎	Nov. 28–Dec. 18	♏	Sept. 26–Dec. 31	♏
Oct. 14–Nov. 3	♏	Dec. 19–Dec. 31	♑		
Nov. 4–Nov. 25	♑				
Nov. 26–Dec. 17	♐				
Dec. 18–Dec. 31	♑				

1923		1924		1925	
Dates	*Sign*	*Dates*	*Sign*	*Dates*	*Sign*
Jan. 1–Jan. 20	♏	Jan. 1–Jan. 21	♑	Jan. 1	♏
Jan. 21–Feb. 16	♑	Jan. 22–Feb. 12	♒	Jan. 2–Jan. 22	♑
Feb. 17–Mar. 11	♐	Feb. 13–Mar. 5	♓	Jan. 23–Feb. 12	♐
Mar. 12–Apr. 2	♑	Mar. 6–Mar. 27	♈	Feb. 13–Mar. 5	♑
Apr. 3–Apr. 26	♒	Mar. 28–Apr. 19	♎	Mar. 6–Mar. 27	♒
Apr. 27–May 17	♓	Apr. 20–May 20	♉	Mar. 28–Apr. 17	♓
May 18–June 7	♈	May 21–June 29	♊	Apr. 18–May 7	♈
June 8–June 27	♎	June 30–Aug. 16	♉	May 8–May 27	♎
June 28–July 18	♉	Aug. 17–Sept. 14	♊	May 28–June 17	♉
July 19–Aug. 7	♊	Sept. 15–Oct. 7	♋	June 18–July 7	♊
Aug. 8–Aug. 27	♋	Oct. 8–Oct. 29	♌	July 8–July 27	♋
Aug. 28–Sept. 17	♌	Oct. 30–Nov. 20	♍	July 28–Aug. 17	♌
Sept. 18–Oct. 7	♍	Nov. 21–Dec. 11	♎	Aug. 18–Sept. 8	♍
Oct. 8–Oct. 28	♎	Dec. 12–Dec. 31	♏	Sept. 9–Sept. 30	♎
Oct. 29–Nov. 18	♏			Oct. 1–Oct. 22	♏
Nov. 19–Dec. 10	♑			Oct. 23–Nov. 16	♑
Dec. 11–Dec. 31	♐			Nov. 17–Dec. 12	♐
				Dec. 13–Dec. 31	♑

1926		1927		1928	
Dates	*Sign*	*Dates*	*Sign*	*Dates*	*Sign*
Jan. 1–Apr. 8	♑	Jan. 1–Jan. 14	♐	Jan. 1–Jan. 14	♏
Apr. 9–May 6	♒	Jan. 15–Feb. 3	♑	Jan. 15–Feb. 6	☊
May 7–May 29	♓	Feb. 4–Feb. 26	♒	Feb. 7–Feb. 27	♐
May 30–June 20	♈	Feb. 27–Mar. 18	♓	Feb. 28–Mar. 19	♑
June 21–July 11	♉	Mar. 19–Apr. 8	♈	Mar. 20–Apr. 11	♒
July 12–Aug. 1	♉	Apr. 9–Apr. 29	♉	Apr. 12–May 1	♓
Aug. 2–Aug. 22	♊	Apr. 30–May 21	♉	May 2–May 22	♈
Aug. 23–Sept. 11	♋	May 22–June 12	♊	May 23–June 11	♉
Sept. 12–Oct. 1	♌	June 13–July 7	♋	June 12–July 2	♉
Oct. 2–Oct. 22	♍	July 8–Nov. 4	♌	July 3–July 22	♊
Oct. 23–Nov. 12	♎	Nov. 5–Nov. 30	♍	July 23–Aug. 11	♋
Nov. 13–Dec. 3	♏	Dec. 1–Dec. 23	♎	Aug. 12–Aug. 31	♌
Dec. 4–Dec. 24	☊	Dec. 24–Dec. 31	♏	Sept. 1–Sept. 22	♍
Dec. 25–Dec. 31	♐			Sept. 23–Oct. 13	♎
				Oct. 14–Nov. 3	♏
				Nov. 4–Nov. 25	☊
				Nov. 26–Dec. 17	♐
				Dec. 18–Dec. 31	♑

1929		1930		1931	
Dates	*Sign*	*Dates*	*Sign*	*Dates*	*Sign*
Jan. 1–Jan. 8	♑	Jan. 1–Jan. 8	☊	Jan. 1–Jan. 20	♏
Jan. 9–Feb. 2	♒	Jan. 9–Jan. 28	♐	Jan. 21–Feb. 16	☊
Feb. 3–Mar. 1	♓	Jan. 29–Feb. 18	♑	Feb. 17–Mar. 11	♐
Mar. 2–Apr. 26	♈	Feb. 19–Mar. 12	♒	Mar. 12–Apr. 2	♑
Apr. 27–May 26	♓	Mar. 13–Apr. 2	♓	Apr. 3–Apr. 25	♒
May 27–June 28	♈	Apr. 3–Apr. 22	♈	Apr. 26–May 16	♓
June 29–July 22	♉	Apr. 23–May 12	♉	May 17–June 6	♈
July 23–Aug. 14	♉	May 13–June 2	♉	June 7–June 27	♉
Aug. 15–Sept. 4	♊	June 3–June 23	♊	June 28–July 17	♉
Sept. 5–Sept. 25	♋	June 24–July 14	♋	July 18–Aug. 7	♊
Sept. 26–Oct. 16	♌	July 15–Aug. 5	♌	Aug. 8–Aug. 26	♋
Oct. 17–Nov. 6	♍	Aug. 6–Aug. 29	♍	Aug. 27–Sept. 16	♌
Nov. 7–Nov. 26	♎	Aug. 30–Sept. 25	♎	Sept. 17–Oct. 7	♍
Nov. 27–Dec. 17	♏	Sept. 26–Dec. 31	♏	Oct. 8–Oct. 28	♎
Dec. 18–Dec. 31	☊			Oct. 29–Nov. 18	♏
				Nov. 19–Dec. 9	☊
				Dec. 10–Dec. 30	♐
				Dec. 31	♑

TABLE 6 263

1932		1933		1934	
Dates	*Sign*	*Dates*	*Sign*	*Dates*	*Sign*
Jan. 1–Jan. 20	♑	Jan. 1–Jan. 22	⛎	Jan. 1–Apr. 8	♑
Jan. 21–Feb. 12	♒	Jan. 23–Feb. 12	♐	Apr. 9–May 5	♒
Feb. 13–Mar. 4	♓	Feb. 13–Mar. 5	♑	May 6–May 29	♓
Mar. 5–Mar. 26	♈	Mar. 6–Mar. 27	♒	May 30–June 19	♈
Mar. 27–Apr. 19	♎	Mar. 28–Apr. 16	♓	June 20–July 11	♎
Apr. 20–May 21	♉	Apr. 17–May 6	♈	July 12–Aug. 1	♉
May 22–June 23	♊	May 7–May 27	♎	Aug. 2–Aug. 21	♊
June 24–Aug. 17	♉	May 28–June 16	♉	Aug. 22–Sept. 10	♋
Aug. 18–Sept. 13	♊	June 17–July 7	♊	Sept. 11–Oct. 1	♌
Sept. 14–Oct. 6	♋	July 8–July 27	♋	Oct. 2–Oct. 22	♍
Oct. 7–Oct. 28	♌	July 28–Aug. 17	♌	Oct. 23–Nov. 11	♎
Oct. 29–Nov. 19	♍	Aug. 18–Sept. 8	♍	Nov. 12–Dec. 2	♏
Nov. 20–Dec. 10	♎	Sept. 9–Sept. 30	♎	Dec. 3–Dec. 24	⛎
Dec. 11–Dec. 31	♏	Oct. 1–Oct. 22	♏	Dec. 25–Dec. 31	♐
		Oct. 23–Nov. 16	⛎		
		Nov. 17–Dec. 12	♐		
		Dec. 13–Dec. 31	♑		

1935		1936		1937	
Dates	*Sign*	*Dates*	*Sign*	*Dates*	*Sign*
Jan. 1–Jan. 13	♐	Jan. 1–Jan. 14	♏	Jan. 1–Jan. 7	♑
Jan. 14–Feb. 3	♑	Jan. 15–Feb. 5	⛎	Jan. 8–Feb. 1	♒
Feb. 4–Feb. 25	♒	Feb. 6–Feb. 27	♐	Feb. 2–Mar. 2	♓
Feb. 26–Mar. 18	♓	Feb. 28–Mar. 19	♑	Mar. 3–Apr. 20	♈
Mar. 19–Apr. 7	♈	Mar. 20–Apr. 10	♒	Apr. 21–May 28	♓
Apr. 8–Apr. 29	♎	Apr. 11–May 1	♓	May 29–June 27	♈
Apr. 30–May 20	♉	May 2–May 21	♈	June 28–July 22	♎
May 21–June 12	♊	May 22–June 11	♎	July 23–Aug. 13	♉
June 13–July 7	♋	June 12–July 1	♉	Aug. 14–Sept. 4	♊
July 8–Nov. 4	♌	July 2–July 21	♊	Sept. 5–Sept. 24	♋
Nov. 5–Nov. 30	♍	July 22–Aug. 10	♋	Sept. 25–Oct. 15	♌
Dec. 1–Dec. 23	♎	Aug. 11–Aug. 31	♌	Oct. 16–Nov. 5	♍
Dec. 24–Dec. 31	♏	Sept. 1–Sept. 21	♍	Nov. 6–Nov. 26	♎
		Sept. 22–Oct. 12	♎	Nov. 27–Dec. 17	♏
		Oct. 13–Nov. 2	♏	Dec. 18–Dec. 31	⛎
		Nov. 3–Nov. 25	⛎		
		Nov. 26–Dec. 16	♐		
		Dec. 17–Dec. 31	♑		

1938		1939		1940	
Dates	*Sign*	*Dates*	*Sign*	*Dates*	*Sign*
Jan. 1–Jan. 7	⛎	Jan. 1–Jan. 20	♏	Jan. 1–Jan. 20	♑
Jan. 8–Jan 28	♐	Jan. 21–Feb. 15	⛎	Jan. 21–Feb. 11	♒
Jan. 29–Feb. 17	♑	Feb. 16–Mar. 10	♐	Feb. 12–Mar. 4	♓
Feb. 18–Mar. 11	♒	Mar. 11–Apr. 2	♑	Mar. 5–Mar. 26	♈
Mar. 12–Apr. 1	♓	Apr. 3–Apr. 25	♒	Mar. 27–Apr. 19	♋︎(Cetus)
Apr. 2–Apr. 21	♈	Apr. 26–May 16	♓	Apr. 20–May 23	♉
Apr. 22–May 12	(Cetus)	May 17–June 6	♈	May 24–June 16	♊
May 13–June 1	♉	June 7–June 26	(Cetus)	June 17–Aug. 17	♉
June 2–June 22	♊	June 27–July 17	♉	Aug. 18–Sept. 13	♊
June 23–July 13	♋	July 18–Aug. 6	♊	Sept. 14–Oct. 6	♋
July 14–Aug. 5	♌	Aug. 7–Aug. 26	♋	Oct. 7–Oct. 28	♌
Aug. 6–Aug. 29	♍	Aug. 27–Sept. 16	♌	Oct. 29–Nov. 19	♍
Aug. 30–Sept. 25	♎	Sept. 17–Oct. 6	♍	Nov. 20–Dec. 10	♎
Sept. 26–Dec. 31	♏	Oct. 7–Oct. 27	♎	Dec. 11–Dec. 31	♏
		Oct. 28–Nov. 17	♏		
		Nov. 18–Dec. 9	⛎		
		Dec. 10–Dec. 30	♐		
		Dec. 31	♑		

1941		1942		1943	
Dates	*Sign*	*Dates*	*Sign*	*Dates*	*Sign*
Jan. 1–Jan. 21	⛎	Jan. 1–Feb. 15	♑	Jan. 1–Jan. 13	♐
Jan. 22–Feb. 11	♐	Feb. 16–Mar. 2	♐	Jan. 14–Feb. 2	♑
Feb. 12–Mar. 4	♑	Mar. 3–Apr. 8	♑	Feb. 3–Feb. 24	♒
Mar. 5–Mar. 26	♒	Apr. 9–May 5	♒	Feb. 25–Mar. 17	♓
Mar. 27–Apr. 16	♓	May 6–May 28	♓	Mar. 18–Apr. 7	♈
Apr. 17–May 6	♈	May 29–June 19	♈	Apr. 8–Apr. 28	(Cetus)
May 7–May 26	(Cetus)	June 20–July 10	(Cetus)	Apr. 29–May 20	♉
May 27–June 16	♉	July 11–July 31	♉	May 21–June 12	♊
June 17–July 6	♊	Aug. 1–Aug. 21	♊	June 13–July 7	♋
July 7–July 26	♋	Aug. 22–Sept. 10	♋	July 8–Nov. 4	♌
July 27–Aug. 16	♌	Sept. 11–Sept. 30	♌	Nov. 5–Nov. 30	♍
Aug. 17–Sept. 7	♍	Oct. 1–Oct. 21	♍	Dec. 1–Dec. 23	♎
Sept. 8–Sept. 29	♎	Oct. 22–Nov. 11	♎	Dec. 24–Dec. 31	♏
Sept. 30–Oct. 22	♏	Nov. 12–Dec. 2	♏		
Oct. 23–Nov. 15	⛎	Dec. 3–Dec. 23	⛎		
Nov. 16–Dec. 13	♐	Dec. 24–Dec. 31	♐		
Dec. 14–Dec. 31	♑				

TABLE 6 265

1944 Dates	Sign	**1945** Dates	Sign	**1946** Dates	Sign
Jan. 1–Jan. 14	♏	Jan. 1–Jan. 7	♑	Jan. 1–Jan. 7	♐
Jan. 15–Feb. 5	♐	Jan. 8–Feb. 1	♒	Jan. 8–Jan. 27	♐
Feb. 6–Feb. 26	♐	Feb. 2–Mar. 3	♓	Jan. 28–Feb. 17	♑
Feb. 27–Mar. 18	♑	Mar. 4–Apr. 14	♈	Feb. 18–Mar. 11	♒
Mar. 19–Apr. 9	♒	Apr. 15–May 29	♓	Mar. 12–Apr. 1	♓
Apr. 10–Apr. 30	♓	May 30–June 27	♈	Apr. 2–Apr. 21	♈
May 1–May 21	♈	June 28–July 21	♈	Apr. 22–May 11	♈
May 22–June 10	♈	July 22–Aug. 13	♉	May 12–June 1	♉
June 11–June 30	♉	Aug. 14–Sept. 3	♊	June 2–June 22	♊
July 1–July 21	♊	Sept. 4–Sept. 24	♋	June 23–July 13	♋
July 22–Aug. 10	♋	Sept. 25–Oct. 15	♌	July 14–Aug. 4	♌
Aug. 11–Aug. 30	♌	Oct. 16–Nov. 5	♍	Aug. 5–Aug. 29	♍
Aug. 31–Sept. 20	♍	Nov. 6–Nov. 25	♎	Aug. 30–Sept. 26	♎
Sept. 21–Oct. 12	♎	Nov. 26–Dec. 16	♏	Sept. 27–Dec. 2	♏
Oct. 13–Nov. 2	♏	Dec. 17–Dec. 31	♐	Dec. 3–Dec. 13	♎
Nov. 3–Nov. 24	♐			Dec. 14–Dec. 31	♏
Nov. 25–Dec. 16	♐				
Dec. 17–Dec. 31	♑				

1947 Dates	Sign	**1948** Dates	Sign	**1949** Dates	Sign
Jan. 1–Jan. 20	♏	Jan. 1–Jan. 19	♑	Jan. 1–Jan. 21	♐
Jan. 21–Feb. 15	♐	Jan. 20–Feb. 11	♒	Jan. 22–Feb. 11	♐
Feb. 16–Mar. 10	♐	Feb. 12–Mar. 4	♓	Feb. 12–Mar. 4	♑
Mar. 11–Apr. 1	♑	Mar. 5–Mar. 26	♈	Mar. 5–Mar. 25	♒
Apr. 2–Apr. 24	♒	Mar. 27–Apr. 19	♈	Mar. 26–Apr. 15	♓
Apr. 25–May 15	♓	Apr. 20–May 28	♉	Apr. 16–May 5	♈
May 16–June 5	♈	May 29–June 7	♊	May 6–May 26	♈
June 6–June 26	♈	June 8–Aug. 17	♉	May 27–June 15	♉
June 27–July 16	♉	Aug. 18–Sept. 13	♊	June 16–July 6	♊
July 17–Aug. 6	♊	Sept. 14–Oct. 6	♋	July 7–July 26	♋
Aug. 7–Aug. 25	♋	Oct. 7–Oct. 28	♌	July 27–Aug. 16	♌
Aug. 26–Sept. 15	♌	Oct. 29–Nov. 18	♍	Aug. 17–Sept. 7	♍
Sept. 16–Oct. 6	♍	Nov. 19–Dec. 9	♎	Sept. 8–Sept. 29	♎
Oct. 7–Oct. 27	♎	Dec. 10–Dec. 30	♏	Sept. 30–Oct. 21	♏
Oct. 28–Nov. 17	♏	Dec. 31	♐	Oct. 22–Nov. 15	♐
Nov. 18–Dec. 8	♐			Nov. 16–Dec. 13	♐
Dec. 9–Dec. 29	♐			Dec. 14–Dec. 31	♑
Dec. 30–Dec. 31	♑				

1950		1951		1952	
Dates	*Sign*	*Dates*	*Sign*	*Dates*	*Sign*
Jan. 1–Feb. 7	♑	Jan. 1–Jan. 12	♐	Jan. 1–Jan. 13	♏
Feb. 8–Mar. 6	♐	Jan. 13–Feb. 2	♑	Jan. 14–Feb. 4	⛎
Mar. 7–Apr. 8	♑	Feb. 3–Feb. 24	♒	Feb. 5–Feb. 26	♐
Apr. 9–May 5	♒	Feb. 25–Mar. 17	♓	Feb. 27–Mar. 18	♑
May 6–May 28	♓	Mar. 18–Apr. 6	♈	Mar. 19–Apr. 9	♒
May 29–June 18	♈	Apr. 7–Apr. 28	↝	Apr. 10–Apr. 30	♓
June 19–July 10	↝	Apr. 29–May 19	♉	May 1–May 20	♈
July 11–July 31	♉	May 20–June 12	♊	May 21–June 10	↝
Aug. 1–Aug. 20	♊	June 13–July 7	♋	June 11–June 30	♉
Aug. 21–Sept. 9	♋	July 8–Nov. 4	♌	July 1–July 20	♊
Sept. 10–Sept. 30	♌	Nov. 5–Nov. 30	♍	July 21–Aug. 9	♋
Oct. 1–Oct. 21	♍	Dec. 1–Dec. 22	♎	Aug. 10–Aug. 30	♌
Oct. 22–Nov. 10	♎	Dec. 23–Dec. 31	♏	Aug. 31–Sept. 20	♍
Nov. 11–Dec. 1	♏			Sept. 21–Oct. 11	♎
Dec. 2–Dec. 22	⛎			Oct. 12–Nov. 1	♏
Dec. 23–Dec. 31	♐			Nov. 2–Nov. 24	⛎
				Nov. 25–Dec. 15	♐
				Dec. 16–Dec. 31	♑

1953		1954		1955	
Dates	*Sign*	*Dates*	*Sign*	*Dates*	*Sign*
Jan. 1–Jan. 7	♑	Jan. 1–Jan. 6	⛎	Jan. 1–Jan. 20	♏
Jan. 8–Feb. 1	♒	Jan. 7–Jan. 27	♐	Jan. 21–Feb. 15	⛎
Feb. 2–Mar. 4	♓	Jan. 28–Feb. 16	♑	Feb. 16–Mar. 10	♐
Mar. 5–Apr. 8	♈	Feb. 17–Mar. 10	♒	Mar. 11–Apr. 1	♑
Apr. 9–May 30	♓	Mar. 11–Mar. 31	♓	Apr. 2–Apr. 24	♒
May 31–June 27	♈	Apr. 1–Apr. 20	♈	Apr. 25–May 15	♓
June 28–July 21	↝	Apr. 21–May 11	↝	May 16–June 5	♈
July 22–Aug. 12	♉	May 12–May 31	♉	June 6–June 25	↝
Aug. 13–Sept. 3	♊	June 1–June 21	♊	June 26–July 16	♉
Sept. 4–Sept. 23	♋	June 22–July 12	♋	July 17–Aug. 5	♊
Sept. 24–Oct. 14	♌	July 13–Aug. 4	♌	Aug. 6–Aug. 25	♋
Oct. 15–Nov. 4	♍	Aug. 5–Aug. 29	♍	Aug. 26–Sept. 14	♌
Nov. 5–Nov. 25	♎	Aug. 30–Sept. 26	♎	Sept. 15–Oct. 5	♍
Nov. 26–Dec. 16	♏	Sept. 27–Nov. 23	♏	Oct. 6–Oct. 26	♎
Dec. 17–Dec. 31	⛎	Nov. 24–Dec. 18	♎	Oct. 27–Nov. 16	♏
		Dec. 19–Dec. 31	♏	Nov. 17–Dec. 8	⛎
				Dec. 9–Dec. 29	♐
				Dec. 30–Dec. 31	♑

TABLE 6 267

1956		1957		1958	
Dates	*Sign*	*Dates*	*Sign*	*Dates*	*Sign*
Jan. 1–Jan. 19	♑	Jan. 1–Jan. 20	♇	Jan. 1–Jan. 31	♑
Jan. 20–Feb. 10	♒	Jan. 21–Feb. 10	♐	Feb. 1–Mar. 8	♐
Feb. 11–Mar. 3	♓	Feb. 11–Mar. 3	♑	Mar. 9–Apr. 8	♑
Mar. 4–Mar. 25	♈	Mar. 4–Mar. 25	♒	Apr. 9–May 4	♒
Mar. 26–Apr. 19	♎	Mar. 26–Apr. 15	♓	May 5–May 27	♓
Apr. 20–Aug. 18	♉	Apr. 16–May 5	♈	May 28–June 18	♈
Aug. 19–Sept. 13	♊	May 6–May 25	♎	June 19–July 9	♎
Sept. 14–Oct. 5	♋	May 26–June 15	♉	July 10–July 30	♉
Oct. 6–Oct. 27	♌	June 16–July 5	♊	July 31–Aug. 20	♊
Oct. 28–Nov. 18	♍	July 6–July 25	♋	Aug. 21–Sept. 9	♋
Nov. 19–Dec. 9	♎	July 26–Aug. 15	♌	Sept. 10–Sept. 29	♌
Dec. 10–Dec. 30	♏	Aug. 16–Sept. 6	♍	Sept. 30–Oct. 20	♍
Dec. 31	♇	Sept. 7–Sept. 28	♎	Oct. 21–Nov. 10	♎
		Sept. 29–Oct. 21	♏	Nov. 11–Nov. 30	♏
		Oct. 22–Nov. 15	♇	Dec. 1–Dec. 22	♇
		Nov. 16–Dec. 14	♐	Dec. 23–Dec. 31	♐
		Dec. 15–Dec. 31	♑		

1959		1960		1961	
Dates	*Sign*	*Dates*	*Sign*	*Dates*	*Sign*
Jan. 1–Jan. 12	♐	Jan. 1–Jan. 13	♏	Jan. 1–Jan. 7	♑
Jan. 13–Feb. 1	♑	Jan. 14–Feb. 4	♇	Jan. 8–Feb. 2	♒
Feb. 2–Feb. 23	♒	Feb. 5–Feb. 25	♐	Feb. 3–Mar. 7	♓
Feb. 24–Mar. 16	♓	Feb. 26–Mar. 17	♑	Mar. 8–Apr. 2	♈
Mar. 17–Apr. 6	♈	Mar. 18–Apr. 8	♒	Apr. 3–May 31	♓
Apr. 7–Apr. 27	♎	Apr. 9–Apr. 29	♓	June 1–June 28	♈
Apr. 28–May 19	♉	Apr. 30–May 20	♈	June 29–July 21	♎
May 20–June 11	♊	May 21–June 9	♎	July 22–Aug. 12	♉
June 12–July 8	♋	June 10–June 29	♉	Aug. 13–Sept. 3	♊
July 9–Sept. 19	♌	June 30–July 20	♊	Sept. 4–Sept. 23	♋
Sept. 20–Sept. 24	♋	July 21–Aug. 8	♋	Sept. 24–Oct. 14	♌
Sept. 25–Nov. 4	♌	Aug. 9–Aug. 29	♌	Oct. 15–Nov. 4	♍
Nov. 5–Nov. 29	♍	Aug. 30–Sept. 19	♍	Nov. 5–Nov. 25	♎
Nov. 30–Dec. 22	♎	Sept. 20–Oct. 11	♎	Nov. 26–Dec. 16	♏
Dec. 23–Dec. 31	♏	Oct. 12–Nov. 1	♏	Dec. 17–Dec. 31	♇
		Nov. 2–Nov. 23	♇		
		Nov. 24–Dec. 15	♐		
		Dec. 16–Dec. 31	♑		

1962		1963		1964	
Dates	*Sign*	*Dates*	*Sign*	*Dates*	*Sign*
Jan. 1–Jan. 6	⛎	Jan. 1–Jan. 21	♏	Jan. 1–Jan. 19	♑
Jan. 7–Jan. 27	♐	Jan. 22–Feb. 15	⛎	Jan. 20–Feb. 10	♒
Jan. 28–Feb. 16	♑	Feb. 16–Mar. 10	♐	Feb. 11–Mar. 3	♓
Feb. 17–Mar. 10	♒	Mar. 11–Apr. 1	♑	Mar. 4–Mar. 26	♈
Mar. 11–Mar. 31	♓	Apr. 2–Apr. 24	♒	Mar. 27–Apr. 20	↼
Apr. 1–Apr. 20	♈	Apr. 25–May 15	♓	Apr. 21–Aug. 18	♉
Apr. 21–May 11	↼	May 16–June 5	♈	Aug. 19–Sept. 13	♊
May 12–May 31	♉	June 6–June 25	↼	Sept. 14–Oct. 5	♋
June 1–June 22	♊	June 26–July 16	♉	Oct. 6–Oct. 27	♌
June 23–July 12	♋	July 17–Aug. 5	♊	Oct. 28–Nov. 18	♍
July 13–Aug. 4	♌	Aug. 6–Aug. 25	♋	Nov. 19–Dec. 9	♎
Aug. 5–Aug. 29	♍	Aug. 26–Sept. 14	♌	Dec. 10–Dec. 30	♏
Aug. 30–Sept. 28	♎	Sept. 15–Oct. 5	♍	Dec. 31	⛎
Sept. 29–Nov. 16	♏	Oct. 6–Oct. 26	♎		
Nov. 17–Dec. 20	♎	Oct. 27–Nov. 16	♏		
Dec. 21–Dec. 31	♏	Nov. 17–Dec. 8	⛎		
		Dec. 9–Dec. 29	♐		
		Dec. 30–Dec. 31	♑		

1965		1966		1967	
Dates	*Sign*	*Dates*	*Sign*	*Dates*	*Sign*
Jan. 1–Jan. 20	⛎	Jan. 1–Jan. 25	♑	Jan. 1–Jan. 12	♐
Jan. 21–Feb. 10	♐	Jan. 26–Mar. 10	♐	Jan. 13–Feb. 1	♑
Feb. 11–Mar. 3	♑	Mar. 11–Apr. 9	♑	Feb. 2–Feb. 23	♒
Mar. 4–Mar. 25	♒	Apr. 10–May 5	♒	Feb. 24–Mar. 16	♓
Mar. 26–Apr. 15	♓	May 6–May 27	♓	Mar. 17–Apr. 6	♈
Apr. 16–May 5	♈	May 28–June 18	♈	Apr. 7–Apr. 27	↼
May 6–May 25	↼	June 19–July 9	↼	Apr. 28–May 19	♉
May 26–June 15	♉	July 10–July 30	♉	May 20–June 12	♊
June 16–July 5	♊	July 31–Aug. 20	♊	June 13–July 8	♋
July 6–July 25	♋	Aug. 21–Sept. 8	♋	July 9–Sept. 9	♌
July 26–Aug. 15	♌	Sept. 9–Sept. 29	♌	Sept. 10–Oct. 1	♋
Aug. 16–Sept. 6	♍	Sept. 30–Oct. 20	♍	Oct. 2–Nov. 5	♌
Sept. 7–Sept. 28	♎	Oct. 21–Nov. 10	♎	Nov. 6–Nov. 29	♍
Sept. 29–Oct. 21	♏	Nov. 11–Nov. 30	♏	Nov. 30–Dec. 22	♎
Oct. 22–Nov. 16	⛎	Dec. 1–Dec. 22	⛎	Dec. 23–Dec. 31	♏
Nov. 17–Dec. 16	♐	Dec. 23–Dec. 31	♐		
Dec. 17–Dec. 31	♑				

TABLE 6 269

1968		1969		1970	
Dates	*Sign*	*Dates*	*Sign*	*Dates*	*Sign*
Jan. 1–Jan. 13	♏	Jan. 1–Jan. 7	♑	Jan. 1–Jan. 5	⛎
Jan. 14–Feb. 4	⛎	Jan. 8–Feb. 2	♒	Jan. 6–Jan. 26	♐
Feb. 5–Feb. 25	♐	Feb. 3–Mar. 10	♓	Jan. 27–Feb. 16	♑
Feb. 26–Mar. 17	♑	Mar. 11–Mar. 26	♈	Feb. 17–Mar. 10	♒
Mar. 18–Apr. 8	♒	Mar. 27–May 31	♓	Mar. 11–Mar. 30	♓
Apr. 9–Apr. 29	♓	June 1–June 27	♈	Mar. 31–Apr. 20	♈
Apr. 30–May 20	♈	June 28–July 21	⟋	Apr. 21–May 10	⟋
May 21–June 9	⟋	July 22–Aug. 12	♉	May 11–May 31	♉
June 10–June 29	♉	Aug. 13–Sept. 2	♊	June 1–June 21	♊
June 30–July 20	♊	Sept. 3–Sept. 23	♋	June 22–July 12	♋
July 21–Aug. 8	♋	Sept. 24–Oct. 13	♌	July 13–Aug. 4	♌
Aug. 9–Aug. 29	♌	Oct. 14–Nov. 3	♍	Aug. 5–Aug. 29	♍
Aug. 30–Sept. 19	♍	Nov. 4–Nov. 24	♎	Aug. 30–Sept. 29	♎
Sept. 20–Oct. 11	♎	Nov. 25–Dec. 15	♏	Sept. 30–Nov. 10	♏
Oct. 12–Nov. 1	♏	Dec. 16–Dec. 31	⛎	Nov. 11–Dec. 22	♎
Nov. 2–Nov. 23	⛎			Dec. 23–Dec. 31	♏
Nov. 24–Dec. 15	♐				
Dec. 16–Dec. 31	♑				

1971		1972		1973	
Dates	*Sign*	*Dates*	*Sign*	*Dates*	*Sign*
Jan. 1–Jan. 21	♏	Jan. 1–Jan. 18	♑	Jan. 1–Jan. 20	⛎
Jan. 22–Feb. 15	⛎	Jan. 19–Feb. 10	♒	Jan. 21–Feb. 9	♐
Feb. 16–Mar. 9	♐	Feb. 11–Mar. 3	♓	Feb. 10–Mar. 2	♑
Mar. 10–Mar. 31	♑	Mar. 4–Mar. 25	♈	Mar. 3–Mar. 24	♒
Apr. 1–Apr. 23	♒	Mar. 26–Apr. 20	⟋	Mar. 25–Apr. 14	♓
Apr. 24–May 14	♓	Apr. 21–Aug. 18	♉	Apr. 15–May 4	♈
May 15–June 4	♈	Aug. 19–Sept. 13	♊	May 5–May 24	⟋
June 5–June 25	⟋	Sept. 14–Oct. 5	♋	May 25–June 14	♉
June 26–July 15	♉	Oct. 6–Oct. 27	♌	June 15–July 4	♊
July 16–Aug. 4	♊	Oct. 28–Nov. 17	♍	July 5–July 25	♋
Aug. 5–Aug. 24	♋	Nov. 18–Dec. 8	♎	July 26–Aug. 15	♌
Aug. 25–Sept. 14	♌	Dec. 9–Dec. 29	♏	Aug. 16–Sept. 6	♍
Sept. 15–Oct. 5	♍	Dec. 30–Dec. 31	⛎	Sept. 7–Sept. 28	♎
Oct. 6–Oct. 25	♎			Sept. 29–Oct. 21	♏
Oct. 26–Nov. 15	♏			Oct. 22–Nov. 15	⛎
Nov. 16–Dec. 7	⛎			Nov. 16–Dec. 17	♐
Dec. 8–Dec. 28	♐			Dec. 18–Dec. 31	♑
Dec. 29–Dec. 31	♑				

1974		1975	
Dates	*Sign*	*Dates*	*Sign*
Jan. 1–Jan. 18	♑	Jan. 1–Jan. 11	♐
Jan. 19–Mar. 11	♐	Jan. 12–Feb. 1	♑
Mar. 12–Apr. 9	♑	Feb. 2–Feb. 23	♒
Apr. 10–May 4	♒	Feb. 24–Mar. 16	♓
May 5–May 27	♓	Mar. 17–Apr. 5	♈
May 28–June 17	♈	Apr. 6–Apr. 27	♉
June 18–July 9	♉	Apr. 28–May 19	♉
July 10–July 29	♉	May 20–June 11	♊
July 30–Aug. 19	♊	June 12–July 9	♋
Aug. 20–Sept. 8	♋	July 10–Sept. 2	♌
Sept. 9–Sept. 28	♌	Sept. 3–Oct. 4	♋
Sept. 29–Oct. 19	♍	Oct. 5–Nov. 5	♌
Oct. 20–Nov. 9	♎	Nov. 6–Nov. 29	♍
Nov. 10–Nov. 30	♏	Nov. 30–Dec. 22	♎
Dec. 1–Dec. 21	♐	Dec. 23–Dec. 31	♏
Dec. 22–Dec. 31	♐		

6: Mars

EARTH'S OTHER NEIGHBOR in the heavens, not counting our moon, is the red planet Mars. Farther from us than Venus, and smaller than either earth or Venus, Mars is easier to observe than the veiled planet because it is farther from the sun than the earth and its atmosphere is usually clear. Named for the ancient god of war (the Greek Ares), Mars is the fourth of the nine known planets. It has been much in the news recently, and will probably be the next goal of our astronauts.

Although photographs sent back by *Mariner* spacecraft show a pocked surface, much like that of the moon, an old legend persists that there was an ancient civilization on Mars, which died when the planet lost its oxygen (hence its reddish color). This legend received an added boost when the Italian astronomer Schiaparelli, in 1877, reported observing *canali* on the surface of Mars. The Italian word *canali* means channels or grooves, but the word was translated into English as "canals" and speculation immediately began that there were great artificial waterways, like the Panama Canal, on Mars. An American, Percival Lowell, reported seeing hundreds of canals on the red planet, and the subject of ancient Martian cities linked by a network of canals became a great favorite of science-fiction writers (my own favorite is the poetic and often profound *The Martian Chronicles* of Ray Bradbury).

Mars has two satellites, Deimos and Phobos. These are so small that, a few years ago, a Russian scientist postulated that they might be artificial, put into orbit by the ancient Martians just as earthmen have recently put up *Sputnik*, *Explorer*, and other satellites. However, when *Mariner 9* went into orbit around Mars in 1971, it sent back a series of remarkably clear pictures, not only of the Martian surface but of these two moonlets. Deimos and Phobos are irregularly shaped chunks of rock, their surfaces pitted by meteorites.

Thus, as science advances, the legends die. But who knows? Life on earth is known to exist under "impossible" conditions of temperature and pressure; why not elsewhere in the solar system? Von Braun, in a story, advanced the ingenious idea that the Martians had moved underground as their planet lost most of its atmospheric oxygen, deliberately leaving no artifacts on the surface to attract unwelcome visitors. (In *The Martian Chronicles*, Bradbury has two Martians speculating on the possibility of life on the third planet, Earth. They decide that Earth's atmosphere is too rich in oxygen to support intelligent life.) The mystery, if there is one, may be solved when two U.S. *Viking* spacecraft, equipped with life detectors, land on the Martian surface in 1976.

As stated above, Mars is the fourth of the nine known planets of the solar system. Being farther from the sun, its orbit (or year) is longer than the earth's. It takes Mars 780 days to make one circuit of the sun, as compared with faster-moving Venus (225 days). Mars also exhibits the retrograde motion described earlier for Mercury and Venus, so that at times it appears to be moving backward. However, it does so less frequently, so that—from our point of view on earth—Mars has a slower and more orderly movement than either Mercury or Venus.

MEANING OF MARS IN HOROSCOPE

As previously mentioned, Mars moves slower than the earth. Its orbit is 780 days, and it moves through 191 degrees per year.

Named for the god of war, Mars represents the *masculine* principle— the exact opposite of Venus, who is symbolic of the feminine principle. Astrologically, Mars stands for such "masculine" qualities as energy, action, heat, aggression, and power. It is a powerful influence in any horoscope. For good or for bad? Mars is so powerful that in ancient times it was thought to be an evil planet (because of its association with war and its attendant suffering and destruction). Some of this feeling has come down to the present day, so that we find contemporary astrologers referring to Mars as "a necessary evil." This is not necessarily so. For one thing, the influence of *any* planet is not absolute; its effect in your chart is strongly dependent upon its relationship to the other elements. Also, aggression is an ambivalent drive (or emotion), and its effects can be either good or bad, depending upon the direction it takes. War and crime are obvious examples of negative aggression. On the other hand, man's aggressive drive is also responsible for the building of great civilizations. Without this drive, we certainly would not have seen men walking on the moon.

As we noted in the last chapter, Mars is complementary with Venus. Whether we think of them as male or female, mind and emotions, *logos* and *eros*, or Mars and Venus, we know that the human personality contains both elements—and that a well-balanced and mature personality cannot be achieved without a proper balance between the two. Therefore, particular attention should be paid to the relationship (aspect) of Mars to the feminine elements in your horoscope: Venus and the moon.

Mars is the planetary ruler of two signs, Aries and Scorpio, so this planet is especially important if one of these is your sun sign.

In our century, we have paid a heavy price for man's unbridled aggressiveness. Two world wars, Korea, Vietnam, assassinations, increased crime, rebellion, and general unrest have resulted from our failure to balance warlike Mars with Venus, the bringer of peace and love. The situation has become so extreme that a behavioral psychologist has recently advocated the *conditioning* of human beings so that our aggressiveness cannot find such easy and terrible outlet. This is a frightening thought. Most of us value our individual freedom above all else, and "conditioning" sounds a little too much like brainwashing. However, such an extreme measure may have to be taken. Man's inhumanity to man cannot be allowed to continue and accelerate. If it does, the earth may soon be just another lifeless chunk of rock in the sky.

More optimistic thinkers, however, feel that the worst is over. We now stand at the dawn of the Age of Aquarius. They feel that the waters of life, borne on the shoulder of the water-bearer, symbolize a new era of peace, brotherhood, and increasing spiritual rather than materialistic striving. Let's hope so! But universal good must begin with individual good; we must first make peace with ourselves before we can bring it about in nations, races, and over the entire earth. Within your mind, if Mars is dominating Venus (or vice versa), you must first resolve this conflict before you can effectively extend a helping hand to others. It is obvious that the more individuals work on this task, bringing about harmony and well-balanced personalities, the better off the world will be. There is no job more urgent.

Mars is a key element in your horoscope. Examine carefully its relationship with your rising sign and with the other planets. These aspects are invaluable clues to the working out of your personal problems and conflicts. In effect, your horoscope is a map of your personality, both actual and potential, and a wise traveler will use his map to reach the goal of self-betterment.

To place the symbol of Mars (♂) on your chart, turn to Table 7 at the end of this chapter. Here the positions of Mars are listed for each year from 1890 to 1975. Turn to the year of your birth, and find the span of time that includes your birthdate. It should be noted that Table 7 lists *inclusive* sets of dates. That is, if you were born on July 24 and the table lists Mars in Cancer from June 16 to July 24, Mars was still in Cancer on your birthdate, since it did not enter Leo until July 25. As a reminder, the symbols of the 14 signs are given in a key at the beginning of Table 7.

To continue our example of someone born on January 1, 1940, with Aquarius rising, Figure 7 shows his chart with the symbol of Mars entered. In Table 7, it is shown that Mars was in Aquarius on January 1, 1940; therefore, the symbol of Mars is entered in the House occupied by Aquarius, which (on his chart) is the first House.

INTERPRETATION

General interpretations of the meaning of Mars in each of the 14 signs are given below. In reading these, it should be remembered that Mars does not have an *absolute* meaning; whether it is a help or a hindrance depends upon its relationship to other elements of your chart. Also, the House occupied by Mars affects its interpretation. Our imaginary subject (Figure 7) was born with Mars in Aquarius, which is his first House. After reading the interpretation of Mars in Aquarius, he should turn back to Table 1 (p. 4), which lists the basic meanings of the Houses. The life activity governed by that particular House will be enhanced by the presence of Mars. This is also true of the other planets, which we will be placing in the chapters to follow.

MARS IN PISCES ♂ ♓

Mars in Pisces on your chart will probably affect the power of your will as regards your belief, including your belief in yourself as well as spiritual and philosophical matters of belief. The planetary ruler of Pisces is Neptune, which is often associated with spiritual concerns. Mars is a strongly masculine, "willful" planet, and its presence in this sign usually adds a vein of iron to your will to believe. If well aspected to other elements in your chart, Mars will strengthen your belief—in your religion, political party, or personal philosophy of life. What do you believe? This is a question people often ask themselves in our unsettling times; persons with a strongly aspected Mars in Pisces are usually not troubled by such self-questioning. Aries is ruled by Mars, and we have seen that Aries types generally are quite firm about who they are and what they want. If your Mars is poorly aspected, however, you may tend to cling *too* firmly to your

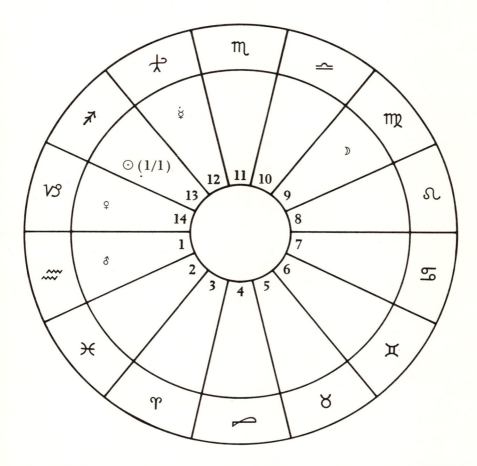

Figure 7. Placement of Mars on chart of subject born on January 1, 1940, with Aquarius rising

beliefs and to defend them the more passionately the less you are truly sure of their validity. Flexibility as well as firmness are needed if we are to grow and mature spiritually. The meaning of the aspects will be taken up in Chapter 12. Meanwhile, check the life activity governed by the House occupied by Pisces on your chart (see Table 1) for a clearer picture of the influence of Mars on the strength of your will in regard to matters of belief.

MARS IN ARIES ♂ ♈

Mars in Aries on your chart should have a powerful effect on all matters concerning the will. Mars is the planetary ruler of Aries. This means that the influence of both planet and sign is approximately doubled with Mars in this sign. A "double" Mars usually denotes great power. If well aspected to other elements, it can greatly increase your chances of success in the arena of life, which all too often resembles a battleground. You have both drive and endurance. If public life attracts you, you should do well in politics; if the arts are your forte, this combination is especially favorable for a career in literature. Whatever your field, you will tend to be a forceful personality in your group—the one others depend on to get things done. On the other hand, if your Mars is poorly aspected to other elements, you may tend to be overly stubborn about the rightness of your ideas and reluctant to listen to another point of view. If strongly opposed, you may brood over the injustice done to you, dogmatically insisting that your way is best. This overweening stubbornness should be guarded against. Group endeavors are impossible without cooperative give and take. The meaning of the aspects will be taken up in Chapter 12. Meanwhile, check the life activity governed by the House occupied by Aries on your chart (see Table 1) for a clearer picture of the influence of Mars in matters concerning the will.

MARS IN CETUS ♂ ♎

Mars in Cetus on your chart is another powerful combination. Cetus is ruled by Jupiter, the "greater fortune," and two strong, masculine planets together will often mean strength of will and a dominant personality. If your Mars is well aspected to other elements, it will provide not only the strong will associated with this planet, but the generosity, benevolence, and good nature associated with Jupiter. Your personality has charm as well as force; you are probably popular with members of both sexes and do not lack for friends and "disciples." You have a good opinion of yourself, without descending to conceit or narcissism, and tend to be a hard, efficient worker. If you are talented, either entertainment or the graphic arts would be excellent fields for you to enter. If your Mars is poorly aspected, however, you may let your drive and leadership qualities get out of hand, forcing through issues that may not be of real advantage either to yourself or to others. Strive for balance in all things. As Landor reminds us in a famous poem, there is a time to be the anvil as well as a time to be the hammer. The meaning of the aspects will be taken up in Chapter 12. Meanwhile, check the life activity governed by the House occupied by Cetus on your chart (see Table 1) for a clearer picture of the influence of Mars on the proper use of your will and drive to succeed.

MARS IN TAURUS ♂ ♉

Mars in Taurus on your chart will probably affect the strength of your emotions, especially where romance and marriage are concerned. Taurus is ruled by Venus, the "lesser fortune," which represents the feminine principle—the exact opposite of Mars, which represents the masculine principle. If well aspected to other elements, Mars in Taurus should help to balance your personality, the sometimes rough edges of the Martian will to power being tempered by the pliancy and cooperative effect of Venus. We all have masculine and feminine elements in our makeup, of course; maturity is to be gained by not letting one overshadow the other too completely. This combination is very good for a career in music, mathematics, the physical sciences, or any branch of technology. It also makes for success with the opposite sex. If your Mars is poorly aspected, on the other hand, you may find yourself being too forceful where gentleness and cooperation are called for. A proper balance between the qualities symbolized by Mars and Venus is the ideal; where one gets the upper hand, the results may be disappointing (if not disastrous), affecting your love life, your career, and your basic personality. The meaning of the aspects will be taken up in Chapter 12. Meanwhile, check the life activity governed by the House occupied by Taurus on your chart (see Table 1) for a clearer picture of the influence of Mars on the strength of your emotions and the balance of your personality.

MARS IN GEMINI ♂ ♊

Mars in Gemini on your chart affects the quickness of your mind, your versatility, and your ability to communicate. Gemini is ruled by Mercury, which is associated with these traits. If well aspected to other elements, Mars in this sign can add will power and endurance to the mercurial elements in your personality; thus, your mind is powerful as well as flexible, and you have the ability not only to conceive an original project, but to stick with it to the end. This combination can make for a powerful and colorful personality, with strength of character added to mental agility and a quick wit. Mars in Gemini is especially favorable for careers that involve writing, speaking, and all fields of communication, such as advertising and broadcasting—and all of us are involved in oral and written expression. If your Mars is poorly aspected, however, it may reinforce the negative Geminian traits of duplicity, fickleness, and untrustworthiness in general. Mercury is the god of thieves and liars as well as intellectuals and communicators, so guard against any tendency to "con" your way through life rather than meeting it with honesty and candor. The meaning of the aspects will be taken up in Chapter 12. Meanwhile, check the life activity governed by the House occupied by Gemini on your chart (see Table 1) for a clearer picture of the influence of Mars on your versatility, intellectual strength, and communicative powers.

MARS IN CANCER ♂ ♋

Mars in Cancer on your chart affects the strength of your emotions and the quality and sensitivity of your feelings. Cancer is ruled by the feminine moon, and its combination with ultra-masculine Mars can mean a fortunate balance of the masculine and feminine elements in your personality if Mars is well aspected to other elements in your chart. Your chances of achieving a well-rounded personality and maturity (both mental and emotional) are good. You have the strength of will to succeed in your chosen profession, along with the sensitivity and compassion necessary to prevent your achieving this end at the expense of your family, friends, and associates. Your romantic life, including marriage and parenthood, should be equally successful, as these especially require strength without brutality, sensitivity without weakness. Be careful of a tendency to engage in dangerous sports, and you should live long and keep a youthful attitude to the end. On the other hand, if your Mars is poorly aspected, you may tend to be overemotional in situations needing a cool head. Also, you may have to fight a tendency to brood and to take secret satisfaction in unhappiness (your own and others'). The meaning of the aspects will be taken up in Chapter 12. Meanwhile, check the life activity governed by the House occupied by Cancer on your chart (see Table 1) for a clearer picture of the influence of Mars on the strength and quality of your emotions.

MARS IN LEO ♂ ♌

Mars in Leo on your chart affects the strength of your sense of personal independence. Leo is the only sign ruled by the sun. Therefore, the

Mars/sun combination in Leo is a strongly masculine one and indicates great potential for power. If your Mars is in good aspect to other elements of your chart, a strongly independent personality is indicated. You are probably a leader and pace-setter rather than a follower, disciple, or aper of current trends. You are a person with definite ideas and opinions. You tend to make strong, lasting friendships and other alliances, and you make an unswerving foe if you are crossed. You would probably do well in either politics or business, if you could play a leading role in the party or firm; you do not take kindly to being bossed and would be unhappy in a sub-servient position. If your Mars is badly aspected to other elements, how-ever, you may have trouble adapting to established ways of doing things and engaging in cooperative efforts. Only a hermit can afford to live in a personal vacuum; remember that too strong a sense of independence can make you a thorn in the side to your spouse, friends, and associates. The meaning of the aspects will be taken up in Chapter 12. Meanwhile, check the life activity governed by the House occupied by Leo on your chart (see Table 1) for a clearer picture of the influence of Mars on the force of your personal independence.

MARS IN VIRGO ♂ ♍

Mars in Virgo on your chart affects the force of your individualism and the strength of your analytical ability. Virgo is ruled by Mercury. Virgo types, as we have noted previously, tend to be strongly individualistic and to have an innate ability to analyze people, situations, and products. What-ever your sun sign, these traits will be reinforced by Mars in Virgo and —if your Mars is well aspected to other elements in your chart—will tend to make you a "one of a kind" type of personality. You probably bear a nickname and are well known to everyone around you (and liked by most). Your ability to analyze makes you hard to fool. It is a quality that makes you a valuable employee in many fields and can be of great personal advantage, as false assumptions of trust, love, or friendship are seen through by your analytical eye as if they were made of glass. If your Mars is badly aspected, on the other hand, your individualism may be so extreme that many will shun you as an odd-ball or fanatic. Your analytical ability may also be overdone, as it is quite possible to analyze a thing, person, or event "to death," and too-sharp criticism can cut like a razor. The meaning of the aspects will be taken up in Chapter 12. Meanwhile, check the life activity governed by the House occupied by Virgo on your chart (see Table 1) for a clearer picture of the influence of Mars on the strength of your individualism and analytical ability.

MARS IN LIBRA ♂ ♎

Mars in Libra on your chart probably affects the quality of your judgment, especially concerning matters of the will. Libra is ruled by Venus. As we have noted previously, the Mars/Venus combination symbolizes the masculine/feminine qualities at the root of our nature, whether we are men or women. If your Mars is in good aspect to other elements, this combination can aid in the achievement of a beautifully balanced personality, the strength of Mars being tempered by the gentleness of Venus, so that your character is neither too hard nor too soft. You can be objective in judging situations and people, and have the strength to stick to your decision, however unpopular it may be. A career in politics or the law would probably work out well for you. You may well have a good natural singing voice, and could succeed as a singer if the arts are your forte. If your Mars is in bad aspect to other elements, however, you may tend to be too forceful in the expression of your opinions. Also, there is a danger that your skill at judgment may lead you to think you have the wisdom of Solomon in such matters. Firmness is fine, but beware of dogmatism. The meaning of the aspects will be taken up in Chapter 12. Meanwhile, check the life activity governed by the House occupied by Libra on your chart (see Table 1) for a clearer picture of the influence of Mars on the strength and quality of your judgment.

MARS IN SCORPIO ♂ ♏

Mars in Scorpio on your chart affects the strength of your empathy (your sensitivity to the feelings of others) and the depth of your emotions. Mars is the ruling planet of Scorpio; therefore, the influence of both sign and planet is approximately doubled. If your Mars is well aspected to other elements in your chart, your humanistic sympathies will be strengthened, which may prompt you to take an active part in causes dedicated to relieve the sufferings of mankind. You are able to put yourself in the other fellow's place and truly "feel for" his problems. This quality makes you a wonderful friend and lover, and you are probably popular—especially with members of the opposite sex. You may have a touch of the poet or the mystic in your makeup; if you do, your "double" Mars can make you more active than Scorpio types usually are in these areas—you will attempt to publish your poems or share your visions, not just muse over them in private. On the other hand, if your Mars is poorly aspected, you may become so sensitive that you cannot stand the sufferings of others, which could force you into the life of a recluse. The meaning of the aspects will be taken up in Chapter 12. Meanwhile, check the life activity governed by the House occupied by Scorpio on your chart (see Table 1) for a clearer picture of the influence of Mars on the strength of your empathy and humanistic ideals.

MARS IN OPHIUCHUS ♂ ♇

Mars in Ophiuchus on your chart affects the strength of your resourcefulness and the range of your versatility. Ophiuchus is ruled by Pluto, a far-off but by no means "cold" planet, as its influence is often associated with wealth. If your Mars is well aspected to other elements in your chart, you could well be the type of person who is seldom at a loss in any situation. If one way doesn't work, you try another, rather than giving up, and will continue until you succeed. You probably tend to be proficient in several fields rather than specializing in one, and you may well have a talent for entertainment. If you have, your talent will have many facets. If music is your field, for example, you can probably sing, play the piano, double in other instruments, and even compose. If your Mars is in bad aspect to other elements, however, you may try too hard to be *Johannes Factotum* (Johnny Do-Everything) and spread your resourcefulness too thin. He who tries to do everything may well end up being unable to do *anything* well. There is also a danger of burning out your talent by applying it too intensively. The meaning of the aspects will be taken up in Chapter 12. Meanwhile, check the life activity governed by the House occupied by Ophiuchus on your chart (see Table 1) for a clearer picture of the influence of Mars on the strength of your resourcefulness and versatility.

MARS IN SAGITTARIUS ♂ ♐

Mars in Sagittarius on your chart affects your tendencies to be extraverted and to play an active part in humanitarian activities. Sagittarius is ruled by Jupiter, which is associated with good fortune and such positive traits as generosity, good humor, sociability, and friendliness. If your Mars is well aspected to other elements, these fine traits will be strengthened and force of will added. You may well be the type of person who can be a leader or boss and still be popular with those subservient to you. A good sense of humor and spontaneous generosity toward your associates are not the traits of a tyrant. You are probably popular with members of both sexes, and success may well come easily to you—especially if your field brings you into direct contact with others. On the other hand, if your Mars is badly aspected to other elements, you may alienate others by expecting too much of them. You drive yourself hard and feel it only natural that others drive themselves equally hard—an attitude that can easily lead to resentment and opposition. The meaning of the aspects will be taken up in Chapter 12. Meanwhile, check the life activity governed by the House occupied by Sagittarius on your chart (see Table 1) for a clearer picture of the influence of Mars on the strength of your conscience and extraverted tendencies.

MARS IN CAPRICORN ♂ ♑

Mars in Capricorn on your chart affects the strength of your conservatism and your tendency to be "realistic" in your approach to life. Capricorn is ruled by Saturn—usually considered by astrologers to be the "bad guy" of the Zodiac. But the Mars/Saturn combination is not necessarily a bad one. On the contrary, if your Mars is in good aspect to other elements of your horoscope, you probably have will power, a firm character, and the ability to keep your head, as Kipling wrote, "when all about you/ Are losing theirs and blaming it on you." Are these bad traits? No. A conservative approach is often the only sensible one, and if you are not realistic about your problems, you will spend most of your life treading hot water! Also, you probably have a dry, subtle sense of humor to offset the Saturnian "gloom"—and creative genius is not uncommon in Capricorn types. If your Mars is poorly aspected to other elements, however, you may insist that your conservative "realism" is the only approach to all of life's problems, thus ruling out large, rich areas of experience; a certain childishness may result, whatever your age or I.Q., preventing full maturity. The meaning of the aspects will be taken up in Chapter 12. Meanwhile, check the life activity governed by the House occupied by Capricorn on your chart (see Table 1) for a clearer picture of the influence of Mars on your drive to be conservative and realistic in your outlook.

MARS IN AQUARIUS ♂ ♒

Mars in Aquarius on your chart affects your temperament and your drive to acquire knowledge, especially in scientific or technical fields. Aquarius is ruled by Uranus, nicknamed "the disruptor" because of its eccentric orbit. If your Mars is in good aspect to other elements in your chart, you probably have a strong drive for individual success—and your chances of achieving it are good, as you have an original approach backed by a keen analytical and critical faculty. You are attracted to novelty and are usually ingenious at working out new ways of doing things. A career in a scientific or technical field would seem to be indicated; or, if attracted to the arts, entertainment might well be a good arena for your talent. You have the drive and original approach needed for success in many fields. If your Mars is in bad aspect to other elements, on the other hand, you may not only have drive but be willful and insist on your own way, thus bringing out the "disruptive" trait symbolized by the orbit of Uranus. Being too analytical or critical will, of course, result in unpopularity. The meaning of the aspects will be taken up in Chapter 12. Meanwhile, check the life activity governed by the House occupied by Aquarius on your chart (see Table 1) for a clearer picture of the influence of Mars on your will to succeed, temperament, and possible "disruptive" traits.

Table 7

POSITIONS OF MARS BY
YEAR (1890 TO 1975)

Key

⧓	Pisces	♍	Virgo
♈	Aries	♎	Libra
⬭	Cetus	♏	Scorpio
♉	Taurus	⚕	Ophiuchus
♊	Gemini	♐	Sagittarius
♋	Cancer	♑	Capricorn
♌	Leo	♒	Aquarius

TABLE 7 285

1890		1891		1892	
Dates	*Sign*	*Dates*	*Sign*	*Dates*	*Sign*
Jan. 1–Jan. 2	♎	Jan. 1–Jan. 25	♒	Jan. 1–Jan. 4	♎
Feb. 3–Aug. 25	♏	Jan. 26–Mar. 1	♓	Jan. 5–Feb. 15	♏
Aug. 26–Oct. 9	⛎	Mar. 2–Apr. 6	♈	Feb. 16–Mar. 31	⛎
Oct. 10–Nov. 15	♐	Apr. 7–May 12	♈	Apr. 1–May 21	♐
Nov. 16–Dec. 20	♑	May 13–June 19	♉	May 22–Nov. 13	♑
Dec. 21–Dec. 31	♒	June 20–July 28	♊	Nov. 14–Dec. 27	♒
		July 29–Sept. 4	♋	Dec. 28–Dec. 31	♓
		Sept. 5–Oct. 14	♌		
		Oct. 15–Nov. 24	♍		
		Nov. 25–Dec. 31	♎		

1893		1894		1895	
Dates	*Sign*	*Dates*	*Sign*	*Dates*	*Sign*
Jan. 1–Feb. 4	♓	Jan. 1–Jan. 20	♏	Jan. 1–Feb. 12	♈
Feb. 5–Mar. 14	♈	Jan. 21–Feb. 28	⛎	Feb. 13–Mar. 28	♈
Mar. 15–Apr. 21	♈	Mar. 1–Apr. 6	♐	Mar. 29–May 9	♉
Apr. 22–May 30	♉	Apr. 7–May 13	♑	May 10–June 19	♊
May 31–July 8	♊	May 14–June 22	♒	June 20–July 28	♋
July 9–Aug. 15	♋	June 23–Aug. 7	♓	July 29–Sept. 7	♌
Aug. 16–Sept. 25	♌	Aug. 8–Oct. 26	♈	Sept. 8–Oct. 16	♍
Sept. 26–Oct. 4	♍	Oct. 27–Dec. 18	♓	Oct. 17–Nov. 23	♎
Oct. 5–Dec. 13	♎	Dec. 19–Dec. 31	♈	Nov. 24–Dec. 30	♏
Dec. 14–Dec. 31	♏			Dec. 31	⛎

1896		. 1897		1898	
Dates	*Sign*	*Dates*	*Sign*	*Dates*	*Sign*
Jan. 1–Feb. 6	⛎	Jan. 1–Feb. 11	♈	Jan. 1–Jan. 15	⛎
Feb. 7–Mar. 11	♐	Feb. 12–Apr. 12	♉	Jan. 16–Feb. 18	♐
Mar. 12–Apr. 15	♑	Apr. 13–May 27	♊	Feb. 19–Mar. 24	♑
Apr. 16–May 21	♒	May 28–July 8	♋	Mar. 25–Apr. 28	♒
May 22–June 25	♓	July 9–Aug. 18	♌	Apr. 29–June 1	♓
June 26–July 31	♈	Aug. 19–Sept. 27	♍	June 2–July 5	♈
Aug. 1–Sept. 13	♈	Sept. 28–Nov. 3	♎	July 6–Aug. 10	♈
Sept. 14–Dec. 19	♉	Nov. 4–Dec. 10	♏	Aug. 11–Sept. 20	♉
Dec. 20–Dec. 31	♈	Dec. 11–Dec. 31	⛎	Sept. 21–Nov. 16	♊
				Nov. 17–Dec. 30	♋
				Dec. 31	♊

1899	
Dates	Sign
Jan. 1–Apr. 28	♊
Apr. 29–June 15	♋
June 16–July 29	♌
July 30–Sept. 8	♍
Sept. 9–Oct. 16	♎
Oct. 17–Nov. 21	♏
Nov. 22–Dec. 27	♐
Dec. 28–Dec. 31	♐

1900	
Dates	Sign
Jan. 1–Jan. 29	♐
Jan. 30–Mar. 3	♑
Mar. 4–Apr. 7	♒
Apr. 8–May 11	♓
May 12–June 13	♈
June 14–July 19	♉
July 20–Aug. 25	♉
Aug. 26–Oct. 5	♊
Oct. 6–Nov. 22	♋
Nov. 23–Dec. 31	♌

1901	
Dates	Sign
Jan. 1–Mar. 1	♌
Mar. 2–May 10	♋
May 11–July 5	♌
July 6–Aug. 18	♍
Aug. 19–Sept. 26	♎
Sept. 27–Nov. 1	♏
Nov. 2–Dec. 7	♐
Dec. 8–Dec. 31	♐

1902	
Dates	Sign
Jan. 1–Jan. 9	♐
Jan. 10–Feb. 11	♑
Feb. 12–Mar. 18	♒
Mar. 19–Apr. 21	♓
Apr. 22–May 24	♈
May 25–June 29	♉
June 30–Aug. 5	♉
Aug. 6–Sept. 13	♊
Sept. 14–Oct. 23	♋
Oct. 24–Dec. 10	♌
Dec. 11–Dec. 31	♍

1903	
Dates	Sign
Jan. 1–July 22	♍
July 23–Sept. 3	♎
Sept. 4–Oct. 11	♏
Oct. 12–Nov. 16	♐
Nov. 17–Dec. 20	♐
Dec. 21–Dec. 31	♑

1904	
Dates	Sign
Jan. 1–Jan. 22	♑
Jan. 23–Feb. 26	♒
Feb. 27–Mar. 31	♓
Apr. 1–May 4	♈
May 5–June 9	♉
June 10–July 16	♉
July 17–Aug. 23	♊
Aug. 24–Oct. 1	♋
Oct. 2–Nov. 12	♌
Nov. 13–Dec. 28	♍
Dec. 29–Dec. 31	♎

1905	
Dates	Sign
Jan. 1–Feb. 22	♎
Feb. 23–May 8	♏
May 9–July 27	♎
July 28–Sept. 13	♏
Sept. 14–Oct. 22	♐
Oct. 23–Nov. 26	♐
Nov. 27–Dec. 30	♑
Dec. 31	♒

1906	
Dates	Sign
Jan. 1–Feb. 4	♒
Feb. 5–Mar. 11	♓
Mar. 12–Apr. 14	♈
Apr. 15–May 20	♉
May 21–June 27	♉
June 28–Aug. 4	♊
Aug. 5–Sept. 12	♋
Sept. 13–Oct. 22	♌
Oct. 23–Dec. 3	♍
Dec. 4–Dec. 31	♎

1907	
Dates	Sign
Jan. 1–Jan. 15	♎
Jan. 16–Feb. 28	♏
Mar. 1–Apr. 26	♐
Apr. 27–July 15	♐
July 16–Sept. 1	♐
Sept. 2–Oct. 24	♐
Oct. 25–Dec. 2	♑
Dec. 3–Dec. 31	♒

TABLE 7 287

1908		1909		1910	
Dates	*Sign*	*Dates*	*Sign*	*Dates*	*Sign*
Jan. 1–Jan. 10	♒	Jan. 1–Jan. 30	♏	Jan. 1–Jan. 14	♓
Jan. 11–Feb. 16	♓	Jan. 31–Mar. 11	♏	Jan. 15–Feb. 26	♈
Feb. 17–Mar. 23	♈	Mar. 12–Apr. 19	♐	Feb. 27–Apr. 8	♈
Mar. 24–Apr. 30	♈	Apr. 20–May 29	♑	Apr. 9–May 18	♉
May 1–June 7	♉	May 30–July 20	♒	May 19–June 27	♊
June 8–July 16	♊	July 21–Sept. 26	♓	June 28–Aug. 5	♋
July 17–Aug. 23	♋	Sept. 27–Nov. 20	♒	Aug. 6–Sept. 14	♌
Aug. 24–Oct. 2	♌	Nov. 21–Dec. 31	♓	Sept. 15–Oct. 24	♍
Oct. 3–Nov. 12	♍			Oct. 25–Dec. 2	♎
Nov. 13–Dec. 21	♎			Dec. 3–Dec. 31	♏

1911		1912		1913	
Dates	*Sign*	*Dates*	*Sign*	*Dates*	*Sign*
Jan. 1–Jan. 8	♏	Jan. 1–Mar. 8	♈	Jan. 1–Jan. 24	♏
Jan. 9–Feb. 15	♏	Mar. 9–Apr. 24	♉	Jan. 25–Feb. 27	♐
Feb. 16–Mar. 22	♐	Apr. 25–June 6	♊	Feb. 28–Apr. 2	♑
Mar. 23–Apr. 26	♑	June 7–July 16	♋	Apr. 3–May 7	♒
Apr. 27–June 2	♒	July 17–Aug. 26	♌	May 8–June 10	♓
June 3–July 8	♓	Aug. 27–Oct. 5	♍	June 11–July 15	♈
July 9–Aug. 17	♈	Oct. 6–Nov. 12	♎	July 16–Aug. 21	♈
Aug. 18–Dec. 31	♈	Nov. 13–Dec. 18	♏	Aug. 22–Oct. 6	♉
		Dec. 19–Dec. 31	♏	Oct. 7–Dec. 31	♊

1914		1915		1916	
Dates	*Sign*	*Dates*	*Sign*	*Dates*	*Sign*
Jan. 1–Jan. 15	♊	Jan. 1–Jan. 4	♏	Jan. 1–May 28	♋
Jan. 16–Mar. 15	♉	Jan. 5–Feb. 7	♐	May 29–July 15	♌
Mar. 16–May 12	♊	Feb. 8–Mar. 12	♑	July 16–Aug. 26	♍
May 13–June 25	♋	Mar. 13–Apr. 16	♒	Aug. 27–Oct. 4	♎
June 26–Aug. 7	♌	Apr. 17–May 19	♓	Oct. 5–Nov. 9	♏
Aug. 8–Sept. 16	♍	May 20–June 22	♈	Nov. 10–Dec. 15	♏
Sept. 17–Oct. 24	♎	June 23–July 28	♈	Dec. 16–Dec. 31	♐
Oct. 25–Nov. 29	♏	July 29–Sept. 4	♉		
Nov. 30–Dec. 31	♏	Sept. 5–Oct. 17	♊		
		Oct. 18–Dec. 31	♋		

1917		1918		1919	
Dates	*Sign*	*Dates*	*Sign*	*Dates*	*Sign*
Jan. 1–Jan. 17	♐	Jan. 1–Mar. 10	♍	Jan. 1–Jan. 30	♑
Jan. 18–Feb. 19	♑	Mar. 11–June 13	♌	Jan. 31–Mar. 6	♒
Feb. 20–Mar. 26	♒	June 14–Aug. 2	♍	Mar. 7–Apr. 8	♓
Mar. 27–Apr. 28	♓	Aug. 3–Sept. 12	♎	Apr. 9–May 12	♈
Apr. 29–June 1	♈	Sept. 13–Oct. 19	♏	May 13–June 17	↞
June 2–July 6	↞	Oct. 20–Nov. 24	⛎	June 18–July 24	♉
July 7–Aug. 12	♉	Nov. 25–Dec. 28	♐	July 25–Aug. 31	♊
Aug. 13–Sept. 21	♊	Dec. 29–Dec. 31	♑	Sept. 1–Oct. 9	♋
Sept. 22–Nov. 1	♋			Oct. 10–Nov. 22	♌
Nov. 2–Dec. 27	♌			Nov. 23–Dec. 31	♍
Dec. 28–Dec. 31	♍				

1920		1921		1922	
Dates	*Sign*	*Dates*	*Sign*	*Dates*	*Sign*
Jan. 1–Jan. 11	♍	Jan. 1–Jan. 8	♑	Jan. 1–Jan. 25	♎
Jan. 12–May 23	♎	Jan. 9–Feb. 12	♒	Jan. 26–Mar. 19	♏
May 24–June 8	♍	Feb. 13–Mar. 18	♓	Mar. 20–June 27	⛎
June 9–Aug. 15	♎	Mar. 19–Apr. 22	♈	June 28–Aug. 5	♏
Aug. 16–Sept. 24	♏	Apr. 23–May 28	↞	Aug. 6–Oct. 1	⛎
Sept. 25–Nov. 1	⛎	May 29–July 4	♉	Oct. 2–Nov. 8	♐
Nov. 2–Dec. 5	♐	July 5–Aug. 12	♊	Nov. 9–Dec. 14	♑
Dec. 6–Dec. 31	♑	Aug. 13–Sept. 18	♋	Dec. 15–Dec. 31	♒
		Sept. 19–Oct. 30	♌		
		Oct. 31–Dec. 11	♍		
		Dec. 12–Dec. 31	♎		

1923		1924		1925	
Dates	*Sign*	*Dates*	*Sign*	*Dates*	*Sign*
Jan. 1–Jan. 20	♒	Jan. 1–Feb. 9	♏	Jan. 1–Jan. 29	♓
Jan. 21–Feb. 25	♓	Feb. 10–Mar. 23	⛎	Jan. 30–Mar. 9	♈
Feb. 26–Apr. 2	♈	Mar. 24–May 5	♐	Mar. 10–Apr. 16	↞
Apr. 3–May 8	↞	May 6–July 3	♑	Apr. 17–May 26	♉
May 9–June 15	♉	July 4–Aug. 13	♒	May 27–July 4	♊
June 16–July 24	♊	Aug. 14–Oct. 26	♑	July 5–Aug. 12	♋
July 25–Aug. 31	♋	Oct. 27–Dec. 18	♒	Aug. 13–Sept. 21	♌
Sept. 1–Oct. 10	♌	Dec. 19–Dec. 31	♓	Sept. 22–Oct. 31	♍
Oct. 11–Nov. 20	♍			Nov. 1–Dec. 9	♎
Nov. 21–Dec. 31	♎			Dec. 10–Dec. 31	♏

TABLE 7 289

1926		1927		1928	
Dates	*Sign*	*Dates*	*Sign*	*Dates*	*Sign*
Jan. 1–Jan. 16	♏	Jan. 1–Feb. 2	♈	Jan. 1–Feb. 1	⛎
Jan. 17–Feb. 23	⛎	Feb. 3–Mar. 22	⊶	Feb. 2–Mar. 7	♐
Feb. 24–Mar. 31	♐	Mar. 23–May 4	♉	Mar. 8–Apr. 10	♑
Apr. 1–May 6	♑	May 5–June 15	♊	Apr. 11–May 16	♒
May 7–June 14	♒	June 16–July 24	♋	May 17–June 19	♓
June 15–July 24	♓	July 25–Sept. 3	♌	June 20–July 25	♈
July 25–Dec. 31	♈	Sept. 4–Oct. 13	♍	July 26–Sept. 3	⊶
		Oct. 14–Nov. 20	♎	Sept. 4–Dec. 31	♉
		Nov. 21–Dec. 27	♏		
		Dec. 28–Dec. 31	⛎		

1929		1930		1931	
Dates	*Sign*	*Dates*	*Sign*	*Dates*	*Sign*
Jan. 1–Apr. 4	♉	Jan. 1–Jan. 12	⛎	Jan. 1–Jan. 30	♋
Apr. 5–May 22	♊	Jan. 13–Feb. 14	♐	Jan. 31–Apr. 17	♊
May 23–July 3	♋	Feb. 15–Mar. 20	♑	Apr. 18–June 10	♋
July 4–Aug. 14	♌	Mar. 21–Apr. 24	♒	June 11–July 25	♌
Aug. 15–Sept. 23	♍	Apr. 25–May 27	♓	July 26–Sept. 4	♍
Sept. 24–Oct. 31	♎	May 28–June 30	♈	Sept. 5–Oct. 12	♎
Nov. 1–Dec. 6	♏	July 1–Aug. 5	⊶	Oct. 13–Nov. 17	♏
Dec. 7–Dec. 31	⛎	Aug. 6–Sept. 14	♉	Nov. 18–Dec. 23	⛎
		Sept. 15–Nov. 1	♊	Dec. 24–Dec. 31	♐
		Nov. 2–Dec. 31	♋		

1932		1933		1934	
Dates	*Sign*	*Dates*	*Sign*	*Dates*	*Sign*
Jan. 1–Jan. 26	♐	Jan. 1–June 28	♌	Jan. 1–Jan. 5	♐
Jan. 27–Feb. 28	♑	June 29–Aug. 12	♍	Jan. 6–Feb. 7	♑
Feb. 29–Apr. 2	♒	Aug. 13–Sept. 21	♎	Feb. 8–Mar. 13	♒
Apr. 3–May 6	♓	Sept. 22–Oct. 27	♏	Mar. 14–Apr. 16	♓
May 7–June 8	♈	Oct. 28–Dec. 2	⛎	Apr. 17–May 20	♈
June 9–July 14	⊶	Dec. 3–Dec. 31	♐	May 21–June 24	⊶
July 15–Aug. 20	♉			June 25–July 31	♉
Aug. 21–Sept. 29	♊			Aug. 1–Sept. 7	♊
Sept. 30–Nov. 13	♋			Sept. 8–Oct. 17	♋
Nov. 14–Dec. 31	♌			Oct. 18–Dec. 2	♌
				Dec. 3–Dec. 31	♍

1935		1936		1937	
Dates	*Sign*	*Dates*	*Sign*	*Dates*	*Sign*
Jan. 1–Feb. 3	♍	Jan. 1–Jan. 17	♑	Jan. 1–Feb. 9	♎
Feb. 4–Mar. 20	♎	Jan. 18–Feb. 21	♒	Feb. 10–Sept. 3	♏
Mar. 21–July 12	♍	Feb. 22–Mar. 26	♓	Sept. 4–Oct. 15	♐
July 13–Aug. 28	♎	Mar. 27–Apr. 29	♈	Oct. 16–Nov. 20	♐
Aug. 29–Oct. 5	♏	Apr. 30–June 4	♉	Nov. 21–Dec. 24	♑
Oct. 6–Nov. 11	♐	June 5–July 11	♉	Dec. 25–Dec. 31	♒
Nov. 12–Dec. 15	♐	July 12–Aug. 18	♊		
Dec. 16–Dec. 31	♑	Aug. 19–Sept. 26	♋		
		Sept. 27–Nov. 6	♌		
		Nov. 7–Dec. 21	♍		
		Dec. 22–Dec. 31	♎		

1938		1939		1940	
Dates	*Sign*	*Dates*	*Sign*	*Dates*	*Sign*
Jan. 1–Jan. 30	♒	Jan. 1–Jan. 8	♎	Jan. 1–Jan. 3	♒
Jan. 31–Mar. 5	♓	Jan. 9–Feb. 20	♏	Jan. 4–Feb. 10	♓
Mar. 6–Apr. 9	♈	Feb. 21–Apr. 9	♐	Feb. 11–Mar. 18	♈
Apr. 10–May 16	♉	Apr. 10–Oct. 9	♐	Mar. 25–Apr. 25	♉
May 17–June 22	♉	Oct. 10–Nov. 23	♑	Apr. 26–June 2	♉
June 23–July 31	♊	Nov. 24–Dec. 31	♒	June 3–July 11	♊
Aug. 1–Sept. 7	♋			July 12–Aug. 19	♋
Sept. 8–Oct. 17	♌			Aug. 20–Sept. 28	♌
Oct. 18–Nov. 28	♍			Sept. 29–Nov. 7	♍
Nov. 29–Dec. 31	♎			Nov. 8–Dec. 16	♎
				Dec. 17–Dec. 31	♏

1941		1942		1943	
Dates	*Sign*	*Dates*	*Sign*	*Dates*	*Sign*
Jan. 1–Jan. 24	♏	Jan. 1–Jan. 2	♓	Jan. 1–Jan. 3	♏
Jan. 25–Mar. 4	♐	Jan. 3–Feb. 18	♈	Jan. 4–Feb. 9	♐
Mar. 5–Apr. 11	♐	Feb. 19–Apr. 2	♉	Feb. 10–Mar. 16	♐
Apr. 12–May 19	♑	Apr. 3–May 13	♉	Mar. 17–Apr. 20	♑
May 20–July 1	♒	May 14–June 22	♊	Apr. 21–May 26	♒
July 2–Dec. 31	♓	June 23–July 31	♋	May 27–July 1	♓
		Aug. 1–Sept. 10	♌	July 2–Aug. 7	♈
		Sept. 11–Oct. 19	♍	Aug. 8–Sept. 25	♉
		Oct. 20–Nov. 27	♎	Sept. 26–Nov. 24	♉
		Nov. 28–Dec. 31	♏	Nov. 25–Dec. 31	♉

TABLE 7 291

1944		1945		1946	
Dates	*Sign*	*Dates*	*Sign*	*Dates*	*Sign*
Jan. 1–Feb. 25	♎	Jan. 1–Jan. 19	♇	Jan. 1–May 4	♊
Feb. 26–Apr. 17	♉	Jan. 30–Feb. 22	♐	May 5–June 19	♋
Apr. 18–May 31	♊	Feb. 23–Mar. 28	♑	June 20–Aug. 2	♌
June 1–July 11	♋	Mar. 29–May 2	♒	Aug. 3–Sept. 11	♍
July 12–Aug. 21	♌	May 3–June 5	♓	Sept. 12–Oct. 19	♎
Aug. 22–Sept. 30	♍	June 6–July 9	♈	Oct. 20–Nov. 25	♏
Oct. 1–Nov. 7	♎	July 10–Aug. 15	♎	Nov. 26–Dec. 30	♇
Nov. 8–Dec. 14	♏	Aug. 16–Sept. 26	♉	Dec. 31	♐
Dec. 15–Dec. 31	♇	Sept. 27–Dec. 31	♊		

1947		1948		1949	
Dates	*Sign*	*Dates*	*Sign*	*Dates*	*Sign*
Jan. 1–Feb. 2	♐	Jan. 1–Feb. 11	♌	Jan. 1–Jan. 12	♐
Feb. 3–Mar. 7	♑	Feb. 12–May 18	♋	Jan. 13–Feb. 14	♑
Mar. 8–Apr. 11	♒	May 19–July 9	♌	Feb. 15–Mar. 21	♒
Apr. 12–May 14	♓	July 10–Aug. 21	♍	Mar. 22–Apr. 23	♓
May 15–June 17	♈	Aug. 22–Sept. 29	♎	Apr. 24–May 27	♈
June 18–July 23	♎	Sept. 30–Nov. 4	♏	May 28–July 1	♎
July 24–Aug. 29	♉	Nov. 5–Dec. 10	♇	July 2–Aug. 7	♉
Aug. 30–Oct. 10	♊	Dec. 11–Dec. 31	♐	Aug. 8–Sept. 15	♊
Oct. 11–Nov. 30	♋			Sept. 16–Oct. 26	♋
Dec. 1–Dec. 31	♌			Oct. 27–Dec. 15	♌
				Dec. 16–Dec. 31	♍

1950		1951		1952	
Dates	*Sign*	*Dates*	*Sign*	*Dates*	*Sign*
Jan. 1–Apr. 9	♍	Jan. 1–Jan. 25	♑	Jan. 1–Jan. 2	♍
Apr. 10–May 28	♌	Jan. 26–Mar. 1	♒	Jan. 3–Mar. 13	♎
May 29–July 26	♍	Mar. 2–Apr. 4	♓	Mar. 14–Apr. 5	♏
July 27–Sept. 7	♎	Apr. 5–May 8	♈	Apr. 6–Aug. 5	♎
Sept. 8–Oct. 14	♏	May 9–June 12	♎	Aug. 6–Sept. 17	♏
Oct. 15–Nov. 19	♇	June 13–July 19	♉	Sept. 18–Oct. 26	♇
Nov. 20–Dec. 23	♐	July 20–Aug. 26	♊	Oct. 27–Nov. 30	♐
Dec. 24–Dec. 31	♑	Aug. 27–Oct. 4	♋	Dec. 1–Dec. 31	♑
		Oct. 5–Nov. 16	♌		
		Nov. 17–Dec. 31	♍		

1953		1954		1955	
Dates	Sign	Dates	Sign	Dates	Sign
Jan. 1–Jan. 2	♑	Jan. 1–Jan. 18	♎	Jan. 1–Jan. 14	♒
Jan. 3–Feb. 7	♒	Jan. 19–Mar. 6	♏	Jan. 15–Feb. 19	♓
Feb. 8–Mar. 13	♓	Mar. 7–Sept. 18	♃	Feb. 20–Mar. 27	♈
Mar. 14–Apr. 17	♈	Sept. 19–Oct. 31	♐	Mar. 28–May 3	♎
Apr. 18–May 23	♎	Nov. 1–Dec. 7	♑	May 4–June 10	♉
May 24–June 29	♉	Dec. 8–Dec. 31	♒	June 11–July 19	♊
June 30–Aug. 7	♊			July 20–Aug. 26	♋
Aug. 8–Sept. 14	♋			Aug. 27–Oct. 6	♌
Sept. 15–Oct. 25	♌			Oct. 7–Nov. 15	♍
Oct. 26–Dec. 6	♍			Nov. 16–Dec. 25	♎
Dec. 7–Dec. 31	♎			Dec. 26–Dec. 31	♏

1956		1957		1958	
Dates	Sign	Dates	Sign	Dates	Sign
Jan. 1–Feb. 3	♏	Jan. 1–Jan. 20	♓	Jan. 1–Jan. 11	♏
Feb. 4–Mar. 15	♃	Jan. 21–Mar. 2	♈	Jan. 12–Feb. 18	♃
Mar. 16–Apr. 24	♐	Mar. 3–Apr. 11	♎	Feb. 19–Mar. 25	♐
Apr. 25–June 7	♑	Apr. 12–May 21	♉	Mar. 26–Apr. 30	♑
June 8–Dec. 5	♒	May 22–June 30	♊	May 1–June 6	♒
Dec. 6–Dec. 31	♓	July 1–Aug. 7	♋	June 7–July 14	♓
		Aug. 8–Sept. 16	♌	July 15–Aug. 26	♈
		Sept. 17–Oct. 26	♍	Aug. 27–Nov. 25	♎
		Oct. 27–Dec. 4	♎	Nov. 26–Dec. 31	♈
		Dec. 5–Dec. 31	♏		

1959		1960		1961	
Dates	Sign	Dates	Sign	Dates	Sign
Jan. 1–Jan. 15	♈	Jan. 1–Jan. 28	♃	Jan. 1–Mar. 25	♉
Jan. 16–Mar. 14	♎	Jan. 29–Mar. 2	♐	Mar. 26–May 16	♊
Mar. 15–Apr. 28	♉	Mar. 3–Apr. 5	♑	May 17–June 28	♋
Apr. 29–June 10	♊	Apr. 6–May 10	♒	June 29–Aug. 10	♌
June 11–July 19	♋	May 11–June 13	♓	Aug. 11–Sept. 19	♍
July 20–Aug. 29	♌	June 14–July 18	♈	Sept. 20–Oct. 27	♎
Aug. 30–Oct. 8	♍	July 19–Aug. 26	♎	Oct. 28–Dec. 2	♏
Oct. 9–Nov. 15	♎	Aug. 27–Oct. 13	♉	Dec. 3–Dec. 31	♃
Nov. 16–Dec. 22	♏	Oct. 14–Dec. 25	♊		
Dec. 23–Dec. 31	♃	Dec. 26–Dec. 31	♉		

TABLE 7 293

1962 Dates	Sign	1963 Dates	Sign	1964 Dates	Sign
Jan. 1–Jan. 7	♏	Jan. 1–Mar. 9	♋	Jan. 1–Jan. 21	♐
Jan. 8–Feb. 10	♐	Mar. 10–Mar. 24	♊	Jan. 22–Feb. 23	♑
Feb. 11–Mar. 15	♑	Mar. 25–June 3	♋	Feb. 24–Mar. 29	♒
Mar. 16–Apr. 19	♒	June 4–July 19	♌	Mar. 30–May 1	♓
Apr. 20–May 23	♓	July 20–Aug. 30	♍	May 2–June 4	♈
May 24–June 26	♈	Aug. 31–Oct. 8	♎	June 5–July 9	♎
June 27–July 31	♎	Oct. 9–Nov. 13	♏	July 10–Aug. 15	♉
Aug. 1–Sept. 8	♉	Nov. 14–Dec. 19	♐	Aug. 16–Sept. 24	♊
Sept. 9–Oct. 23	♊	Dec. 20–Dec. 31	♐	Sept. 25–Nov. 6	♋
Oct. 24–Dec. 31	♋			Nov. 7–Dec. 31	♌

1965 Dates	Sign	1966 Dates	Sign	1967 Dates	Sign
Jan. 1–Jan. 8	♌	Jan. 1–Feb. 2	♑	Jan. 1–Jan. 18	♍
Jan. 9–Feb. 17	♍	Feb. 3–Mar. 9	♒	Jan. 19–Apr. 23	♎
Feb. 18–June 20	♌	Mar. 10–Apr. 12	♓	Apr. 24–June 29	♍
June 21–Aug. 7	♍	Apr. 13–May 15	♈	June 30–Aug. 21	♎
Aug. 8–Sept. 16	♎	May 16–June 20	♎	Aug. 22–Sept. 30	♏
Sept. 17–Oct. 23	♏	June 21–July 27	♉	Oct. 1–Nov. 6	♐
Oct. 24–Nov. 28	♐	July 28–Sept. 3	♊	Nov. 7–Dec. 10	♐
Nov. 29–Dec. 31	♐	Sept. 4–Oct. 12	♋	Dec. 11–Dec. 31	♑
		Oct. 13–Nov. 26	♌		
		Nov. 27–Dec. 31	♍		

1968 Dates	Sign	1969 Dates	Sign	1970 Dates	Sign
Jan. 1–Jan. 12	♑	Jan. 1–Jan. 31	♎	Jan. 1–Jan. 24	♒
Jan. 13–Feb. 17	♒	Feb. 1–Apr. 3	♏	Jan. 25–Mar. 1	♓
Feb. 18–Mar. 22	♓	Apr. 4–May 19	♐	Mar. 2–Apr. 5	♈
Mar. 23–Apr. 25	♈	May 20–Aug. 22	♏	Apr. 6–May 11	♎
Apr. 26–May 31	♎	Aug. 23–Oct. 7	♐	May 12–June 18	♉
June 1–July 7	♉	Oct. 8–Nov. 14	♐	June 19–July 27	♊
July 8–Aug. 14	♊	Nov. 15–Dec. 19	♑	July 28–Sept. 3	♋
Aug. 15–Sept. 21	♋	Dec. 20–Dec. 31	♒	Sept. 4–Oct. 13	♌
Sept. 22–Nov. 2	♌			Oct. 14–Nov. 23	♍
Nov. 3–Dec. 15	♍			Nov. 24–Dec. 31	♎
Dec. 16–Dec. 31	♎				

1971		1972		1973	
Dates	*Sign*	*Dates*	*Sign*	*Dates*	*Sign*
Jan. 1–Jan. 3	♎	Jan. 1–Feb. 4	♓	Jan. 1–Jan. 19	♏
Jan. 4–Feb. 13	♏	Feb. 5–Mar. 12	♈	Jan. 20–Feb. 27	⛎
Feb. 14–Mar. 30	⛎	Mar. 13–Apr. 20	⌐	Feb. 28–Apr. 5	♐
Mar. 31–May 17	♐	Apr. 21–May 29	♉	Apr. 6–May 11	♑
May 18–Nov. 11	♑	May 30–July 7	♊	May 12–June 20	♒
Nov. 12–Dec. 26	♒	July 8–Aug. 15	♋	June 21–Aug. 3	♓
Dec. 27–Dec. 31	♓	Aug. 16–Sept. 24	♌	Aug. 4–Nov. 18	♈
		Sept. 25–Nov. 3	♍	Nov. 19–Dec. 3	♓
		Nov. 4–Dec. 12	♎	Dec. 4–Dec. 31	♈
		Dec. 13–Dec. 31	♏		

1974		1975	
Dates	*Sign*	*Dates*	*Sign*
Jan. 1–Feb. 10	♈	Jan. 1–Feb. 5	⛎
Feb. 11–Mar. 26	⌐	Feb. 6–Mar. 12	♐
Mar. 27–May 8	♉	Mar. 13–Apr. 15	♑
May 9–June 18	♊	Apr. 16–May 21	♒
June 19–July 27	♋	May 22–June 25	♓
July 28–Sept. 6	♌	June 26–July 31	♈
Sept. 7–Oct. 15	♍	Aug. 1–Sept. 11	⌐
Oct. 16–Nov. 23	♎	Sept. 12–Dec. 31	♉
Nov. 24–Dec. 30	♏		
Dec. 31	⛎		

7: Jupiter

♃

FIFTH of the nine known planets of the solar system, giant Jupiter is the largest of the planets that circle our sun and commands a central position (that is, four planets are closer to the sun and four are farther out). Jupiter is so huge that its mass is twice as great as that of all the other planets combined. It is quite apt, then, that it should be named for the chief god of the ancients (called Zeus by the Greeks).

Jupiter has no less than 12 moons, one of which (Titan) is large enough to have an atmosphere. Men will probably not be able to explore Jupiter directly—its gravity would crush a human being—so these moons will most likely be the bases for our astronauts when they have ventured beyond Mars and the asteroid belt.

Could life exist on Jupiter? Not only is it too massive for human beings, but its atmosphere would be poisonous to us. However, scientists have learned not to say "no" too quickly to such questions. There is life right here on earth that thrives under "impossible" conditions of pressure and temperature. So, although the possibility cannot be ruled out, Jovian life—if it exists—would have to be much different from human life on earth. Some science-fiction writers have speculated in their stories on what forms such life would take, and a few of them—especially Poul Anderson—have come up with ingenious theories.

Jupiter is so far away that it has not been an object of immediate interest to our space program. As is only natural, heavenly bodies closer to the earth have been (and are) their initial targets—the moon first, then Mars and Venus. However, an unmanned spacecraft, Pioneer 10, has been launched on a voyage to Jupiter that will take 600 to 700 days. If all goes as planned, *Pioneer 10* will send back pictures and information that may include clues to possible life in the Jovian atmosphere. This ambitious project (nicknamed the Grand Tour) will not end at Jupiter; *Pioneer 10* has been programmed to fly by the other major planets—Saturn, Uranus, and Neptune—as well. All knowledge of these planets gained so far has been astronomical. If the Grand Tour is successful, it will represent our first direct contact with the giants of the solar system.

As stated above, Jupiter is the fifth of the nine known planets. Being farther from the sun, its orbit (or year) is longer than that of earth or Mars. It takes Jupiter 11.86 years to make one circuit of the sun, as compared with 780 days for Mars. Jupiter also exhibits the retrograde motion described earlier for Mercury, Venus, and Mars, so that at times it appears to be moving backward. However, it does so less frequently, so that—from our point of view on earth—Jupiter has a slower and more orderly movement than these planets.

MEANING OF JUPITER IN HOROSCOPE

As previously mentioned, Jupiter moves slower than the earth. Its orbit is 11.86 years, and it moves through 30 degrees per year.

Named for the chief deity of the ancients, Jupiter is the "greater fortune" in the horoscope. (We noted above that Venus is the "lesser fortune.") This god was also known as Jove, from which we have our adjective "jovial" for good-humored, big-hearted people. Jupiter is definitely a beneficent element in your chart. Its keywords are *expansion* and *preservation*.

Because of its great size and commanding position in the solar system, Jupiter is a powerful element in any horoscope—and usually its influence is good. No planet has an absolute, fixed meaning, however; its influence depends largely on its aspects to other elements. If these aspects are good (or neutral), Jupiter will bring good luck, benevolence, and strength. If it is in bad aspect to another planet, Jupiter will strengthen any negative qualities of that planet. Jupiter is like a good king who rules a powerful nation. He is generous and just to his subjects. If he should be betrayed, however, or if another nation should make war on him, his benevolent smile will disappear, and down will come the iron fist of kingly displeasure!

The gods and most of the rulers of our era have been male. This has been reflected in the family, where—until quite recently, at least—the father was the head of the family. This picture has begun to change, at the dawn of the Age of Aquarius, and women are finally making some progress in their long, uphill struggle for equal rights. However, for most of us, the father-figure is still the dominant one in our lives. Even after we have become parents and grandparents ourselves, this powerful male figure continues to exert his influence on our lives, if only in the unconscious mind—and psychoanalytical literature is full of the struggles of patients with father-figures. Thus, the influence of Jupiter is one to be reckoned with. Venus can also bring good luck, if well aspected, and is necessary to offset the more aggressive influence of Mars, but Venus is still the lesser fortune, Jupiter the greater.

Perhaps this will change. We may yet see a woman elected President of the United States, and the nuclear family (if it survives) may yet be dominated by the mother. The Age of Aquarius could have many such changes in store, but true astrology does not attempt to predict the future. It gives you, in the horoscope, a tool to help you know yourself, to see your potential strengths and weaknesses. How you use this knowledge is up to you. As far as we know, fate is still largely a matter of character, and individual character can be molded. The horoscope can point to possible directions for us to take, but we must choose which road to take and how far to travel along it. As Cassius said:

> Men at some time are masters of their fates:
> The fault, dear Brutus, is not in our stars,
> But in ourselves, that we are underlings.

Jupiter's influence can help to keep us from being underlings.

Jupiter is the planetary ruler of two signs, Cetus and Sagittarius, so this planet is especially important if one of these is your sun sign.

To place the symbol of Jupiter (♃) on your chart, turn to Table 8 at the end of this chapter. Here the positions of Jupiter are listed for each year from 1890 to 1975. Turn to the year of your birth and find the span of time that includes your birthdate. It should be noted that Table 8 lists *inclusive* sets of dates. That is, if you were born on October 8 and the table lists Jupiter in Gemini from June 7 to October 8, Jupiter was still in Gemini on your birthdate, since it did not enter Cancer until October 9.

To continue our example of someone born on January 1, 1940, with Aquarius rising, Figure 8 shows his chart with the symbol of Jupiter entered. In Table 8, it is shown that Jupiter was in Pisces on January 1, 1940; therefore, the symbol of Jupiter is entered in the House occupied by Pisces, which (on his chart) is the second House.

INTERPRETATION

General interpretations of the meaning of Jupiter in each of the 14 signs are given below. In reading these, it should be remembered that Jupiter does not have an *absolute* meaning; whether it is a help or a hindrance depends upon its relationship to other elements of your chart. Also, the House occupied by Jupiter affects its interpretation. Our imaginary subject (Figure 8) was born with Jupiter in Pisces, which is his second House. After reading the interpretation of Jupiter in Pisces, he should turn back to Table 1 (p. 4), which lists the basic meanings of the Houses. The life activity governed by that particular House will be enhanced by the presence of Jupiter. This is also true of the other planets, which we will be placing in the chapters to follow.

JUPITER IN PISCES ♃ ♓

Jupiter in Pisces on your chart enhances your belief, not only in spiritual and philosophical matters, but your belief in yourself; that is, your self-confidence and real inner opinion of yourself. Pisces is ruled by a planet named for another chief god of the classic pantheon, Neptune, which is often associated with spiritual concerns. The presence of Jupiter, the "greater fortune," in this sign will probably have a powerful effect on all of your spiritual (or psychic) interests. If well aspected to other elements in your chart, Jupiter will strengthen and bring good fortune to you. If you attend church or temple, you are probably devout and attend services regularly, without being fanatical or dogmatic in insisting that yours is the only "right" creed. You are too generous and even-tempered to fall into such stances. You believe in yourself, without conceit, and the openness of your personality easily attracts friends and lovers. If your Jupiter is in poor aspect to other elements, however, you may be *too* generous in your outlook, so that you cannot see the evil in nefarious schemes and are taken advantage of by people with only their own self-interest in mind. The meaning of the aspects will be taken up in Chapter 12. In the meantime, check the life activity governed by the House occupied by Pisces on your chart (see Table 1) for a clearer picture of Jupiter's influence on your belief.

JUPITER IN ARIES ♃ ♈

Jupiter in Aries on your chart enhances your will and its use in achieving success in all areas of life. Aries is ruled by Mars, so we have here a combination of two strong, masculine planets. The aggressive nature of Mars has been discussed previously. Jupiter, if in good aspect to other elements, brings a stabilizing effect to the will and drive to power of Mars. You have strong convictions and are probably a natural leader, whatever your field. Your courage and will to succeed can carry you through long, difficult projects, without discouragement at temporary

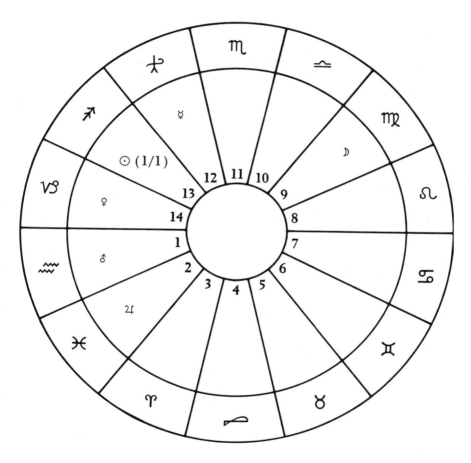

Figure 8. Placement of Jupiter on chart of subject born on January 1, 1940, with Aquarius rising

setbacks. If met with opposition, you simply try harder. Success should come easily to you, especially since you tend to be lucky as well as unafraid of hard work. This combination would seem to be excellent for politicians, military men, executives, and all whose work requires responsibility and supervision of others. If your Jupiter is badly aspected, on the other hand, you may find it tempting to use your strength to dominate others in situations where equal give-and-take is called for. The meaning of the aspects will be taken up in Chapter 12. In the meantime, check the life activity governed by the House occupied by Aries on your chart (see Table 1) for a clearer picture of Jupiter's influence on your will and its uses in the power struggles of life.

JUPITER IN CETUS ♃ ♍

Jupiter in Cetus on your chart enhances the development of your personality, your career, and your personal fortune. Cetus is ruled by Jupiter, so the presence of the planetary ruler in this sign approximately doubles its influence (for good or ill). A "double" Jupiter can be a sign of great good fortune, if your Jupiter is in good aspect to other elements, and Lady Luck will probably often smile upon your ventures. Most things come easily to you, but you are conscientious and fair, always willing to lend a helping hand and to let others have the benefit of your experience and knowledge. You have a good opinion of yourself, without being conceited, and your personal charm and magnetism are considerable. You are probably highly popular with members of both sexes. You also have an innate sense of good taste and proper form, which could help greatly in a career in the entertainment world or the graphic arts. If your Jupiter is badly aspected, however, you may come to depend too much on luck and charisma to carry you through situations calling for sound planning and hard work. Also, you may let yourself be spoiled by the easiness of your popularity. The meaning of the aspects will be taken up in Chapter 12. In the meantime, check the life activity governed by the House occupied by Cetus on your chart (see Table 1) for a clearer picture of Jupiter's influence on your personal fortunes.

JUPITER IN TAURUS ♃ ♉

Jupiter in Taurus on your chart enhances the emotional side of your nature and affects your talent, especially in the field of music. Taurus is ruled by Venus, the "lesser fortune," so the combination of the two fortunes, greater and lesser, bodes well for success if your Jupiter is well aspected to other elements. If it is, you are probably that rare person whose great emotional sensitivity does not make him shy, but adds depth to a pleasant, outgoing personality. Though anything but narcissistic, you think well of yourself and probably have many friends (of both sexes). Though your emotions are strong, you can generally keep them under control. Your attitude is well balanced, and you appreciate both the masculine and feminine elements in human beings. You could do well in many fields, especially those connected with music, mathematics, or the physical sciences. If your Jupiter is in bad aspect to other elements, on the other hand, you may lose that fine control of your emotions that should be the hallmark of your personality—and this can result in either a violent temper or in a brooding, shy, withdrawn attitude in social situations. The meaning of the aspects will be taken up in Chapter 12. In the meantime, check the life activity governed by the House occupied by Taurus on your chart (see Table 1) for a clearer picture of Jupiter's influence on your emotional life and talent.

JUPITER IN GEMINI ♃ ♊

Jupiter in Gemini on your chart enhances the strength of your intellect, your versatility, and your communicative powers (both oral and written). Gemini is ruled by Mercury, which is associated with these characteristics. If your Jupiter is well aspected to other elements, its presence in this sign can add toughness to a flexible intellect, warmth to a quick wit, and steadiness to a personality that may be all too willing to jump from job to job—or even from spouse to spouse! The mercurial traits often make for a fascinating personality; when to these are added the strength and generosity of Jupiter, the outcome may well be an outstanding individual in many ways. Success is highly likely, especially if your field involves communication of the written or oral word. You are attractive to members of the opposite sex and probably are a center of attention at parties and other social occasions. If your Jupiter is badly aspected, however, you may develop a tendency to get by on your looks and charm, avoiding the spadework needed to build a solid character. Do not let yourself be flattered by well-meaning friends; "brilliance" is often not enough. The meaning of the aspects will be taken up in Chapter 12. In the meantime, check the life activity governed by the House occupied by Gemini on your chart (see Table 1) for a clearer picture of Jupiter's influence on your intellect, versatility, and ability to communicate.

JUPITER IN CANCER ♃ ♋

Jupiter in Cancer on your chart enhances the sensitivity of your feelings and your conservative tendencies. Cancer is the only sign ruled by the moon. As we have noted previously, the moon is feminine and symbolizes the unconscious. Male and highly conscious Jupiter in this sign can mean a good balance between the masculine and feminine sides of your nature if Jupiter is in good aspect to other elements. Thus, if you are a man, your sensitivity does not make you effeminate; if you are a woman, your strength does not make you "mannish." You have a strong sense of responsibility and are good at running things in a quiet way. A well-aspected Jupiter generally means good luck, but you do not depend on luck; you play your cards with care, and like to keep an ace in the hole. Your chances of success, both professionally and personally, are good. On the other hand, if your Jupiter is in bad aspect to other elements, the strength of your emotions may occasionally get out of hand, and an overaccented sensitivity may make you too touchy for normal social contacts. Any such tendencies should, of course, be faced up to and resolved. The meaning of the aspects will be taken up in Chapter 12. In the meantime, check the life activity governed by the House occupied by Cancer on your chart (see Table 1) for a clearer picture of Jupiter's influence on your emotional life and conservatism.

JUPITER IN LEO ♃ ♌

Jupiter in Leo on your chart enhances your personal sense of independence. Leo is ruled by the sun, and it is hard to think of a more "kingly" combination than Jupiter and the sun. If your Jupiter is well aspected to other elements, your sense of independence—of being on your own and doing things your own way—is not only strengthened, but rounded out by the other positive traits of Jupiter. There is strong leadership potential here. You may very well be the innovator and pace-setter in your group, the one to whom others look for guidance. If you are in such a position, you do not let it go to your head; you feel comfortable in the driver's seat and are glad to help others when they feel lost or confused. If you could assume a leading role, you would probably do well in either politics or business, but would find it difficult to follow a routine or simply do piecework. If your Jupiter is poorly aspected, however, you may feel that you *always* have to be the leader, and build up resentment toward others who try to usurp your position, even if they are experts and you are not. Remember Donne's dictum: "No man is an island." The meaning of the aspects will be taken up in Chapter 12. In the meantime, check the life activity governed by the House occupied by Leo on your chart (see Table 1) for a clearer picture of Jupiter's influence on your sense of independence.

JUPITER IN VIRGO ♃ ♍

Jupiter in Virgo on your chart enhances your individualism and your analytical ability. Virgo is ruled by Mercury, which—in this sign—tends to bring out individualistic traits and the ability to analyze people, products, and situations. If your Jupiter is in good aspect to other elements in your chart, you may well be a "one of a kind" type of personality. You stand out in any group without making any effort to be noticed, are known to all around you, and probably have a nickname. The more we are propagandized to conform and be alike, the more you insist on being different, and you are admired for this trait. You have the ability to quickly size up people and events; it is almost impossible to fool you. You could be successful in many fields, especially those requiring analytical or critical ability. If your Jupiter is in bad aspect, however, you may carry your individualism to extremes, so that people think your eccentricities freakish. Also, you may become so sharply critical that you hurt others' feelings, and this can be the route to loneliness and frustration. The meaning of the aspects will be taken up in Chapter 12. In the meantime, check the life activity governed by the House occupied by Virgo on your chart (see Table 1) for a clearer picture of Jupiter's influence on your individualism and analytical ability.

JUPITER IN LIBRA ♃ ♎

Jupiter in Libra on your chart enhances the quality of your judgment. Libra is ruled by Venus, and the combination of Jupiter and Venus—the greater and lesser fortunes—can mean a well-balanced personality as well as good luck and material prosperity. If your Jupiter is well aspected to other elements, your ability to judge is probably superb. Though always objective and just, you are even-handed and generous in forgiving faults in others. You can keep a cool head in situations where strong emotions are aroused, but you are never cold or ruthless. Success should come to you fairly easily, and you will probably prosper in most of your ventures. Politics or the law would be excellent fields for you; or, if musically talented, you could probably do well as a singer, as you may well have a good natural singing voice. If your Jupiter is badly aspected, on the other hand, you may judge yourself too harshly, and either become unsure of your opinions or let them harden into dogmatism. The meaning of the aspects will be taken up in Chapter 12. In the meantime, check the life activity governed by the House occupied by Libra on your chart (see Table 1) for a clearer picture of Jupiter's influence on the quality of your judgment.

JUPITER IN SCORPIO ♃ ♏

Jupiter in Scorpio on your chart enhances your empathy, sympathy, and humanistic ideals. Scorpio is ruled by Mars, and we have observed that Scorpio types could be called the *humanists* of the Zodiac. If your Jupiter is in good aspect to other elements, the Mars/Jupiter combination could lead you to be a real force for good in the world. You are very sensitive to the feelings of others, which is intuitive and may be guided by extrasensory perception (ESP). You not only "feel for" others in bad straits, but are perfectly willing to give your time and energy to try to help them. You are idealistic, and probably dream of a world where no one is in want and justice is done to all. There may be a mystic streak in your nature and a talent for the arts (especially poetry). You will probably succeed in your efforts to make the world a little better, and may make a genuine spiritual or poetic contribution to wisdom or art. If your Jupiter is in bad aspect to other elements, however, you may lose your sense of proportion, giving too much of yourself to others—who may be all too willing to give nothing in return. The meaning of the aspects will be taken up in Chapter 12. In the meantime, check the life activity governed by the House occupied by Scorpio on your chart (see Table 1) for a clearer picture of Jupiter's influence on your empathy and humanistic ideals.

JUPITER IN OPHIUCHUS ♃ ⚕

Jupiter in Ophiuchus on your chart enhances your resourcefulness and versatility. Ophiuchus is ruled by Pluto, which is often associated with wealth, so the presence of the "greater fortune" in this sign could mean that your chances of attaining material prosperity—and possibly fame—are good. If your Jupiter is well aspected to other elements, you are probably a highly resourceful and energetic type of person. Temporary setbacks and even failure do not throw you for a loss. If one of your ideas or projects should fail, you always have another one up your sleeve. You also have the trait (usually associated with Mercury) of being able to do more than one thing at a time or hold down more than one job. You are probably popular with members of both sexes, have a good sense of humor, and may well have a gift for entertainment. You are sensitive as well as genial, and are probably considered lucky. If your Jupiter is badly aspected to other elements, on the other hand, you may tend to let your popularity carry you, shunning the hard work nearly always necessary for success. Or you may become the victim of too-early success. The meaning of the aspects will be taken up in Chapter 12. In the meantime, check the life activity governed by the House occupied by Ophiuchus on your chart (see Table 1) for a clearer picture of Jupiter's influence on your versatility, talent, and resourcefulness.

JUPITER IN SAGITTARIUS ♃ ♐

Jupiter in Sagittarius on your chart enhances your extraversion, your conscience, and your desire to play an active role in humanitarian activities. Sagittarius is ruled by Jupiter, and the presence of the planetary ruler in this sign approximately doubles the influence of Jupiter. If your Jupiter is in good aspect to other elements, one is tempted to say that "the sky is no limit." Sagittarius is usually considered the luckiest sign in the Zodiac, and a "double" Jupiter almost certainly means success, material prosperity, and popularity. You are good at organization and other executive duties, and are probably a natural leader. You are popular with subordinates as well as friends because, no matter how much wealth and power you may amass, you are never tempted to play the tyrant; your good humor and generosity keep you from narrow views, and you make a real effort to help your less fortunate fellows. If your Jupiter is in bad aspect, however, you may become insensitive to the weaknesses of others, expecting them to be as strong and able as yourself. A touch of Scorpio's empathy would then be called for. The meaning of the aspects will be taken up in Chapter 12. In the meantime, check the life activity governed by the House occupied by Sagittarius on your chart (see Table 1) for a clearer picture of Jupiter's influence on your conscience and extraverted tendencies.

JUPITER IN CAPRICORN ♃ ♑

Jupiter in Capricorn on your chart enhances your conservatism and your tendency to face life "realistically" rather than dream about it. Capricorn is ruled by Saturn, as conservative as Jupiter is open-handed, and whose "cold" is usually contrasted to the Jovian warmth. If your Jupiter is well aspected to other elements in your chart, these contrasting traits can balance out. You could then achieve a nice balance between recklessness and overcaution, the spendthrift and the miser, the social leader and the hermit. This is the "golden mean" that Aristotle said was the ideal of human conduct. Without being tight-fisted, you are cautious in spending your time and energy, as well as your money, and always have something put by for a possible rainy day. Your sight is clear, you have few illusions, and your personality is enlivened by a dry, ironic wit. On the other hand, if your Jupiter is badly aspected, you may become confused as to when to spend, when to save; and if you choose to retreat into a too-conservative stance, you may fail to develop all sides of your personality.

This could result in psychic childishness, whatever your age. The meaning of the aspects will be taken up in Chapter 12. In the meantime, check the life activity governed by the House occupied by Capricorn on your chart (see Table 1) for a clearer picture of Jupiter's influence on your conservative and "realistic" tendencies.

JUPITER IN AQUARIUS ♃ ♒

Jupiter in Aquarius on your chart enhances the stability of your personality and your ability to acquire knowledge, especially in scientific or technical fields. Aquarius is ruled by Uranus, which is sometimes called "the disruptor" because of its eccentric orbit. If your Jupiter is in good aspect to other elements, your chances of achieving a well-balanced personality are good, as the strength and steadiness of Jupiter will offset any wayward or "disruptive" tendencies. You could succeed in fields of science or technology, as your analytical faculties are keen. You have a novel approach to most things and are attracted by the new. If the arts attract you, you would probably do well in the field of entertainment. Whatever the field, your critical sense and novel approach can make you a valuable employee—and a colorful friend or lover. If your Jupiter is in bad aspect to other elements, however, you may go so far in your offbeat tastes that you will be considered a "kook" rather than a lovable "character." You will have to curb a tendency to be overanalytical and too sharp in your criticism of others. The meaning of the aspects will be taken up in Chapter 12. In the meantime, check the life activity governed by the House occupied by Aquarius on your chart (see Table 1) for a clearer picture of Jupiter's influence on your stability and analytical tendencies.

TABLE 8 307

Table 8
POSITIONS OF JUPITER (1890 TO 1975)

Dates	Sign	Symbol
Jan. 1 to Mar. 29, 1890	Sagittarius	♐
Mar. 30 to Aug. 3, 1890	Capricorn	♑
Aug. 4 to Nov. 20, 1890	Sagittarius	♐
Nov. 21, 1890 to Mar. 19, 1891	Capricorn	♑
Mar. 20, 1891 to Mar. 16, 1892	Aquarius	♒
Mar. 17, 1892 to Mar. 5, 1893	Pisces	♓
Mar. 6 to June 22, 1893	Aries	♈
June 23, 1893 to June 11, 1894	Cetus	⊷
June 12, 1894 to June 6, 1895	Taurus	♉
June 7 to Oct. 8, 1895	Gemini	♊
Oct. 9, 1895 to Jan. 12, 1896	Cancer	♋
Jan. 13 to June 1, 1896	Gemini	♊
June 2 to Sept. 27, 1896	Cancer	♋
Sept. 28, 1896 to Oct. 5, 1897	Leo	♌
Oct. 6, 1897 to Oct. 18, 1898	Virgo	♍
Oct. 19, 1898 to Oct. 29, 1899	Libra	♎
Oct. 30, 1899 to Nov. 6, 1900	Scorpio	♏
Nov. 7, 1900 to Mar. 21, 1901	Ophiuchus	⚕
Mar. 22 to June 9, 1901	Sagittarius	♐
June 10 to Nov. 11, 1901	Ophiuchus	⚕
Nov. 12, 1901 to Mar. 8, 1902	Sagittarius	♐
Mar. 9, 1902 to Mar. 2, 1903	Capricorn	♑
Mar. 3, 1903 to Feb. 29, 1904	Aquarius	♒
Mar. 1 to June 25, 1904	Pisces	♓
June 26 to Oct. 14, 1904	Aries	♈
Oct. 15, 1904 to Feb. 12, 1905	Pisces	♓
Feb. 13 to June 4, 1905	Aries	♈
June 5, 1905 to May 27, 1906	Cetus	⊷
May 28 to Oct. 13, 1906	Taurus	♉
Oct. 14 to Nov. 14, 1906	Gemini	♊
Nov. 15, 1906 to May 21, 1907	Taurus	♉
May 22 to Sept. 15, 1907	Gemini	♊
Sept. 16, 1907 to Feb. 22, 1908	Cancer	♋
Feb. 23 to May 6, 1908	Gemini	♊
May 7 to Sept. 11, 1908	Cancer	♋
Sept. 12, 1908 to Sept. 21, 1909	Leo	♌
Sept. 22, 1909 to Oct. 3, 1910	Virgo	♍
Oct. 4, 1910 to Oct. 14, 1911	Libra	♎

continued

Dates	Sign	Symbol
Oct. 15, 1911 to Feb. 27, 1912	Scorpio	♏
Feb. 28 to May 5, 1912	Ophiuchus	⚕
May 6 to Oct. 18, 1912	Scorpio	♏
Oct. 19, 1912 to Feb. 22, 1913	Ophiuchus	⚕
Feb. 23 to July 23, 1913	Sagittarius	♐
July 24 to Oct. 15, 1913	Ophiuchus	⚕
Oct. 16, 1913 to Feb. 18, 1914	Sagittarius	♐
Feb. 19, 1914 to Feb. 14, 1915	Capricorn	♑
Feb. 15, 1915 to Feb. 11, 1916	Aquarius	♒
Feb. 12 to June 1, 1916	Pisces	♓
June 2 to Dec. 8, 1916	Aries	♈
Dec. 9, 1916 to Jan. 1, 1917	Pisces	♓
Jan. 2 to May 19, 1917	Aries	♈
May 20, 1917 to May 10, 1918	Cetus	⬄
May 11 to Sept. 4, 1918	Taurus	♉
Sept. 5, 1918 to Jan. 2, 1919	Gemini	♊
Jan. 3 to Apr. 29, 1919	Taurus	♉
Apr. 30 to Aug. 28, 1919	Gemini	♊
Aug. 29, 1919 to Aug. 26, 1920	Cancer	♋
Aug. 27, 1920 to Sept. 5, 1921	Leo	♌
Sept. 6, 1921 to Sept. 17, 1922	Virgo	♍
Sept. 18, 1922 to Feb. 4, 1923	Libra	♎
Feb. 5 to Apr. 3, 1923	Scorpio	♏
Apr. 4 to Sept. 26, 1923	Libra	♎
Sept. 27, 1923 to Jan. 29, 1924	Scorpio	♏
Jan. 30 to June 16, 1924	Ophiuchus	⚕
June 17 to Sept. 25, 1924	Scorpio	♏
Sept. 26, 1924 to Feb. 3, 1925	Ophiuchus	⚕
Feb. 4, 1925 to Feb. 2, 1926	Sagittarius	♐
Feb. 3, 1926 to Jan. 29, 1927	Capricorn	♑
Jan. 30 to June 5, 1927	Aquarius	♒
June 6 to Sept. 10, 1927	Pisces	♓
Sept. 11, 1927 to Jan. 22, 1928	Aquarius	♒
Jan. 23 to May 14, 1928	Pisces	♓
May 15, 1928 to May 3, 1929	Aries	♈
May 14 to Sept. 13, 1929	Cetus	⬄
Sept. 14 to Oct. 26, 1929	Taurus	♉
Oct. 27, 1929 to Apr. 22, 1930	Cetus	⬄
Apr. 23 to Aug. 14, 1930	Taurus	♉
Aug. 15, 1930 to Feb. 23, 1931	Gemini	♊
Feb. 24 to Mar. 18, 1931	Taurus	♉

TABLE 8 309

continued

Dates	Sign	Symbol
Mar. 19 to Aug. 11, 1931	Gemini	♊
Aug. 12, 1931 to Aug. 10, 1932	Cancer	♋
Aug. 11, 1932 to Aug. 19, 1933	Leo	♌
Aug. 20, 1933 to Jan. 5, 1934	Virgo	♍
Jan. 6 to Mar. 10, 1934	Libra	♎
Mar. 11 to Aug. 30, 1934	Virgo	♍
Aug. 31, 1934 to Jan. 5, 1935	Libra	♎
Jan. 6 to May 15, 1935	Scorpio	♏
May 16 to Sept. 4, 1935	Libra	♎
Sept. 5, 1935 to Jan. 10, 1936	Scorpio	♏
Jan. 11, 1936 to Jan. 17, 1937	Ophiuchus	⛎
Jan. 18, 1937 to Jan. 17, 1938	Sagittarius	♐
Jan. 18, 1938 to Jan. 11, 1939	Capricorn	♑
Jan. 12 to May 11, 1939	Aquarius	♒
May 12 to Oct. 28, 1939	Pisces	♓
Oct. 29 to Dec. 20, 1939	Aquarius	♒
Dec. 21, 1939 to Apr. 27, 1940	Pisces	♓
Apr. 28, 1940 to Apr. 15, 1941	Aries	♈
Apr. 16 to Aug. 8, 1941	Cetus	⚲
Aug. 9 to Dec. 6, 1941	Taurus	♉
Dec. 7, 1941 to Mar. 29, 1942	Cetus	⚲
Mar. 30 to July 27, 1942	Taurus	♉
July 28, 1942 to July 26, 1943	Gemini	♊
July 27, 1943 to July 25, 1944	Cancer	♋
July 26 to Dec. 8, 1944	Leo	♌
Dec. 9, 1944 to Feb. 15, 1945	Virgo	♍
Feb. 16 to Aug. 1, 1945	Leo	♌
Aug. 2 to Dec. 9, 1945	Virgo	♍
Dec. 10, 1945 to Apr. 18, 1946	Libra	♎
Apr. 19 to Aug. 8, 1946	Virgo	♍
Aug. 9 to Dec. 16, 1946	Libra	♎
Dec. 17, 1946 to Dec. 24, 1947	Scorpio	♏
Dec. 25, 1947 to Jan. 1, 1949	Ophiuchus	⛎
Jan. 2, 1949 to Jan. 1, 1950	Sagittarius	♐
Jan. 2 to Apr. 30, 1950	Capricorn	♑
May 1 to Aug. 24, 1950	Aquarius	♒
Aug. 25 to Dec. 20, 1950	Capricorn	♑
Dec. 21, 1950 to Apr. 21, 1951	Aquarius	♒
Apr. 22, 1951 to Apr. 10, 1952	Pisces	♓
Apr. 11 to Aug. 26, 1952	Aries	♈
Aug. 27 to Sept. 22, 1952	Cetus	⚲

continued

Dates	Sign	Symbol
Sept. 23, 1952 to Mar. 27, 1953	Aries	♈
Mar. 28 to July 17, 1953	Cetus	⌁
July 18, 1953 to July 10, 1954	Taurus	♉
July 11, 1954 to July 9, 1955	Gemini	♊
July 10 to Nov. 16, 1955	Cancer	♋
Nov. 17, 1955 to Jan. 17, 1956	Leo	♌
Jan. 18 to July 7, 1956	Cancer	♋
July 8 to Nov. 10, 1956	Leo	♌
Nov. 11, 1956 to Mar. 26, 1957	Virgo	♍
Mar. 27 to July 10, 1957	Leo	♌
July 11 to Nov. 19, 1957	Virgo	♍
Nov. 20, 1957 to Nov. 29, 1958	Libra	♎
Nov. 30, 1958 to Dec. 8, 1959	Scorpio	♏
Dec. 9, 1959 to Dec. 16, 1960	Ophiuchus	⛎
Dec. 17, 1960 to May 8, 1961	Sagittarius	♐
May 9 to June 12, 1961	Capricorn	♑
June 13 to Dec. 14, 1961	Sagittarius	♐
Dec. 15, 1961 to Apr. 7, 1962	Capricorn	♑
Apr. 8, 1962 to Apr. 4, 1963	Aquarius	♒
Apr. 5, 1963 to Mar. 24, 1964	Pisces	♓
Mar. 25 to July 16, 1964	Aries	♈
July 17 to Nov. 16, 1964	Cetus	⌁
Nov. 17, 1964 to Mar. 5, 1965	Aries	♈
Mar. 6 to June 29, 1965	Cetus	⌁
June 30, 1965 to June 24, 1966	Taurus	♉
June 25, 1966 to June 23, 1967	Gemini	♊
June 24 to Oct. 19, 1967	Cancer	♋
Oct. 20, 1967 to Feb. 27, 1968	Leo	♌
Feb. 28 to June 15, 1968	Cancer	♋
June 16 to Oct. 23, 1968	Leo	♌
Oct. 24, 1968 to Nov. 3, 1969	Virgo	♍
Nov. 4, 1969 to Nov. 14, 1970	Libra	♎
Nov. 15, 1970 to Nov. 23, 1971	Scorpio	♏
Nov. 24, 1971 to Nov. 30, 1972	Ophiuchus	⛎
Dec. 1, 1972 to Mar. 30, 1973	Sagittarius	♐
Mar. 31 to Aug. 3, 1973	Capricorn	♑
Aug. 4 to Nov. 21, 1973	Sagittarius	♐
Nov. 22, 1973 to Mar. 19, 1974	Capricorn	♑
Mar. 20, 1974 to Mar. 18, 1975	Aquarius	♒
Mar. 19 to Dec. 31, 1975	Pisces	♓

8: Saturn

ħ

SATURN is another giant among the planets, second in size only to Jupiter. Sixth of the nine known planets of the solar system, it was named for the ancient god of the underworld (the Greek Kronos) and was also identified with Cronus—Father Time. For a long time, Saturn was thought to have nine moons, but a tenth, Janus, was discovered in 1966. Saturn is distinguished by its famous rings, which make it the most beautiful of the planets. These rings are fairly broad, but quite thin; it was the "edge-on" appearance of the rings that enabled the recent discovery of Janus.

As is the case with Jupiter, men will probably not be able to explore Saturn directly, as its gravity would crush a human being. The moons, then, will most likely be the bases for our astronauts when they have ventured beyond Jupiter.

It is unlikely that life will be found on Saturn. Besides its mass and poisonous atmosphere, it has an extremely low density (less than that of water). Anything like the mammalian life on earth would find it impossible to develop in such an environment. But life takes a myriad of shapes and forms, even here on earth, so we must not rule out the possibility of Saturnian life until we have proof.

One of Saturn's moons, Titan, is large (3,550 miles in diameter) and is known to have an atmosphere. This is illustrated in a beautiful painting by Chesley Bonestell, which shows Saturn seen through the blue sky of Titan (the sky seen from our moon is black because the moon does not have an atmosphere). Therefore, it would seem more likely that what we recognize as life could exist on Titan rather than on the surface of Saturn.

As mentioned in the last chapter, an unmanned spacecraft, *Pioneer 10*, has been launched on a Grand Tour of the outer planets. It will take *Pioneer 10* about two years to reach Jupiter, and much longer to reach Saturn, but—if the mission is successful—we will gain our first non-astronomical knowledge of the giant planets.

As stated above, Saturn is the sixth of the nine known planets of the solar system. Being farther from the sun, its orbit (or year) is longer than that of the inner planets or Jupiter. It takes Saturn 29.46 years to make one circuit of the sun, as compared with 11.86 years for Jupiter and 780 days for Mars. Saturn also exhibits the retrograde motion described earlier for the inner planets and Jupiter, so that it sometimes appears to be moving backward.

MEANING OF SATURN IN HOROSCOPE

As previously mentioned, Saturn moves slower than the earth. Its orbit is 29.46 years, and it moves through only 12 degrees a year. This means that it takes Saturn nearly thirty years to move through all 14 signs (constellations) of the Zodiac. It sometimes remains in one sign for more than two years, then (because of its retrograde motion) will remain in another for only a few months.

Named for the ancient god of the underworld, Saturn is traditionally considered to be the exact opposite of Jupiter. It is thought to be as negative as Jupiter is positive, as malefic as Jupiter is beneficent. It is the governor of old age and its keyword is *limitation*. Gloomy, cold, taciturn, the traditional portrait of the individual ruled by Saturn is that of a bitter old miser desperately clutching his few remaining shreds of life. However, as we have discussed previously, no planet has an *absolute* meaning: its influence is dictated by its aspects to other elements in your chart. So the traditional portrait of Saturn is not necessarily true. Its intrinsic "evil" can be neutralized by other planets that are in good aspect.

Conservatism in itself is not a bad trait; in our flamboyant and reckless age, it could be considered a virtue. Nor does Saturn's influence rule out a sense of humor. Just as the adjective "jovial" is derived from Jupiter (Jove), the adjective "saturnine" is derived from Saturn—and, although it means "heavy, grave, sullen," saturnine *humor* is a type that has become highly popular in recent years; that is, "black" humor.

The individual ruled by Saturn, then, is not necessarily "star-crossed." He may simply be conservative in his tastes and conduct, realistic in his approach to life, and have a dry, ironic sense of humor.

However, the astrological tradition that calls Saturn *malefic* is a strong one. If we think about it, it is also seen to be necessary. Evil certainly exists in our world, and a horoscope would be untrue or incomplete if all of its aspects were positive. Although sometimes popular with the public, the "goody-goody" type of writing on astrology that simply tells us how wonderful we are is false to the realities of human life. Very few (if any) of us can look back on our lives and say there were more good times than bad, more prosperity than trouble. The Golden Age (ruled by Saturn, incidentally) is a myth of the distant past. We live in a time of transition from one era to another, and such times are not known for their tranquillity. Although great progress was made during the Renaissance, for example, it was a time of wars, revolutions, unrest, and suffering for the great majority. Our twentieth century is similar, with the important differences that man now has the technical means to commit racial suicide (genocide), is swiftly polluting the atmosphere of the earth, running out of raw materials, and is threatened by overpopulation. Living in such a threatening environment, the individual often feels at a loss. If he turns to astrology for help and advice, and is told that everything is just lovely, he has every right to reject astrology as a bogus science.

No, we need Saturn. The cosmos must truly reflect the microcosmos, which is man. Good could not exist without evil—the light cannot be seen except in contrast to the darkness. "As above, so below."

Albert Camus wrote that the only truly philosophical question is that of suicide. If we elect to live, then we must live—not, perhaps, without hope, as he suggests—but with our eyes open to the reality of life. And that reality includes the *potential* evil symbolized by Saturn in the horoscope. We must always bear in mind, however, that the force of Saturn, like all the other planets, is dependent upon its aspects.

Saturn is the planetary ruler of Capricorn, so this planet is especially important if Capricorn is your sun sign.

To place the symbol of Saturn (♄) on your chart, turn to Table 9 at the end of this chapter. Here the positions of Saturn are listed for each year from 1890 to 1975. Turn to the year of your birth and find the span of time that includes your birthdate. It should be noted that Table 9 lists *inclusive* sets of dates. That is, if you were born on December 4 and the table lists Saturn in Ophiuchus from June 1 to December 4, Saturn was still in Ophiuchus on your birthdate, since it did not enter Sagittarius until December 5.

To continue our example of someone born on January 1, 1940, with Aquarius rising, Figure 9 shows his chart with the symbol of Saturn entered. In Table 9, it is shown that Saturn was in Pisces on January 1, 1940; therefore, the symbol of Saturn is entered in the House occupied by Pisces, which (on his chart) is the second House.

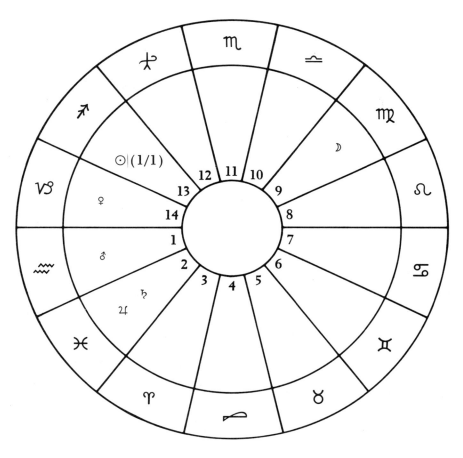

Figure 9. Placement of Saturn on chart of subject born on January 1, 1940, with Aquarius rising

INTERPRETATION

General interpretations of the meaning of Saturn in each of the 14 signs are given below. In reading these, it should be remembered that Saturn, though potentially malefic, does not have an *absolute* meaning; whether it is a help or a hindrance (or neutral) depends upon its relationship to other elements of your chart. Also, the House occupied by Saturn affects its interpretation. Our imaginary subject (Figure 9) was born with Saturn in Pisces, which is his second House. After reading the interpretation of Saturn in Pisces, he should turn back to Table 1 (p. 4), which lists the basic meanings of the Houses. The life activity governed by that particular House will be enhanced by the presence of Saturn. This is also true of the other planets, which we will be placing in the chapters to follow.

SATURN IN PISCES ♄ ♓

Saturn in Pisces on your chart affects your belief in yourself—the strength or weakness of your values—as well as in a spiritual or philosophical sense. Pisces is ruled by Neptune, named for the ancient god of the sea, which is often associated with spiritual matters. Both the underworld and the sea represent the *unconscious*, which is the true source of our beliefs. If your Saturn is in good aspect to other elements in your chart, it will strengthen your conservatism and sense of reality in such matters. It is highly unlikely that you could be a fanatic or wild-eyed visionary. If you are religious in a formal sense, you are quietly devout, attend services regularly, and tend to resist changes in the form of your worship. You feel that you know yourself well and try to achieve your goals by steady, enduring effort; you do not trust quick flashes of intuition. You exert a steadying influence on those around you. If your Saturn is in bad aspect, however, you may well be *too* conservative and cautious for your own good. Balance is always necessary; too prudent is as bad as too rash. The meaning of the aspects will be taken up in Chapter 12. Meanwhile, check the life activity governed by the House occupied by Pisces on your chart (see Table 1) for a clearer picture of Saturn's influence on your belief.

SATURN IN ARIES ♄ ♈

Saturn in Aries on your chart affects the strength of your will and its use in solving the problems of your life. Aries is ruled by Mars. The masculine, aggressive nature of Mars is usually expressed through the will to power. Your Saturn, if it is well aspected to other elements, may create a good balance between the sometimes rash impulsiveness of Mars and

316 THE ASTROLOGY 14 HOROSCOPE

the conservative, "realistic" influence of Saturn. You have strong convictions and are probably a hard worker. You may well be one of those fortunate people who have the self-control neither to be the first to rush into the new nor the last to give up the old. You are clear-eyed about the possibilities and limitations of your life and career, and feel that a good deal can be accomplished through the steady (but nonviolent) application of your will—as indeed it can! If your Saturn is badly aspected, on the other hand, you may tend to let the aggressive impulse overrule your innate caution and try to force your way through life by sheer will power, whatever the odds. This may lead to temporary success, but will result in one-sidedness, if not disaster. The meaning of the aspects will be taken up in Chapter 12. Meanwhile, check the life activity governed by the House occupied by Aries on your chart (see Table 1) for a clearer picture of Saturn's influence on your will and its uses.

SATURN IN CETUS ♄ ♎

Saturn in Cetus on your chart affects your basic personality and your career. Cetus is ruled by Jupiter, the "greater fortune," so the two giants of the solar system are here combined. If your Saturn is in good aspect to other elements, your personality may be well balanced between the two extremes symbolized by "positive" Jupiter and "negative" Saturn. You have charm and an outgoing attitude that will probably ensure your popularity with members of both sexes. You like people and activity around you, even when you are working, and can concentrate on your task even in the midst of uproar. A career in the world of entertainment or the graphic arts may be indicated, as you have color and magnetism without too much "artistic" temperament, and an innate sense of good taste and proper form. If your Saturn is in bad aspect, however, your talent and enthusiasm may be dampened by feelings of personal insecurity that will prevent you from taking necessary chances. Too strong a sense of "realism" can water down the colors of your personality and prevent its development to full flower. Be bold when boldness is called for, prudent when caution is necessary. The meaning of the aspects will be taken up in Chapter 12. Meanwhile, check the life activity governed by the House occupied by Cetus on your chart (see Table 1) for a clearer picture of Saturn's influence on the development of your personality and career.

SATURN IN TAURUS ♄ ♉

Saturn in Taurus on your chart affects the emotional side of your personality and your talent, especially if you should be musically gifted.

Taurus is ruled by Venus, and the association of Venus with the emotions and the art of music has been discussed previously. If your Saturn is well aspected to other elements, the masculine strength of Saturn can balance the emotional sensitivity of Venus, resulting in a well-balanced personality. You are appreciative of both the mental and emotional, masculine and feminine sides of everyone you meet, and this quality usually leads to popularity and a successful love life. If music is your field, you achieve a good synthesis of the old and the new, between the extremes of eighteenth-century minuets and the latest acid rock. You could also do well in mathematics or the physical sciences, which are allied to music. If your Saturn is badly aspected, on the other hand, your conservatism may override your emotional sensitivity, making you shy and withdrawn in social situations and putting a block in the path of your love life. The beloved must be sought, not simply gazed on from afar! The meaning of the aspects will be taken up in Chapter 12. Meanwhile, check the life activity governed by the House occupied by Taurus on your chart (see Table 1) for a clearer picture of Saturn's influence on your emotional life and talent.

SATURN IN GEMINI ♄ ♊

Saturn in Gemini on your chart affects your versatility, your intellectual powers, and your ability to communicate. Gemini is ruled by Mercury. If your Saturn is in good aspect to other elements, this can be an excellent combination. The mercurial traits usually require the balance of the conservative ones symbolized by Saturn; the "negative" traits of Saturn often need a touch of the color and dash of Mercury. A proper synthesis of these extremes can result in a well-rounded personality—colorful without being merely flashy, solid and steady without being dull. You have a quick mind and a talent for communicating your thoughts and feelings, both in conversation and in written form. You are versatile and interested in many things, but have the good sense not to spread yourself too thin or "ride off in all directions." You are probably quite popular, and your chances for success are good. If your Saturn is in bad aspect, however, your mercurial side may overbalance the conservative elements, and you will rush into situations that should first have been carefully and realistically assessed. Keep your horses in rein, but don't hobble them! The meaning of the aspects will be taken up in Chapter 12. Meanwhile, check the life activity governed by the House occupied by Gemini on your chart (see Table 1) for a clearer picture of Saturn's influence on your intellect, versatility, and communicative ability.

SATURN IN CANCER ♄ ♋

Saturn in Cancer on your chart affects your emotional sensitivity and your conservative tendencies. Cancer is ruled by the moon. Since the moon is feminine and Saturn is masculine, a good balance can be achieved between them if your Saturn is well aspected to other elements. If it is, your chances of achieving a mature personality are good. Although you tend to be conservative and cautious, both in business and in your personal life, you are sensitive to the needs of others—especially their emotional needs—and this quality can make you popular and successful, even if you prefer to remain in the background. Though quiet, you are at ease on social occasions and have a good sense of humor. You have a strong sense of duty and responsibility; these will serve you well, both in marriage and in your career. If your Saturn is badly aspected, on the other hand, you can easily become *too* conservative—an attitude that will make you shy with others and may prevent you from taking the bold leap that is often necessary both in romance and in pursuit of your career. The meaning of the aspects will be taken up in Chapter 12. Meanwhile, check the life activity governed by the House occupied by Cancer on your chart (see Table 1) for a clearer picture of Saturn's influence on your emotional life and conservative traits.

SATURN IN LEO ♄ ♌

Saturn in Leo on your chart affects your attitude of personal independence. Leo is the only sign ruled by the sun. Just as the sun shines alone at the center of the solar system, so Leo types often feel they have to be on their own and depend on no one else. If your Saturn is in good aspect to other elements, the opposites can be reconciled, the extremes avoided, and a nice balance between independence and conservatism may be achieved. You probably have strong leadership qualities, and may well be the innovator and pace-setter for your group. You like to originate projects and see them through to the end, but realize that very little can be gained without the help and cooperation of others. A fiercely independent will can often be unrealistic and lead one into blind alleys; you know this, and check your bold enthusiasm with a proper leavening of caution and good sense. If your Saturn is in bad aspect, however, you may let your independent drive to succeed on your terms overrule Saturnian caution and realism. He who is overly independent will often end up too lonely. The meaning of the aspects will be taken up in Chapter 12. Meanwhile, check the life activity governed by the House occupied by Leo on your chart (see Table 1) for a clearer picture of Saturn's influence on your independent attitude.

SATURN IN VIRGO ♄ ♍

Saturn in Virgo on your chart affects your individualism and your analytical ability. Virgo is ruled by Mercury. If your Saturn is well aspected to other elements, this could be a good combination, as the restricting influence of Saturn should be complemented by traits such as those symbolized by Mercury. You are strongly individualistic in your life style and have the ability to analyze (or criticize) people, things, and situations. The conservatism and caution of a well-aspected Saturn can nicely balance these traits, keeping you from being too much "one of a kind" or too sharp in your analysis and criticism. Your personality is distinct, and you probably bear a nickname. You are a hard person to fool, either in personal matters or in business. These traits can make you a valuable employee in many fields and an interesting friend. If your Saturn is badly aspected, on the other hand, your individualistic streak may get out of hand; it is fine to stand out, but few people like to be considered freakish. Also, your analytical ability may make you unpopular if you wield it with too sharp an edge. The meaning of the aspects will be taken up in Chapter 12. Meanwhile, check the life activity governed by the House occupied by Virgo on your chart (see Table 1) for a clearer picture of Saturn's influence on your individualism and analytical talent.

SATURN IN LIBRA ♄ ♎

Saturn in Libra on your chart affects your ability to judge and, if you are talented, the use of that talent (especially if your field is music). Libra is ruled by Venus. The emotional warmth of "the lesser fortune" can be a good foil for the restrictive "cold" of Saturn. If your Saturn is in good aspect to other elements, this combination of traits can lead to a well-balanced personality, which is only right in one whose forte is often that of judgment. If you achieve this mental and emotional balance, you have excellent chances for success, especially in any field that makes contact with the law. No matter how strong your feelings may be, you can hold them in abeyance and be objective when it comes to matters of judgment. You may well have an excellent voice, and it could probably be trained for a successful career as a singer. If your Saturn is in bad aspect, however, you may tend to be too conservative and cautious in your judgments (of yourself and others) or let your emotions sway you unduly in making a choice. There is also a danger that your opinions may become dogmatic. The meaning of the aspects will be taken up in Chapter 12. Meanwhile, check the life activity governed by the House occupied by Libra on your chart (see Table 1) for a clearer picture of Saturn's influence on your judgment and talent.

SATURN IN SCORPIO ♄ ♏

Saturn in Scorpio on your chart affects your empathy (sensitivity to others' feelings) and humanistic ideals. Scorpio is ruled by Mars. In this sign, the Saturn/Mars combination will probably mean that empathy and humanistic ideals will be kept to a more conservative and realistic level than is often the case with Scorpio types. If your Saturn is well aspected to other elements, your concern for the plight of humanity is great, and you are willing to give your time, energy, and money for causes that seem worthy to you. But you prefer to remain in the background, and your contributions are probably anonymous. Your humanistic ideals are high, but there may well be a fatalistic streak in your nature. Your philosophy is stoic. There have always been suffering, illness, and poverty; you feel that the fight against them is a noble one, but is really a lost cause. Nevertheless, you are on the side of the angels. If your Saturn is badly aspected, on the other hand, you may become so pessimistic as to feel that the lot of human beings is hopeless, and your quiet endurance may relapse into bitterness. The meaning of the aspects will be taken up in Chapter 12. Meanwhile, check the life activity governed by the House occupied by Scorpio on your chart (see Table 1) for a clearer picture of Saturn's influence on your humanistic ideals and philosophical attitude.

SATURN IN OPHIUCHUS ♄ ⚕

Saturn in Ophiuchus on your chart affects your resourcefulness and the versatility of your talent. Ophiuchus is ruled by Pluto, which is named for a personification of wealth. On the material level, rich people are often Saturnian types, so good chances for prosperity are indicated by this combination. If your Saturn is in good aspect to other elements, you can achieve a well-balanced personality because the realistic conservatism symbolized by Saturn will not allow you to squander your wealth of talents and resourcefulness. You are a person of many parts and can easily switch from one to another. You could be successful in many fields and probably have a talent for entertainment. If you do, you can do more than one "turn." You are probably highly popular with members of both sexes. You have a colorful personality, but have the good sense not to spend your energy and talent too lavishly. If your Saturn is in bad aspect to other elements, however, you may become too careful, and hesitate to answer when opportunity knocks at your door. The meaning of the aspects will be taken up in Chapter 12. Meanwhile, check the life activity governed by the House occupied by Ophiuchus on your chart (see Table 1) for a clearer picture of Saturn's influence on your resourcefulness and the versatility of your talent.

SATURN IN SAGITTARIUS ♄ ♐

Saturn in Sagittarius on your chart affects your conscience and your extraverted tendencies. Sagittarius is ruled by Jupiter, whose traits are considered the opposite of Saturn's. If your Saturn is well aspected to other elements, this combination could mean that your personality will achieve a good balance between the "positive" traits of Jupiter and the "negative" ones of Saturn. You tend to be outgoing and sociable, but are not headstrong or too impulsive. Your humanistic ideals are strong, and you desire to act on them rather than simply think or talk about the problems of humanity. You could be a strong, steady influence in any organization, pulling back the hotheads and urging on the timid ones. You are probably popular and have many friends who share the sensitivity of your conscience. If your Saturn is poorly aspected, on the other hand, you may develop your extraverted side to the extent that your inner life of intuition and dreams becomes meaningless to you. This will make your personality lopsided and prevent you from enjoying the richness of a fully developed personality. The meaning of the aspects will be taken up in Chapter 12. Meanwhile, check the life activity governed by the House occupied by Sagittarius on your chart (see Table 1) for a clearer picture of Saturn's influence on your extraversion and your conscience.

SATURN IN CAPRICORN ♄ ♑

Saturn in Capricorn on your chart affects your "realistic" attitude to life and your conservatism. Capricorn is ruled by Saturn, so the presence of the planetary ruler in this sign approximately doubles its influence. If your Saturn is in good aspect to other elements, your conservatism will not be carried to the point where you are thought a reactionary or isolationist. Although you have a down-to-earth attitude and believe in facing life's problems realistically and without illusions, you do not expect everyone else to feel and act as you do. There is great variety in the human condition; you appreciate this fact without feeling that you have to join extreme or radical movements. You play your cards close to the vest.

Caution, along with an open-eyed and tolerant attitude, is often the best way for personal success and often for sheer survival. If your Saturn is in bad aspect, however, your attitude may shift to one of intolerance and you may feel it necessary to retreat from a "crazy" society. This could cripple the development of your personality, and you might retain an emotional childishness throughout your life. The meaning of the aspects will be taken up in Chapter 12. Meanwhile, check the life activity governed by the House occupied by Capricorn on your chart (see Table 1) for a clearer picture of Saturn's influence on your conservatism and "realistic" attitude.

SATURN IN AQUARIUS ♄ ♒

Saturn in Aquarius on your chart affects the stability of your personality (or lack of it) and your ability to acquire knowledge, especially scientific or technical knowledge. Aquarius is ruled by Uranus, which has been nicknamed "the disruptor" because of its eccentric orbit. If your Saturn is well aspected to other elements, the stable influence of this planet can offset any extremes in your personality, either in your temperament or tastes, so that your chances of becoming well rounded are good. You have a natural flair for science or technology, as your analytical sense is keen, and could probably do well in these fields. You may well have talent that could be exploited successfully in the world of entertainment. You have an original approach and are attracted to novelty, but realize the foolishness of going to the extreme edge of fashion, deportment, etc. If your Saturn is badly aspected, on the other hand, the eccentricities of your personality may be accented, and there can be a tendency to "nerves" or unstable temperament, especially if entertainment is your field. You will need to keep in good shape, mentally and physically. The meaning of the aspects will be taken up in Chapter 12. Meanwhile, check the life activity governed by the House occupied by Aquarius on your chart (see Table 1) for a clearer picture of Saturn's influence on your stability and analytical traits.

TABLE 9 323

Table 9. POSITIONS OF SATURN (1890 TO 1975)

Dates	Sign	Symbol
Jan. 1 to Feb. 24, 1890	Leo	♌
Feb. 25 to June 27, 1890	Cancer	♋
June 28, 1890 to Oct. 26, 1891	Leo	♌
Oct. 27, 1891 to Mar. 30, 1892	Virgo	♍
Mar. 31 to July 17, 1892	Leo	♌
July 18, 1892 to Nov. 28, 1893	Virgo	♍
Nov. 29, 1893 to Apr. 13, 1894	Libra	♎
Apr. 14 to Aug. 24, 1894	Virgo	♍
Aug. 25, 1894 to Jan. 15, 1896	Libra	♎
Jan. 16 to Apr. 9, 1896	Scorpio	♏
Apr. 10 to Oct. 8, 1896	Libra	♎
Oct. 9, 1896 to Nov. 27, 1898	Scorpio	♏
Nov. 28, 1898 to Jan. 26, 1901	Ophiuchus	⚕
Jan. 27 to Aug. 11, 1901	Sagittarius	♐
Aug. 12 to Oct. 16, 1901	Ophiuchus	⚕
Oct. 17, 1901 to Mar. 22, 1903	Sagittarius	♐
Mar. 23 to July 20, 1903	Capricorn	♑
July 21 to Dec. 18, 1903	Sagittarius	♐
Dec. 19, 1903 to May 27, 1905	Capricorn	♑
May 28 to June 30, 1905	Aquarius	♒
July 1, 1905 to Feb. 1, 1906	Capricorn	♑
Feb. 2, 1906 to Mar. 18, 1908	Aquarius	♒
Mar. 19, 1908 to Apr. 11, 1910	Pisces	♓
Apr. 12, 1910 to Apr. 21, 1912	Aries	♈
Apr. 22, 1912 to Aug. 7, 1913	Cetus	⬎
Aug. 8 to Nov. 24, 1913	Taurus	♉
Nov. 25, 1913 to Apr. 25, 1914	Cetus	⬎
Apr. 26, 1914 to Aug. 4, 1915	Taurus	♉
Aug. 5, 1915 to Feb. 4, 1916	Gemini	♊
Feb. 5 to Apr. 15, 1916	Taurus	♉
Apr. 16, 1916 to Aug. 7, 1917	Gemini	♊
Aug. 8, 1917 to Aug. 11, 1919	Cancer	♋
Aug. 12, 1919 to Sept. 1, 1921	Leo	♌
Sept. 2, 1921 to Oct. 5, 1923	Virgo	♍
Oct. 6, 1923 to Nov. 14, 1925	Libra	♎
Nov. 15, 1925 to Jan. 1, 1928	Scorpio	♏
Jan. 2 to July 8, 1928	Ophiuchus	⚕
July 9 to Sept. 23, 1928	Scorpio	♏
Sept. 24, 1928 to Mar. 12, 1930	Ophiuchus	⚕

continued

Dates	Sign	Symbol
Mar. 13 to May 31, 1930	Sagittarius	♐
June 1 to Dec. 4, 1930	Ophiuchus	⛎
Dec. 5, 1930 to Jan. 22, 1933	Sagittarius	♐
Jan. 23, 1933 to Mar. 8, 1935	Capricorn	♑
Mar. 9, 1935 to Apr. 24, 1937	Aquarius	♒
Apr. 25 to Oct. 17, 1937	Pisces	♓
Oct. 18, 1937 to Jan. 13, 1938	Aquarius	♒
Jan. 14, 1938 to May 19, 1939	Pisces	♓
May 20 to Nov. 19, 1939	Aries	♈
Nov. 20, 1939 to Feb. 2, 1940	Pisces	♓
Feb. 3, 1940 to May 29, 1941	Aries	♈
May 30, 1941 to June 4, 1943	Cetus	⬎
June 5, 1943 to Oct. 10, 1944	Taurus	♉
Oct. 11 to Nov. 3, 1944	Gemini	♊
Nov. 4, 1944 to June 7, 1945	Taurus	♉
June 8, 1945 to Sept. 19, 1946	Gemini	♊
Sept. 20, 1946 to Jan 23, 1947	Cancer	♋
Jan. 24 to June 9, 1947	Gemini	♊
June 10, 1947 to Sept. 18, 1948	Cancer	♋
Sept. 19, 1948 to Apr. 2, 1949	Leo	♌
Apr. 3 to May 28, 1949	Cancer	♋
May 29, 1949 to Oct. 9, 1950	Leo	♌
Oct. 10, 1950 to May 15, 1951	Virgo	♍
May 16 to June 9, 1951	Leo	♌
June 10, 1951 to Nov. 10, 1952	Virgo	♍
Nov. 11, 1952 to May 16, 1953	Libra	♎
May 17 to July 30, 1953	Virgo	♍
July 31, 1953 to Dec. 24, 1954	Libra	♎
Dec. 25, 1954 to May 11, 1955	Scorpio	♏
May 12 to Sept. 21, 1955	Libra	♎
Sept. 22, 1955 to Feb. 23, 1957	Scorpio	♏
Feb. 24 to Apr. 20, 1957	Ophiuchus	⛎
Apr. 21 to Nov. 11, 1957	Scorpio	♏
Nov. 12, 1957 to Jan. 10, 1960	Ophiuchus	⛎
Jan. 11, 1960 to Mar. 2, 1962	Sagittarius	♐
Mar. 3 to Aug. 20, 1962	Capricorn	♑
Aug. 21 to Nov. 27, 1962	Sagittarius	♐
Nov. 28, 1962 to Apr. 20, 1964	Capricorn	♑
Apr. 21 to Aug. 11, 1964	Aquarius	♒
Aug. 12, 1964 to Jan. 14, 1965	Capricorn	♑
Jan. 15, 1965 to Mar. 3, 1967	Aquarius	♒

TABLE 9 325

continued

Dates	Sign	Symbol
Mar. 4, 1967 to Mar. 26, 1969	Pisces	♓
Mar. 27, 1969 to July 18, 1970	Aries	♈
July 19 to Oct. 23, 1970	Cetus	⬯
Oct. 24, 1970 to Apr. 4, 1971	Aries	♈
Apr. 5, 1971 to July 16, 1972	Cetus	⬯
July 17 to Dec. 14, 1972	Taurus	♉
Dec. 15, 1972 to Apr. 2, 1973	Cetus	⬯
Apr. 3, 1973 to July 18, 1974	Taurus	♉
July 19, 1974 to Dec. 31, 1975	Gemini	♊

9: Uranus

♅

ALTHOUGH MUCH SMALLER than the giants Jupiter and Saturn, Uranus is so much larger than Mercury, Venus, the earth, and Mars that it is classed as a giant planet of the solar system. Seventh of the nine known planets, it was named for the ancient sky god. Uranus has a slightly greenish color and is the center of a family of five moons.

Uranus is truly one of the outer planets. All of the planets we have studied so far are visible with the naked eye if you know where to look; Uranus can be seen only through a large telescope. It was unknown to the ancients, who had no such instruments, and was not discovered until 1781 by Sir William Herschel.

The surface of Uranus is frozen solid. This planet is so far from the sun that, even on its sunlit side, its temperature never rises above 274°F. below zero. When our astronauts eventually reach Uranus, they will need well-heated suits! It is highly unlikely that they will find any kind of life there.

The unmanned spacecraft *Pioneer 10*, which is on its way to Jupiter at this writing, has been programmed to fly by Uranus on its Grand Tour of the outer planets. It will take years for *Pioneer 10* to reach Uranus, of course, but—if the mission is successful—it will send back the first non-astronomical data on this far planet.

A notable feature of Uranus is the eccentricity of its orbit. Its distance from the sun can vary by as much as 166 million miles, and its axis is tilted so that the north pole of Uranus is sometimes pointed at the earth.

As stated above, Uranus is the seventh of the nine known planets of the solar system. Being farther from the sun, its orbit (or year) is much longer than that of any of the planets we have studied so far. It takes Uranus 84 years to make one circuit of the sun, as compared with 29.46 years for Saturn and 11.86 years for Jupiter. Uranus also exhibits the retrograde motion described earlier, so that it sometimes appears to be moving backward.

MEANING OF URANUS IN HOROSCOPE

As previously mentioned, Uranus moves much slower than the earth. Its orbit is 84 years, and it moves through only 4 degrees a year. You would have to live a long life to observe the motion of Uranus through all 14 constellations (signs) of the Zodiac. It sometimes remains in one sign for six or seven years, then (because of its retrograde motion) will remain in another for only a few months.

Uranus is an object of dispute among astrologers. Some claim that its influence is beneficent, especially where science, mechanics, and invention are concerned; others have nicknamed this planet "the disruptor" (because of its eccentric orbit) and say that Uranus-ruled natives tend to have disruptive personalities because of this planet's rule. It must be remembered, however, that the influence of any planet can be strengthened or lessened by its relationship (aspects) to other elements in the horoscope.

The fact that the discovery of Uranus more or less coincided with the industrial revolution of the nineteenth century may be responsible for the association many astrologers make of this planet with drastic changes and revolution or rebellion. It may also account for Uranus being identified with mechanical invention, technology, and analysis. In any case, Uranus, with its eccentric orbit, does seem to affect these areas in natives with this planet strongly placed in their horoscopes.

Uranus is the planetary ruler of Aquarius, so this planet is especially important if Aquarius is your sun sign. Whether or not you were born when the sun was in Aquarius (February 22 to March 20), you may be an Aquarius type if you have a group of strong planets in this sign. Since we have now entered (or are about to enter—another dispute) the Age of Aquarius, the planetary ruler of this sign has come into some prominence in astrological circles. Thus, although it is so far from the sun, Uranus can be an important element in your chart.

What does the Age of Aquarius mean for us? I mentioned some of the spiritual possibilities at the end of Chapter 2. At the moment, there seems to be a strong resurgence of religious feeling, especially among the young. "Jesus freaks" are to be seen everywhere, and *Jesus Christ Superstar* has been a hit musical on Broadway. There is no abatement in the interest in eastern religions and philosophies. A friend of mine (a Leo) is writing a book, *Now and Zen*, to bring Zen Buddhism into line with western consciousness. And the interest in the occult goes on. At the same time, science and technology are surging ahead. The moon shots are still the most spectacular, but the discoveries in biology, genetics, medicine, and cryonics will probably have a more far-reaching effect upon mankind. Wars, rebellion, riots, crime, and general unrest continue to plague the planet Earth.

This is the situation as the Age of Aquarius dawns. Its overall meaning to you is still largely unknown. Your horoscope will help you to understand your place in this often bewildering and frightening environment, but too much faith should not be placed in it. The horoscope can be a valuable tool, an aid in self-understanding, but there are so many unknowns in the human equation that it would be foolish to rely exclusively on one source of knowledge and possible comfort. "Progress" is accelerating, and chaos is apparently waiting in the wings. What is urgently needed is for each individual to learn to know himself *and* his world. The Age of Aquarius is potentially a great one for the human race, but we must be prepared for changes that may come faster than we can digest them.

To place the symbol of Uranus (♅) on your chart, turn to Table 10 at the end of this chapter. Here the positions of Uranus are listed for each year from 1890 to 1975. Find the span of time that includes your birthdate. It should be noted that Table 10 lists *inclusive* sets of dates. That is, if you were born on July 17, 1945, and the table lists Uranus in Cetus from April 19, 1940 to July 17, 1945, Uranus was still in Cetus on your birthdate, since it did not enter Taurus until July 18, 1945.

To continue our example of someone born on January 1, 1940, with Aquarius rising, Figure 10 shows his chart with the symbol of Uranus entered. In Table 10, it is shown that Uranus was in Aries on January 1, 1940; therefore, the symbol of Uranus is entered in the House occupied by Aries, which (on his chart) is the third House.

INTERPRETATION

General interpretations of the meaning of Uranus in each of the 14 signs are given below. In reading these, it should be remembered that Uranus does not have an *absolute* meaning; whether it is a help or a hindrance depends upon its relationship to other elements of your chart. Also, the House occupied by Uranus affects its interpretation. Our imaginary subject (Figure 10) was born with Uranus in Aries, which is his third House. After reading the interpretation of Uranus in Aries, he should turn back to Table 1 (p. 4), which lists the basic meanings of the Houses.

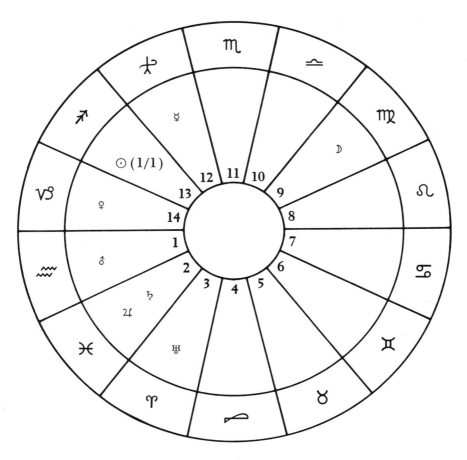

Figure 10. Placement of Uranus on chart of subject born on January 1, 1940, with Aquarius rising

The life activity governed by that particular House will be enhanced by the presence of Uranus. This is also true of the two remaining planets, Neptune and Pluto, which we will be placing in the chapters to follow.

URANUS IN PISCES ♅ ♓

Uranus in Pisces on your chart enhances the strength and quality of your belief. This includes your belief in yourself as well as religious convictions, political affiliations, etc. Pisces is ruled by Neptune, which is often associated with spiritual (psychic) matters. The combination of the sky god (Uranus) and the sea god (Neptune) symbolizes a synthesis of consciousness (ego) with the unconscious. If your Uranus is in good aspect to other elements, you can achieve this synthesis that Jung called *individuation*, which is necessary for the development of a well-balanced and mature personality. Whether or not you attend church or temple, you are a deeply religious person. You believe in yourself and in mankind; that is, you believe in God. You are strongly individualistic, analytical without being overly critical, and are attracted to the new. If your Uranus is in bad aspect, however, the eccentricity symbolized by the orbit of Uranus may overcome the steadiness of your faith. This could result in dogmatism or in nervousness and displays of temperament, along with too-sharp criticism of your associates and friends. The meaning of the aspects will be taken up in Chapter 12. In the meantime, check the life activity governed by the House occupied by Pisces on your chart (see Table 1) for a clearer picture of the influence of Uranus on your belief.

URANUS IN ARIES ♅ ♈

Uranus in Aries on your chart enhances the strength of your will and its application to the problems of life. Aries is ruled by Mars, whose aggressive nature we have discussed earlier. If your Uranus is well aspected to other elements, your will may find a good outlet in being applied to scientific, technical, or mechanical problems. Whether or not you enter a field dealing with such, your strong analytical ability can be applied to many areas of life. Your chances for success are good, as you have both drive and the type of mind most called for in our twentieth-century technocracy. You may very well be inventive, a good leader or boss, and clever at working out novel solutions to old problems. If you do not place too much reliance on your will but give intuition its due place, a happy and successful life is within your grasp. If your Uranus is badly aspected, on the other hand, you may be tempted to use your will power in an overbearing way (which usually ensures unpopularity) or to become cranky and inconsistent in its applications. You will need to strive for balance and keep in top condition, both mentally and physically. The meaning of the aspects will be taken up in Chapter 12. In the meantime, check the life activity governed by the House occupied by Aries on your chart (see Table 1) for a clearer picture of the influence of Uranus on your will and its application to life.

URANUS IN CETUS ♅ ♎

Uranus in Cetus on your chart enhances the color and strength of your personality and your career potential. Cetus is ruled by Jupiter, the "greater fortune," so here we have a combination of the sky god Uranus with the chief god Jupiter. These deities both symbolize consciousness, so their combination should make for an alert, highly aware person. If your Uranus is in good aspect to other elements, you are probably well-rounded in your tastes and abilities. You have a good deal of charm and are popular with members of both sexes. A happy balance between the mind and the emotions can well lead to personal fulfillment and success in many fields, although you may have a special talent for entertainment or the graphic arts. You like people, and prefer to do your work in human surroundings rather than in an ivory tower. If your Uranus is in bad aspect, however, you may become a victim of "artistic" temperament, be subject to fits of "nerves," and use your analytical ability too sharply in criticizing your friends, co-workers, and spouse. Another danger is being too conscious, ignoring the messages from the unconscious that come in dreams and "visions." The meaning of the aspects will be taken up in Chapter 12. In the meantime, check the life activity governed by the House occupied by Cetus on your chart (see Table 1) for a clearer picture of the influence of Uranus on your personality traits and career possibilities.

URANUS IN TAURUS ♅ ♉

Uranus in Taurus on your chart enhances the emotional side of your nature and your talent, especially for music. Taurus is ruled by Venus. The combination of masculine Uranus and feminine Venus can lead to the development of a beautifully balanced personality, provided that your Uranus is well aspected to other elements in your chart. If it is, the analytical, inventive, mental side symbolized by Uranus can be properly synthesized with the emotional, feminine side represented by Venus. You probably make friends easily and are popular, especially with members of the opposite sex. You are not baffled by social contacts, and have an intuitive understanding of nearly everyone you meet. You could well be gifted musically, especially as a composer or arranger, or could have a successful career in the physical sciences, mathematics, or technology. If your Uranus is badly aspected to other elements, however, you may become erratic in your emotional attachments, being too shy where you should be bold or overreacting to emotional situations. Try not to let any emotional uncertainty make you withdraw from the society of your fellows. You need them, and they need you. The meaning of the aspects will be taken up in Chapter 12. In the meantime, check the life activity governed by the House occupied by Taurus on your chart (see Table 1) for a clearer picture of the influence of Uranus on your emotional life and the deployment of your talent.

URANUS IN GEMINI ♅ ♊

Uranus in Gemini on your chart enhances your intellect, versatility, and communicative powers. Gemini is ruled by Mercury. If your Uranus is in good aspect to other elements, this combination could well mean the development of a powerful mind, an agile wit, and ease in communicating your thoughts and feelings (both orally and in writing). You tend to be mentally alert at all times, and the scientific advances of our era have a special fascination for you, whether or not you are employed in a scientific or technical field. You speak well without being overly aggressive in attempts to dominate the conversation, and probably have a gift for writing. If you do, your talent is badly needed in our confusing times, as you can make the most complex subject clear and comprehensible to the layman. You would also make an excellent editor. If your Uranus is in bad aspect, on the other hand, your versatility may lead you into extreme situations; you may find yourself wearing too many hats or taking on more commitments than you have time or energy for. Keep a check on your enthusiasm for new projects when you already have a full schedule. The meaning of the aspects will be taken up in Chapter 12. In the meantime, check the life activity governed by the House occupied by Gemini on your chart (see Table 1) for a clearer picture of the influence of Uranus on your intellect and versatility.

URANUS IN CANCER ♅ ♋

Uranus in Cancer on your chart enhances the sensitivity of your emotional life and your conservatism. Cancer is ruled by the feminine moon, so the presence of masculine Uranus in this sign can mean a favorable balance between the mind and emotions, conscious and unconscious, masculine and feminine. If your Uranus is well aspected to other elements, your emotional sensitivity will be kept from dominating your personality by a strong analytical sense. You are at ease on social occasions and probably very popular with members of the opposite sex. Your sense of humor tends to be impish, and you may love to play practical jokes, especially if no one knows you are the originator. You can be successful in many fields; your innate understanding of both sexes serves you well, both socially and professionally. If your Uranus is badly aspected, however, there is a danger of emotional instability. This may be expressed in shyness, even with close friends, or in sudden bursts of temper followed by periods of depression. Always strive for balance in your outlook, and listen closely to that "inner" voice. The meaning of the aspects will be taken up in Chapter 12. In the meantime, check the life activity governed by the House occupied by Cancer on your chart (see Table 1) for a clearer picture of the influence of Uranus on your emotional sensitivity and conservative tendencies.

URANUS IN LEO ♅ ♌

Uranus in Leo on your chart enhances your sense of personal independence. Leo is ruled by the sun, the all-powerful center of our system of planets. If your Uranus is in good aspect to other elements, your analytical and critical faculties will be strengthened by this combination. You are independent in your thoughts and (within the law) your actions. You pride yourself on being self-supporting and a good provider for your dependents. In business, you would make an excellent executive, as you are probably a natural leader and unafraid of bold steps in such areas as the introduction of a new product or service. You are attracted to the new and different, but able to see through people and products whose only virtue is their novelty. You probably have many friends and are equally popular with your associates and subordinates. If your Uranus is in bad aspect, on the other hand, you may carry your independent attitude too far, alienating those around you by your inability to cooperate and give way when you are wrong. Or your analytical ability may go too far in the direction of destructive criticism. The meaning of the aspects will be taken up in Chapter 12. In the meantime, check the life activity governed by the House occupied by Leo on your chart (see Table 1) for a clearer picture of the influence of Uranus on your sense of personal independence.

URANUS IN VIRGO ♅ ♍

Uranus in Virgo on your chart enhances your individualistic traits and your analytical ability. Virgo is ruled by Mercury. If your Uranus is well aspected to other elements, your individualism will be strengthened and your personality made more colorful and progressive by the presence of this planet. Virgo types are known for their keen analytical ability, and this trait will receive a boost from Uranus, which is associated with analytical science, technology, and mechanical invention. You have the makings of a scientist or technician—the field of computer technology, for example, should be a natural for you. Your individualism, which may have earned you a nickname, keeps you from being just another cog in the machine, however; if the position you occupy demands too much conformity, and you cannot improve it, you will not hesitate to move on to one that gives freer play to your need for self-expression. If your Uranus is badly aspected, however, there is a real danger that your analysis may be misapplied. Picking a thing or person to pieces may well result in unpopularity and loneliness. The meaning of the aspects will be taken up in Chapter 12. In the meantime, check the life activity governed by the House occupied by Virgo on your chart (see Table 1) for a clearer picture of the influence of Uranus on your individualism and analytical ability.

URANUS IN LIBRA ♅ ♎

Uranus in Libra on your chart enhances your judgment and the expression of your talent, especially if you are gifted musically. Libra is ruled by Venus. If your Uranus is in good aspect to other elements, a good balance can be achieved between the masculine, analytical traits of Uranus and the feminine, intuitive qualities of Venus, resulting in a well-balanced personality. The law may be less a science than an art, but your innate talent for judgment, fortified by a strong analytical and critical faculty, could make you an excellent judge or lawyer, and would also be good for a career in politics. The ability to judge objectively can be equally valuable in all walks of life, of course, in personal and social life as well as in your career. You may also have a talent for music, which will probably seek expression in vocal rather than instrumental music. If your Uranus is in bad aspect, on the other hand, you may become erratic in your judgments and find your objectivity slipping into subjective prejudice and bias. A judge, above all else, must be able to keep his balance! The meaning of the aspects will be taken up in Chapter 12. In the meantime, check the life activity governed by the House occupied by Libra on your chart (see Table 1) for a clearer picture of the influence of Uranus on your ability to judge and possible musical talent.

URANUS IN SCORPIO ♅ ♏

Uranus in Scorpio on your chart enhances your humanistic ideals and your empathy—your sensitivity to the feelings and needs of others. Scorpio is ruled by Mars. If your Uranus is well aspected to other elements, the analytical traits associated with this planet can strengthen and make more active the intuitive sensitivity associated with Scorpio types. Your feeling for the needs of others, and willingness to help when you can, make you sought after as a friend and lover, and you are probably popular with members of both sexes. You would truly like to see a better, happier world for the human race, and your ability to analyze existing trends and situations leads you to formulate new and better ways and means of improving the human condition (whether on a personal, familial, or universal level). There is mysticism or poetry in your makeup, and you may well have an intuition for prophecy. Your extrasensory perception (ESP) may also be well developed. If your Uranus is badly aspected, however, your efforts to help your fellows may become erratic or you may feel overwhelmingly discouraged when your efforts fail. The meaning of the aspects will be taken up in Chapter 12. In the meantime, check the life activity governed by the House occupied by Scorpio on your chart (see Table 1) for a clearer picture of the influence of Uranus on your humanistic ideals and empathy.

URANUS IN OPHIUCHUS ♅ ⚕

Uranus in Ophiuchus on your chart enhances your resourcefulness and versatility, especially where talent is concerned. Ophiuchus is ruled by Pluto, which was named for a god of the underworld (the source of jewels, minerals, and other riches). If your Uranus is in good aspect to other elements, this combination could mean that you are endowed with a wealth of talents, as many Ophiuchus types are. If this is the case, your talent may well find good expression in the world of entertainment, where versatility and resourcefulness are highly valuable traits. Not only can you do several different "acts," but you can analyze current trends and come up with new and original ways of doing things. You like people, especially at parties, and are probably popular with members of both sexes. If your Uranus is in bad aspect, on the other hand, your talent may become untrustworthy so that you come to depend too much on inspiration and too little on hard work. Also, there is a danger that you may become overly critical of your contemporaries, when the target for such close analysis should be yourself! The meaning of the aspects will be taken up in Chapter 12. In the meantime, check the life activity governed by the House occupied by Ophiuchus on your chart (see Table 1) for a clearer picture of the influence of Uranus on your resourcefulness, talent, and versatility.

URANUS IN SAGITTARIUS ♅ ♐

Uranus in Sagittarius on your chart enhances your humanitarian conscience and your extraversion. Sagittarius is ruled by Jupiter, the "greater fortune," and is often thought to be the luckiest sign in the Zodiac. If your Uranus is well aspected to other elements, the generosity and "joviality" of Jupiter can be strengthened by the presence of Uranus, which supplies intellectual energy and analytical ability that Jupiter-ruled natives often lack. A love of the society of other people permeates almost everything you do. This trait makes you popular with members of both sexes, as your outgoing personality makes it hard not to like you. Although sociable and usually easygoing, you are also capable of hard work and would make an excellent executive; your subordinates would respect as well as like you, and you would be able to lead rather than drive them. If your Uranus is badly aspected, however, your analytical sense may not help you to spot phonies and bogus friends, who will take advantage of your friendliness and generosity. Be as sociable as you like, but it is foolish to expect honesty and fairness in everyone you meet. The meaning of the aspects will be taken up in Chapter 12. In the meantime, check the life activity governed by the House occupied by Sagittarius on your chart (see Table 1) for a clearer picture of the influence of Uranus on your humanitarian conscience and extraverted tendencies.

URANUS IN CAPRICORN ♅ ♑

Uranus in Capricorn on your chart enhances your sense of conservatism and tendency to be "realistic" in your view of life. Capricorn is ruled by Saturn. This combination is not necessarily a bad one. The restrictive traits symbolized by Saturn can be nicely balanced by the Uranian urge to analyze and to seek out the new and different. If your Uranus is in good aspect to other elements, you could well achieve such a balance in your personality. You like to get to the bottom of things and situations, and have the ability to see through the hastily erected facades that are often thrown up in our culture. You have your feet on the ground and don't like to make a move until you have examined all aspects of the situation. Your caution and conservatism can serve you well, both socially and in your career. If your Uranus is in bad aspect, on the other hand, you may become "hung up" on your desire to analyze and proceed with caution. If carried to extremes, this tendency could cripple the development of your personality so that an emotional childishness would prevail throughout your life. The meaning of the aspects will be taken up in Chapter 12. In the meantime, check the life activity governed by the House occupied by Capricorn on your chart (see Table 1) for a clearer picture of the influence of Uranus on your conservatism and "realistic" approach to life.

URANUS IN AQUARIUS ♅ ♒

Uranus in Aquarius on your chart enhances the stability of your personality (or its instability) and your analytical ability. Uranus is the planetary ruler of Aquarius, and the presence of Uranus in this sign approximately doubles its influence. If your Uranus is well aspected to other elements, you can be colorful and original without going to eccentric extremes so that people think you "weird." You have an original approach to life that makes you popular with people (of both sexes) who have similar tastes. You have a good mind, and are able to soak up knowledge easily, especially in scientific or technical fields. You have a flair for analysis, which can make you a valuable employee and possibly lead to a career as an inventor. You may also have a talent for entertainment. If your Uranus is badly aspected, however, you may develop an overly sensitive temperament that will make you difficult to work with. Also, your analytical ability can be overdone and make you unpopular. Analysis (taking apart) must be complemented by synthesis (putting together). The meaning of the aspects will be taken up in Chapter 12. In the meantime, check the life activity governed by the House occupied by Aquarius on your chart (see Table 1) for a clearer picture of the influence of Uranus on the stability of your personality and your analytical/critical sense.

Table 10. POSITIONS OF URANUS (1890 to 1975)

Dates	Sign	Symbol
Jan. 1, 1890 to Dec. 10, 1894	Libra	♎
Dec. 11, 1894 to May 15, 1895	Scorpio	♏
May 16 to Sept. 28, 1895	Libra	♎
Sept. 29, 1895 to Dec. 20, 1900	Scorpio	♏
Dec. 21, 1900 to July 8, 1901	Ophiuchus	⛎
July 9 to Oct. 4, 1901	Scorpio	♏
Oct. 5, 1901 to Feb. 4, 1907	Ophiuchus	⛎
Feb. 5 to July 5, 1907	Sagittarius	♐
July 6 to Nov. 26, 1907	Ophiuchus	⛎
Nov. 27, 1907 to Mar. 26, 1913	Sagittarius	♐
Mar. 27 to June 29, 1913	Capricorn	♑
June 30, 1913 to Jan. 11, 1914	Sagittarius	♐
Jan. 12, 1914 to Mar. 9, 1920	Capricorn	♑
Mar. 10 to Sept. 22, 1920	Aquarius	♒
Sept. 23 to Dec. 27, 1920	Capricorn	♑
Dec. 28, 1920 to Mar. 30, 1927	Aquarius	♒
Mar. 31 to Nov. 4, 1927	Pisces	♓
Nov. 5, 1927 to Jan. 12, 1928	Aquarius	♒
Jan. 13, 1928 to May 25, 1933	Pisces	♓
May 26 to Oct. 12, 1933	Aries	♈
Oct. 13, 1933 to Mar. 17, 1934	Pisces	♓
Mar. 18 1934 to July 2, 1939	Aries	♈
July 3 to Oct. 26, 1939	Cetus	⚲
Oct. 27, 1939 to Apr. 18, 1940	Aries	♈
Apr. 19, 1940 to July 17, 1945	Cetus	⚲
July 18 to Dec. 1, 1945	Taurus	♉
Dec. 2, 1945 to May 6, 1946	Cetus	⚲
May 7, 1946 to July 18, 1951	Taurus	♉
July 19, 1951 to Feb. 3, 1952	Gemini	♊
Feb. 4 to Apr. 28, 1952	Taurus	♉
Apr. 29, 1952 to Sept. 17, 1956	Gemini	♊
Sept. 18, 1956 to Jan. 7, 1957	Cancer	♋
Jan. 8 to July 2, 1957	Gemini	♊
July 3, 1957 to Nov. 1, 1961	Cancer	♋
Nov. 2, 1961 to Jan. 10, 1962	Leo	♌
Jan. 11 to Aug. 10, 1962	Cancer	♋
Aug. 11, 1962 to Oct. 1, 1967	Leo	♌
Oct. 2, 1967 to Apr. 25, 1968	Virgo	♍
Apr. 26 to July 8, 1968	Leo	♌

TABLE 10 339

continued

Dates	Sign	Symbol
July 9, 1968 to Dec. 2, 1972	Virgo	♍
Dec. 3, 1972 to Mar. 27, 1973	Libra	♎
Mar. 28 to Sept. 17, 1973	Virgo	♍
Sept. 18, 1973 to Dec. 31, 1975	Libra	♎

10: Neptune

Like Uranus, Neptune is much smaller than Jupiter and Saturn, but so much larger than the inner planets (and Pluto) that it is classed as a giant planet of the solar system. Eighth of the nine known planets, it was named for the ancient god of the sea. Neptune is blue-green in color, and is circled by two moons, appropriately named Triton and Nereid.

Only Pluto is farther from the sun than Neptune. It is invisible to the naked eye, and a large telescope is necessary to observe it. It was, of course, unknown to the ancients, who knew of no planets beyond Saturn. Neptune was discovered in 1846 by Johann Galle. Before its actual discovery, its existence was predicted by Urbain Leverrier and John C. Adams, who (working independently) concluded that, because of an irregularity in the movement of Uranus, another planet must exist beyond the orbit of Uranus.

The surface of Neptune is frozen, of course, and it is unlikely that our astronauts will find any kind of life on this planet. It is so far away that it will probably be a long time before they venture that far into space.

The Grand Tour of the outer planets that is being conducted by the unmanned spacecraft *Pioneer 10* will include Neptune in its itinerary. If the mission is successful, *Pioneer 10* will send back the first nonastronomical information on this planet. At this writing, however, the spacecraft is still on its way to Jupiter, so it will be many years before it can reach Neptune.

As stated above, Neptune is the eighth of the nine known planets of the solar system. Being farther from the sun, its orbit (or year) is much longer than that of the other planets we have so far studied. It takes

Neptune 164.79 years to make one circuit of the sun, as compared with 84 years for Uranus and 29.46 years for Saturn. Neptune also exhibits the retrograde motion described earlier, so that it sometimes appears to be moving backward.

MEANING OF NEPTUNE IN HOROSCOPE

As previously mentioned, Neptune moves much slower than the earth. Its orbit is 164.79 years, and it moves through only 2 degrees a year. Thus, in the span of time covered by this book (1890 to 1975), it has not moved through all of the constellations (signs) of the Zodiac. Neptune was in Cetus on New Year's Day, 1890, and will be in Scorpio on New Year's Eve, 1975. In 86 years, then, it passes through only 8 of the 14 signs. It sometimes remains in one sign for ten or eleven years, then (because of its retrograde motion) will remain in another for only a few months.

Neptune was named for the ancient god of the sea, whom the Greeks knew as Poseidon. Like Saturn, he was the ruler of a vast and mysterious realm. Even today, we know more about the surface of the moon than we do of the farthest depths of the sea. The keywords of Neptune are *nebulousness* and *impressionability*. This planet is usually associated with matters of the spirit—with belief that goes beyond rational science and everyday affairs.

Since Neptune was not discovered until the nineteenth century, it is only natural that there should be dispute among astrologers as to its meaning and influence in the horoscope. This is indeed the case. There being no ancient body of writings about this planet, one astrologer has called Neptune "sinister," whereas others think it a beneficent influence in your chart. It must be remembered, however, that the influence of any planet can be strengthened or lessened by its relationship (aspects) to other elements of the horoscope.

Neptune is the planetary ruler of Pisces, so this planet is especially important if Pisces is your sun sign. The connection of Neptune and Pisces is a natural one, since the symbol of Pisces is a stylized image of two fish, swimming in opposite directions, and a fish is obviously at home in the sea.

We are entering the Age of Aquarius, which means that we are leaving the Age of Pisces. Each such age lasts for over two thousand years. It can be said that the Age of Pisces was dominated by the figure of Jesus Christ and the impact of his teachings upon mankind. The age that is closing was one of a great spiritual revolution—the birth and spread of Christianity. This is symbolized well by Pisces, for an ancient symbol of Christ was the fish. The early Christians used to identify one another by drawing (and then hastily erasing) a stylized fish. It is well known that St. Peter was a fisherman, and Jesus said to him: "Come with me, and I will teach you to be a fisher of men."

Does this mean that mankind is leaving an age of faith and is entering an age of faithlessness or one that will see a revival of pagan idolatry? I do not think so. The Age of Pisces began with the Christian revolution against the idols of Rome, and western consciousness was dominated by the Church for many centuries. After the Renaissance had revived interest in classical knowledge, the Age of Pisces began to draw to a close with the rise of scientific "enlightenment" in the eighteenth century. Science has been in the driver's seat ever since. As ages go, however, the rise of science has been quite recent. The Age of Pisces was an age of faith; the dawning Age of Aquarius will, I feel, be an age of even greater faith. Most people have learned by now that science is not enough. A greater and more all-embracing faith is needed for men and women of the twentieth century, their children, and their descendants.

What form this faith will take is hard to see at the moment, but we can see its harbingers in the widespread rebellion of the young against the ways of their parents. The psyche is just as real as the world of material "reality." The young intuit this, and their rebellion (which sometimes takes foolish forms) is founded on their belief that a richer and more meaningful life is possible than what is offered by bigger and better computers, faster and more expensive cars, and the suburban battle against crabgrass. They may go off in wrong directions, but the spirit of their rebellion is as true and pure as that of the Christian revolt against the iron rule of Rome.

It should be clear, then, why Pisces is associated with spiritual matters. If Pisces is concerned with them, then so is its ruling planet, Neptune.

To place the symbol of Neptune (Ψ) on your chart, turn to Table 11 at the end of this chapter. Here the positions of Neptune are listed for each year from 1890 to 1975. Find the span of time that includes your birthdate. It should be noted that Table 11 lists *inclusive* sets of dates. That is, if you were born on July 29, 1941, and the table lists Neptune in Leo from April 11 to July 29, 1941, Neptune was still in Leo on your birthdate, since it did not enter Virgo until July 30, 1941.

To continue our example of someone born on January 1, 1940, with Aquarius rising, Figure 11 shows his chart with the symbol of Neptune entered. In Table 11, it is shown that Neptune was in Virgo on January 1, 1940; therefore, the symbol of Neptune is entered in the House occupied by Virgo, which (on his chart) is the ninth House.

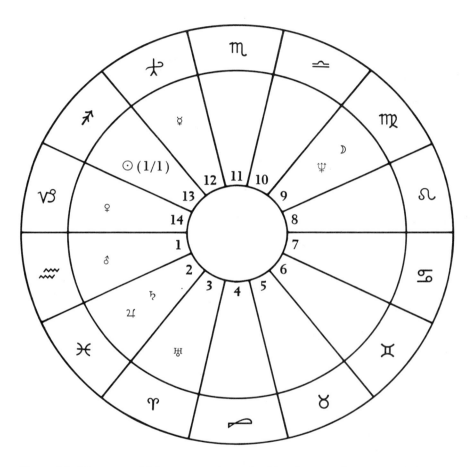

Figure 11. Placement of Neptune on chart of subject born on January 1, 1940, with Aquarius rising

INTERPRETATION

General interpretations of the meaning of Neptune are given below. It should be noted that, in the span of time covered by this book (1890 to 1975), Neptune did not enter all 14 signs. Therefore, interpretations of Neptune in the signs from Cetus to Scorpio are given, and none is made for Ophiuchus, Sagittarius, Capricorn, Aquarius, Pisces, and Aries. In reading these, it should be remembered that Neptune does not have an *absolute* meaning; whether it is a help or a hindrance depends upon its relationship to other elements of your chart. Also, the House occupied by Neptune affects its interpretation. Our imaginary subject (Figure 11) was born with Neptune in Virgo, which is his ninth House. After reading the interpretation of Neptune in Virgo, he should turn back to Table 1 (p. 4), which lists the basic meanings of the Houses. The life activity governed by that particular House will be enhanced by the presence of Neptune. This is also true of Pluto, which we will be placing in the next chapter.

NEPTUNE IN CETUS ♆ ♋

Neptune in Cetus on your chart affects your spiritual (or psychic) life, especially as it is expressed in your basic personality and career or life style. Cetus is ruled by Jupiter, the "greater fortune," so—if your Neptune is in good aspect to other elements in your chart—this combination can mean good luck, fortune, and success in all of your affairs that have to do with the spirit. The unconscious part of the psyche is the source of all religious or spiritual knowledge and inspiration, and the sea (Neptune's realm) is a prime symbol of the unconscious. A happy blend of consciousness (symbolized by Jupiter) and the "dark" country below the level of consciousness is thus possible for you. You are mature in your outlook, and enjoy the society of all kinds of people, especially the young. If your Neptune is in bad aspect to other elements, however, you may lose some of your spiritual autonomy and come to rely too much on Authority, especially if represented by the iron-clad rules of your church, temple, or sect. Remember that the spirit can only flower in freedom; do not attempt to enclose it in a cage. The meaning of the aspects will be taken up in Chapter 12. Meanwhile, check the life activity governed by the House occupied by Cetus on your chart (see Table 1) for a clearer picture of Neptune's influence on the spiritual side of your personality and life style.

NEPTUNE IN TAURUS ♆ ♉

Neptune in Taurus on your chart affects the emotional side of your spiritual nature and enhances your talent, especially if your field is music. Taurus is ruled by Venus. If your Neptune is well aspected to other elements, this combination of feminine Venus and masculine Neptune can bode well for the full development of a well-balanced personality. Jung said that the goal of individual development is *individuation:* the mature state where all parts of the psyche, conscious and unconscious, are brought into a state of mutually complementary balance. You can achieve this poise and maturity, especially necessary in the second half of life, when the outer battles of life have been faced and it is necessary to look within. Your emotions are under control without being unduly suppressed. You are probably strongly religious, whether or not you attend church or temple, and your emotional spirituality may well find expression in the field of music. If your Neptune is badly aspected, on the other hand, your emotions may get the better of your mind, thus losing for you that precious state of equilibrium. The meaning of the aspects will be taken up in Chapter 12. Meanwhile, check the life activity governed by the House occupied by Taurus on your chart (see Table 1) for a clearer picture of Neptune's influence on the emotional side of your psyche and its possible expression in music.

NEPTUNE IN GEMINI ♆ ♊

Neptune in Gemini on your chart affects your intellect, communicative powers, and versatility as these are used in the service of your spirit (or psyche). Gemini is ruled by Mercury. Although "spirited," Mercury-ruled natives often rely too exclusively on their conscious minds, wits, and ability to express themselves, tending to ignore the powerful spiritual upthrusts from the unconscious. If your Neptune is in good aspect to other elements, you can avoid this top-heavy state and let *all* sides of your personality develop harmoniously. You have a good mind, a ready sense of humor, and are able to express yourself clearly. These valuable traits, when bolstered by a properly exercised spirit, can mean a well-rounded personality. You are probably both popular and successful, especially if your field involves communication (oral or written). If your Neptune is in bad aspect, however, you may let your versatility and widespread interests lead you to spread yourself too thin; *concentration* is also necessary for success and fulfillment. Or you may let "mental" occupations distract you from the spirit, which should receive equal attention. The meaning of the aspects will be taken up in Chapter 12. Meanwhile, check

346 THE ASTROLOGY 14 HOROSCOPE

the life activity governed by the House occupied by Gemini on your chart (see Table 1) for a clearer picture of Neptune's influence on the spiritual uses of your intellect, wit, and versatility.

NEPTUNE IN CANCER ♆ ♋

Neptune in Cancer on your chart affects your emotional sensitivity to spiritual concerns and your conservative tendencies. Cancer is ruled by the moon. If your Neptune is well aspected to other elements, the femininity symbolized by the moon can be in excellent balance with the masculine traits represented by Neptune, leading to the full development of all sides of your personality. Women are often more "spiritual" than men; they are in closer touch with the emotion and thus with the unconscious, which is the source of most spiritual life. The moon's influence can increase this sensitivity if you are a woman and bring it into fuller play if you are a man. You are probably strongly religious and may even be regarded as psychic. Being in touch with your psychic roots lends you strength and endurance for life's trials. If your Neptune is badly aspected, on the other hand, you may react overemotionally to situations that call for a cool head and clear thinking. Remember that *both* sides of the psyche, conscious and unconscious, must be developed if you are to attain happiness and maturity. The meaning of the aspects will be taken up in Chapter 12. Meanwhile, check the life activity governed by the House occupied by Cancer on your chart (see Table 1) for a clearer picture of Neptune's influence on your conservatism and emotional approach to matters of the spirit.

NEPTUNE IN LEO ♆ ♌

Neptune in Leo on your chart affects your personal sense of independence concerning spiritual affairs. Leo is ruled by the sun. Just as the sun shines alone at the center of the solar system, you, too—however small your realm—would like to stand and shine alone. If your Neptune is in good aspect to other elements, you may be able to achieve this (within the limits of human possibility). The conscious, "mental" drive symbolized by the sun can be balanced by the spirituality represented by Neptune, which has its source in the unconscious. You are probably a natural leader and would rather work alone than be subservient to others. In spiritual matters, you insist on making up your own mind and listening to the voice of your conscience. Though your belief may be strong, you find it hard to be just another sheep in the fold. The world needs such free spirits. If your Neptune is in bad aspect, however, you can easily go too far in your desire for independence. Remember that the spiritual wisdom of the past has much to teach you, however strongly you insist on interpreting it your own way. A lost sheep can be a very lonely creature. The meaning of the aspects will be taken up in Chapter 12. Meanwhile, check the life activity governed by the House occupied by Leo on your chart (see Table 1) for a clearer picture of Neptune's influence on your spiritual independence.

NEPTUNE IN VIRGO ♆ ♍

Neptune in Virgo on your chart affects your individualism and analytical ability, especially as these are applied to matters of belief. Virgo is ruled by Mercury. If your Neptune is well aspected to other elements, it is possible for you to achieve a good balance between the mental, analytical traits symbolized by Mercury in this sign and the emotional, spiritual values represented by Neptune. Although it is necessary for you to understand and check something out before you can believe in it, your belief may still be strong. Some of the most powerful analytical minds in history were those of people who were also deeply spiritual. Your pronounced individualism may keep you from joining a church or temple, but this does not mean that you are "outside the fold." Your individualism and analytical streak can stand you in as good stead in matters of the spirit as they do in business or everyday affairs. If your Neptune is badly aspected, on the other hand, you may find it hard to join any group and can misuse your analysis, trying to apply it to matters that call for faith or intuition. The meaning of the aspects will be taken up in Chapter 12. Meanwhile, check the life activity governed by the House occupied by Virgo on your chart (see Table 1) for a clearer picture of Neptune's influence on the spiritual application of your individualism and analytical ability.

NEPTUNE IN LIBRA ♆ ♎

Neptune in Libra on your chart affects the spiritual quality of your judgment and, if you are talented, the expression of that talent in music. Libra is ruled by Venus. If your Neptune is in good aspect to other elements, the feminine, emotional side symbolized by Venus can be balanced by the spiritual drive of masculine Neptune to permit the achievement of a happy, well-balanced personality. Your innate ability to make correct, objective judgments of people, things, and situations can be applied not only in a legal (mundane) sense, but also in spiritual affairs and matters of belief. This includes belief in yourself, your country or political party, and in the philosophical attitude with which you interpret life. You are not fooled by Bible-thumpers, but can judge just what faith and belief are right for you. If talented, your art may well be that of vocal music. If your Neptune is in bad aspect, however, you may develop lack of self-confidence in your judgments and opinions, or may become dogmatic in your assertions. A proper balance is necessary to avoid the extremes of fanaticism and atheism. The meaning of the aspects will be taken up in Chapter 12. Meanwhile, check the life activity governed by the House occupied by Libra on your chart (see Table 1) for a clearer picture of Neptune's influence on your judgment and talent, especially in spiritual applications.

NEPTUNE IN SCORPIO ♆ ♏

Neptune in Scorpio on your chart affects your empathy—your ability to "feel for" others—and your spiritual sensitivity. Scorpio is ruled by Mars, whose masculine aggressiveness is mainly *conscious*; this tendency can be offset by the spiritual depths represented by Neptune. If your Neptune is well aspected to other elements, you can achieve such a balance in your personality. You are probably a deeply spiritual person, whether or not you are religious in a formal sense, and idealistic in your belief that man's lot on earth can be greatly improved—if each of us will see to his own development and be willing to lend a helping hand to his neighbor. Your extrasensory perception (ESP) may be well developed, and you are sensitive to the "inner" voice of conscience as well as to the needs of others. If your Neptune is badly aspected, on the other hand, you may let yourself be unduly discouraged when your idealism and efforts to help meet with coldness or indifference in the world of human affairs. Many less sensitive people mistake kindness for weakness, and this often happens to Scorpio types. The meaning of the aspects will be taken up in Chapter 12. Meanwhile, check the life activity governed by the House occupied by Scorpio on your chart (see Table 1) for a clearer picture of Neptune's influence on your spiritual empathy and humanistic ideals.

TABLE 11 349

Table 11. POSITIONS OF NEPTUNE (1890 TO 1975)

Dates	Sign	Symbol
Jan. 1, 1890 to Aug. 25, 1894	Cetus	♉︎
Aug. 26 to Oct. 12, 1894	Taurus	♉
Oct. 13, 1894 to June 9, 1895	Cetus	♉︎
June 10, 1895 to Jan. 16, 1896	Taurus	♉
Jan. 17 to Apr. 2, 1896	Cetus	♉︎
Apr. 3, 1896 to July 16, 1906	Taurus	♉
July 17, 1906 to Jan. 23, 1907	Gemini	♊
Jan. 24 to May 15, 1907	Taurus	♉
May 16, 1907 to Aug. 25, 1917	Gemini	♊
Aug. 26, 1917 to Jan. 28, 1918	Cancer	♋
Jan. 29 to June 27, 1918	Gemini	♊
June 28, 1918 to Sept. 20, 1928	Cancer	♋
Sept. 21, 1928 to Feb. 19, 1929	Leo	♌
Feb. 20 to July 23, 1929	Cancer	♋
July 24, 1929 to Dec. 22, 1939	Leo	♌
Dec. 23, 1939 to Jan. 3, 1940	Virgo	♍
Jan. 4 to Sept. 24, 1940	Leo	♌
Sept. 25, 1940 to Apr. 10, 1941	Virgo	♍
Apr. 11 to July 29, 1941	Leo	♌
July 30, 1941 to Jan. 9, 1952	Virgo	♍
Jan. 10 to Feb. 3, 1952	Libra	♎
Feb. 4 to Oct. 19, 1952	Virgo	♍
Oct. 20, 1952 to May 16, 1953	Libra	♎
May 17 to Aug. 17, 1953	Virgo	♍
Aug. 18, 1953 to Jan. 24, 1964	Libra	♎
Jan. 25 to Mar. 15, 1964	Scorpio	♏
Mar. 16 to Nov. 12, 1964	Libra	♎
Nov. 13, 1964 to June 18, 1965	Scorpio	♏
June 19 to Sept. 7, 1965	Libra	♎
Sept. 8, 1965 to Dec. 31, 1975	Scorpio	♏

II: Pluto

♇

THE FARTHEST from the sun of all the planets in the solar system, Pluto —unlike the other outer planets—is not a giant planet. Its size is not known exactly, but it is probably smaller than any of the planets except Mercury. Ninth of the known planets, it was named for an ancient god of the underworld (Plutus), who is also a personification of wealth. Pluto has no moons.

This little planet is so far from the sun that, if you could stand on its surface, the sun would appear to be only another large star. It was unknown to the ancients, who were unable to detect any planets beyond Saturn. Pluto was not discovered until 1930, when Clyde Tombaugh confirmed the prediction of Percival Lowell (in 1914) that another planet must exist beyond Neptune.

The surface of Pluto is even colder than that of Uranus and Neptune, and it has little or no atmosphere. It will probably be a very long time before our astronauts will be able to venture so far into space, and the possibility of their finding life on Pluto is extremely unlikely.

The Grand Tour of the outer planets that will be made by the unmanned spacecraft *Pioneer 10* is limited to the giant planets. We will have to wait for a still more ambitious project before nonastronomical data on Pluto can be received on earth.

As stated above, Pluto is the outermost of the nine known planets of the solar system. Being farther from the sun, its orbit (or year) is much longer than that of the other planets we have studied. It takes Pluto 248.4 years to make one circuit of the sun, as compared with 164.79 years for

Neptune and 84 years for Uranus. Pluto also exhibits the retrograde motion described earlier, so that it sometimes appears to be moving backward.

MEANING OF PLUTO IN HOROSCOPE

As previously mentioned, Pluto moves much slower than the earth. Its orbit is 248.4 years, and it moves through only about 1.5 degrees a year. Thus, in the span of time covered by this book (1890 to 1975), it has not moved through all of the constellations (signs) of the Zodiac. Pluto was in Cetus on January 1, 1890, and will be in Virgo on December 31, 1975. In 86 years, then, it passes through only 6 of the 14 signs. It sometimes remains in one sign for more than twenty years, then (because of its retrograde motion) will remain in another for only a few months.

Pluto was named for an ancient god of the underworld, Plutus, who is also known as Hades. However, a pagan god of the underworld does not necessarily correspond to the Christian conception of the devil in hell, which was once thought to lie beneath the earth's surface. On the contrary: we receive jewels, minerals, and other riches from the depths of the earth, which explains Plutus as a personification of *wealth*. As keywords for Pluto, one astrologer has suggested *elimination, renewal,* and *regeneration.* An association with the House of death (see Table 1, p. 4) and further associations of Pluto with World Wars I and II, dictatorship, and nuclear weapons have led some astrologers to conclude that this planet is a malefic influence in the horoscope.

Since Pluto was not discovered until 1930, it is a Johnny-come-lately among the planets, and it is naturally an object of dispute among astrologers. Although it has been over four decades since its discovery, some astrologers still do not recognize the existence of Pluto. It is so small and so far from the sun that they regard is as insignificant and leave it out of their calculations. Such an attitude is far from the scientific spirit of Astrology 14. Pluto is known to exist; therefore, it should be included if your horoscope is to be complete. Since there is no ancient body of knowledge about this planet, it can be tentatively assumed that its influence is malefic (like that of Saturn), with two provisions: (1) The association of Pluto with *wealth* should not be forgotten, and (2) it must be remembered that the influence of *any* planet can be strengthened or lessened by its relationship (aspects) to other elements of the horoscope.

Pluto is the planetary ruler of Ophiuchus, so this planet is especially important if Ophiuchus is your sun sign. The sun is in Ophiuchus from December 6 to December 31, which includes the winter solstice, so it seems appropriate that fast-frozen Pluto should rule this sign.

The influence of this recently discovered planet is an area that needs research, which is also needed for the "new" sun signs, Cetus and Ophiuchus, and for the significance of the movement of the spring point from Aries into Pisces, signifying the dawn of the Age of Aquarius. Many astrologers, especially the older ones, have been unwilling to engage in such "far out" research. To them, astrology (despite its name) is really a game with fixed rules, like chess, that must not be altered. To them, the actual positions of the stars are of no importance; the zodiacal constellations remain "fixed" in the positions they occupied two thousand years ago.

I am not going to repeat the arguments I set forth in my previous book, *Astrology 14*, for a more scientific astrology that keeps up with the stars' movements and the precession of the equinoxes. I will only repeat that, as Einstein and others have clearly demonstrated, the universe is *dynamic*— not one particle stands still. If astrology is ever to attain the standing of a true science and not simply another occult art, it too must be dynamic and flexible. This is the philosophy of Astrology 14, and if another planet —beyond the orbit of Pluto—were to be discovered tomorrow, a scientific astrologer would not hesitate to include it in his calculations as soon as data on it were known.

Let us, then, give Pluto its due place in the family of planets that circle the sun.

To place the symbol of Pluto (♇) on your chart, turn to Table 12 at the end of this chapter. Here the positions of Pluto are listed for each year from 1890 to 1975. Find the span of time that includes your birthdate. It should be noted that Table 12 lists *inclusive* sets of dates. That is, if you were born on December 2, 1941, and the table lists Pluto in Cancer from October 11 to December 2, 1941, Pluto was still in Cancer on your birthdate, since it did not go back into Gemini until December 3, 1941.

To continue our example of someone born on January 1, 1940, with Aquarius rising, Figure 12 shows his chart with the symbol of Pluto entered. In Table 12, it is shown that Pluto was in Gemini on January 1, 1940; therefore, the symbol of Pluto is entered in the House occupied by Gemini, which (on his chart) is the sixth House.

INTERPRETATION

General interpretations of the meaning of Pluto are given below. It should be noted that, in the span of time covered by this book (1890 to 1975), Pluto did not enter all 14 signs. Therefore, interpretations of Pluto in the signs from Cetus to Virgo are given, and none is made for Libra, Scorpio, Ophiuchus, Sagittarius, Capricorn, Aquarius, Pisces, and Aries.

In reading these, it should be remembered that Pluto does not have an *absolute* meaning; whether it is a help or a hindrance depends upon its relationship to other elements of your chart. Also, the House occupied by Pluto affects its interpretation. Our imaginary subject (Figure 12) was born with Pluto in Gemini, which is his sixth House. After reading the interpretation of Pluto in Gemini, he should turn back to Table 1 (p. 4), which lists the basic meanings of the Houses. The life activity governed by that particular House will be enhanced by the presence of Pluto.

PLUTO IN CETUS ♇ ♒︎

Pluto in Cetus on your chart enhances the possibility of your amassing wealth (both material and spiritual). Cetus is ruled by Jupiter, the "greater fortune." If your Pluto is in good aspect to other elements of your chart, the beneficent influence of Jupiter will overrule any malefic influence of Pluto. Your chances for prosperity are good. We all know that money is insignificant compared to mental, emotional, and spiritual riches—but it is not "nothing" (nor is it the root of all evil). Material prosperity will free you to develop the sides of your nature that have nothing to do with business. Your well-aspected Pluto in this sign should ensure luck, good fortune, and the development of a genial, well-rounded personality that will bring popularity as well as success. If your Pluto is in bad aspect, however, you may find that the success of your ventures is illusory; temporary material gains may be more than offset by the cost to your spirit of acquiring these gains. Beware of making the acquirement of the things of this world your chief (or only) goal. Loneliness and frustration may result. The meaning of the aspects will be taken up in Chapter 12. In the meantime, check the life activity governed by the House occupied by Cetus on your chart (see Table 1) for a clearer picture of Pluto's influence on the possibilities of your acquiring wealth.

PLUTO IN TAURUS ♇ ♉

Pluto in Taurus on your chart enhances the emotional aspects of acquiring wealth of all kinds and—if you are talented—the successful deployment of your art, especially if your field is music. Taurus is ruled by Venus. If your Pluto is well aspected to other elements, the feminine "warmth" of this planet can offset the masculine "cold" of Pluto, making possible the development of a mature, well-rounded personality. There is a good chance that you will achieve material prosperity, and your emotional sensitivity will prevent you from clutching at the brass ring if your success means loss to others. You are hardly the type of cold, ruthless,

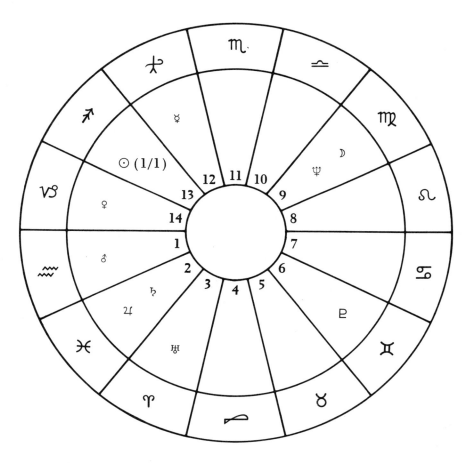

Figure 12. Placement of Pluto on chart of subject born on January 1, 1940, with Aquarius rising

greedy businessman whose path to "the top" is strewn with the wreckage of others' hopes. Your ethical sense is well developed. Also, you may be musically gifted; if so, you could probably build a successful career on this talent. If your Pluto is badly aspected, on the other hand, you may become too emotionally involved with your associates to attain the objectivity necessary for most careers. The wisdom of the heart must be balanced by that of the mind. The meaning of the aspects will be taken up in Chapter 12. In the meantime, check the life activity governed by the House occupied by Taurus on your chart (see Table 1) for a clearer picture of Pluto's influence on the emotional side of your career and possible musical talent.

PLUTO IN GEMINI ♇ ♊

Pluto in Gemini on your chart enhances your versatility, intellect, and ability to communicate as these are employed to amass both spiritual and material wealth. Gemini is ruled by Mercury. Since Mercury is the fastest-moving planet in the solar system, and Pluto the slowest, this combination can lead to a good balance: the impetuosity symbolized by Mercury restrained by the "sluggishness" represented by Pluto. If your Pluto is in good aspect to other elements, you can tread this middle way (the "golden mean" of Aristotle) between the extremes. The quickness of your mind and wit, your versatility, and your communicative powers (both oral and written) can all serve you well in your career, bringing the prospects of material security well within your grasp. Your drive and colorful personality bring friends as well as success. If your Pluto is in bad aspect, however, you may overdo the mercurial traits of nimbleness and versatility, as these can develop into such negative traits as fickleness, untrustworthiness, and restlessness. It is fine to be able to wear more than one hat; a job-hopper is something else again. The meaning of the aspects will be taken up in Chapter 12. In the meantime, check the life activity governed by the House occupied by Gemini on your chart (see Table 1) for a clearer picture of Pluto's influence on your mercurial quickness in the acquisition of wealth.

PLUTO IN CANCER ♇ ♋

Pluto in Cancer on your chart enhances your emotional sensitivity and conservative attitude to the amassing of riches (which can, of course, be both material and spiritual). Cancer is the only sign ruled by the moon. If your Pluto is well aspected to other elements, you can achieve a nice balance between the masculine objectivity symbolized by Pluto and the feminine subjectivity represented by the moon. Whether your goal is spiritual enlightenment or a well-filled bank account (or both—as it should be), this combination can be a fortunate one. The greatest spiritual lessons are not read in books, but are *lived* with the whole being; the truly successful man of business, sensitive as well as shrewd, is not motivated by simple greed. Your approach may be conservative, but you are always aware of the needs of others. If your Pluto is badly aspected, on the other hand, your emotional sensitivity may make you hesitate to take the hard but necessary steps often required for success. Or your conservatism may deteriorate into timidity, preventing you from the boldness often necessary if you are to reach your goal. The meaning of the aspects will be taken up in Chapter 12. In the meantime, check the life activity governed by the House occupied by Cancer on your chart (see Table 1) for a clearer picture of Pluto's influence on your emotional sensitivity and conservatism in acquiring wealth.

PLUTO IN LEO ♇ ♌

Pluto in Leo on your chart enhances the independence of your attitude toward acquiring wealth. Leo is the only sign ruled by the sun. There is only one sun in the solar system, of course, and you would rather shine by your own efforts than merely reflect the light of others. This is a commendable attitude in an age of conformity, and if your Pluto is in good aspect to other elements you may well achieve success by means of "operation bootstrap." You like to make up your own mind about things and (if possible) to be your own boss. Whether your goal is money, knowledge, a rich life style, or the wealth of the spirit, you tend to try to hew your own path to it rather than follow one carved out by others. This is often difficult, but the rewards of such effort can be great. You may well reach the top. If your Pluto is in bad aspect, however, your independent attitude may lead you to reject good counsel and advice. The days of *laissez faire* enterprise are nearly over; the cooperation of others and the support of outside forces are usually necessary, and it would be foolish to pretend they are not. The meaning of the aspects will be taken up in Chapter 12. In the meantime, check the life activity governed by the House occupied by Leo on your chart (see Table 1) for a clearer picture of Pluto's influence on your independent attitude toward the acquirement of riches.

PLUTO IN VIRGO ♇ ♍

Pluto in Virgo on your chart enhances your individualism and analytical ability as these are applied in the acquirement of wealth. Virgo is ruled by Mercury. If your Pluto is well aspected to other elements, your individualistic traits will keep you from being just another "face in the crowd," and your ability to analyze and criticize can be put to good use in amassing your fortune. By riches, of course, is meant spiritual as well as material gain. You have an original approach to things that, coupled with your analytical ability, can make you a highly valuable employee. The inventor is not always the one rewarded in this world, of course, but your ability to "see through" people as well as products should stand you in good stead when it comes to protecting your rights. Your chances for success are good. If your Pluto is badly aspected, on the other hand, your individualism may lead you to reject the ideas of others, whatever their value, simply because they are not your own. Your gift for analysis can also be misused if you develop into a nit-picker, critical of everything and everyone. The meaning of the aspects will be taken up in Chapter 12. In the meantime, check the life activity governed by the House occupied by Virgo on your chart (see Table 1) for a clearer picture of Pluto's influence on your individualism and analytical approach to the amassing of wealth.

Table 12. POSITIONS OF PLUTO (1890 TO 1975)

Dates	Sign	Symbol
Jan. 1, 1890 to June 29, 1899	Cetus	♉︎
June 30 to Dec. 4, 1899	Taurus	♉
Dec. 5, 1899 to May 18, 1900	Cetus	♉︎
May 19, 1900 to Aug. 20, 1922	Taurus	♉
Aug. 21 to Dec. 3, 1922	Gemini	♊
Dec. 4, 1922 to June 30, 1923	Taurus	♉
July 1, 1923 to Feb. 4, 1924	Gemini	♊
Feb. 5 to May 11, 1924	Taurus	♉
May 12, 1924 to Oct. 10, 1941	Gemini	♊
Oct. 11 to Dec. 2, 1941	Cancer	♋
Dec. 3, 1941 to Aug. 8, 1942	Gemini	♊
Aug. 9, 1942 to Feb. 14, 1943	Cancer	♋
Feb. 15 to June 15, 1943	Gemini	♊
June 16, 1943 to Oct. 27, 1956	Cancer	♋
Oct. 28, 1956 to Jan. 6, 1957	Leo	♌
Jan. 7 to Aug. 11, 1957	Cancer	♋
Aug. 12, 1957 to Apr. 2, 1958	Leo	♌
Apr. 3 to June 26, 1958	Cancer	♋
June 27, 1958 to Oct. 7, 1969	Leo	♌
Oct. 8, 1969 to Mar. 31, 1970	Virgo	♍
Apr. 1 to Aug. 6, 1970	Leo	♌
Aug. 7, 1970 to Dec. 31, 1975	Virgo	♍

12: The Aspects

WE HAVE NOW considered the rising sign, sun, moon, and planets from innermost Mercury to outermost Pluto. The horoscope, then, is complete. Or is it? You have erected your chart; that is, you have found your rising sign, which determines your first House, and entered the signs of the Zodiac in their correct order in the outer circle of the wheel of the horoscope; then entered the symbols of the sun, moon, and planets in their proper Houses. You have read a general interpretation of the meaning of each of these elements. Before we can proceed to the interpretation of the horoscope as a whole, however, a final, all-important step remains: determining the *aspects*.

The horoscope chart is drawn in the form of a circle, and a circle always consists of 360 degrees. Whether the circle is divided into 12 or 14 slices (Houses), the number of degrees is always the same. You can, then, compute the number of degrees separating two elements in your chart. If the number of degrees separating two elements is astrologically meaningful, these elements are *in aspect* to one another. Five major aspects are used in astrology. Let us define these before going into their interpretations.

DEFINITIONS OF MAJOR ASPECTS

CONJUNCTION ☌

Two planets that are close together on the chart are in conjunction. They need not occupy the same degree of the circle, but should be within 10 degrees of each other for the conjunction to be effective. (The allowable margin for any aspect is called the *orb*.)

OPPOSITION ☍

Two planets that are opposed or opposite to each other are in opposition. That is, they are approximately 180 degrees apart on the wheel of the horoscope. Orb: 10 degrees.

SEXTILE ⚹

Two planets that are approximately 60 degrees apart are in sextile. Orb: 7 degrees.

SQUARE ☐

Two planets that are approximately 90 degrees apart are in square. Orb: 9 degrees.

TRINE △

Two planets that are approximately 120 degrees apart are in trine. Orb: 9 degrees.

These major aspects are the ones astrologers are chiefly concerned with. In preparing a very detailed chart, some astrologers also compute the minor aspects. Some of these are the quintile (72 degrees), the sesquadrate (135 degrees), and the quincunx (150 degrees). Their use has often been disputed, so we will not consider them in interpreting the Astrology 14 horoscope.

One of the major aspects is variable in its meaning, two are good, and two are bad. The variable aspect is the conjunction. It can be good or bad, depending upon which planets are in conjunction and the sign (and House) in which they are conjoined. The good or favorable aspects are the sextile and the trine. The bad or unfavorable aspects are the opposition and the square. Just how good or bad these aspects are depends upon many factors—the intrinsic nature of the planet must be considered, as well as its placement by sign and House. Before aspects can be interpreted, they obviously must be known; that is, you must compute the degree of the sign occupied by each planet.

COMPUTING THE ASPECTS

To find the exact position of the sun, moon, and each planet at the moment of the subject's birth, an astrologer uses a reference book called an ephemeris (plural: ephimerides). These are published, by year, in inexpensive paper editions, and are available in most bookstores. Before you can proceed much further with your personal horoscope, you will need the ephemeris for the year of your birth.

The ephimerides are calculated according to the system of traditional astrology. That is, they show the sun entering Aries at the vernal equinox and are limited to the 12 traditional sun signs. In the system of Astrology 14, the sun enters *Pisces* at the vernal equinox, and all 14 sun signs are included. Since Astrology 14 ephemerides are not yet available, it will be necessary to convert the figures in your ephemeris. Remember that, although the circle always contains 360 degrees, Astrology 14 cuts the pie of the Zodiac into two more pieces, so each sign (or House) occupies fewer degrees. Traditional astrology divides the Zodiac into 12 sectors of 30 degrees each. In the system of Astrology 14, the sectors are naturally smaller: each sign (or House) occupies approximately 26 degrees, or 25.71 degrees to be exact.

Find the month and day of your birth in your ephemeris. The column headings show the symbol of each planet and the symbol of the sun sign the planet is in. The planetary positions are given in degrees and minutes (a degree, like an hour, is divided into 60 minutes). Before writing down these positions, convert each figure to the nearest whole degree. For example: 17°49′ is closer to 18 degrees than to 17 degrees. Be sure to include the symbol of the sun sign—18 degrees Libra should be written 18°♎.

Table 13 is a conversion chart that will help you to convert the positions found in your ephemeris to the proper positions for your Astrology 14 horoscope. The first column of this table lists the 14 signs of the Zodiac. The second column lists the ephemeris position when the planet entered that sign. Obviously, Cetus and Ophiuchus are not listed in the ephemeris. When did the planet enter Cetus? At the position listed in the ephemeris as 21° ♉. When did it enter Ophiuchus? At the position listed in the ephemeris as 14° ♐.

It will take some figuring, but Table 13 will aid you in finding the correct sign and degree for each element of your horoscope. Bear in mind that 26 degrees separate each of the signs according to Astrology 14, whereas 30 degrees separated each sign under the system of traditional astrology.

To make this vital step clearer, let us continue the example of a subject born on January 1, 1940, with Aquarius rising. Consulting the ephemeris for 1940, I find the following data:

Day: 1 January	Jupiter: 01°13′♈
Sun: 09°56′♑	Saturn: 24°26′♈
Moon: 00°45′♎	Uranus: 18°15′♉
Mercury: 22°54′♐	Neptune: 25°31′♍
Venus: 08°56′♒	Pluto: 02°14′♌
Mars: 28°18′♓	

TABLE 13. ASTROLOGY 14 CONVERSION CHART

Planet enters	Ephemeris position
Sagittarius at	10 degrees Capricorn (10°♑)
Capricorn at	6 degrees Aquarius (6°♒)
Aquarius at	2 degrees Pisces (2°♓)
Pisces at	0 degrees Aries (0°♈)
Aries at	26 degrees Aries (26°♈)
Cetus at	21 degrees Taurus (21°♉)
Taurus at	16 degrees Gemini (16°♊)
Gemini at	11 degrees Cancer (11°♋)
Cancer at	6 degrees Leo (6°♌)
Leo at	0 degrees Virgo (0°♍)
Virgo at	26 degrees Virgo (26°♍)
Libra at	22 degrees Libra (22°♎)
Scorpio at	18 degrees Scorpio (18°♏)
Ophiuchus at	14 degrees Sagittarius (14°♐)

Converting to whole degrees:

Sun:	10°♑	Jupiter:	1°♈
Moon:	1°♎	Saturn:	24°♈
Mercury:	23°♐	Uranus:	18°♉
Venus:	9°♒	Neptune:	26°♍
Mars:	28°♓	Pluto:	2°♌

I am now ready to convert to Astrology 14 positions. The sun comes first. We already know that our subject's sun sign is Sagittarius. Table 13 shows that the sun enters Sagittarius at 10 degrees Capricorn (10° ♑), so it is obvious that the sun was in 0° ♐ at the moment of our subject's birth. In Figure 13, therefore, I erase the date of his birth beside the sun symbol in Sagittarius and replace it with its position (0°). That one was easy! Now for the moon. Table 4 showed that the moon was in Virgo on his birthdate, and the ephemeris position is 1°♎. Since the moon entered Virgo at the ephemeris position of 26°♍ (Table 13), a little figuring shows that the ephemeris position of 1° ♎ equals the true position of 6°♍. I enter this position beside his moon symbol.

The figuring is really not difficult. You must simply remember that the movement is always counterclockwise, from the first degree of the first House ("9 o'clock") to the last degree of the fourteenth House; that each sign in the ephemeris occupies 30 degrees; and that each sign in your Astrology 14 horoscope occupies 26 degrees.

Let us go on to Mercury. I know that his Mercury is in Ophiuchus, and the ephemeris position is 23° ♐. Table 13 shows that Mercury entered Ophiuchus at the ephemeris position of 14° ♐. Simply by adding 9 degrees, I know that the true position of his Mercury was 9°⚷, and I enter this

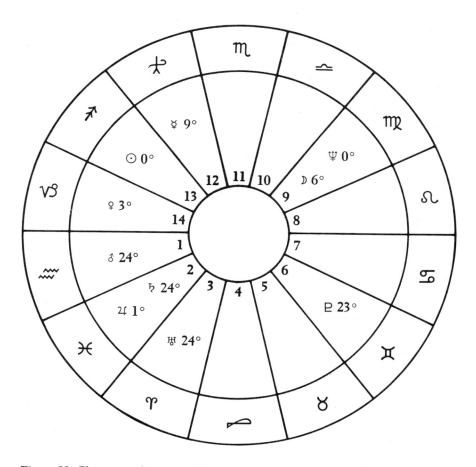

Figure 13. Placement of exact positions on chart of subject born on January 1, 1940, with Aquarius rising

position on Figure 13. Proceeding in the same way with the remaining planets, I compute:

$$
\begin{array}{rcl}
\text{Venus:} & 9°\,\text{♒} & = & 3°\,\text{♑} \\
\text{Mars:} & 28°\,\text{♓} & = & 24°\,\text{♒} \\
\text{Jupiter:} & 1°\,\text{♈} & = & 1°\,\text{♓} \\
\text{Saturn:} & 24°\,\text{♈} & = & 24°\,\text{♓} \\
\text{Uranus:} & 18°\,\text{♉} & = & 24°\,\text{♈} \\
\text{Neptune:} & 26°\,\text{♍} & = & 0°\,\text{♍} \\
\text{Pluto:} & 2°\,\text{♌} & = & 23°\,\text{♊}
\end{array}
$$

After entering these positions on Figure 13, I am ready at last to compute the aspects.

Does our subject have any conjunctions? We noted above that two planets must be within 10 degrees of each other to be in conjunction. In his first House (Aquarius), Mars is at 24°. In his second House, Jupiter is at 1°♓. Although Mars and Jupiter are in different Houses, they are only 3 degrees apart and so are in conjunction. This is written ♂ ☌ ♃. In his ninth House, Neptune (0°♍) and the moon (6°♍) are close enough together to form a conjunction, which is written ☽ ☌ ♆.

The conjunction is the easiest aspect to see on your chart. Our imaginary subject has two of them, but you may have more (or less). Remember that the ascendant line (0 degrees of your first House) must be included as if it were another planet. Its symbol is the abbreviation Asc. After you have computed your conjunctions, enter them in the space provided at the bottom of your chart.

We noted above that, to be in *opposition*, two planets must be approximately 180 degrees apart, with an allowable orb of 10 degrees. In general, the first House is opposed to the eighth House, the second House to the ninth House, etc. Planets in opposition are usually in opposed Houses, but it again depends upon their exact degree. Since each House covers a span of 26 degrees, planets in opposed Houses may not be in opposition; also, planets near the cusp may be in opposition although their Houses are not opposed.

Turning again to our imaginary subject, let us see if he has any oppositions. To help in these (and other) computations, Figure 14 shows the circle of the horoscope, divided into the 14 Houses, with the degree of each cusp shown progressively. For convenience, the line perpendicular to the ascendant line (the midheaven and nadir of traditional astrology) is shown as a dotted line. Use of Figure 14 should make it fairly easy to see which planets on your chart are in opposition (approximately 180 degrees apart).

A little figuring shows that our subject's Mars (24°♒) is 183 degrees from his Neptune (0°♍) and 189 degrees from his moon (6°♍). These

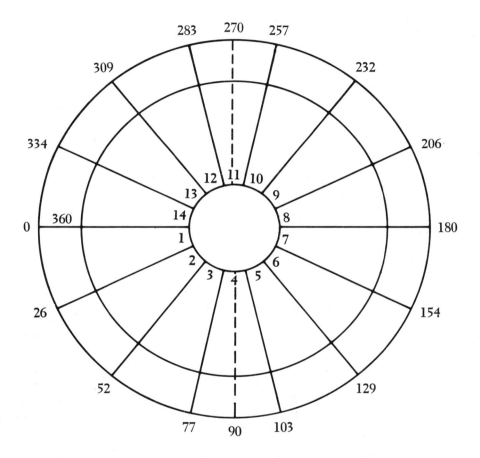

Figure 14. Cusps of Astrology 14 horoscope shown by progressive degrees

planets, then, are in opposition—written as ♂ ☍ ♆ and ☽ ☍ ♂. Proceeding counterclockwise, we see that his Jupiter (1°♓) is in near-exact opposition to his Neptune and is also in opposition to his moon. These aspects are written ♃ ☍ ♆ and ☽ ☍ ♃. In his sixth House, Pluto (23°♊) is in opposition to Venus (3°♑), which is written ♀ ☍ ♇. So our subject has five oppositions.

After you have computed your oppositions (if any) and entered them at the bottom of your chart, we will proceed to the *sextile*. As mentioned above, two planets are in sextile when they are approximately 60 degrees apart, the allowable orb being 7 degrees. Examination of our imaginary subject's chart (Figure 13), along with Figure 14, shows that his Pluto (23°♊) is in sextile to his Neptune (0°♍) and to his moon (6°♍). These aspects are written ♆ ✶ ♇ and ☽ ✶ ♇. Compute your sextile aspects; if you have any, enter them at the bottom of your chart.

We will now consider the *square*. You will remember that two planets are in square when they are approximately 90 degrees apart, with an allowable orb of 9 degrees. This aspect is fairly easy to see because planets in square will be at nearly right angles to each other.

Our imaginary subject's chart shows that his Mercury (9°♈) is in square with three planets: Neptune (0°♍), Mars (24°♒), and Jupiter (1°♓). These aspects are written ☿ □ ♆, ☿ □ ♂, and ☿ □ ♃. Also, his sun (0°♐) is in square with his moon (6°♍), which is written ☉ □ ☽. Now compute your own square aspects (if any), bearing in mind that, with an orb of 9 degrees, two planets are in square if they are in a range of 81 to 99 degrees of each other. Enter these aspects at the bottom of your chart.

The last of the major aspects is the *trine*. Two planets are in trine if they are approximately 120 degrees apart. The allowable orb is again 9 degrees. Examination of our imaginary subject's chart shows that he has four trine aspects: Jupiter and Pluto, Mars and Pluto, Mercury and Saturn, and sun and Uranus. These are written ♃ △ ♇, ♂ △ ♇, ☿ △ ♄, and ☉ △ ♅. Examine your own chart for possible trine aspects. These should be entered at the bottom of your chart.

INTERPRETATION

With all aspects entered at the bottom of your chart, your horoscope is now complete. It remains to interpret the meaning of your horoscope *as a whole*. This will be taken up in the next chapter. It should be remembered, however, that we have been interpreting the *general* meaning of your horoscope all through this book. By now you should know the life activities of each House, as outlined in Table 1 (p. 4); the general meaning of your sun sign; what each planet signifies; and the general meaning of each planet on your chart in relation to the sign (and House) occupied by that planet. In addition, you have learned that a conjunction is a variable aspect, its significance depending upon the planets conjoined, and that the sextile and trine are favorable aspects, the square and opposition unfavorable aspects.

Bearing all of these things in mind, let us proceed to the detailed interpretation of the completed horoscope.

13: Bringing It All Together

As I MENTIONED in my previous book, *Astrology 14*, the real art of astrology lies in the interpretation of the completed chart. This is a subject that can (and has) filled volumes. Except for the basic interpretations, the steps we have taken so far have been more or less mechanical—erecting the horoscope and filling in its elements, one by one. Now that you have completed your chart and entered the aspects, the great question remains to be answered: What does it *mean*?

The completed horoscope is a picture of yourself—a self-portrait—but it is a *symbolic* picture, hence the need for interpretation. A baby, when it draws its first breath, bears little resemblance to the adult it will one day be. Why, then, a natal chart? Why not a symbolic representation of the heavens as they appeared on your twenty-first birthday, or today, or next year? Such charts are erected, of course, and are known as *progressed* horoscopes. However, these are outside the scope of this book, which is concerned only with the erection and interpretation of the natal chart. This picture of the heavens as they appeared at the moment of your birth is so important, astrologically, because the horoscope does not simply represent the heavenly bodies as they appeared at that moment, but is a symbolic picture of your *entire life*. One of the basic tenets of astrology is that your character (and thus your fate) is, to a certain extent, fixed at the moment of your birth by the arrangement of the heavenly bodies at that moment. I say "to a certain extent" because I do not believe our lives are *determined* by the stars. There are so many variables in the human equation that environment probably plays an equally important part in your individual development. It obviously makes a difference if you were born in a native village in Africa or in New York City; if your parents were poor and life was a constant struggle or if they were wealthy and gave you security and a good education; if you are a male or a female; if you were an only child, or the eldest of the children, or the youngest. The list could be extended indefinitely.

Your natal chart, then, does not pretend to predict the events in your life exactly or in great detail. What it does is show your *potential* development. The word "potential" is important. We all have strengths and weaknesses. Almost everyone is "good at"—has a talent for—something. Musicians, for example, are often *born* with a good ear for pitch and a natural sense of rhythm; others may have a "tin ear" or be unable to keep time with their foot to a Sousa march. An eye for color and form are frequently *inherent* in the artist, as are mechanical aptitude in a machinist and a flair for working with numbers in a mathematician or accountant. If we take aptitude tests, we may discover what field would be best for the exploitation of our talents and abilities—something a properly erected and interpreted horoscope could probably have told us long ago. In short, then, a natal chart is a projection of your inherent strengths and weaknesses: a picture, in symbols, of your potential character. It is up to you, of course, to use this picture as a key to your personality. If you know your strengths, you can exploit them in your pursuit of success and happiness; if you know your weaknesses, you can work or study to bolster them, and avoid fields where you would have your worst foot forward from the first day of work!

Hard work, schooling, and the drive of ambition can, of course, often overcome the lack of an inherent gift. In Aesop's famous fable, the tortoise beat the speedier hare simply by not giving up. But a great deal of disappointment and heartbreak could be avoided if people knew themselves better and built their ambitions on their strong points. A girl with crossed eyes, buck teeth, and lumpy thighs may win a beauty contest, but the odds against it are so great that it takes no crystal ball to foresee heartbreak for her if she has pinned her hopes on winning the contest. The same girl may have a strong aptitude to be a teacher, say, and could find happiness and fulfillment in helping children to develop *their* potential. But potential is like muscle—it must be exercised if it is to be developed. And first of all, of course, you must *know* your potential before you can take steps to develop it. Which brings us back to the natal chart and its interpretation.

Picture yourself at the center of your chart, on the earth, looking up at the heavens. This is your sky. In a symbolic sense, it is yourself. The sun, moon, and planets are in motion against a background of starry space. The outer circle represents the ecliptic—the path of the sun on its yearly voyage—and the symbols of the 14 signs represent the zodiacal constellations through which the sun passes in the course of a year. As we learned in Chapter 1, the constellations also are in motion, rising and setting as the earth turns on its axis. What, then, remains fixed in this picture? Only the Houses, those 14 "slices of the pie"—they form the stationary background against which the heavenly bodies move.

When interpreting your chart, bear in mind that the *aspects* are the heart of the horoscope. You learned how to compute these in the last chapter, and entered them at the bottom of your chart. The meanings of all possible aspects will now be given. Later, our imaginary subject's aspects will be interpreted and we shall see how these fit into the overall interpretation of his chart.

INTERPRETATION OF ASPECTS

The aspects will be interpreted in the following order:

1. Ascendant (Asc.)
2. Sun (☉)
3. Moon (☽)
4. Mercury (☿)
5. Venus (♀)
6. Mars (♂)
7. Jupiter (♃)
8. Saturn (♄)
9. Uranus (♅)
10. Neptune (♆)
11. Pluto (♇)

To avoid repetitions, it must be remembered that ☉ ☌ ♇ means exactly the same as ♇ ☌ ☉. That is, the first element will always be given according to the order listed above.

INTERPRETATION OF COMPLETED HOROSCOPE

Figure 15 shows the completed horoscope, with aspects, of our imaginary subject born on January 1, 1940, with Aquarius rising. All of the necessary information has now been given. It remains only to bring it all together to interpret the completed chart. By following this process closely, you will be able to apply it to your own horoscope.

The process is not one of simple addition. Remember that the horoscope is a symbolic picture of a whole human being, not bits and pieces of him spread throughout a circle. That is, just as your mind and body are inseparable, so are the various elements in your horoscope. Thus, the

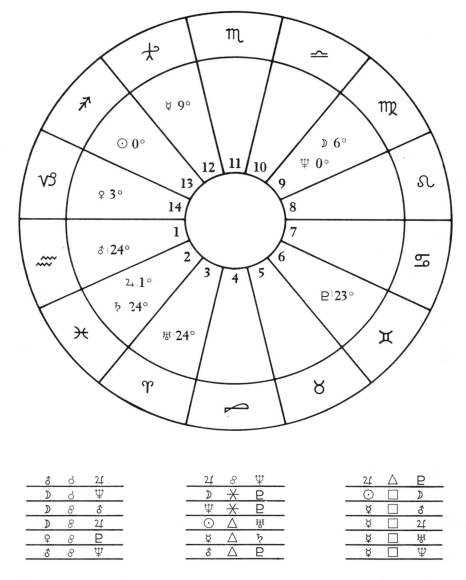

Figure 15. Completed horoscope, with aspects, for subject born on January 1, 1940, with Aquarius rising

process of interpretation is one of *synthesis*—a bringing together of the separate elements that we have analyzed (taken apart) in previous chapters.

Our subject's sun sign is Sagittarius, the "lucky" sign, ruled by Jupiter, so we should expect generosity and benevolence among his basic traits. Since Aquarius is his rising sign, the sun was in his thirteenth House, which governs friends, group objectives, hopes, wishes, and benefits. The influence of Jupiter should bring good fortune to these life activities. However, the sun had just passed the cusp separating Sagittarius from Ophiuchus at the moment of his birth. Therefore, the versatility and resourcefulness of Ophiuchus must be included among his basic potential traits.

Ophiuchus occupied his twelfth House, and Mercury was in this House when he was born. Since the twelfth House governs his career, material responsibility, social life and status, reputation, honors, etc., we would expect these life activities to be affected by the "mercurial" traits of versatility, quick intellect, and wit. However, his Mercury is also in aspect to several other planets, so we will consider this influence when we study his aspects below.

His rising sign (Aquarius) occupies his first House, of course, which governs the most *personal* portion of one's character—his individual life, including body and egocentric concerns, and his personal potential. So we would expect to find, in his basic personality, the Aquarian traits of a critical mind, ability to acquire knowledge easily, especially in scientific or technical fields, attraction to novelty, and a certain amount of temperament or "nerves." His Mars is in Aquarius; therefore, along with basic Sagittarian and Aquarian traits, he should have some of the will power, aggressiveness, and stubbornness associated with Mars.

We already have a rough outline of his personality. Let us go on to his aspects, which—to repeat—are the heart of any horoscope. We will take them in the same order in which they were listed. Since our subject has no ascendant aspects (*Asc.*), we will start with the sun.

His sun and moon are in square (☉ □ ☽). This is a bad aspect, its basic interpretation being "low vitality, self-centered; success in doubt." This influence runs counter to the positive influences described above, so we should expect a weakening of his drive for success; also, his "jovial" temperament may be hurt by an egocentric attitude. His sun, however, is also in trine to his Uranus (☉ △ ♅), which is a very good aspect. The basic interpretation is "original, resourceful, colorful, very creative." This strengthens his basic Ophiuchan resourcefulness and adds originality and creativity to his Jovian generosity and Martian energy and will power. The signs (and Houses) occupied by his moon and Uranus must also be noted. With moon in Virgo (ninth House), his individualistic and analytical traits are stressed—negatively, because of the square. The ninth House governs death and inheritances, sex expression, and self-sacrifice. He should be prepared, then, for possible trouble in these areas. Uranus in Aries (third House) positively affects the strength of his will and its application to the problems of life. The third House governs education and communications. This aspect bolsters the influence of Mercury in Ophiuchus, so we would expect him to be a good student, a hard worker, and someone with facility at expression, in both oral and written communication.

Our subject has four moon aspects besides sun in square with moon just discussed. It should be remembered that the moon basically affects *personality*—the opposite of the sun, which affects *individuality*. The associations of the moon with feminine traits and the unconscious should also be borne in mind. His moon and Mars are in opposition (☽ ☍ ♂). This is a bad aspect, its basic interpretation being "rash, headstrong, destructive, passionate." His Martian traits and tendencies are strengthened negatively, especially with Mars in his first House, which governs his basic personality. A danger of over-aggressiveness thus exists. His moon is also in opposition to his Jupiter (☽ ☍ ♃). Basic interpretation: "extravagant, hypocritical, careless, arrogant." His Jupiter is in Pisces (second House), which affects belief—in himself as well as in spiritual matters—so that his self-esteem is negatively strengthened. The second House governs money, financial concerns, physical possessions, and securities. There is a danger of extravagance or carelessness in these areas. His moon is also in conjunction with Neptune (☽ ☌ ♆), which is a variable aspect. Basic interpretation: "spiritually sensitive; may be too introverted." Both moon and Neptune are in Virgo (ninth House), whose meanings were discussed under sun aspects. With his strong Mars, it is doubtful that he would become too introverted, but egotism and willfulness seem to be strongly indicated. There is a danger that he could become morbidly preoccupied with death. On the positive side, his moon is in sextile with Pluto (☽ ⚹ ♇). Basic interpretation: "imperturbable, steady, ambitious, very perceptive." This is a good aspect, and should help to offset his Martian aggressiveness. Pluto is in Gemini (sixth House), which strengthens his mercurial traits—versatility, intellect, and communicative powers—especially as these apply to the acquisition of wealth. The sixth House governs children, amusements, recreation, and display. This aspect positively increases his chances of attaining success, both materially and spiritually, and indicates that he will be a good provider and family man, whatever his business associates may think of him!

Our subject has five Mercury aspects. His Mercury is in square with Mars (☿ □ ♂). Basic interpretation: "irritable, dogmatic, argumentative, vindictive." Since the square is a bad aspect, his negative Martian traits are strengthened (especially with Mars in his first House) and positive mercurial and Ophiuchan traits correspondingly weakened. We would expect to see his versatility, resourcefulness, etc., perverted to personal, selfish ends. This is backed up by the next aspect. His Mercury is also in square with Jupiter (☿ □ ♃). Basic interpretation: "biased opinions, exaggerates, tries to bluff." With Jupiter in his second House, governing money, possessions, etc., our subject appears less and less attractive as a business partner! However, his Mercury is also in trine to his Saturn (☿ △ ♄), which is a very good aspect. Basic interpretation: "deep-thinking, persistent, realistic, reflective." These more sober traits are ones our subject seems greatly to need. Like his Jupiter, his Saturn is in Pisces (second House), so the concern is again with his *belief*, in himself as well as in a religious or philosophical sense. We have seen that the second House governs money, possessions, etc., so his ability to achieve success through hard, steady effort is strengthened by this aspect. On the other hand, his Mercury is in square with his Uranus (☿ □ ♅)—a bad aspect. Basic interpretation: "eccentric, overly analytical, high-strung, critical." We have noted that Uranus in Aries (third House) has to do with the will and its application to life's problems; also that the third House governs education and communications. So our subject tends to be too temperamental to be as good a student and worker as his ☉△♅ first led us to expect. Finally, his Mercury is also in square with his Neptune (☿ □ ♆). Basic interpretation: "dreamy, absent-minded, morbid, manic-depressive." Like his moon, his Neptune is in Virgo (ninth House), so again his individualism and analytical ability are negatively affected, especially where death, sex expression, etc., are concerned. This aspect points up the danger of a neurotic condition developing in these areas, so that, if things go against him, he could become obsessed by sex or even end up as a suicide.

Our subject has only one Venus aspect—his Venus is in opposition to his Pluto (♀ ☍ ♇). Basic interpretation: "erotic, overly sensitive, easily infatuated." This is a bad aspect that again points to possible trouble in his love life. His Venus is in Capricorn (fourteenth House), which indicates a clash between conservatism and eroticism. The fourteenth House governs possible trouble, imprisonment, self-betrayal, illness, escapism, and disgrace. At this point, it is safe to say that our subject should be warned of weaknesses and possible deep trouble regarding his emotional life. However, he has other, more positive aspects to be considered.

His Mars is in conjunction with his Jupiter (♂ ☌ ♃)—a variable aspect. Basic interpretation: "expansively energetic; may be overly ambitious." The basic meanings of Mars in Aquarius (first House) and Jupiter in Pisces (second House) have already been discussed. From other aspects studied so far, it would seem that he has plenty of energy already, and that his ambitions may lie in selfish directions. His Mars is in opposition to his Neptune (♂ ☍ ♆). Basic interpretation: "fanatic, obsessed, self-glorifying, neurotic." A bad aspect. We have already noted that Neptune in Aries (third House) has to do with education and communications, so there is a danger of our subject specializing too narrowly in one field or subject, and of becoming obsessed with the "rightness" of his chosen views and dogmatic in their defense. His final Mars aspect, however, is a very good one. His Mars is in trine to his Pluto (♂ △ ♇). Basic interpretation: "energetic but controlled; success very probable." With Pluto in Gemini (sixth House), the emphasis is again on children, amusements, etc., and the use of his mercurial traits to gather wealth. The trine is the strongest positive aspect, so his potential as a good family man and provider is strengthened. This aspect will tend to ameliorate the bad aspects that could lead him into dead ends of selfishness and neuroticism.

He has two remaining Jupiter aspects, one good and one bad. His Jupiter is in opposition to his Neptune (♃ ☍ ♆). Basic interpretation: "unsound, dreamy, superstitious, hysterical." A bad aspect that again points to the possibility that he may develop unrealistic, neurotic tendencies. The basic meanings of Jupiter in Aries (second House) and Neptune in Virgo (ninth House) have already been discussed. He could have serious financial troubles, especially where deaths and inheritances are concerned. His Jupiter is in trine to his Pluto (♃ △ ♇). Basic interpretation: "enjoys all sides of life, tolerant, dignified." A very good aspect. Again the emphasis is on children, recreation, etc. (Pluto in the sixth House), so it seems that our subject will probably be a good father, although his ☉ □ ☽ , discussed above, may cause him trouble as a lover and husband.

Our subject has one remaining aspect to be considered. His Neptune is in sextile to his Pluto (♆ ⚹ ♇). Basic interpretation: "mystical, truly religious, prophetic." This is a good aspect and should help to offset the influence of his bad aspects as they apply to his spiritual life. He is certainly religious, but whether this will deepen and strengthen his character or lead him into the narrow path of the fanatic or zealot probably depends on factors outside the horoscope (parental influence, schooling, and his environment in general). The aspects clearly indicate that either way is open to him.

SUMMARY

We have now examined the 18 aspects on our imaginary subject's chart. These aspects, in sum, are a little more negative than the average. With one variable aspect, two good ones, and two bad ones, the odds are in favor of an even split between good and bad aspects; in fact, the odds slightly favor the good aspects, since aspects of the sun with Mercury and

Venus can only be good or variable. But our subject has two conjunctions (variable), six good aspects, and ten bad aspects. This does not mean that he is "star-crossed" and doomed to end up as a failure, neurotic, or suicide. Not at all! To repeat an important point: the horoscope can only point up *potential* strengths and weaknesses in the life of an individual. Of course, our subject may succumb to the influence of the negative aspects in his chart; but he may just as well overcome these tendencies and lead the full and happy life suggested by his good aspects. He will probably have to work a little harder than the average to achieve this end, and be stronger in resisting temptation, but his fate is in his own hands. It is up to him. His horoscope neither dooms him to failure nor guarantees his success. It is simply a tool that will help him to self-knowledge if he uses it to warn him of possible pitfalls and to point up potential areas of strength that it would be advisable for him to exploit to further his ambition and reach his goal.

Like the moon, which is always half in shadow, we all have our "light" side and our "dark" side. Our imaginary subject is no exception. If one were simply to add up all the traits listed for his aspects, the result would be self-contradictory and ultimately meaningless. His success is both "doubtful" and "very probable." He is both "dignified" and "hysterical." However, the aspects are both strengthened and weakened by other aspects, and opposite traits sometimes tend to cancel each other out. That is why an astrologer must ponder the complete chart and try to achieve a *synthesis* of all the elements. Bearing this in mind, I would say of our subject that his is a many-sided personality. He is basically both resourceful and versatile, and many different careers are open to him. His energy, drive, inventiveness, and ambition should make him an excellent businessman, for instance. However, he will probably have to fight off the temptation to take short cuts to success that are less than honest. He will try to put up a good appearance and convince others of his worth; however, he has secret doubts and fears, which may make him overcompensate by being all the more aggressive and self-centered. If he fails, or is caught in a dishonest venture, he will probably try to "save face" in the Oriental tradition. He may earn a bad reputation in his early career, and will have to work doubly hard to redeem the trust and respect of his associates. His love life is liable to be stormy. His drive and occasionally ruthless emotions will be attractive to many women—but may drive away the very one he wants to keep. Nevertheless, after many affairs, he will marry, and his marriage will probably be lasting. At any rate, he will be a good father to his children and an excellent provider for his family. The development of his spiritual side will probably also have many ups and downs—veering, perhaps, from atheism to fanaticism as a young man. If he can win life's other battles, his mature years will see the fruition of a quiet but deep and heartfelt faith.

CONCLUSION

You have now learned how to erect and interpret your Astrology 14 horoscope. It is a complex task, but I have tried to keep the directions simple without leaving out anything important. There are too many elements in your chart to keep all the meanings and interpretations in your head at once. To get the complete picture, I would advise you to go back and copy down the points that are salient to your horoscope. That is, if your rising sign is Pisces, make notes on the meaning of Pisces rising given in Chapter 1. If your sun sign is Cancer, go to Chapter 2 and make notes on the basic interpretation of Cancer as a sun sign. Do the same with all the chapters. Then copy out the basic interpretations of the aspects you have entered at the bottom of your chart. Summarize as much as possible (without losing important details) and you will then have proper "working papers" to help you interpret your horoscope.

It may be objected that the horoscope described in this book is not wholly accurate because emphasis is placed on the rising sign rather than the ascendant. As I mentioned earlier, the ascendant is 0 degrees of the first House. A House, however, does not usually coincide with a sign. To be truly accurate, the horoscope should be plotted on the ascendant. That is, if Aries is your rising sign, and your ascendant is 15 degrees Aries, your first House will start at 15 degrees Aries. Only if your ascendant should happen to be at 0 degrees will your rising sign and first House coincide. In a general work such as this book, it is impossible to be so precise. Plotting the ascendant is an individual matter, whether you do it yourself or have an astrologer do it for you. If you wish to plot your own ascendant, you will find directions in many books on astrology. It must be remembered, however, that the figure you derive will have to be converted to the correct Astrology 14 figure (see Chapter 12, especially Table 13).

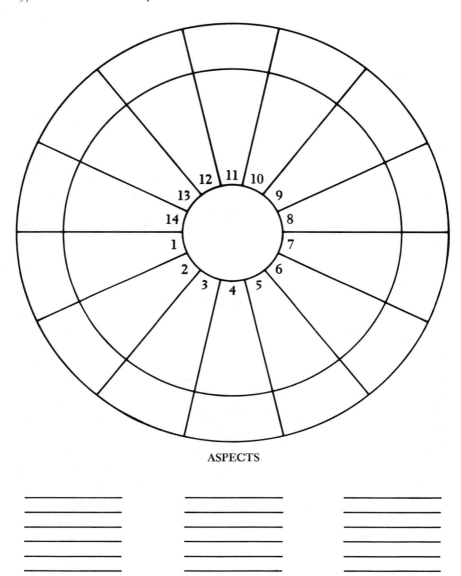

ASPECTS

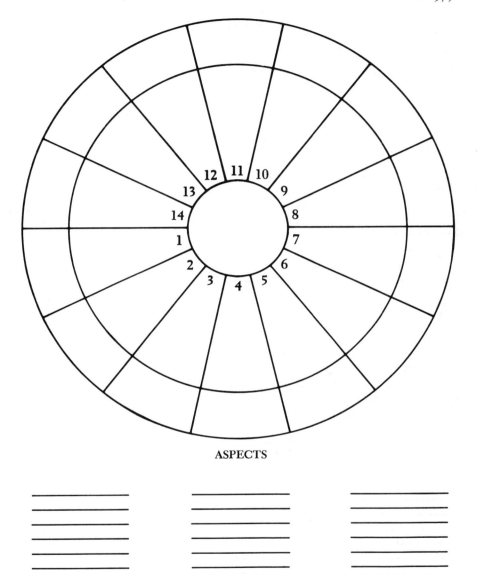

ASPECTS

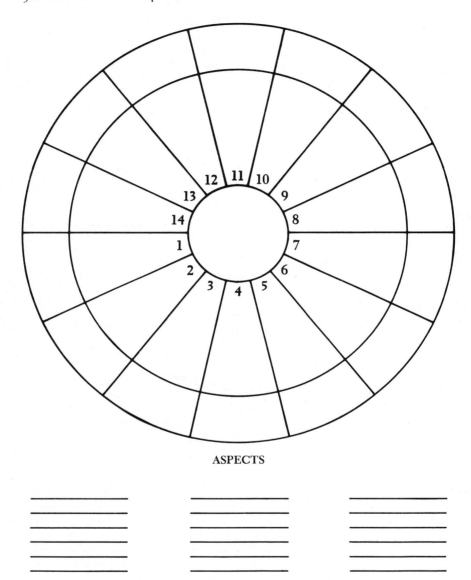

ASPECTS

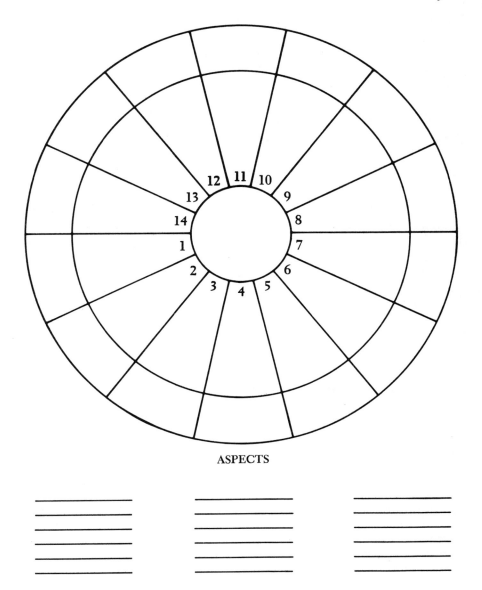

ASPECTS

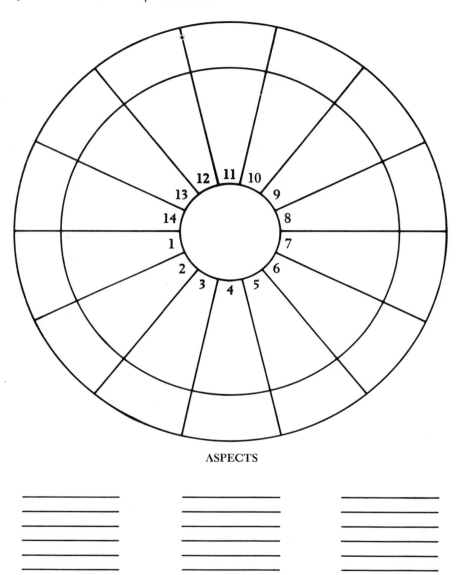

ASPECTS

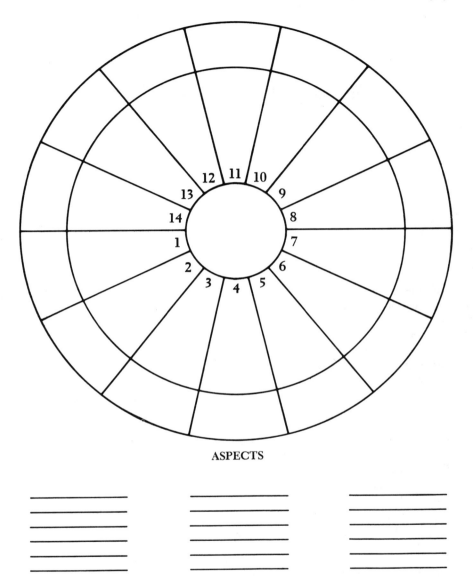

ASPECTS

Glossary of Astrological Terms

Ascendant: Degree of sign rising on eastern horizon at moment of birth. In Astrology 14, 0° of first House. Sometimes used as synonym for *rising sign*.

Aspect: Astrologically significant number of degrees between planets in horoscope. Major aspects: *conjunction, opposition, sextile, square, trine.* Minor aspects: *quincunx, quintile, sesquadrate.*

Astrology: Science or art of determining human destiny by positions of heavenly bodies.

Astrology 14: Modern, scientific system of astrology that places spring point at 0° Pisces, includes all 14 constellations (signs) actually in Zodiac, and determines characteristics from study of individuals.

Conjunction: Major aspect, variable: two planets close together on chart. Allowable orb: 10°. Symbol: ☌ .

Constellation: Group of stars related only by appearance from earth. Zodiacal constellations are source of *signs.*

Cusp: Dividing line between two signs (or Houses) on horoscope. A planet near cusp affects and is affected by both signs (or Houses).

Descendant: Point on horoscope opposite to *ascendant.* Not used in Astrology 14.

Ephemeris: Source book for positions of planets by date. Plural: ephemerides.

Horoscope: Circular symbolic representation of heavens at a particular moment, usually moment of subject's birth. Divided into 14 Houses (12 in traditional astrology), with earth at center. Synonym: *chart.*

House: One of 14 divisions of horoscope (12 in traditional astrology), which remain stationary. Each House governs a life activity.

Midheaven: Point at top of horoscope determined by line perpendicular to ascendant/descendant line. Abbreviation: MC. Not used in Astrology 14.

Nadir: Point at bottom of horoscope determined by line perpendicular to ascendant/descendant line. Abbreviation: IC. Not used in Astrology 14.

Opposition: Major aspect, unfavorable: two planets opposite each other on chart (180° apart). Allowable orb: 10°. Symbol: ☍.

Orb: Allowable variation from exact aspects.

Planet: Nine heavenly bodies that circle the sun. In astrology, sun and moon are also called planets.

Progressed chart: Horoscope with planets advanced to a point past moment of birth, based on some system such as "a day for a year."

Quincunx: Minor aspect, unfavorable: two planets 150° apart on chart. Allowable orb: 3 to 4°. Not used in Astrology 14.

Quintile: Minor aspect, when two planets are 72° apart on chart. Not used in Astrology 14.

Rising sign: Sign rising on eastern horizon at moment of birth. Sometimes used as synonym for *ascendant*.

Sesquadrate: Minor aspect, unfavorable: two planets 135° apart on chart. Allowable orb: 3 to 4°. Not used in Astrology 14.

Sextile: Major aspect, favorable: two planets 60° apart on chart. Allowable orb: 7°. Symbol: ✳.

Sign: One of 14 zodiacal constellations. *Sun sign* is sign sun was in at moment of birth. Traditional astrology recognizes only 12 signs, which do not correspond to constellations.

Spring point: Beginning of zodiacal year when sun is at 0° Pisces (0° Aries in traditional astrology); *vernal equinox* (first day of spring).

Square: Major aspect, unfavorable: two planets 90° apart on chart. Allowable orb: 9°. Symbol: □.

Time twin: Someone born in same area and at same moment as yourself, so that horoscope is nearly identical to yours.

Trine: Major aspect, favorable: two planets 120° apart on chart. Allowable orb: 9°. Symbol: △.

Vernal equinox: First day of spring; beginning of zodiacal year when sun is at 0° Pisces (0° Aries in traditional astrology).

Zodiac: Band in heavens extending 8° on each side of *ecliptic* (apparent sun path). Planets move within boundaries of Zodiac. Basis of science or art of astrology.

Bibliography

Adler, Alfred. *Understanding Human Nature*. New York: Greenberg: Publisher, 1927.

Benares, Camden. *Now and Zen* (in preparation).

Bradbury, Ray. *The Martian Chronicles*. New York: Doubleday and Co., Inc., 1950.

Camus, Albert. *The Myth of Sisyphus*. New York: Alfred A. Knopf, Inc., 1955.

Davison, Ronald C. *Astrology*. New York: Bell Publishing Co., 1963.

Ephemeriden 1890–1950. Zürich: Verlag Max S. Metz AG., 1971.

Freud, Sigmund. *The Interpretation of Dreams*. New York: The Modern Library, Random House, Inc., 1950.

Golgge Ephemeride, 1961–1965, 1966–1970, 1971–1975. Freiburg, Germany: Verlag Hermann Bauer, 1961, 1965, 1969.

Goodavage, Joseph F. *Write Your Own Horoscope*. New York: The New American Library, 1968.

Jung, Carl G. *Psychological Types* (Collected Works: Vol. 6). Princeton, N.J.: Princeton University Press, 1971.

Jung, Carl G. "Synchronicity: An Acausal Connecting Principle." (*Collected Works: Vol. 8. The Structure and Dynamics of the Psyche.*) New York: Bollingen Foundation, Pantheon Books, 1960.

Jung, Carl G., and Pauli, W. *The Interpretation of Nature and the Psyche*. New York: Bollingen Foundation, Pantheon Books, 1955.

Larousse Encyclopedia of Astronomy. New York: Prometheus Press, 1959.

Ley, Willy, and Bonestell, Chesley. *The Conquest of Space*. New York: The Viking Press, 1958.

Long, L. H. (Editor). *The 1971 World Almanac and Book of Facts*. New York: Newspaper Enterprise Association, Inc., 1970.

MacCraig, Hugh. *The Ephemeris of the Moon.* Richmond, Va.: Macoy Publishing Co., 1951.

MacNeice, Louis. *Astrology.* London: Aldus Books, 1964.

Menzel, Donald H. *Astronomy.* New York: Random House, Inc., 1970.

Rand, Ayn. *The Fountainhead.* New York: The Bobbs-Merrill Co., Inc., 1943.

Rudhyar, Dane. *The Astrology of Personality.* Lucis Publishing Co., 1936; Doubleday Paperback edition, 1970.

Schmidt, Steven. *Astrology 14: Your New Sun Sign.* New York: The Bobbs-Merrill Co., Inc., 1970.

Shakespeare, William. *Hamlet, Julius Caesar,* and *Romeo and Juliet.*

Simplified Scientific Ephemeris, 1951–1960. Oceanside, Calif.: The Rosicrucian Fellowship, 1950–1959.

The Bible, King James Version.

Time Magazine. "The Revised Zodiac," Nov. 23, 1970; "Is There Life on Mars—or Beyond?" Dec. 13, 1971.

West, John Anthony, and Toonder, Jan Gerhard. *The Case for Astrology.* New York: Coward-McCann, Inc., 1970.

Zain, C. C. *Spiritual Astrology.* Los Angeles: The Church of Light, 1935.

Index